Designing Mental Health Services and Systems for Children and Adolescents: A Shrewd Investment

THE BOOK SERIES OF THE INTERNATIONAL ASSOCIATION FOR CHILD AND ADOLESCENT PSYCHIATRY AND ALLIED PROFESSIONS

THE LEADERSHIP SERIES

Titles in this series address topics of current international interest in the field of child and adolescent psychiatry, psychology, and social work. Each book reports on the most up-to-date research and clinical care methods, worldwide, by internationally known experts. Volumes provide authoritative IACAPAP policy statements and overviews, and also strive to be readable and practical contributions to topics of immediate concern.

Titles available in this series:

New Approaches to Mental Health from Birth to Adolescence (Volume 9)
Colette Chiland, M.D., Ph.D. and J. Gerald Young, M.D., Editors
Yale University Press

Why Children Reject School: Views from Seven Countries (Volume 10)
Colette Chiland, M.D., Ph.D. and J. Gerald Young, M.D., Editors
Yale University Press

Children and Violence (Volume 11)
Colette Chiland, M.D., Ph.D. and J. Gerald Young, M.D., Editors
Jason Aronson Inc.

*Designing Mental Health Services and Systems for Children and
    Adolescents: A Shrewd Investment* (Volume 12)
J. Gerald Young, M.D. and Pierre Ferrari, M.D., Editors
Brunner/Mazel Publishers

THE MENTOR SERIES

This new series will feature books by distinguished invited authors and editors. It will also address topics of current interest, with a strong emphasis on education and dissemination of the most current knowledge for clinicians. For more details, please contact Brunner/Mazel Publishers.

Designing Mental Health Services and Systems for Children and Adolescents: A Shrewd Investment

EDITED BY

J. GERALD YOUNG, M.D.

PIERRE FERRARI, M.D.

Diana Kaplan, Ph.D.
Associate Editor

USA	Publishing Office:	BRUNNER/MAZEL
		A member of the Taylor & Francis Group
		325 Chestnut Street
		Philadelphia, PA 19106
		Tel: (215) 625-8900
		Fax: (215) 625-2940
	Distribution Center:	BRUNNER/MAZEL
		A member of the Taylor & Francis Group
		47 Runway Road, Suite G
		Levittown, PA 19057
		Tel: (215) 269-0400
		Fax: (215) 269-0363
UK		BRUNNER/MAZEL
		A member of the Taylor & Francis Group
		1 Gunpowder Square
		London EC4A 3DE
		Tel: +44 171 583 0490
		Fax: +44 171 583 0581

DESIGNING MENTAL HEALTH SERVICES AND SYSTEMS FOR CHILDREN AND ADOLESCENTS: A Shrewd Investment

1 2 3 4 5 6 7 8 9 0

Printed by Edwards Brothers, Ann Arbor, MI, 1998.
A CIP catalog record for this book is available from the British Library.
⊗The paper in this publication meets the requirements of the ANSI Standard Z39.48-1984 (Permanence of Paper). Library of Congress Cataloging-in-Publication Data available from publisher.

1-56032-794-4

CONTENTS

The Utilization and Outcomes of Current Treatments for Developmental Psychopathology

Models of Treatment and Preventive Interventions for Developmental Psychopathology

**International Models of Mental Health
Systems for Children and Adolescents:
What is the Reality When We Put
Principles into Practice?**

Contents

Summary: Reconciling Evolving Economic Strategies and the Needs of Children in 21st Century Systems of Care

**Recommendations of the International
Association for Child and Adolescent
Psychiatry and Allied Professions
(IACAPAP)**

CONTRIBUTORS

Veira F. A. Bailey, F.R.C. Psych.
Consultant in Child and Adolescent
Psychiatry
Hounslow Department of Child and
Adolescent Psychiatry
London, England

Mario Bertolini, M.D.
Professor and Director
Clinica di Neuropsichiatria Infantile
Ospedale San Gerardo di Monza
Universitá degli Studi di Milano
Monza, Italy

B. Blanz, M.D.
Clinic for Child and Adolescent
Psychiatry
Friedrich-Schiller University
Jena, Germany

Jacek Bomba, M.D., Ph.D.
Professor of Psychiatry
Department of Psychiatry
Collegium Medicum
The Jagiellonian University
Krakow, Poland

Margaret J. Briggs-Gowan, M.D.
Child Psychiatry and Pediatrics
Yale Child Study Center
New Haven, Connecticut
U.S.A.

Ernesto Caffo, M.D.
Professor of Child Psychiatry
University of Modena
Modena, Italy
President, iL TELEFONO AZZURO
Bologna, Italy

Salvador Celia, M.D., Ph.D.
Leo Kanner Institute
Porto Alegre, Brazil

Miguel Cherro-Aguerre, M.D.
Professor and Director
Child and Adolescent Psychiatry
The University of the Republic
School of Medicine
Montevideo, Uruguay

Colette Chiland, M.D., Ph.D.
Professor Emeritus of Clinical
Psychology
René Déscartes University
(Sorbonne-Human Sciences)
Paris, France

Donald J. Cohen, M.D.
Irving B. Harris Professor of Child
Psychiatry, Pediatrics, and Psychology
Yale University School of Medicine
Director, Yale Child Study Center
Chief, Child Psychiatry
Children's Hospital at Yale-New
Haven
New Haven, Connecticut
U.S.A.

Ronald A. Feldman, Ph.D.
Professor and Dean
School of Social Work
Columbia University
New York, New York
U.S.A.

Pierre Ferrari, M.D.
Professor of Child and Adolescent
Psychiatry
University of Paris XI
Medical Director, Department of
Child and Adolescent Psychiatry
Fondation Vallée
Gentilly, France

Ian M. Goodyer, M.D.
Professor of Child and Adolescent
Psychiatry
Department of Psychiatry
Developmental Psychiatry Section
University of Cambridge
Cambrige, England

C. Göpel, M.D.
Department of Child and Adolescent
Psychiatry and Psychotherapy
Central Institute of Mental Health
Mannheim, Germany

Helga Hannesdóttir, M.D.
Department of Child and
Adolescent Psychiatry
National University Hospital
Reykjávik, Iceland

T.-P. Ho, M.D., M.R.C. Psych.
Consultant Child Psychiatrist
Department of Psychiatry
Queen Mary Hospital
The University of Hong Kong
Pokfulam, Hong Kong

Peter S. Jensen, M.D.
Chief, Child and Adolescent
Disorders Research Branch
National Institute of Mental
Health
Rockville, Maryland
U.S.A.

Diana Kaplan, Ph.D.
Bellevue Hospital Center
New York, New York
U.S.A.

Robert A. King, M.D.
Associate Professor of Child
Psychiatry and Pediatrics
Yale Child Study Center
New Haven, Connecticut
U.S.A.

B. Lay, M.D.
Department of Child and Adolescent
Psychiatry and Psychotherapy
Central Institute of Mental Health
Mannheim, Germany

Philip J. Leaf, Ph.D.
Professor, Department of Mental
Hygiene
The Johns Hopkins University
School of Hygiene and Public Health
Baltimore, Maryland
U.S.A.

Gabriel Levi, M.D.
Professor of Child Neuropsychiatry
Department of Child and
Adolescent Neurology and
Psychiatry
Universitá di Roma "La Sapienza"
Roma, Italia

Donald W. Light, Ph.D.
Professor of Comparative Health
Care Systems
Chief, Division of Social and
Behavioral Medicine
Department of Psychiatry
University of Medicine and Dentistry
of New Jersey
Stratford, New Jersey
President, Light and Associates
Princeton, New Jersey
U.S.A.

Savita Malhotra, M.D., Ph.D.
Additional Professor
Department of Psychiatry
Postgraduate Institute of Medical
Education and Research
Chandigarh, India

Linda C. Mayes, M.D.
Associate Professor of Pediatrics and
Child Psychiatry
Yale Child Study Center
New Haven, Connecticut
U.S.A.

Tiberiu Mircea, M.D.
Associate Professor of Child and
Adolescent Psychiatry
Catedra de Psihiatrie Infantila
Universitátea de Medicina si
Farmacie
Timisoara, Romania

Tamar Mozes, M.D.
Sackler School of Medicine
Tel Aviv University
Petah-Tiqva, Israel

Francesca Neri, M.D.
Vice Director
Clinica di Neuropsichiatria Infantile
Ospedale San Gerardo di Monza
Universitá degli Studi di Milano
Monza, Italy

R. Penge, M.D.
Department of Child and Adolescent
Neurology and Psychiatry
Universitá di Roma "La Sapienza"
Rome, Italy

Helmut Remschmidt, M.D., Ph.D.
Professor and Director
Department of Child and
Adolescent Psychiatry
Philipps-University
Marburg, Germany

Leonard Saxe, Ph.D.
Research Professor
Family and Children's Policy Center
Heller School
Brandeis University
Waltham, Massachusetts
U.S.A.

Kari Schleimer, M.D., Ph.D.
Assistant Director
Department of Child and
Adolescent Psychiatry
University Hospital
University of Lund
Malmo, Sweden

Martin H. Schmidt, M.D., Sc.D.
Professor and Chairman
Department of Child and Adolescent
Psychiatry and Psychotherapy
Central Institute of Mental Health
Mannheim, Germany

John E. Schowalter, M.D.
Albert J. Solnit Professor of Child
Psychiatry and Pediatrics
Yale Child Study Center
Clinical Chief, Child Psychiatry
Children's Hospital at Yale-New
Haven
New Haven, Connecticut
U.S.A.

Mary E. Schwab-Stone, M.D.
Associate Professor of Child
Psychiatry and Pediatrics
Yale Child Study Center
New Haven, Connecticut
U.S.A.

Anatoly A. Severny, M.D., Ph.D.
President, Independent Association
of Child Psychiatrists and
Psychologists in Russia
Moscow, Russia

Alexander Yu. Smirnov, M.D., Ph.D.
Deputy Director, Moscow
Psychological Center
Member, Executive Board
Independent Association of Child
Psychiatrists and Psychologists in
Russia
Moscow, Russia

Sylvie Tordjman, M.D.
Department of Child and
Adolescent Psychiatry
Fondation Vallée
Gentilly, France

Sam Tyano, M.D.
Professor of Psychiatry
Gehah Mental Health Center
Sackler School of Medicine
Tel Aviv University
Petah-Tiqva, Israel

Agnes Vetró, M.D., Ph.D.
Associate Professor, Department of
Child and Adolescent Psychiatry
Department of Psychiatry
Albert Szent-Gyorgyi Medical
University
Szeged, Semmelweis, Hungary

Reinhard Walter, Ph.D.
Department of Child and
Adolescent Psychiatry
Philipps-University
Marburg, Germany

J. Gerald Young, M.D.
Professor of Psychiatry
Division of Child and Adolescent
Psychiatry
New York University School of
Medicine
Bellevue Hospital Center
New York, New York
U.S.A.

Mario Zanetti
Professor
Universitá di Bologna
Direttore della Programmazione
Sanitaria
Regione Emilia Romagna
Bologna, Italy

PREFACE AND DEDICATION

Throughout this book there is a recurring theme, that of the tension between the *clinical needs* of children and adolescents at multiple levels and the *economic forces* that press administrators to find rapid, often simplified answers. The sudden demand to reduce costs has been a frustrating experience for all participating in mental health services for children and adolescents, a notorious "low income producer" among medical specialties that was already underfunded. It has been an easy shift for many clinician administrators to resort to repeated injunctions to clinicians to be "more practical" or to "be more realistic about expenses;" while this is needed, and is a welcome improvement in management, the underlying problems are infinitely more complex. Simple answers to these challenges have a common feature: they use administrative procedures to reduce costs while neglecting the very difficult problems of providing the best clinical response to a child's and family's problem. For example, psychosocial therapies are often the first to be devalued, criticized, and dismissed by managers; this is because they are time-intensive and are based on mechanisms of action that are difficult to measure, such as therapeutic relationships and the use of language. Nevertheless, we have learned from some administrators that a wide range of professional disciplines, guiding theories, and treatment approaches can be embraced within pragmatic and successful management of mental health systems for children and adolescents.

In spite of the challenges, a number of child and adolescent psychiatrists have been able to respond with success to the serious economic and administrative issues that have always confronted our field, and to promote the advancement of clinical care, research, and education. For more than 60 years, the officers of the International Association for Child and Adolescent Psychiatry and Allied Professions (IACAPAP) have been at the helm of the field of child and adolescent psychiatry internationally. They have moved the field forward as a serious, clinical and scientific profession with broadly shared values. It is to these individuals that we wish to dedicate this book, recalling their unusual principles and imagination. We especially wish to acknowledge the Presidents of IACAPAP, who have set high standards and have consistently shown how clinical care and science are mutually enriching, and that the various intellectual traditions within the field of child mental health can be integrated. All have managed to achieve a remarkable merging within themselves of multiple roles not easily integrated. Each has been a wise and practical administrator of a clinical unit while remaining attentive to the inner lives of children in their consulting rooms.

The Venice International Working Group, organized by IACAPAP to examine mental health services and systems for children, represented the efforts of many individuals in Italy and other nations. We especially wish to acknowledge the contributions of Professor Ernesto Caffo of the University of Modena. As founder and President of Il Telefono Azzurro, he has applied his vision to create an exceptional range of programs for children and families in Italy. His spirited collaboration with Dr. Myron Belfer, Dr. Donald Cohen and others, including the editors of this volume, have made this book possible.

It has been the tradition of IACAPAP to find ways to improve the quality of the lives of vulnerable children, those in need of treatment, and their families. One sector of this effort has been to facilitate the work of mental health professionals committed to children and families. Clinicians who have been administrators, researchers, and educators have embodied the values of IACAPAP throughout the world over many decades, and they serve as models for the field. They also stand before us as proof that the tensions between economic pragmatism and clinical needs can be reduced, and that the effort to provide optimal clinical care is a worthy and increasingly achievable goal.

J. Gerald Young, M.D.
Pierre Ferrari, M.D.

ACKNOWLEDGEMENTS

Several people were especially helpful during the editing and production of this book and we are grateful to them. Dr. Donald

Cohen was characteristically generous and constructive in his careful reading and comments on parts of the manuscript. In a more general way, we also recognize that the good spirits and wisdom of Professor Colette Chiland infuse this book. Ms. Zuzel Guerra carried out diverse secretarial and administrative tasks accurately at all phases of preparing this volume, and did so with a welcome cheerfulness. Ms. Alison Mudditt, Editorial Director for Behavioral Sciences at Taylor and Francis, was a reliable source of good judgement, strategies, and encouragement. Similarly, Ms. Catherine Kovacs, the Production Editor, combined her excellent editing skills with flexibility and good humor, enabling us to complete the myriad of tasks associated with the book's production. Finally, Jessica, Nicole, Sabina, and Lara Young were both agreeably patient during our long months of work and an inspiration for this book about children.

INTRODUCTION

Clinicians treating the mental health disorders of childhood quickly learn that treatment expenditures for children are a shrewd investment for the future. A clinician caring for children and their families often witnesses untreated early childhood symptoms smoldering over the years, boiling into a disorder sufficiently significant to require very expensive treatment and cause unquestioned suffering for the child and family. The lack of resources for treating these children leaves the clinician, who fruitlessly recommended treatment, feeling helpless and increasingly alarmed about the obvious costs at a time of purported efforts to reduce expenditures for healthcare. As families are followed clinically over the years, moreover, both the development of adult psychiatric disorders and multigenerational transmission of disorders—through both genetic and social transmission—adds to the magnification of problems. The clinician observes a new escalation of troubles, this time affecting multiple members of a family, compounding both the suffering and the expenses. This understanding of the genesis of psychiatric disorders in childhood seemed, in the past, to rely too much on clinical observations, which were scientifically suspect. However, sufficient scientific data has now been accumulated so that the potential savings of psychiatric morbidity and behavioral health expenditures through childhood prevention efforts cannot be disputed. Financial estimates of very substantial lifetime savings for individual cases treated during childhood or adolescence, as described later in this book, can now be projected using practical and conservative analyses. Nevertheless, policies to implement adequate mental health services and systems for children and adolescents continue to appear slowly.

A recent example of expenditures is illuminating. Autism and the pervasive developmental disorders have long been recognized as highly disabling, and therefore expensive, lifelong conditions. Yet, funding for research remained at a low level, due, at various times, to views that not enough was known about the disorders or that they were too rare (an inaccurate view of their prevalence, prolonged by insufficient research funding) to warrant substantial funding. Recently there has been a large increase in funding for autism in the United States. The National Institutes of Health, using maximum figures that are somewhat inflated, spent $10 million in 1995 for autism research and $12 million in 1996; in 1997 the amount was increased to $20 million and the four subsequent years will see this higher level of funding sustained. While this is very gratifying, contrasting it to the total of $13 billion spent on the care of patients with autism per year in the United States makes the startling underinvestment clear (M. Bristol, personal communication, March 1998).

How do we explain the neglect of childhood psychiatric disorders? In brief, it is accounted for by the lack of political and economic power and productivity of children. They do not vote, nor influence policies, and they do not generate income or funding for other individuals or entities. They rely upon the generous and nurturing feelings of adults who care very much for their welfare. This is a fragile foundation for support.

In the privacy of their consulting rooms, child and adolescent psychiatrists listen to men and women tell with unquestioned sincerity of their devotion to their children as the first purpose of their lives. In the public meetings in which child and adolescent psychiatrists participate in decisions that affect the lives and well-being of thousands of children, to mention this devotion to *children*, as a group, would be a ruinous and humiliating error. No sensible professional would quote Emily Dickinson's poem:

> If I can stop one heart from breaking,
> I shall not live in vain;
> If I can ease one life the aching,
> Or cool one pain,
> Or help one fainting robin
> Unto his nest again,
> I shall not live in vain.

> *If I Can Stop One Heart from Breaking*
> Emily Dickinson

Seeing these tender, compassionate words on one of the first pages of this book evokes a feeling of awkward vulnerability for having put them there. Yet, it is just these sentiments about their children that clinicians hear from parents with such predictability; it does not matter whether they are eminent and powerful or diminished and exhausted. And these same sentiments are never to be mentioned in the course of deliberations among serious adults concerning programs for children. How do we account for this paradox? Is it enough to say that we cannot afford such compassion? This quandary lies at the core of the problems discussed in this book.

An international group of professionals came together in Venice in the spring of 1996 to discuss the mounting problems associated with changes in the mental health systems for children and adolescents in countries across the globe. Sponsored by the International Association for Child and Adolescent Psychiatry and Allied Professions, the Venice International Working Group had a difficult task. It was to consider all aspects of mental healthcare for children and adolescents necessary for building the best clinical services and systems, from developmental psychopathology, epidemiology, and treatment outcome to the economics of healthcare delivery systems and the problems of individual countries. The goal was to develop a clear statement describing the elements fundamentally necessary for an adequate mental health system for children and adolescents. It is hoped that the resulting statement can be used by clinicians and healthcare managers across the world as they establish or refine their own service systems. More important, this statement can be used in defense of children and families in dire need of these services, but for whom they are unavailable.

While developing these services for children is an ambitious mission, and it is well known that there are many obstacles, the benefits are compelling and the dangers of inactivity are disagreeable: "If clinicians are not going to lead the effort to provide effective services, there is a significant risk that efforts to develop services will continue to be driven more by economic factors than clinical outcomes" (Leaf, Chapter 8, this volume). Further, we are warned that "If the majority of clinicians remain uninterested in documenting the outcomes they achieve, someone else will fill this void. How likely is it that these efforts will be consistent with the best interests of those children and adolescents experiencing emotional and behavioral problems?" (Leaf, Chapter 8).

Taking up this challenge means establishing the base of knowledge necessary to accomplish our goals. Mental health services for children and adolescents utilize a broad array of treatments and prevention strategies. Skeptics view this as an indication of their ineffectiveness. The reality is, however, that it reflects the complexity of these disorders of the developing brain and mind, and the intricacy of needs for each child. Building systems of psychiatric care for children and adolescents requires an understanding of the factors and pathways leading to psychiatric morbidity during childhood and adolescence, knowledge sufficient to guide treatment. We also need data indicating the number of children characterized by a standardized method as having a psychiatric disorder with sufficient functional impairment to require treatment. It is essential to review the economic systems that structure the manner in which mental healthcare for children is funded and delivered, and how management strategies might be developed to enable us to generate a sensible financial plan for the services to be provided. Similarly, we should have information about the number of children currently utilizing such services. It is essential to review the available treatments, both the principles that underlie them and our best current knowledge of the outcomes of these treatments. Prevention must be given priority as the best means to reduce overall expenditures over longer time periods, so recent prevention research and strategies merit our scrutiny. Once again, reassessment of existing model prevention programs will be a good gauge of the practicality of prevention programs. Moreover, as clinicians, we recognize that we must determine the best manner of structuring programs for different age groups of children. Finally, we need models for the systems that we are attempting to set up: active systems of services in various parts of the world that we can discuss and that will guide us past pitfalls that otherwise would undermine our activities. These considerations form the structure of this book, which maps some of the chief topics that must be considered in any plan for building mental health services for children and adolescents.

This tactic attempts to elucidate common strategies for developing these systems that can be applied to essentially all nations of the world. Yet there are other facets of these problems that differ according to the country involved. For example, 40% of the total population of India is below 14 years of age (350 million children). A minimum estimate would suggest that 10% of these children, or 35 million children, have a severe psychiatric disorder urgently requiring immediate treatment. These figures do not include about two thirds of the adolescents in India, who are 14 and above. Regrettably, psychiatric services for children and adolescents are almost nonexistent. Special strategies obviously will be needed to begin to aid the children of India within these restrictive realities. "The wide gap between the need for service, the existing infrastructure, and the resources, at hand or in the future, seems insurmountable. This is the challenge for the whole profession, the nation, and also the world" (Malhotra, Chapter 27).

Finally, to function successfully we need to see clearly the competitive forces active in the field, and not only to understand what is occurring but to have the courage to say what we all see. As an example, we can appraise the forces of healthcare management and economics in relation to the clinical challenges that never evaporate: the policies embodied in managed care are useful for cost containment, but will also be destructive if not melded with inventive clinical strategies for providing services to children within these constraints. Clinicians must respond actively to these economic forces.

We close this set of thoughts with lines from a poem that again risk sentimentality, but have the ring of uncontested truth when applied to the "slow compassion" of international public policy for children:

> For life is all too short, dear,
>   And sorrow is all too great,
> To suffer our slow compassion
>   That tarries until too late;
> And it isn't the thing you do, dear,
>   It's the thing you leave undone
> Which gives you a bit of a heartache
>   At the setting of the sun.
>
>   *The Sin of Omission*
>   Margaret E. Sangster

J. Gerald Young
Pierre Ferrari

THE GENESIS AND PREVALENCE OF DEVELOPMENTAL PSYCHOPATHOLOGY: DEFINING THE NEED FOR MENTAL HEALTH SERVICES FOR CHILDREN AND ADOLESCENTS

1

Developmental Psychopathology and Child Mental Health Services: Risk and Protective Factors in Children, Families, and Society

DONALD J. COHEN

ERNESTO CAFFO

Developmental psychopathology emphasizes the intimate connections between biological and psychological development, the role of parents and other caregivers in shaping children's competence, the social and historical context of development, and the psychobiological pathways that lead from one stage to another and that are marked by continuities and discontinuities (Cicchetti & Cohen, 1995; Cicchetti & Rogosch, 1996). This developmental knowledge illuminates the sensitive points when risk is likely to be expressed, as well as optimal times for prevention and intervention. These developmental epochs include the critically important early childhood as well as early adolescence, when children experience the increasing power of community and peer groups.

The scientific study of children's development provides a framework for effective intervention. At each point in a child's life, from gestation through adolescence, children and families are confronted by expectable challenges as well as threatening risks and vulnerabilities. When problems arise, the child and family mobilize their own modes of adaptation (Masten, Best, & Garmezy, 1990). Their success will set the stage for future strengths or lead to increased vulnerability. As tasks of personal and family development are mastered, the child and parents can move ahead with new competence and confidence. Failures in adaptation, however, set the stage for the child and parents to move further from the normal growth curve and to follow a trajectory that leads to increasing dysfunction. Failure in a developmental task is a risk factor for the next phase of development. For example, children who fail to learn how to read by age 8 are likely to then fail in school and drop out by age 12 or 13.

Stage by stage, strengths generally build upon strengths, and risks are compounded by failures. Healthy babies in loving families acquire the preconditions for later achievement in school and community. Fragile infants in impoverished homes slip behind developmentally, with each delay setting the stage for subsequent problems.

Small, vulnerable, drug-exposed infants who are raised in chaotic and dysfunctional families fail to thrive as infants. They will be 2 or 3 years behind in language and social skills when they reach school, and they are likely to fail academically and to drop out of school early in adolescence, to become the young parents of the next generation of infants at risk (Mayes & Granger, 1996; Mayes & Bornstein, 1998). Today, millions of children like this are placed on a conveyor belt at birth that will lead them from one failure to another. It is no surprise when they succumb to drugs, prostitution, and crime in adolescence.

This perspective emphasizes the multigenerational nature of the child mental health field. Risk and protective factors are transmitted from one generation to the next. Compared with the fortunate child in an "average expectable environment," the dysfunctional child and adolescent is more likely to grow up to become the inadequate parent for the next generation. Yet, not all vulnerable children in situations of danger become impaired, and policy planners and clinicians must be aware of the dangers of any linear, mechanistic model that could become a self-fulfilling prophecy of doom for millions of children (Cicchetti, 1994). Mathematical methods for assessing the likelihood that a child will succeed or fail are applicable only to large groups of children. Using empirical information about correlations between factors and outcomes, it is possible to calculate the likelihood that one specific risk factor (such as exposure to maltreatment) will either increase or decrease the chance that a child will have an adverse outcome. Yet, in the real world, there are very many complicated interactions among factors, modifying variables, and other complications (such as degree of exposure). Thus, great care must be used in making any generalization about the effect of an experience on specific children. Even empirically, well-supported generalizations from large populations can be used only with great caution in relation to any individual child.

From clinical and research studies, we know that some children are able to overcome external challenges and to learn and achieve, even in the most difficult situations. This type of decreased vulnerability may relate to the age of exposure (e.g., babies are more sensitive to separations or to poor nutrition), biological differences (e.g., some children are genetically at higher risk for disorders), and dosage effects (e.g., even in situations of trauma, the children who are closest to the event are at highest risk). Sometimes, there are hints about the source of resilience for particular children, e.g., a determined parent, a caring mentor, unusual talents or intelligence. By studying children who move ahead, in spite of risk, clinical investigators can learn about inborn strengths, protective factors, and what helps children cope with adversity. This knowledge can lead to better preventive programs.

Just as in other branches of public health, this knowledge of normal tasks of development, as well as the threats to specific individuals and groups, provides a framework for community- and family-based interventions. Support at each phase of development and early detection of difficulties are far more efficient and clinically sensitive—for the child, family, and society—than later attempts at remediation when things have gone badly. However, no child or group should ever be ignored, however serious or persistent their problems may be. Even in situations of the greatest adversity, such as the experiences and life-course of street children, children who have suffered from years of abuse, and children who are truant from school and already delinquent or in reformatories, communities and clinicians can offer children opportunities and hope for their self-righting and future achievement. Giving a child hope and skills can literally be life saving.

The work of child mental health professionals with hundreds of thousands of children and families throughout the world has generated important new knowledge about vulnerable children as well as about what can be helpful to children. This cumulative experience has the capacity to provide hope and resources.

Mental health professionals can provide authentic information about children to parents, teachers, and government. While there is far more to learn about young children, scientific knowledge already is available and should be used to help assure that children receive the care that will move them forward. This available knowledge about risk and protective factors can also help families, teachers, and clinicians recognize when a child is first starting to have problems and to provide effective treatment to help put development back on course.

THE FIRST YEARS OF LIFE

Children provided with warm care and attention become attached to their parents and then to one or two adults who take care of them on a regular basis. They build up an internal, emotional portrait of their parents. When the parents are not there—when they are at work or busy with something else—or when children are upset, they remember the internal portrait and comfort themselves. The more securely children are attached, the more easily they can cope with new experiences, including the normal traumas of life, such as separations from parents. However, no degree of warm attachment will immunize a child from the greatest tragedies that occur during war or serious illness (Apfel & Simon, 1996).

The experiences during the first years of life—at home, in daycare, in the community—are especially important because they lay down the foundations for all future development (Cicchetti, 1994). Fortunate children who have been loved, stimulated, talked with, comforted, and given predictable care will see the world as basically safe and secure, will feel valued and effective, will have trust in themselves and others, and will be able to use their intellectual potentials to their limits. Children who have had difficult experiences—and these are the children of greatest concern to all clinicians and policy planners—are likely to have serious problems in their social, emotional, or intellectual development.

In subsequent years, there may be opportunities for such a child's earlier brain and behavior problems to be reshaped. Children with low self esteem from repeated failures and neglect can blossom if they are provided with mentors and chances for success, and anxious children can be helped with therapy and emotional supports. Overactive children can learn how to calm down in kindergarten. Clinicians and educators should always nurture every child's potential for recovery. But they cannot count on the success of such renovations when maladaptive processes have gone on too long or too badly.

While the first years of life are extremely important in shaping children's development, there is no magic period of development. Children who have had a good start in life require continuing support from families and community. And children who have started life with difficulties may compensate with interventions. At each phase, children require developmentally suitable care from parents and others, continuity of relations, affection, intellectual stimulation, protection from harm, and security. These are met by parents, childcare workers, the school, and the community. With maturation, the child's world widens to include peers, neighborhood, and the broader society. These progressively take over some of the influence and even the authority earlier vested in parents. Thus, developmental support begins to include the media, police who provide security, and employers who offer jobs and a future role in the economy.

SOCIAL CHANGES AND TRAUMA

To an increasing degree, children's opportunities for continuity of nurturance by loving parents are being eroded. Broad social changes are affecting families of all social classes.

One century ago, in the United States and in Europe, the average family had many children (seven in the United States), two parents, and a mother at home to care for the children. Divorce was rare. Today, the situation is vastly different. In Europe and the United States, the average family has two children, both parents work, and infants are placed in daycare the first year or two of life. Many children are born out of wedlock and divorce rates are reaching 50%. Thus, most children will live with only one parent sometime during their childhood.

Children's needs and parents' styles of caring for children evolved over hundreds of thousands of years of human evolution. During the past century, society has changed much more rapidly than our brains can evolve. As families have become smaller and more mobile, many young families can no longer turn to their own parents for help and guidance. Increasingly, there must be social systems to support young families and to intervene when there are problems.

During the past 10 years, new models of intervention have been devised. These emphasize prevention, family support, and the integration of a spectrum of community-based services for those with serious problems. These models also underscore the synergism of professionals, parents, and the community and draw upon the expertise of many different professions: child and adolescent psychiatry, pediatrics, social work, nursing, psychology, childcare, and others.

In addition to these pervasive changes in family life, the lives of children during the past decade have been burdened by special risks. These risks have been the particular concern of child and adolescent psychiatrists and other mental health professionals, and include the impact of urban violence, multigenerational poverty, poor living conditions, bad nutrition, drugs and AIDS, abuse and neglect, child labor and exploitation, and the impact of parental physical and psychiatric illness on children. Also, children have become the major victims of political upheaval in Africa, Asia, Europe, and South America. Indeed, during warfare, women and children are no longer spared but have increasingly been specifically targeted as victims. Thus, children are killed in schools and bombed in hospitals, and they are disproportionately represented among those who are hit by shells or exploded by landmines. Today, millions of children are refugees and live in camps or as undocumented aliens, often separated from their parents by intentional government policy. Traumatized by war in their own homelands, they are then exposed to illness, danger, lack of schooling, and the risks of sexual and other types of exploitation. There is a cascade of developmental disruption from acute and persistent trauma (Pynoos, Steinberg, & Wrath, 1995).

When a child is abused at home and victimized in the community, he is unable to evoke any secure, emotional, internal portrait of a caring adult. His internal world is blank, or, worse, it is filled with frightening images. Children who grow up attacked from the outside are attacked by demons from within. They may turn their passivity into active forms of aggression to preserve their sense of selfhood—literally, to survive as people. Thus, we see children move from being witnesses and victims of violence to perpetrators of violence. Their aggression allows them to maintain a sense of personal coherence and effectiveness. Often, such children are recruited into youth gangs and paramilitary groups, and they organize their entire lives around the themes of retaliation and revenge.

TREATMENT, SERVICES, AND POLICY

Child psychiatric treatment and mental health systems have a relatively short history in medicine. The pioneers in child psychiatry, child psychoanalysis, pediatrics, and social work began to explore the vast domain of childhood emotional, developmental, and psychiatric disorders during the 1930s. Formal training programs in child psychiatry were established only during the 1950s, and systematic research in the field of child mental health is only several decades old. Today, in many nations, child and adolescent psychiatry is still emerging as a distinct profession, and there are few developmental psychologists, child mental health social workers, child psychiatric nurses, or special educators. Yet, a wide range of psychosocial therapies has been developed for broad classes of disturbances and conditions; more recently, child psychiatrists have been able to use medications that are effective for specific types of psychiatric disorders in children and adolescents. These treatments can ameliorate specific symptoms, reduce the burden of suffering, and markedly improve the quality of life of children and families. A challenge for clinical researchers is to carefully evaluate the available treatments and approaches to determine which are most effective for specific children and to define areas in need of more systematic research.

However, it is also broadly recognized that some of the traditional approaches to clinical care, such as the office-based provision of intensive, long-term, individual psychotherapy, cannot be delivered to the vast number of children in need. Also, these traditional approaches may be of only limited effectiveness for children at highest risk, who are constantly exposed to trauma and adversity. During the last several years, mental health workers have been experimenting with alternative methods of delivering care, reducing barriers to services, and providing quick, effective intervention at times of crisis. Some of these innovations offer hope that new effective interventions can be mobilized for vulnerable children. These include the use of schools as the base for family and child services, new methods of early intervention for vulnerable children, new curricula for children with special needs, and partnerships between police and mental health workers (Marans, 1995).

However, to advance the welfare of children at highest risk, further research is required. Developmental, behavioral, and mental disorders are costly both financially and in terms of human suffering. Hundreds of thousands of dollars, and even millions of dollars, may be spent on the lifelong care of a child with a serious developmental or psychiatric disorder. Yet, few societies devote substantial funding for basic research on brain and behavioral development, nor for translating these findings into new types of intervention and treatment. In large part, it will only be through advances in basic and applied research that there can be fundamental change in the prognosis for the most serious conditions, such as autism, language and learning disorders, and intellectual handicap.

Second, systematic research is needed on prevention and new approaches to treatment and intervention. There are effective methods for reducing risk, including good prenatal and childhood health and nutrition, and assuring that all children receive suitable schooling and continuity of family care. But child mental health professionals do not know how to prevent the major disorders that afflict children in high-risk situations who are often burdened by both constitutional and environmental risks. The interactions among genetic, constitutional, and environmental factors shape brain and behavior. Children with serious disorders need more than loving kindness and attention, and current treatments and interventions are often inadequate. This is painfully evident in relation to the early-onset, pervasive disorders. But the lack of generally effective treatment is clear even in relation to the more frequent, later–onset difficulties. For example, the majority of teenagers with drug and conduct disorders do not respond to currently available therapies, nor do we know how to treat parents who are persistently abusive or to repair the psychobiological damage to children who have experienced years of abuse.

To make use of emerging knowledge, the professions dealing with children require training that is soundly based on basic and clinical knowledge, and they need opportunities for continuing education. New knowledge about children's brains and development, about developmental psychopathology, and about treatments will not be useful to children unless the professions who serve them are well informed. This includes teachers and social workers, as well as police officers, childcare workers, nurses, pediatricians, and mental health clinicians.

As a voice for all children, child mental health professionals can do a great deal to decrease risk factors and promote protective factors for populations and individuals. Information about risks, causes, and treatments is vital for government at all levels and of all political persuasions. Governments need authentic information about the state of children, the institutions that serve them, and the preventive and interventive programs that work. The critical evaluation of such data is an important part of shaping rational social policy.

There is a great deal that governments already can use to reduce the burden of suffering and to create opportunities for healthier development. Governments should promote early and sustained healthcare, emotional and intellectual stimulation, regularity and structure, and the availability and support of families. It is critically important to protect children from danger and to provide shelter and continuity of care, including family reunification for refugees and a sense of hope within the mainstream of society for all children. Strengthening democratic society requires children who have been treated fairly, who internalize the values of cooperation and sharing, and who have the capacities and education to become productive and well-compensated workers. Children and adolescents need to feel that there is a basic social structure that is fair and that offers a chance of success, if they apply themselves and use their abilities well.

Today, in all developing nations, the rich are getting richer and the gap between rich and poor is increasing. In many nations, the elderly are rich and financially secure and young families are increasingly burdened and poor. In this situation of increased concentration of wealth in a very affluent upper class, an increasing sense of alienation and bitterness is transmitted to children. By adolescence, the young and poor who feel left out of the mainstream become cynical, socially disconnected, and a threat to the security of others with whom they feel no moral or social engagement. These social facts are of vital importance to those who lead our governments.

This public health perspective on the social development of children is increasingly important in relation to the future security of nations. Throughout the world, leaders are recognizing that a nation's most critical natural resource is its children. To succeed in the future, nations will need physically and emotionally healthy children who are intellectually prepared for modern technology.

At the beginning of this century, child advocates and government leaders predicted that this would be the century of the child. Who would have predicted the holocaust, with 1 million children murdered, or the staggering burdens of racism throughout the world? Now, looking backwards at the fate of children during this century, with millions of children caught in wars, living on the street, and abused in their own homes, we can see that this has been a grim century indeed for children and nations.

Child psychiatrists, psychologists, educators, and social workers have specialized knowledge to share and important care to provide. They are the natural spokespeople for children at risk and those who have been traumatized. And they can be engaged, ethical advocates, not only for patients and families at risk but also for all families and for the power of communities to mobilize on behalf of all their children.

REFERENCES

Apfel, R., & Simon, B. (Eds.). 1996. *Minefields in their hearts: The mental health of children in war and communal violence.* New Haven, CT: Yale University Press.

Cicchetti, D. (Ed.). 1994. Advances and challenges in the study of the sequelae of child maltreatment [Special Issue]. *Development and Psychopathology,* 6(1).

Cicchetti, D., & Cohen, D. J. (Eds.). 1995. *Developmental psychopathology. Volume 1: Theory and methods, Volume 2: Risk, disorder and adaptation.* New York: Wiley.

Cicchetti, D., & Rogosch F. (Eds.). 1996. Developmental pathways: Diversity in process and outcome [Special Issue]. *Development and Psychopathology,* 8(4).

Marans, S. (1996). *The police-mental health partnership.* New Haven, CT: Yale University Press.

Masten, A., Best, K., & Garmezy, N. (1990). Resilience and development: Contributions from the study of children who overcome adversity. *Development and Psychopathology,* 2, 425–444.

Mayes, L., & Granger, R. (1996). Teratologic and developmental effects of prenatal drug exposure: Alcohol, heroin, marijuana, and cocaine. In M. Lewis (Ed.), *Child and adolescent psychiatry: A comprehensive textbook* (pp. 374–382). Philadelphia: Williams and Wilkins.

Mayes, L., & Bornstein, M. (1998). The context of development for young children from cocaine-abusing families. In P. Kato and T. Mann (Eds.), *Health psychology of special populations* (in press). New York: Plenum Press.

Pynoos, R., Steinberg, A., & Wraith, R. (1995). A developmental model of childhood traumatic stress. In D. Cicchetti and D. J. Cohen (Eds.), *Developmental psychopathology, Volume 2: Risk, disorder and adaptation* (pp. 72–95). New York: Wiley.

2

The Scope and Prevalence of Psychiatric Disorders in Childhood and Adolescence

MARY E. SCHWAB-STONE

MARGARET J. BRIGGS-GOWAN

Knowledge of the scope and prevalence of psychiatric disorders in childhood and adolescence is essential for the effective design of mental health treatment services. The field of epidemiology offers a set of methodologies for building a scientific base of information about the distribution of disease in time, place, and persons (Lilienfeld, 1976). This information promotes the scientific understanding of factors involved in the etiology and course of disease and also supports administrative needs for planning treatment and prevention services (Earls, 1989).

The introduction of epidemiological methods into child psychiatry is a fairly recent event. About 40 years ago, LaPouse and Monk (1958) used systematic assessment methods to gather information on the frequency of problem behaviors in a community sample from the northeastern United States. They found high rates of fears and worries among children 6–12 years old in this general population sample, suggesting that these phenomena are in part developmental and are not invariably pathological. In the mid 1960s, Michael Rutter carried out a landmark study of psychiatric disorder in 9– to 11-year-olds on the Isle of Wight in Great Britain (Rutter, Tizard, & Whitmore, 1970; Rutter, Tizard, Yule, Graham, & Whitmore, 1976). Remarkable by virtue of its scope, comprehensive assessment battery, innovative design, attention to measurement issues, and use of multiple informants, this study yielded a rich scientific base of information on psychiatric disorder in children. Among the many findings were a prevalence estimate for psychiatric disorder in this age group of nearly 7% and the finding that only a tenth of those were receiving child psychiatric services.

Over the decades since these two early studies, child psychiatry as a field has doggedly sought to know the prevalence of psychiatric disorders in young people. This chapter will review and synthesize some basic findings on prevalence after considering the basic methodological and historical influences that have daunted this effort.

THE ASSESSMENT OF CHILD PSYCHIATRIC DISORDER

A major task in the development of knowledge about a disorder involves the determination of its prevalence in the general population and its distribution with respect to basic characteristics of people, such as age and gender, and factors that might increase risk (e.g., economic disadvantage), or, conversely, protect against developing disorder (e.g., good family relationships). Such studies require samples from the general population since patients seen in clinical settings do not even closely approximate the numbers in need of psychiatric services. And, because diverse factors other than the presence of disorder are related to help-seeking, clinically based studies cannot be counted on to represent accurately the characteristics of persons who are likely to have particular conditions.

It can be argued that in recent years child psychiatric research has followed in the path of, but at a distance behind, research in adult psychiatry. In the United States, the Epidemiological Catchment Area Study (Regier, Myers, Kramer, Robins, Blazer, Hough et al., 1984) was launched in the late 1970s. This rigorously conducted 5-site community survey spurred the development of methods for evaluating psychopathology with adults in community settings (the Diagnostic Interview Schedule; Robins, Helzer, Croughan, & Ratcliff, 1981) and sparked a major surge of interest in applying such methods to research needs in child psychiatry. The publication of the American Psychiatric Association's Diagnostic and Statistical Manuals, DSM-III in 1980 and DSM-III-R in 1987, and the revision of the International Classification of Diseases (ICD-10, in 1992) marked an important shift toward a phenomenological approach to the classification of psychiatric conditions, an approach compatible with structured diagnostic interview techniques required by large-scale community studies.

Whereas the development and testing of the Diagnostic Interview Schedule for adults proceeded fairly rapidly, the task of developing a worthy instrument for children and adolescents has proved more challenging and time consuming. There are a number of reasons for this, including the need to capture relevant information about symptoms across years, during which many developmental changes occur, and the need to collect and integrate information from both children and parents. Also, the very nature of child and adolescent psychopathology contributes to the challenge of this task, since many "symptoms" are the same behaviors and emotions that, when occurring with lesser intensity and frequency or at a different developmental phase, would be considered normative.

In the 1980s and 1990s, a variety of interviews were developed, tested, and used, in various stages of refinement, in epidemiological studies. From this period of focus on methodology, several basic issues have been settled or at least delineated (Hodges, 1993). These include establishing that children are important as informants about their symptoms and that direct questioning on such topics is not harmful per se. The importance of using direct interviews when determining clinical levels of disorder, rather than checklists, has been affirmed, as has been the need to incorporate an assessment of functioning or impairment in addition to determining levels and types of symptomatology (Hodges, 1993). There are now six fairly widely used structured diagnostic interviews that vary in style, degree of structure, intended use, and level of training required for administration.

The issue of methodology is not a minor one when considering the question of prevalence. Indeed, many factors involved in how and what information is collected bear directly on the determination of the prevalence of disorder. These include, for example, what informants are used, how information from different sources is combined, the choice of instrument, and how impairment is measured and incorporated into the determination of diagnosis. These, in addition to basic features of the study, e.g., where it is conducted and background features of the study population, must be kept in mind in interpreting prevalence results for any purpose and particularly for service planning.

THE PREVALENCE OF CHILD PSYCHIATRIC DISORDER

Concomitant with this period of intense focus on the development of diagnostic instruments, and indeed facilitated by it, a wave of studies has characterized the descriptive epidemiology of child and adolescent psychiatric disorder. These studies have been conducted in geographically diverse populations (e.g., Queensland, Australia, Connell, Irvine, & Rodney, 1982; North Troendelag, Co., Norway, Vikan, 1985; Ontario, Canada, Offord et al., 1987; New York State, U.S.A., Cohen, Velez, Kohn, Schwab-Stone, & Johnson, 1987; Puerto Rico, Bird et al., 1988; Dunedin, New Zealand, Anderson, Williams, McGee, & Silva, 1987, etc.). They have utilized a range of assessment tools including checklists (e.g., the Child Behavior Checklist; Achenbach & Edelbrock, 1983), rating systems derived from the Rutter studies (Rutter et al., 1970) and diagnostic interview measures, such as the Diagnostic Interview Schedule for Children (DISC; Costello, Edelbrock, Dulcan, & Kalas, 1984 and subsequent revisions, e.g., Shaffer et al., 1993; Shaffer et al., 1996) and the Child and Adolescent Psychiatric Assessment (CAPA; Angold & Costello, 1995b, Angold, Prendergast, Cox, Harrington, Simonoff, & Rutter, 1995). For this generation of studies, prevalence rates ranged from 14% to about 20%, with most studies revealing overall rates in the 17% to 20% range (Brandenburg, Friedman, & Silver, 1990; Costello, 1989; Costello et al., 1996; Shaffer et al., 1996). The convergence of findings on prevalence is particularly remarkable given the diverse populations studied and the different methods used for defining caseness (Costello, 1989). Generally, this near 20% includes about 2% with serious disorders, 7% to 8% with disorders of moderate severity, and the remainder with mild disorders (Earls, 1985; Earls, 1989). This prevalence estimate of 20% contrasts with the commonly cited 11.8% derived from a rigorous review of prevalence studies from the period 1928–1975 (Gould, Wunsch-Hitzig, & Dohrenwend, 1980). This difference in rates most likely reflects a combination of methodological advances, including the use of multiple (rather than single) informants in the more recent studies, and increased methodological rigor in instrumentation and data collection (Brandenburg et al., 1990; Costello, 1989).

High levels of comorbidity, or the co-occurrence of two or more disorders, has been a consistent finding in prevalence studies of child and adolescent psychiatric disorder. Comorbidity among the major disorders of young people typically hovers around 50% or over (Anderson et al., 1987; Bird et al., 1988; Bird, Gould, & Staghezza, 1993; Offord, Boyle & Racine, 1989). While there is considerable overlap among the externalizing disorders and, similarly, among the internalizing disorders, there is also comorbidity between internalizing and externalizing disorders (Offord, 1995). This consistent and marked degree of comorbidity carries important implications for clinical diagnostic assessment and treatment, for anticipating service needs, and for the conceptual basis for our understanding of childhood psychopathology. Offord (1995) notes that the high levels of comorbidity and the lack of distinctive features associated with specific disorders have raised the question of whether our current level of knowledge permits the degree of distinction that is currently being made between diagnostic categories.

It is important to note that there is no magic number, no absolute truth about the percentage of children who suffer from psychiatric disturbance in general or from a particular disorder. Prevalence estimates can vary greatly depending on the degree of impairment that is incorporated into the case definition. For example, in the Dutch study by Verhulst, Berden, and Sanders-Woudstra (1985), prevalence ranged from 26% when cases of moderate severity were included to 7% when only those classified as severely disturbed were considered. Similarly, in the recent Methods for the Epidemiology of Child and Adolescent Disorders (MECA) Study, rates ranged from nearly 40% when diagnoses were made on the basis of symptom criteria alone to rates ranging from 20% to 5% when increasing degrees of impairment were required to define a case (Shaffer et al., 1996). Thus, the question of prevalence can honestly be answered in many different ways, and the answer depends mainly on the reason for asking. There are circumstances in which only severely disturbed cases are of concern, and there are other instances in which the occurrence of behaviors generally thought of as "symptoms" is of interest even when they are not accompanied by interference in functioning or perceived need for treatment.

TRENDS IN THE PREVALENCE OF PSYCHIATRIC DISORDERS IN CHILDHOOD AND ADOLESCENCE

Generally, rates of disorder tend to increase from childhood to adolescence (Offord and Fleming, 1996). While the emotional disorders (or internalizing disorders, e.g., anxiety and depression) tend to be the most prevalent overall (Angold & Costello, 1995b; Costello, 1989), it is more revealing to view frequencies and shifts in frequencies by gender and age group. Overall, boys have more disruptive behavior problems and girls more emotional disorders (Costello, 1989). In particular, rates of major depressive disorder have been shown to increase markedly in girls during mid-adolescence when they reach the 2:1 female:male gender ratio characteristic of this disorder in adults (Angold & Costello, 1995a; Angold & Worthman, 1993; Cohen, Cohen, & Brook, 1993; Weissman & Klerman, 1977), and conduct disorders increase among boys after puberty (Costello, 1989). The rate of attention-deficit hyperactivity disorder is substantially higher in boys than girls in childhood and through adolescence (Cohen, Cohen, & Kasen, 1993). Trends such as these point to the importance of incorporating a developmental perspective in studying psychiatric disorders in children and adolescents and in considering the particular service needs of this changing population. It has also been shown that risk for psychiatric disorder is increased in children who do poorly at school; who have chronic health problems, brain disorder, difficult temperament, or parental psychopathology; who grow up in situations of economic disadvantage; and who come from families with high levels of marital discord and family dysfunction (Offord & Fleming, 1996).

In addition to the important task of identifying groups of children and adolescents who are at risk for psychiatric disorder or who may be in need of treatment, the determination of course and persistence of disorder are critical and carry implications for planning and delivery of mental health services. Cohen, Cohen, Brook (1993) examined this issue in a study of 734 children aged 9–18 years who were followed up after a 2 1/2 year period. They found substantial levels of persistence in diagnosis over this period, with one third or more of cases sustaining an equivalent diagnostic level at follow-up. The exception to this finding was major depression, where the episodic nature of the disorder reduces the likelihood that it will have occurred within any specific period. The authors note that findings such as these argue for a view of child psychopathology as persistent, perhaps as persistent as the typical diagnosable disorder in adulthood (Cohen, Cohen, & Brook, 1993).

WHERE WE ARE AND FUTURE DIRECTIONS

Over the past two decades, substantial progress has been made in the development of methodologies for studying childhood psychiatric disorder and in the descriptive epidemiology of this field. The convergence of findings with respect to the prevalence and correlates of disorder is heartening and speaks to their validity. Earls (1989) notes the success of what he calls the "first phase" for epidemiology and child psychiatry but cites two caveats. The first is the relatively greater level of success in studying broadly conceptualized disorders. This contrasts with the current system for classifying and studying disorders which delineates specific entities with relatively sharper edges. The second of Earls's caveats, noted by Offord (1995) as well, involves the need to identify and understand causal risk factors, particularly those that can be changed. While many correlates of disorder are known, considerably less is known about those risk factors that are truly causal and for which it is actually possible to intervene.

With these caveats, Earls suggests that the partnership between child psychiatry and epidemiology is ready to move into a second phase, one of experimentation. In this respect, he is proposing preventive trials, in which interventions would be developed to reduce exposure to causal risk factors or, alternatively, efforts would be directed toward increasing the competence of vulnerable children so that they might more effectively resist the effects of factors that dispose toward disorder. Thus, one future direction involves the use of preventive trials, both to shed light on etiology (i.e., by testing the effects of interventions on hypothesized causal risk factors) and to determine the effectiveness of preventive strategies on the occurrence of disorder.

A second future direction involves the necessity to understand fully the need for child psychiatric treatment services and the major gap that exists between the numbers of children with significant psychopathology and the numbers who actually receive services. Costello, Burns, Angold, and Leaf (1993), summarizing from recent studies, note that while one child in five has a DSM disorder, and one in ten is significantly impaired, only half of the latter receive mental healthcare and far fewer are treated in specialty mental healthcare settings. At a time when systems of care are being scrutinized and restructured, and changes in mental health services are being driven by concerns about healthcare costs (Leaf et al., 1996), it is particularly important that those efforts utilize data on prevalence of child psychiatric disorder, impairment due to disorder, and availability and use of services. It is equally important for child psychiatric epidemiology as a field to develop the base of information that will most effectively serve the planning needs of those charged with the mental healthcare of our next generation.

REFERENCES

Achenbach, T. M., & Edelbrock, C. (1983). *Manual for the child behavior checklist and revised child behavior profile.* Burlington, VT: University of Vermont, Department of Psychiatry.

Anderson, J. C., Williams, S., McGee, R., & Silva, P. A. (1987). DSM-III disorders in preadolescent children: Prevalence in a large sample from the general population. *Archives of General Psychiatry, 44,* 69–76.

Angold, A., Prendergast, M., Cox, A., Harrington, R., Simonoff, E., & Rutter, M. (1995). The Child and Adolescent Psychiatric Assessment (CAPA). *Psychological Medicine, 25,* 739–753.

Angold, A., & Worthman, C. W. (1993). Puberty onset of gender differences in rates of depression: A developmental, epidemiologic and neuroendocrine perspective. *Journal of Affective Disorders, 29,* 145–158.

Angold, A., & Costello, E. J. (1995a). Developmental epidemiology. *Epidemiologic Reviews, 171,* 74–82.

Angold, A., & Costello, E. J. (1995b). A test-retest reliability study of child-reported psychiatric symptoms and diagnoses using the Child and Adolescent Psychiatric Assessment (CAPA-C). *Psychological Medicine, 25,* 755–762.

Bird, H. R., Canino, G., Rubio-Stipec, M., Gould, M. S., Ribera, J., Sesman, M., Woodbury, M., Huertas, S., Pagan, A., Sanchez-Lacay, A., & Moscoso, M. (1988). Estimates of the prevalence of childhood maladjustment in a community survey in Puerto Rico. *Archives of General Psychiatry, 44,* 821–824.

Bird, H., Gould, M., & Staghezza, B. (1993). Patterns of diagnostic comorbidity in a community sample of children aged 9 through 16 years. *Journal of the American Academy of Child and Adolescent Psychiatry, 32,* 361–368.

Brandenburg, N., Friedman, R., & Silver, S. (1990). The epidemiology of childhood psychiatric disorders: Prevalence findings from recent studies. *Journal of the American Academy of Child and Adolescent Psychiatry, 291,* 76–83.

Cohen, P., Cohen, J., & Brook, J. (1993). An epidemiological study of disorders in late childhood and adolescence—II. Persistence of disorders. *Journal of Child Psychology and Psychiatry, 346,* 869–877.

Cohen, P., Cohen, J., Kasen, S., Velez, C. N., Hartmark, C., Johnson, J., Rojas, M., Brook, J., & Streuning, E. L. (1993). An epidemiological study of disorders in late childhood and adolescence—I. Age- and gender-specific prevalence. *Journal of Child Psychology and Psychiatry, 346,* 851–867.

Cohen, P., Velez, N., Kohn, M., Schwab-Stone, M., & Johnson, J. (1987). Child psychiatric diagnosis by computer algorithm: Theoretical issues and empirical tests. *Journal of the American Academy of Child and Adolescent Psychiatry, 26,* 631–638.

Costello, E. (1989). Developments in child psychiatric epidemiology. *Journal of the American Academy of Child and Adolescent Psychiatry, 28*(6), 836–841.

Costello, E. J., Angold, A., Burns, B. J., Stangl, D. K., Tweed, D. L., Erkanli, A., & Worthman, C. M. (1996). The Great Smoky Mountains Study of youth: Goals, design, methods, and the prevalence of DSM-III-R disorders. *Archives of General Psychiatry, 53,* 1129–1136.

Costello, E. J., Burns, B. J., Angold, A., & Leaf, P. J. (1993). How can epidemiology improve mental health services for children and adolescents? *Journal of the American Academy of Child and Adolescent Psychiatry, 32*(6), 1106–1114.

Costello, E. J., Edelbrock, C. S., Dulcan, M., & Kalas, R. (1984). *Testing of the NIMH Diagnostic Interview Schedule for Children (DISC).* Pittsburgh, PA: Western Psychiatric Institute and Clinic, School of Medicine, University of Pittsburgh.

Earls, F. (1985). Epidemiology of psychiatric disorders in children and adolescents. In J. O. Cavenar (Gen. Ed.), *Psychiatry* (Vol. 3, Chap. 12). Philadelphia: J. B. Lippincott.

Earls, F. (1989). Epidemiology and child psychiatry: Entering the second phase. *American Journal of Orthopsychiatry, 592,* 279–283.

Gould, M. S., Wunsch-Hitzig, R., & Dohrenwend, B. P. (1980). Formulation of hypotheses about the prevalence, treatment and prognostic significance of psychiatric disorders in children in the United States. In B. P. Dohrenwend, M. S., Gould, & B. Link (Eds.), *Mental illness in the United States: Epidemiological estimates* (pp. 9–44). New York: Praeger.

Hodges, K. (1993). Structured interviews for assessing children. *Journal of Child Psychology and Psychiatry, 341,* 49–68.

Lapouse, R., & Monk, M. A. (1958). An epidemiological study of behavior characteristics in children. *American Journal of Orthopsychiatry, 48,* 1134–1144.

Leaf, P. J., Alegria, M., Cohen, P., Goodman, S. H., Horwitz, S. M., Hoven, C. W., Narrow, W. E., Vaden-Kiernan, M., & Regier, D. A. (1996). Mental health service use in the community and schools: Results from the four-community MECA study. *Journal of the American Academy of Child Adolescent Psychiatry, 35*(7), 889–897.

Lilienfeld, A. M. (1976). *Foundations of epidemiology.* New York: Oxford University Press.

Offord, D. R. (1995). Child psychiatric epidemiology: Current status and future prospects. *Canadian Journal of Psychiatry, 40,* 284–288.

Offord, D., Boyle, M. H., & Racine, Y. (1989). Ontario Child Health Study: Correlates of disorder. *Journal of the American Academy of Child and Adolescent Psychiatry, 28,* 856–860.

Offord, D., Boyle, M., Szatmari, P., Rae-Grant, N., Links, P., Cadman, D., Byles, J., Crawford, J., Blum, H., Byrne, C., Thomas, H., & Woodward, C. (1987). Ontario Child Health Study: II. Six-month prevalence of disorder and rates of service utilization. *Archives of General Psychiatry, 44,* 832–836.

Offord, D. R., & Fleming, J. E. (1996), Epidemiology. In M. Lewis (Ed.), *Child and adolescent psychiatry: A comprehensive textbook* (pp. 1166–1178). Baltimore,: Williams & Wilkins.

Regier, D. A., Myers, J. K., Kramer, M., Robins, L. N., Blazer, D. G., Hough, R. L., Eaton, W. W., & Locke, B. Z. (1984). The NIMH Epidemiological Catchment Area Program: Historical context, major objectives, and study population characteristics. *Archives of General Psychiatry, 41,* 934–941.

Robins, L., Helzer, J. E., Croughan, J., & Ratcliff, K. S. (1981). NIMH Diagnostic Interview Schedule: Its history, characteristics and validity. *Archives of General Psychiatry, 38,* 381–389.

Rutter, M., Tizard, J., & Whitmore, K. (1970). *Education, health and behavior.* Harlow, England: Longman.

Rutter, M., Tizard, J., Yule, W., Graham, P., & Whitmore, K. (1976). Isle of Wight Studies , 1964–1974. *Psychological Medicine, 6,* 313–332.

Shaffer, D., Fisher, P., Dulcan, M., Davies, M., Piacentini, J., Schwab-Stone, M. E., Lahey, B., Bourdon, K., Jensen, P., Bird, H., Canino, G., & Regier, D. A. (1996). The NIMH Diagnostic Interview Schedule for Children Version 2.3 (DISC-2.3): Description, acceptability, prevalence rates, and performance in the MECA study. *Journal of the American Academy of Child and Adolescent Psychiatry, 35*(7), 1865–877.

Shaffer, D., Schwab-Stone, M., Fisher, P., Cohen, P., Piacentini, J., Davies, M., Conners, K., & Regier, D. (1993). The Diagnostic Interview Schedule for Children-Revised Version (DISC-R): I. Preparation, field testing, interrater reliability, and acceptability. *Journal of the American Academy of Child and Adolescence Psychiatry, 32,* 643–650.

Verhulst, F. C., Berden, G. F. M., & Sanders-Woudstra, J. (1985). Mental health in Dutch children: (II) The prevalence of psychiatric disorder and relationship between measures. *Acta Psychiatrica Scandinavica, 72* (Suppl. 324), 1–45.

Vikan, A. (1985). Psychiatric epidemiology in a sample of 1510 ten-year-old children: I. Prevalence. *Journal of Child Psychology & Psychiatry, 26,* 55–75.

Weissman, M. M., & Klerman, G. L. (1977). Sex differences and the epidemiology of depression. *Archives of General Psychiatry, 38,* 381–389.

THE COSTS OF DEVELOPMENTAL PSYCHOPATHOLOGY: FINANCING, MANAGEMENT, AND QUALITY OF CARE OF MENTAL HEALTH SERVICES FOR CHILDREN AND ADOLESCENTS

3

Trends in Cost Management for Healthcare Services: Managed Care in the 1990s

J. GERALD YOUNG

THE COST OF HEALTHCARE

Twenty-five years ago a book examining the process of designing mental health systems for children and adolescents would have reviewed professional topics and controversies and presented research data, but would have mentioned economic perspectives and financial management little or not at all. Today the emphasis is the opposite. Healthcare has become so expensive for all nations that professional strategies and programs are developed within the context of economic structures that definitively limit many of the options available for these programs.

Healthcare expenditures in the United States increased dramatically, over little more than two decades, from 6% of the gross national product (GNP) to more than 12% by the mid-1990s, and are anticipated to reach 17% by the year 2000. The percentages of the GNP devoted to healthcare expenditures in France and Sweden are similar to that in the United States, but in absolute dollars, the expenditures are less. In the United States, of a total expenditure of more than $800 billion in 1991, it is estimated that more than $100 billion (about 13%) was for the treatment of mental disorders and substance abuse (Sharfstein, Webb, & Stoline, 1996). Moreover, with all of these expenditures, various reports have suggested that the overall health of Americans is not substantially better than the health of citizens of comparable countries spending far less, suggesting that little value is obtained by the high costs. These massive expenditures and nettlesome controversies leave no doubt that economics and financial management are to be essential ingredients of all mental health program development for children and adolescents.

It is not surprising that people and nations choose to spend large amounts of money to improve the health of their families. The challenges for healthcare financing will persist and new solutions will continue to appear, such as the recent strategy of "managed care" in the United States. For other countries it is a useful model of privatization and "for profit" methods of cost containment.

METHODS OF PAYMENT FOR HEALTHCARE AND THE ORIGINS OF MANAGED CARE

The method of payment for medical services in the United States has become a battleground of cost control, competition, worries about quality of care, ethical concerns, corporate maneuvering for market control, consumer rights . . . . The list is long as the century comes to a close. Payment methods affect incentives for providers, medical care opportunities and choices for patients, and costs and their control for the entities who pay for the medical services and the corporations who purchase services on a large scale. When the healthcare industry became the largest industry in the United States, it was inevitable that novel approaches to payment for medical services would emerge. This spawned the health maintenance organizations (HMOs) and managed care organizations (MCOs) that burst onto the scene in the 1980s and 1990s and are now so familiar to Americans. The fundamental change is from a *fee-for-service payment to a physician* or other healthcare provider, to prepaid medicine. Prepayment and group practice were combined to generate a health management strategy designed to provide healthcare that is affordable while maintaining or improving its quality.

Prepaid medicine utilizes an agreement through which a specific package of medical services is provided by an identified healthcare provider to a predetermined group of patients for a preset fee. It has a long history preceding the explosion of activity in the past decade. It initially was a solution to the problem of delivering healthcare services to a geographically remote and sometimes migratory population. These were lean and limited programs that did not resemble conventional medical practice, and mental healthcare was not a component. *Group practice* appeared in the 1880s (e.g., the Mayos and other groups) as a means to improve medical care by providing a range of specialist care that was coordinated organizationally and contained mechanisms for improving quality of care through physician training plans. *Rural cooperatives, city governments, and consortiums of employers and consumers* brought together prepaid medicine and group practice in order to devise an alternative to fee-for-service medicine. As HMOs began to appear and expand in the late 1950s, some independent practitioners drew together into organizations functioning in separate offices while offering prepaid medical care as a unit—the beginning of *independent practice associations (IPAs)*. Psychiatrists participated in only a limited manner in these early IPAs, as psychiatric services were considered to be too expensive (because the treatments were viewed as time-intensive) to be practical for full inclusion (Bittker, 1992).

By the late 1960s and the 1970s, the controversy about payment for medical services was serious and a subject of policy debate at government, corporate, and consumer levels. This was fueled by a growing recognition that medical cost control was looming ever larger as a problem and could not be ignored. Another shift occurred in the early 1970s; this time, it was a shift in perspective that gave incentives for promoting health rather than treating illnesses. President Nixon signed the Health Maintenance Organization Act of 1973 to promote HMO development, although with restrictive conditions by today's standards. The number of HMO plans and patients covered by them remained small (Bittker, 1992). This concern about costs was justified, however, because beginning in the 1960s, healthcare expenditures increased, and the rapid escalation quickly reached a rate of twice the rate of general inflation and stayed at this level until being slowed in the 1990s. This was coupled with poor performance of the general economy, making the problem much more intolerable. By the late 1980s, the annual rate of inflation of health insurance premiums approached 20%, and large employers refused to ignore the problem. The fee-for-service payment system was under attack and corporate employers developed new strategies, including the decision to not insure employees or to shift the cost of healthcare partially to employees by increasing the employees' contribution to health insurance premiums, deductibles, and copayments. In addition, some large employers chose to establish self-insured plans, paying physicians and hospitals directly. Nothing slowed the engine of healthcare inflation, and by 1990 new corporate strategies and decisions grasped the healthcare market more firmly, as large employers began using varied tactics, such as channeling employees into managed care plans, aggregating with other corporate employers into regional purchasing coalitions, and contracting directly with healthcare providers so as to reduce or eliminate the role of managed care insurers.

Additionally, there were too many indicators that healthcare was managed unwisely and the suspicion that existing payment mechanisms actually encouraged it: frequent unnecessary hospitalization, the existence of cost-effective alternatives to hospitalization, the failure of a reduction of length of stays to have a negative impact on outcomes, the observation that a small proportion of enrollees account for a high percentage of outpatient visits, and the striking diversity of patterns of treatment for various types of psychiatric disorders (Iglehart, 1996).

THE COSTS OF MENTAL HEALTHCARE AND THE ENTRY OF MANAGED CARE INTO MENTAL HEALTH SYSTEMS

Anxieties About the Inclusion of Mental Healthcare Within Managed Care Plans

Early experiments with HMOs during the 1960s and 1970s included basic mental health benefits in order to compete with the better psychiatric benefits provided in private insurance programs. This was viewed with apprehension because of the concern that too many patients with chronic mental illness would enter the plans. At the same time the growing number of patients with alcohol and drug abuse problems needed several types of medical care and might enter into the plans through any of several doors. The emphasis was on time-limited services, and specific types of patients were excluded from these early plans. The preferred psychiatric intervention was consultation to primary care practitioners (Bittker, 1992). Moreover, the apparent discrimination against mental illnesses posed ethical and legal problems.

Approximately 20% of the population of the United States has a diagnosable mental disorder, yet only 10% to 20% of these patients receive treatment. Moreover, discrimination against individuals with these disorders results in a disproportionate number not having health insurance of any kind (twice the percentage of patients with general medical disorders). Bias against patients with mental health disorders causes an unjustified portrayal of them as disproportionate contributors to increasing insurance costs and the healthcare crisis generally, while stigmatization prevents these patient groups from responding to these allegations.

The nature of many psychiatric assessment methods and treatments continues to seem dubious and imprecise to many outside the field, in spite of advances that clarify and substantiate them. Professional controversies about therapeutic methods, as well as the expanding number of types of mental health practitioners (many with minimal training) who confuse the public's understanding of the professional status of various therapists, have bred skepticism about the efficacy and legitimacy of mental health treatments. It is ironic that this is a strong factor in economic policy debates now, at a time when neuroscience data are validating many clinical observations of the past and clinical research methods have achieved remarkable progress, from diagnostic sensitivity to functional brain imaging. Nevertheless, these problems and biases continue to undermine the credibility of mental health clinicians and services, leaving them more vulnerable to the more severe elements of cost containment methods.

The Costs of Mental Illnesses

Nevertheless, by the mid-1980s, prepaid behavioral healthcare was growing rapidly, along with prepaid medical care. This was inevitable, because the cost of behavioral healthcare was much too high to be hidden. During the year 1990, $85.1 billion was spent for direct treatment costs for behavioral health disorders by Americans. This amounted to about 10% of all personal health expenditures. Moreover, most of this was paid for by "third party payers": someone other than the patient or the provider, usually the government, an insurance company, or a managed care company. In 1990, 40% of expenditures for mental health and substance abuse services was paid for by private insurance or out-of-pocket payments. Another 22% was paid for by the federal government (through Medicare, Medicaid, the Department of Veterans Affairs, and other programs). The remaining

38% came from state and local government expenditures (Iglehart, 1996). These expenditures were certain to motivate these payers to establish another payment mechanism.

One of the dilemmas facing policy makers is that the estimates of the cost of mental illness and substance abuse are actually underestimates. For example, the estimate quoted above is that more than $100 billion was paid for the treatment of mental disorders and substance abuse in 1991 in the United States. However, the actual total economic cost was estimated by a study to be $273.3 billion for mental illness and substance abuse when including a broad range of factors like reduced productivity, premature death, law enforcement expenses, motor vehicle accidents, and the like (Sharfstein et al., 1996).

Third party payers, on the other hand, have doubts about the efficacy of psychiatric treatments at the same time that costs are escalating. Finding that limitations on insurance coverage for psychiatric treatments appear to be especially effective, cost containment has been the primary focus of all management efforts to restructure the delivery of mental healthcare using managed care and benefit limits.

Deviations of the Healthcare Economy from Traditional Market Economies

All of these factors lead to accelerating costs as the target for reforms in the management of mental health services, and cost containment as the primary goal in the design of mental health systems. This is accomplished using a variety of procedures. They can be grouped according to how they affect the supply or demand for mental health services within a market economy. However, we recall that medicine, and particularly psychiatry, does not fit well within the traditional concept of market-based economics for several reasons. An important element of this is the presence of third party payers instead of just suppliers and consumers of the services. This reflects the fact that the consumers and suppliers (providers) cannot pay for all of these services. For psychiatry in particular, another element makes it an exception to traditional market-based economics. Mental healthcare involves a disproportionate number of patients with chronic, severe disorders, and this, along with various biases, has made insurance companies reluctant to provide mental health services and to assume the perceived risk of caring for too many patients with chronic illnesses that will result in high service utilization among these patients who have few resources with which to pay for the services. This has led to the intervention of the government into the mental healthcare marketplace, altering market dynamics by providing a safety net upon which both insurers and consumers depend. More generally, the presence of third party payers creates an artificial situation in which equilibrium between supply and demand is never achieved and, therefore, prices cannot be determined (Sharfstein et al., 1996).

Who are these third party payors? In the United States the payors from public systems include Medicare (healthcare coverage for persons 65 and over by the federal government), Medicaid (healthcare coverage for indigent patients by the federal and state governments), the Veterans Affairs medical system (for nearly 30 million veterans living in the United States), and state and local hospital and community health systems. The payors from the private sector include private health insurance companies, self-insuring corporations, and managed care organizations.

MANAGED CARE TECHNIQUES FOR COST CONTAINMENT

Methods to achieve cost containment can aim at either the demand or the supply of mental health services, and many examples of each are in active use.

Managed Care Organizations

Managed care has many definitions. Managed care is a system of managing patients and the cost of their healthcare using common business practices to provide the best healthcare services in the most cost-efficient manner, within a defined healthcare organization or network, using techniques that influence and restrict both the provider's and the patient's choices in order to assure cost containment. Managed care utilizes varied techniques to reduce expenditures for healthcare, as described in the following paragraphs. These methods are presented in detail in many books, such as books on managed care published by the American Medical Association and the American Psychiatric Association.

Alternative Payment Methods

A first method for containing healthcare costs is to select a method of payment for healthcare services that does not allow the clinician to control the amount charged for each service, with the possibility of increasing the fee at any time (whether to cover unexpected expenses or to increase the profit margin). A traditional fee-for-service method is one in which a fee is charged by the clinician for each service provided to the patient, who is to pay directly the amount charged. This method contributed to inflation of costs by removing the provider's incentive to provide efficient care. Under capitation and other payment methods, payors do not pay more for an increased volume of services. This is related to the problem that payments by third party payors protect both patients and clinicians from financial responsibility because they are not aware of the actual costs of treatment.

Variations on this method gradually emerged, such as a *costs-plus method* paid by a third party payor (a percentage of the indirect costs are added to the direct costs and reimbursed) or a *usual-customary-reasonable fee method* (these are calculated fees: the *usual fee* is the physician's average past fee, the *customary fee* is a selected percentile such as 80% or 90%, and the *reasonable fee* is a maximum allowable fee to be paid to the provider). *Bundling* of payment for multiple types of services under a single umbrella fee has become common, as has the use of *fee schedules*, which attempt to relate the fee to the complexity of the service provided within a list of fees paid for specific services.

Capitation is the single most significant fee method utilized in managed care organizations. Capitation is a method in which an organization agrees to provide services to a group of enrolled patients for a prepaid fixed fee. The specific amount paid is independent of the frequency and intensity of services later actually provided to the patients, so the provider organization assumes the risks of the illnesses, with functions of both provider and insurer.

The *prospective payment method* is discussed below under the example of the diagnosis-related group (DRG) method.

Cost Sharing

Costs can be affected on the demand side by the third party payor shifting some of the costs to the patient. This can be done in a variety of ways, such as not covering certain disorders (which often include psychiatric disorders) and leaving the patient to assume the risk, excluding certain prior illnesses, utilizing waiting periods before coverage is activated, and cost sharing. In addition, simple restrictions, such as limits on the number of visits to the physician, can be utilized and are common for psychiatric care.

Cost sharing makes patients more aware of the expenses associated with treatment, and include the *deductible* (a specific amount to be paid by the patient before any insurance payment is made), *coinsurance* (a percentage of the agreed upon fee for services that the patient must pay, e.g., 20% for surgical services or 50% for outpatient psychiatric care), and a *copayment* (a flat fee to be paid by the patient for each time the specific service is rendered).

Cost sharing on the supply side consists of mechanisms to reduce the amounts of reimbursements and increase incentives for clinical efficiency. The methods are aimed at both clinicians and hospitals or other healthcare facilities. They include fee schedules, discounted fees, and capitation and other prospective payment methods. These are the most effective cost containment methods, and they shift financial risk to clinicians and facilities. The typical methods include the following.

Fee freezes: Prohibitions by the government against an increase in fees, which, however, when lifted, are followed by subsequent substantial increases. This strategy has not been useful in the long run for cost containment.

Health maintenance organizations: HMOs use the capitation method of a prospective, predetermined payment calculated on a per-person or capitated basis as payment for healthcare services provided by the HMO. The three types of HMOs are a *staff HMO* (direct employment of providers and a group setting for care provision to patients); a *group practice HMO* (the HMO contracts with a separate provider group or multiple groups in the network model); and *independent practice associations (IPAs)* (physicians in private practice in their own offices who organize together and are paid by the HMO on a discounted fee-for-service basis).

Preferred provider organizations (PPOs): This is a network of independent clinicians who negotiate with a payor to arrange a discounted fee schedule (typically 10% to 30% below customary fees) while being guaranteed a specific volume of patients. Strong utilization review guidelines are part of the arrangement. When a patient chooses to use a provider in the PPO, their cost sharing is less than when using a clinician outside the PPO.

Diagnosis-related groups (DRGs): This is a prospective payment system first used by Medicare in the United States. The financial risk of resource use is shifted to hospitals by assigning each patient to a DRG upon admission to the hospital (according to the patient's diagnosis, age, major procedures anticipated, and complications or comorbidity). Each DRG has a preset reimbursement rate, set and adjusted according to multiple influencing factors, which is paid as a lump sum for the hospitalization costs for that patient. The hospital then examines its *case mix*, the number of patients in each DRG, and how it affects overall patient care income. There were nine DRGs for mental disorders and five for substance abuse disorders among the original 470 Medicare DRGs. However, research documented that DRGs did not predict resource consumption for psychiatric disorders and these were exempted from DRGs. Each hospital then arranged another prospective payment system for psychiatric disorders that would be appropriate for its typical patient mix. Many risks in the DRG system indicated that the system was not applicable to psychiatric disorders (Sharfstein, Webb, & Stoline, 1996).

Resource-based relative value system (RBRVS): This method of payment, initiated by Medicare in the United States, was utilized as a variant of a fee schedule in order to hold down escalating fees for physician services. Using a consensus approach, it established a relative value of services in units (not dollars) in relation to a standard nomenclature for all services. The values reflect perceived value to patients and the necessary resource input (physician time, skill, practice expenses, and malpractice costs for each service). A dollar conversion factor set at various times determines the payment for the service. For example, in 1992, the conversion was total relative value units $\times$ \$31.00. This system was anticipated to shift payments from procedure-oriented specialties to cognitive specialties (including psychiatry). However, simulations suggested that average psychiatric reimbursement would actually decrease and regulations were revised after intensive negotiations (Sharfstein et al., 1996).

Utilization Review and Utilization Management

Utilization management affects patients on the demand side as a group of cost containment techniques used by purchasers of health benefits to manage healthcare costs by influencing decisions about the appropriateness of patient care procedures on a case by case basis. This shifts financial risk to the patient. The specific techniques include: *preadmission certification* (the requirement for prior approval by the insurance company for a nonemergency hospitalization), *second opinion programs* (payment by the insurance company for a second opinion when an expensive procedure is recommended), *discharge planning* (the treatment team and patient work with a case manager to facilitate early discharge), *gatekeepers* (the primary care provider who controls the flow of patients to providers by finding the most economical provider and favoring providers within the system), and *high-cost case managers* (providers who focus on those patients who generate high expenditures to facilitate a higher quality of care and keep the cost of care at a lower level).

On the supply side, *utilization review* is aimed at excessive resource use by the evaluation of the management of individual cases and the services provided. It is focused on clinician decisions and uses *peer review* by "professionals" (these can be psychiatrists, nurses, social workers, or medical records technicians, etc.). The peer review is applied at various times as prospective review, concurrent review, or retrospective review. Hospitals initially set up their own peer review groups, but in 1972 this was replaced by the requirement for *professional standards review organizations (PSROs)* and, in 1982, by *peer review organizations (PROs)* who compete for contracts with the state.

IN THE ALPHABET SOUP

Clinicians frustrated by the plethora of ever-changing cost containment techniques and their acronyms tease about the alphabet soup created, while more seriously questioning many aspects of these systems (Shore & Beigel, 1996). Nevertheless, some of the purposes of these systems are at least partially being fulfilled, and the intent to apply better management procedures to mental healthcare is laudable. However, there are many remaining problems being uncovered, as described in Chapter 26. The simplicity of the managed care approach has made it attractive, but is also its Achilles heel, as the clinical complexity of patient care is now becoming evident to managed care organizations, just as it has been to clinicians for centuries.

Child and adolescent psychiatry has been left out or on the periphery of managed care systems in many specific organizational methods that were established. Nevertheless, it is undeniable that these managed care systems have had a major impact on the organization and conduct of mental health services for children and adolescents in the United States. They must be integrated into our design of services and systems, at the same time that we strive to find better solutions.

While the appearance of managed care seemed abrupt and unpredictable to many physicians, the next phases of the evolution of healthcare systems will also contain surprises. For example, it now appears that large corporate employers are developing new strategies for cost containment and achieving increasing influence on the healthcare marketplace. One of the strategies being utilized increasingly is contracting directly with healthcare providers, eliminating or reducing the role of managed care organizations as a further avenue to cost containment for the corporation (Bodenheimer & Sullivan, 1998).

The predictability of change in healthcare financing mechanisms suggests that novel approaches to healthcare will be rewarded as these financing mechanisms evolve. Clinicians and administrators participating in mental healthcare services and systems now have powerful incentives to examine the assessments and treatments which they utilize. As improved treatment and prevention methods are developed, they will shape the delivery of mental healthcare for children and adolescents.

REFERENCES

Bittker, T. E. (1992). The emergence of prepaid psychiatry. In J. L. Feldman & F. J. Fitzpatrick (Eds.), *Managed Mental Health Care: Administrative and Clinical Issues* (pp. 3–10). Washington, D.C.: American Psychiatic Press.

Bodenheimer, T., & Sullivan, K. (1998). How large employers are shaping the health care marketplace. *New England Journal of Medicine. 338,* 1003–1007.

Iglehart, J. K. (1996), Managed care and mental health. *New England Journal of Medicine, 334,* 131–135.

Sharfstein, S. S., Webb, W. L., & Stoline, A. M. (1996). Economics of psychiatry. In H. Kaplan & B. Sadock (Eds.), *Comprehensive Textbook of Psychiatry* (6th ed., pp. 2677–2689). Baltimore: Williams & Wilkins.

Shore, M. F., & Beigel, A. (1996). The challenges posed by managed behavioral health care. *New England Journal of Medicine, 334,* 116–118.

4

The Consequences of Changes in Mental
Health Systems for Individual Children
and Families

JOHN E. SCHOWALTER

Given the brevity of this chapter, I will concentrate on the change in the mental health system with which I am the most familiar. This is the accelerating switch in the United States from insurance companies paying clinicians' fees for the particular services the clinicians deem necessary or appropriate to a new method of financing known as managed care. There are many types of managed care, but all require clinicians to be managed. Care may be managed by one or more of the following techniques: selecting which clinicians and facilities are credentialed for use by an insured population; requiring clinicians to obtain preauthorization for a treatment and continuing authorization throughout a treatment, in order for the clinician to be paid; using the least expensive clinicians possible, as determined by the managed care organization (MCO); lack of confidentiality between clinician and MCO; MCO-determined facility and fee rates; and a 10% to 20% portion of the clinician's fee withheld by the MCO, only to be released back to the clinician at the end of the year if the MCO has fared well financially. It has often been pointed out that managed care is better named "managed cost."

Prior to managed cost, clinicians typically charged a standard fee which, if within "community standards," would be paid to them for any services they or their facility believed necessary. The more care was provided, the more financial compensation was obtained. Clinicians and facilities sometimes overtreated and thus overcharged.

Healthcare costs, including those for mental health services, rose so steeply in the late 1980s and early 1990s that businesses complained that they could no longer continue to pay for employees' (and their dependents') health coverage and still remain competitive in the pricing of their products. Healthcare spending grew during the years between 1960 and 1990 at more than double the growth rate for the rest of the American economy. MCOs approached companies' benefits managers and offered to find clinicians and facilities to provide care to their employees at a preset per-member-per-month cost. The opportunity for companies to obtain a set healthcare cost at the beginning of their budget year was very popular, and today, over 75% of U.S. companies use MCO middlemen to arrange for their employees' healthcare.

There is a tradition in the United States that mentally ill children who live below a given poverty level be provided services financed by tax-supported public funds. These funds are usually a combination of monies from the state and federal governments. Each state has a network of clinics, hospitals, and residential treatment facilities which provides this type of care. This medical network is often informally linked with schools and with children's welfare services. In the mid-1990s, state governments also began to contract with MCOs to deliver care to poor and seriously emotionally disturbed children. This public managed care movement will probably, to some degree, involve all 50 states by the year 2000.

Most polls show that those insured through MCOs like them as well as they did their previous fee-for-service insurance. However, only about 20% of privately insured people use any medical care in a given year, so it is understandable that at least 80% notice no change. Studies of those who have a real need for mental healthcare services tend to be less happy with managed cost and more likely to disenroll if given the choice (Scholle, Kelleher, Childs, Mendeloff, & Gardner, 1997).

As a result of managed cost healthcare, the average length of an inpatient stay for children and adolescents has fallen fast and far in the 1990s. Although there are geographical differences that are linked directly to the severity of cost management, it is not unusual for an inpatient facility's average length of stay in a half-dozen years to have fallen from the range of 30–60 days to the range of 5–14 days. The sole admission criterion for many MCOs is a patient's dangerousness toward self or others. Although management has been most stringent regarding inpatient care, since it makes up the largest percentage of mental health costs, as inpatient dollars are squeezed as dry as possible, outpatient care is coming under much stricter scrutiny. What is most troubling for most clinicians, besides the loss of personal income, is the demand for psychiatrists to concentrate chiefly on medication management (Shore & Beigel, 1996), leaving them no time to form a therapeutic relationship or to be able to involve family and patient as fully as possible in the treatment process (Woolhandler & Himmelstein, 1996). Leon Eisenberg (1995) has made clear that time has always been a crucial factor in all medical care. Time is also required to sustain adequate teaching in academic departments.

The basic dialectic between clinicians and MCO owners is for clinicians to argue that less care hurts patients and for owners to reply: "prove it." Quality of care is very difficult to define and even more difficult to measure in a controlled manner that assesses outcomes. This is a current dilemma for all sections of medicine. Under the previous, fee-for-service reimbursement method, practitioners were not eager for, and often attacked attempts to perform controlled outcome studies. Today, the MCO owners are the ones who drag their feet. Those who are faring well are usually opposed to research that might upset their favorable status quo. There is much clinician reportage of revolving-door inpatient admissions and a deterioration in their child and adolescent patients' quality of life, but there is little data, not even anecdotal, to show a managed-care-caused rise in, for example, suicides, homicides, or worsening of psychosis.

Although managed cost managers have stressed that management will allow the money saved from "right-sizing" benefits to be used to provide mental health services for more persons, this is not true yet. A combination of increased joblessness and more stringent company benefit packages for employees' dependents has recently increased the number of uninsured American children (Newacheck, Hughes, & Cisternas, 1995). In 1997 there were an estimated 3 million American children who were eligible for Medicaid care but who were not enrolled, and an additional 7 million children of working parents whose family income was too high for Medicaid benefits but who did not have employee health benefits and could not afford to buy commercial health insurance.

Although it is very chancy to try to predict future changes in mental health financing and its future consequences, a few factors seem likely. Economic evaluation has become a given part of children's mental care evaluation (Knapp, 1997), and this seems immutable. While managed cost has slowed the steep yearly increases in healthcare costs, this has mainly benefited employers and for-profit MCOs. Few employees have seen either fiscal or personal benefit (Drake, 1997). If the latter does not occur, there could be a "consumer" backlash and a push for more legal oversight of MCO healthcare delivery. Money diverted from clinicians' pockets now goes into the higher MCO administrative costs, salaries, and stockholder payouts. One of the greatest dangers in the for-profit MCO takeover of the mental health service system for poor and severely ill children is that when the profits have all been taken, the for-profit MCOs will pull out of the mental health business. Since century-old public delivery systems are now being dismantled, a for-profit MCO pull-out in the future will leave state and local governments with a public system void and no other options for taking care of the nation's most vulnerable, most complicated, and most difficult children's mental health population. To avoid this nightmare, state and federal lawmakers must be lobbied forcefully to not entirely hand over this awesome responsibility to those who will only be around for as long as the profit is worth it.

REFERENCES

Drake, D. F. (1997). Managed care: A product of market dynamics. *Journal of the American Medical Association, 277,* 560–563.

Eisenberg, L. (1995). The social construction of the human brain. *American Journal of Psychiatry, 152,* 1563–1575.

Knapp, M. (1997). Economic evaluations and interventions for children and adolescents with mental health problems. *Journal of Child Psychology and Psychiatry, 38,* 3–25.

Newacheck, P. W., Hughes, D. C., & Cisternas, M. (1995). Children and health insurance: An overview of recent trends. *Health Affairs, 14(1),* 244–254.

Scholle, S. H., Kelleher, K. J., Childs, G., Mendeloff, J., & Gardner, W. P. (1997). Changes in medicaid managed care enrollment among children. *Health Affairs, 16(2),* 164–170.

Shore, M. F., & Beigel, A. (1996). The challenges posed by managed behavioral healthcare. *New England Journal of Medicine, 334,* 116–118.

Woolhandler, S., & Himmelstein, D. U. (1996). Annotation: Patients on the auction block. *American Journal of Public Health, 86,* 1699–1700.

5

Quality and Economics: The Concept of Equity in Times of Limited Resources

MARIO ZANETTI

This paper explores the relationships between quality and efficiency in healthcare. After first clarifying the differences between equity and equality, the former being seen as an ideal and the latter as "a fact," I will address the issue of cost containment within the Italian context of *aziendalizzazione*. This implies the transformation of large public hospitals into autonomous enterprises, the adoption of competitive mechanisms, and the pursuit of "value for money" in managing health services. Quality is not necessarily incompatible with efficiency; optimizing healthcare delivery and avoiding the inappropriate use of resources is a moral imperative. It is therefore important that clinicians whose daily decisions have, at times, tremendous financial implications get seriously and actively involved in order to avoid unleashing a wildcat market, which would be unfair as well as costly or, worse still, would create a formally equal system offering low-quality care.

When I was invited to contribute my thoughts on this topic, I recognized immediately that while I had no specific knowledge or experience in the field of child psychiatry, I was willing to present a perspective on the current relationship between economics and health. I took this perspective for two reasons: the first is that it would enable me to write on a subject within my sphere of competency, and the second is that, no matter what country one comes from, and no matter what healthcare system one has, we all must come to grips with the fact that, as we approach the beginning of the third millenium, economic resources are being curtailed in every field, including healthcare.

So the great challenge before us will be to maintain a united, equal, efficacious, efficient, and high-quality healthcare system while containing costs.

Will this be possible? Consider the answer to this question while I present a few thoughts on the relationship between quality and economics, with special attention on the concept of equity in times of limited resources.

In order to focus on the topic of this paper, it is necessary to define the current relationship among three elements in the field of healthcare that may apparently have to do with different themes, sometimes even contrasting ones, but that are intrinsically interconnected and complement one another: quality, the economic aspects of healthcare systems, and equity.

When talking about healthcare systems in terms of quality, we find ourselves inevitably pulled in different directions. If we wish to speak of the ''quality'' of care itself with respect to the services rendered and to the outcomes of care expressed in terms of added health for the recipients, it becomes especially important to assess: (a) the efficacy of the care given; (b) the balance between the inevitable risks caused by the care given and the benefits produced by the services rendered; (c) the degree of efficiency of the services rendered (optimality of the relationship between efficacy, necessity, and appropriateness of each service rendered in each specific case); and (d) accessibility to the healthcare system expressed in terms of equity: a healthcare system that offers adequate quality care must guarantee equal opportunity of access to the service requested for all those needing care without regard to level of income, place of residency, level of education, and so on.

It is really not necessary to add anything else, as every possible relationship between quality, equity, and the economic aspects of healthcare is included or implicit in the above considerations. It is, however, important to make one point clear: there are many other perspectives on the quality/economics relationship that will not be considered but that must be mentioned

One such perspective, which is quite common, is that high-quality care cannot be given unless investments are increased; this means that quality is a cost, and that to increase quality, one must add money. We can easily sustain the opposite theory today, thanks to programs of ''continuous quality improvement'' and ''total quality management'' that have in practice proven their own basic principles.

I should also mention the importance of the relationship between quality and the cost of the product, for the very fact that the product of the healthcare system and its quality are not easily definable.

In any event, if we reflect on the problem created by the necessity of maintaining acceptable margins of equity in the system notwithstanding the continuing contraction of available economic resources (or to rephrase the point, to maintain adequate margins of quality of the healthcare product while raising the level of efficiency of the system of production), it is necessary and it would seem feasible to demonstrate that equity need not be automatically lost when economic possibilities are reduced, and to actively demonstrate this in a system in which the contraction of financial resources has coincided, as it has in in just about every country, with the introduction of principles of private enterprise (called *aziendalizzazione* in Italy) into the healthcare system, giving us pause as to the preservation of equality and equity for citizens.

Having made these few preliminary points, I will now turn to the problem of equity in healthcare and to the relationship between equity and aziendalizzazione in terms of cost containment in healthcare.

THE PROBLEM OF EQUITY IN HEALTHCARE

As has been shown repeatedly since *The Black Report* (Townsend, 1982) on inequality in the English National Health Service, even in public healthcare systems that are committed to guaranteeing equal opportunity of access to healthcare for all citizens regardless of income, this objective has never been reached, not even in the more developed countries.

We have many facts to prove that:

1. The fringes of the population that fall into low income brackets have poorer health (for example, higher mortality rates, higher morbidity rates, higher frequency of cases of insomnia and depression, higher frequency of high-risk lifestyles).

2. The fringes of the population that fall into high income brackets interact more easily with the healthcare system and have greater access to its services, especially as regards specialist or preventive care (i.e., better quality healthcare services).

We may conclude by paraphrasing George Orwell that we may all be equal and yet "some are more equal than others."

Having made the above observations, I believe it fitting to consider some of the concepts implicit in the notion of equity. First, what does equity in the field of healthcare mean? Culyer (1993) summarizes equity as follows:

- equality of expenditure pro capita,
- distribution based on needs,
- distribution based on health status,
- equality of access/utilization;

while Leenan summarizes it this way:

- equal access to healthcare,
- equal utilization for equal needs,
- equal quality of healthcare.

Having said this, it is important to point out that equity is not the same thing as equality. The first is a feature of a certain "political" line supported by government, while the latter is the effect of the adopted policy on the members of the community to which the policy has been applied. Or we could say that equity is a just distribution of healthcare resources, and equality is how health is distributed within the population. It is also important to remember what Bobbio, a renowned Italian philosopher still living today, wrote on the subject of justice and equality: "Justice is an ideal, equality is a fact."

Since, when we speak of equality, it is necessary to determine "equality among whom, with respect to what, and what kind of balance there is between the sacrifices asked of those in an advantageous position and the benefits to those at a disadvantage," the establishment of a fair or just policy does not so much mean guaranteeing equal opportunity of access to all members of the community to every service necessary to satisfy every need expressed (the basic notion of the welfare statement), but rather guaranteeing all members of the community equal opportunity of access to those services that the community decides can satisfy a given priority of essential needs.

Therefore, we can safely say that equality in health, meaning equal opportunity of access to priority services, and the quality of healthcare are two concepts that cannot be separated.

THE RELATIONSHIP BETWEEN EQUITY AND AZIENDALIZZAZIONE IN TERMS OF COST CONTAINMENT IN HEALTHCARE

Upon first inspection, it would seem that any form of cost containment in healthcare accompanied by forms of management based on principles similar to those of private enterprise would damage the qualities of solidarity and egalitarianism that the healthcare system may have hitherto defended.

This, in fact, is what is feared by those who, having analyzed the current trends in Italy as well as in other countries, have come to the conclusion that a civilized country's only acceptable answer to its citizens' health problems is to offer a totally public healthcare service structured on solidarity and egalitarian principles. These thinkers have not realized that this is perhaps feasible in theory only.

Yet, as the literature on the subject demonstrates, neither totally public nor completely private healthcare systems exist that have found the exhaustive answer to the health needs of a given population. It is therefore necessary to look for our solution in intermediate systems that include both public and private aspects. This is exactly what countries in Europe and other parts of the world, including Italy, are currently trying to achieve.

In Figures 5.1 and 5.2 we have illustrated what could happen if this trend towards accepting private enterprise principles (aziendalizzazione) into a public healthcare system were to lead to inequality for healthcare recipients.

Public healthcare policy today (Figure 5.1) is based on three major tendencies. The first is toward the contraction of funds, the second, toward giving incentives to boost efficiency, and the third, toward adopting some forms of privatization. In order to reach these

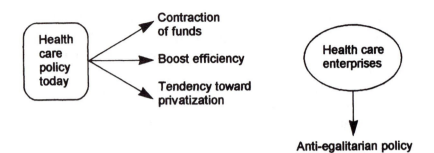

Figure 5.1 *Effects of the introduction of private enterprise principles into a public healthcare system (I)*

goals we have created the *aziende sanitarie* or healthcare enterprises. Taken by itself, a private enterprise or business, if dedicated exclusively to making a profit, could lead to an anti-egalitarian policy, and this is neither desirable nor acceptable in the field of healthcare.

Current public healthcare policy (Figure 5.2) is working towards aziendalizzazione in our public hospitals and other healthcare facilities. The adoption of competitive mechanisms (internal competition

CURRENT HEALTH CARE POLICY

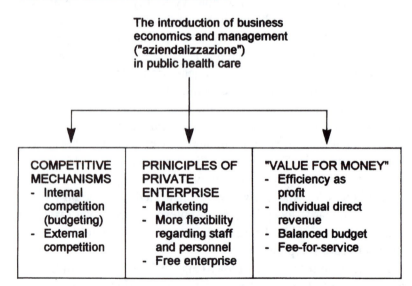

Figure 5.2 *Effects of the introduction of private enterprise principles into a public healthcare system (II)*

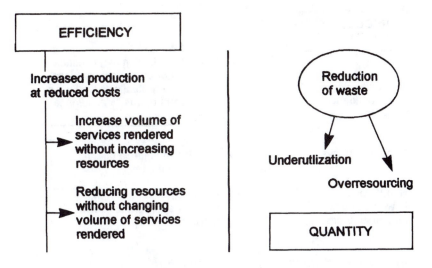

Figure 5.3 *Boosting efficiency through incentives*

through budgeting and external competition with other public and private facilities), principles of private enterprise (marketing, more flexibility regarding staff and personnel, and free enterprise), and "value for money" (efficiency as profit, individual direct revenue, balanced budgeting, and fee-for-service) will become important objectives for all healthcare enterprises.

The fact that we are faced with having to work with limited resources could lead to conditions of inequality that can only be avoided if certain protective mechanisms are put into effect:

1. Boosting efficiency through incentives, thus leading to improved efficiency (Figure 5.3). This means increasing production and reducing costs, increasing the volume of services rendered without increasing resources, reorganizing the services, and a substantial commitment to reducing waste.
2. Reduction of waste (Figure 5.3) in terms of both quantity (waste due to underutilization and/or to overresourcing) and quality (ineffective or unwarranted practices must be eliminated, and incentives must be offered that encourage the choice of giving only necessary and appropriate care; see Figure 5.4).

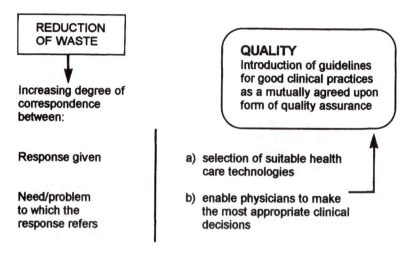

Figure 5.4   *Reduction of waste through the introduction of guidelines*

3. Optimizing healthcare services (Figure 5.5) to avoid the inappropriate use of resources for those patients not needing care, thus leaving valuable resources for those who could benefit from their use.
4. Maintaining certain standards of equity in the delivery of healthcare.

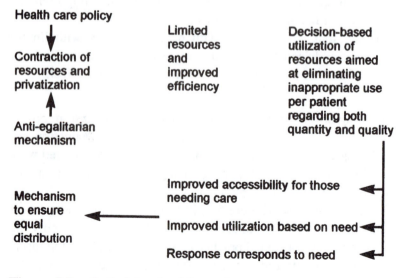

Figure 5.5   *Optimizing health services*

Even if we manage to achieve what has been outlined, inequality and discrimination cannot be totally avoided with respect to equal opportunity of access to care. It must be very clear, however, that if efficiency is to improve, and if the efficacy and quality of the healthcare system and adequate levels of equity are to be guaranteed, we will have to have the full support of our physicians.

The efficiency, efficacy of treatment, and quality we are referring to here are, to use a term dear to Prof. Donabedian, "clinical"; therefore, "managerial" efficiency can at best work as a support mechanism.

So if our clinicians do not get seriously and actively involved, due to lack of either effort on our part or volition on theirs, we may create a free and wildcat market, which would mean an unfair and costly one. Worse still, we could create a formally equal system offering low-quality care. Something of this sort happened in Bologna as far back as the 14th century, when members of the *promedicato* (the Governing Board of Health in Bologna from 1550 to 1700), deciding what tariff to put on theriac, a universal drug compound, realized that not all citizens could afford it and so decided to promote a less expensive product of inferior quality that the poor could afford. Reflections on this story and on what I have discussed in the paper, I will leave to the reader.

REFERENCES

Culyer, A. J. (1993). Health, health expenditures and equity. In E. van Doorslaer et al. (Eds.), *Equity in the finance and delivery of health care. An international perspective* (pp. 191–198). Oxford, England: Oxford University Press.

Townsend P. (1982). *The Black Report.* London: Penguin.

6

A Shrewd Investment: The Economics of Mental Healthcare for Children and Adolescents

D O N A L D   W .   L I G H T

V E I R A   F .   A .   B A I L E Y

Child and adolescent psychiatric services save society many times their cost and therefore are a shrewd investment. A sound financial plan first estimates the incidence and prevalence of need in a community or population and then estimates the costs of effective treatment plans by mental health teams. These actions, together, yield a solidly based budget, to which should be added costs for supervising the team, in-service training, and consultation with and training of other agencies. Early recognition and treatment save money compared to later recognition and treatment. These procedures are obvious and sensible but rarely done.

Child and adolescent psychiatric services catch disabling and maladaptive patterns of behavior early instead of letting them persist for years into adult life and, through poor parenting, into the next generation. This affects not only mental health services but also educational services, the criminal justice system, and social security. Longitudinal studies find that about half the children with psychiatric disorders exhibit the same or similar disorders years later (Robins & Rutter, 1990). This figure is not surprising and may be higher, for disabling symptoms reflect ways that children have learned to defend themselves and cope in what they perceive to be a threatening or troubling world, and they go on coping in those same ways unless they learn new ways.

Tom, for example, was a nice boy but had not attended school for a year when he was referred to a child mental health team at age 13. Even before age 12, he had managed to stay out of school for three weeks or so whenever he got a cold or a "tummy ache," and to miss days because he went to sleep late. His school attendance problems had led to his being removed from his family and put in a children's home, which had no better luck getting him to school.

In addition, the child mental health team found a family of three older children, none of whom had stayed in school, and an unmarried mother on welfare benefits who set no limits on her children. The eldest child was now an 18-year-old unmarried mother of two. The second oldest had been a truant and stayed in his room all day, isolated, unskilled, and collecting welfare checks. The third child saw little of the inside of a classroom and was on her way to a life like her mother, older sister, and brother.

After a complex assessment by a psychiatric team in London. Tom was treated for school refusal using a specialized program of services: a carefully structured intensive group experience, family counseling, and carefully orchestrated integration into school. He has been in school ever since (5 years) and is the only member of his family to stay past age 16. He has passed his national proficiency exams.

As an investment, what would a cost-conscious purchaser pay for this service? What is it worth? Without it, Tom would probably have stayed in the children's home until 18 at a cost of 700 British pounds sterling a week, or 36,400 pounds a year. For 182,000 pounds, society would have purchased a chaotic, run-down holding operation with no benefits. Yet most municipalities and states more readily pay for such homes than invest in psychiatric treatments that are much more effective and save much more money. Tom would have ended up unskilled, semiliterate, and impaired by the unresolved issues about authority and institutions that plague school refusers. Tom would then most likely get and lose a couple of unskilled jobs, go on Social Security, turn to alcohol or drugs or both to salve the wastage of his life, and perhaps steal. By his 30s, if not before, his use of medical services would rise well above that of comparable people who finished school.

At a minimum, an untreated truant who is an agreeable person of normal intelligence is likely to be work-shy and agoraphobic. Such a person will probably cost society and the government 500,000 pounds over a lifetime, and run up a costly sum of medical services. At a maximum, an untreated aggressive truant will cost society and the government much more. Because he was treated, however, Tom is more likely to hold a steady job for life and pay taxes rather than draw welfare checks from the taxes of others.

Is this service then worth 50,000 pounds, that is, one-tenth the minimum cost without treatment? Is a 10-fold return a shrewd investment? Or is it worth 5,000 pounds, a 100-fold return on investment? The actual cost was only 769 pounds, a 650-fold return on investment. Yet school refusers all over the civilized world go untreated for lack of funds.

Conduct-disordered children offer another example of a serious problem with costly, long-term consequences that can be treated (Bailey, 1996). Such children, who have an abnormal rate of lying, cheating, stealing, hitting, disobeying, and not cooperating are increasingly prevalent (Webster-Stratton, 1991). Contributing to and compounding their problems is the fact that they are more likely to be abused by their parents and/or rejected by their peers (Coie, 1990; Reid, Taplin, & Loeber, 1981). Their behaviors tend to persist into adolescence and adult life through drug abuse, juvenile delinquency, adult crime, antisocial behavior, marital problems, poor employee relations, unemployment, interpersonal problems, and poor physical health (Kazdin, 1985; Robins, 1981). Children who exhibit conduct disorders early are more likely to become chronic offenders in later life (Patterson, DeBaryshe, & Ramsey, 1989). Several relatively brief training programs have been shown to be effective, saving many times their cost in medical, educational, criminal, and welfare expenditures (Webster-Stratton, 1991; Bailey, 1996).

Child and adolescent mental health services are the most underrated and neglected investment in healthcare today. They strengthen families, prevent decades of wasted life, teach self-help skills, increase productivity, minimize hospitalization, and reduce medical costs, welfare costs, crime, and police, court, and prison costs.

DEFINING NEEDS

Practically speaking, the economics of mental healthcare for children and adolescents center around defining needs and interventions so that a government, an authority, or another payer knows that it is purchasing something worthwhile. An important issue in defining needs concerns whether the term "needs" should be limited to those who can benefit from treatment. In an era of cost–benefit analysis and economic thinking, this limitation is understandable. Politically, this definition can be used to justify cutting services. Yet, such a definition would exclude all those suffering from a disorder for which no known cure exists, and it would exclude all the caring, comforting, and relief from pain and suffering that can be done. In child and adolescent psychiatry, a major contribution of treatment is to increase the patient's ability to function normally. Thus, one must beware that incentive pay, or budgets, will be structured to reward a narrow concept of "need" that excludes much treatment and caring. Let us agree that needs will refer to those who suffer from a recognized medical/psychological problem, regardless of whether there is a known cure, and that treatment should be given to those who want it. That is to say, all those in need should be assessed and offered treatment, a portion of whom will accept treatment.

One can then estimate need based on prevalence rates, discussed elsewhere, and adjusted for relative deprivation as measured by the Jarman (1983) scale or a similar scale that measures deprivation in a clinically relevant way. Becoming familiar with the Jarman scale and efforts to improve on it is essential for purchasing and paying for mental health and medical services. One also needs to note differences in prevalence between rural and urban ares. In the case of this first needs-based purchasing plan, the rates, total populations for specific age/sex groups, and actual cases are shown in Table 6.1. These estimates are based on British epidemiological studies by Rutter et al. (1970, 1974, 1975), Crisp, Palmer, & Kalncy (1976), Monck, Graham, Richman, & Dobbs (1990), Garralda (1991), and Taylor, Sandberg, Thorley, & Giles (1991).

These figures represent far more than meets the eye, for they highlight how much pathology is not recognized or is not seen for lack of investment in child and adolescent services. They are also unduplicated figures, and many cases have more than one problem. To this total should be added about 10% of mothers suffering from depression (40% of whom have children with psychiatric problems). There are also a significant number of abused children who do not manifest psychiatric disorders but who should be assessed. Overall, from the work of Michael Rutter and others, it is clear that 7% of children aged 0–15 in rural areas and 14% in inner-city areas have behavior, conduct, and emotional disorders. This unduplicated total (about 17,000 in the case of the Hounslow Spelthorne district) equals 10 times the number actually seen. This is generally the case:

Table 6.1   *Prevalence of Child and Adolescent Psychiatric Disorders, Hounslow-Spelthorne District Health Authority*

Specific disorders	Prevalence rates	Population	Cases
Mentally handicapped with psych. disorder	25% of 2.5% IQ 50–70 0–19	1,788	447
	40% of 0.3% IQ < 50 17–19	215	107
			92
Phys. handicapped with psych. disorder	20% of 5% 0–19	3,575	715
Anorexia/bulimia (severe)	1% of 15–19	19,853	198
Psychosis	0.02% of 12–16	17,000	3
	0.5% of 17–19	11,912	60
Sleep disorders	10% of 0–4	18,767	1,876
	4% of 5–9	17,291	692
Encopresis	2% of 5–9	17,291	346
Enuresis, nocturnal	4% of 5–9	17,291	692
	1% of 10–14	15,593	156
diurnal	2% of 5–9	17,291	346
School phobias (severe)	0.1% of 10–16	23,534	24
Hyperkinetic syndrome	1.7% of 5–9	17,291	294
Drug abuse	4% of 12–16	17,000	680
	8% of 17–19	11,912	953
HIV-positive children	Unknown		5
Physical abuse	14.0% of 0–16	59,592	8,342
(56% with beh. disorder;			4,671
25% with psych. disorder)			2,085
(severe)	0.1% of 0–16	59,592	60
Sexual abuse	7.0% of 3–16	46,681	3,268
(35% with psych. disorder)			1,144
(severe)	2.7% of 3–16	46,681	1,260
Neglect (severe)	unknown		
Failure of thrive	3% of 0–4	18,767	563
	1% of 5–9	17,291	173
Behavioral disorders	10% of 0–4	18,767	1,876
Conduct disorders	6% of 5–16	40,825	2,450
Emotional disorders	4% of 5–16	40,825	1,633
Total	10% of 0–16	59,592	5,959
	10% of 17–19	11,912	1,191
Total prevalence of children's disorders needing treatment			7,150
Plus depressed mothers (About 40% have children with psychiatric problems)			
Plus abused children not manifesting disorders			7,873
Total cases needing assessment			16,899

". . . fewer than 10% of children who need mental health services actually receive them" (Webster-Stratton, 1991). The underinvestment is huge. Short of persuading purchasers to provide sufficient funds, one must prioritize in terms of demand, efficacy of treatment, and impact on the lives of people in the area. Conduct disorders, for example, should get high priority, even though a number of mental health teams have not learned how to work effectively with this population.

TREATMENTS: DIAGNOSTICALLY RELATED SERVICE PACKAGES

Practically speaking, the most difficult task in developing a mental health budget is to estimate the cost of treatment. Most therapeutic units have gone through the discipline of documenting how they treat different kinds of cases and what these treatments cost. Further, there are a number of problems that make psychiatric treatment more elusive than many medical and surgical treatments. One tissue is timing. Often we do not know how effective a treatment is until after it has been carried out. A second issue is motivation. A desire for treatment greatly increases the chances of benefiting from it. This is quite different from surgery, where willingness to be treated has a limited influence on effectiveness. Third, symptoms are much more heterogeneous in child psychiatry than in medical or surgical categories, so that even if one can define a need, one cannot so clearly know which treatment will be most effective. Fourth, treatments are more heterogeneous than in medicine and surgery, so that great skill and experience is required in choosing and tailoring the most effective intervention. Fifth, the personalities of and relationship between the therapist and the patient are more important than in surgery. Sixth, measurements of effectiveness are usually not as precise as in other parts of medicine. Seventh, it is difficult to get truly matched controls to gauge effectiveness, and even if one has controls, they too experience various forms of "treatment" as time passes. Eighth, it is difficult to get large enough samples to measure outcomes well. Finally, there is a basic lack of funds to investigate the effectiveness of treatments.

All these technical and clinical problems should not discourage us, but humble us. Anyone serious about cost-effectiveness and sound purchasing should sponsor an effort to think through these limitations and identify Diagnostically Related Service Packages (DRSPs). For now, most payers or purchasers do not know what they are getting for their money, and most providers do not know the cost or value of what they are doing. We spent many hours reflecting on and observing how our treatment team assessed and treated children with different problems. We also need to estimate the cost of different team members. Even this seemingly elementary task was difficult because at that time the care group manager did not have accurate or complete figures on how much people were paid or what the overhead costs were. Thus, Appendix A contains the best estimates of hourly costs based on imperfect data available in 1991.

Appendix B contains the first estimates of DRSPs for all the major disorders. It is subject to revision and refinement as a unit learns from this exercise. The summary of Appendix B is shown in table 6.2, a menu of DRSPs. The goal is to make a profile of prevalences and a menu of DRSPs the basis for a sound financial budget for child and adolescent mental health services (Light & Bailey, 1992).

TRAINING, CONSULTATION, AND ADMINISTRATIVE COSTS

Most units of any size with a senior consultant will incur any number of other demands, and these many consume much of the senior consultant's time. One of the most important and economically sound is training social workers, health visitors, general practitioners, pediatricians, and the staff in schools and childrens' homes how to recognize the symptoms of various disorders, when to refer, and how to respond therapeutically. Clearly, the mental health unit cannot treat all cases alone. The wider the network of skilled staff to treat and follow up, the better. We estimated that these training activities would or should take up about 5% of a well-budgeted unit. Equally, important are the in-depth training programs for the 11 staff, 2 resident specialist trainees, 2 junior doctors, 1 psychologist, 4 staff on the day unit, and 2 community psychiatric nurses that made up the unit. Their training costs consume about 20% of the

Table 6.2   *A Menu of DRSPs for Child Mental Health Services*

	Estimated 1991 average cost (in pounds)
1. Behavioral and conduct disorders	
(a) Preschoolers, mild/moderate	308
(b) Preschoolers, severe, outpatient	702
(c) Preschoolers, severe, preschool group	1,870
(d) School age, preadolescents, mild	462
(e) School age, preadolescent, severe, outpatient	550
(f) School age, preadolescent, day unit	2,783
(g) Adolescents, mild/moderate, outpatient	462
(h) Adolescents, severe, outpatient	550
(i) Adolescents, severe, day unit, 1 year	2,659
(k) Adolescents, severe, day unit, 2 years	4,788
2. Emotional disorders	
(a) Preschoolers, mild/moderate, outpatient	308
(b) Preschoolers, moderate/severe, outpatients	506
(c) Preschoolers, severe, preschool group	1,870
(d) School age, preadolescents, mild/moderate	462
(e) School age, preadolescents, severe	550
(f) School age, preadolescents, severe, day unit	2,783
(g) Adolescents, moderate/severe, outpt. gp.	806
(h) Adolescents, severe, with day unit	2,783
(i) Older adolescents, moderate/severe	748
3. Handicapped with serious psychiatric disorder	See 2
4. Epileptic with serious psychiatric disorder	See 2
5. Abused: Physical, sexual, emotional, neglect	
(a) Preschoolers	6,454
(b) School age, preadolescents, with day unit	2,421
with group therapy	1,158
with individual services	1,298
(c) Sexual abuse, all ages	924
6. Nonorganic failure to thrive	6,454
7. Anorexia nervosa	
(a) Mild	1,677
(b) Severe	17,591
8. Bulimia	2,161
9. Psychosis, outpatient only	2,704
with day unit	3,266

full budget. In addition, the senior consultant had a number of administrative tasks that consumed about 7% of the budget. The administrative analysis showed that serious inefficiencies were being caused by having too few secretarial staff, so that professional therapists were forced to do their own clerical work.

We hope that this brief overview of a complex topic makes clear what a shrewd investment child and adolescent psychiatry is and how one might go about calculating it. A needs-based purchasing plan, when presented in a strategic manner, justifies a significant amount of funding in child and adolescent mental health. The question, always, is where to find the funds, and, paradoxically, they may be in our own backyard. For often there is a great deal of money spent unwisely or squandered on very costly, private, for-profit residential programs. Ironically, district services that refer patients to such programs often get a larger budget than better managed services. For keeping inpatient bed days and costs low, a district service is rewarded by receiving less money/Ma perverse disincentive that should be eliminated.

For example, in the United States, Congressional hearings on the government health insurance program for the U.S. armed services, CHAMPUS, revealed that it was spending 25% of its entire budget on psychiatric services, most of it for residential treatment for a small number of children and adolescents (Baine, 1992; Martin, 1992). This is far more than the usual 10% of healthcare that usually goes to psychiatric services. Thus, while regular outpatient services appeared to be underfunded, large sums of money were being spent on private residential services and hospitalization. The average length of stay was 188 days, and one–third of the admissions were found by an independent body to be unnecessary. Moreover, a Congressional investigation found nationwide exploitation of insurance funds for child and adolescent psychiatric services:

> Our investigation team found that thousands of adolescents, children and adults have been hospitalized for psychiatric care they didn't need. They found hospitals that hired bounty hunters to almost kidnap patients. . . . Patients sometimes were kept against their will until the benefits ran out. Often psychiatrists felt pressured by hospitals to alter diagnoses to increase their profits. Hospitals would go into schools and initiate kickbacks to counselors who could find students that had mental health insurance and would then be put into that hospital. Bonuses were even paid to employees if they could keep the beds filled'' (Schroeder, 1992, p. 1).

Hearings in Texas found that officials of private psychiatric hospitals "told people they needed mental health treatment when they did not, submitted false and inflated billings, changed diagnoses and treatments to match insurance coverage, and admitted filling the psychiatric facilities without proper cause" (Rowland, 1992, p. 4). There is a great need for professionals to police such actions, because they give all psychiatric services a bad name at the same time as they consume the funds that could easily pay for public and nonprofit services focused on home-based and outpatient services.

REFERENCES

Bailey, V. F. A. (1996). Intensive interventions in conduct disorders. *Archives of Disease in Childhood, 74,* 352–356.

Baine, D. (1992). Statement to the hearings before the U.S. House of Representatives Select Committee on Children, Youth, and Families, April 28, 1992. In *The profits of misery: How psychiatric treatment bilks the system and betrays our trust.* Washington, D.C.: U.S. Government Printing Office.

Coie, A. E. (1990). Adapting intervention to the problems of aggressive and disruptive rejected children. In S. R. Asher & J. D. Coie (Eds.), *Peer rejection in childhood.* (pp. 309–337) Cambridge, England: Cambridge University Press.

Crisp, J. J., Palmer, R. L., & Kalucy, R. S. (1976). How common is anorexia nervosa? A prevalence study. *British Journal of Psychiatry, 128,* 549–554.

Garralda, M. E. (1991). Epidemiology and evaluation of child psychiatric disorders. *Current Opinion in Psychiatry, 4,* 524–528.

Jarman, B. (1983). Identification of underprivileged areas. *British Medical Journal, 186,* 1705–1712.

Kazdin, A. E. (1985). *Treatment of antisocial behavior in children and adolescents.* Homewood, IL: Dorsey.

Light, D. W., & Bailey V. (1992). A needs-based purchasing plan for child mental health in the Hounslow-Spelthorne District Health Authority. London: NorthWest Thames Regional Health Authority. Obtainable from the Dept. of Child & Adolescent Psychiatry, 92 Bath Road, Hounslow, Middlesex TW3 3EL.

Martin, E. D. (1992). Statement to the hearings before the U.S. House of Representatives Select Committee on Children, Youth, and Families, April 28, 1992. In *The profits of misery: How psychiatric treatment bilks the system and betrays our trust.* Washington, DC: U.S. Government Printing Office.

Monck, E. Graham, P., Richman, N., & Dobbs, R. (1990). Eating and weight control problems in a community population of adolescent girls aged 15–20. In H. Remschmidt & M. H. Schmidt (Eds.), *Anorexia nervosa: Child and youth psychiatry. European Perspective.* Göttingen, Germany: Hogrefe and Huber.

Patterson, G. R., DeBaryshe, B. D., & Ramsey, E. (1989). A developmental perspective on antisocial behavior. *American Psychologist, 44,* 329–335.

Reid, J., Taplin, P., & Loeber, R. (1981). A social interactional approach to the treatment of abusive families. In R. Stewart (Ed.), *Violent behavior: Social learning approaches to prediction, management and treatment.* New York: Brunner/Mazel.

Robins, L. N. (1981). Epidemiological approaches to natural history research: Antisocial disorders in children. *Journal of the American Academy of Child Psychiatry, 20,* 566–580.

Robins, L. N., & Rutter, M. (Eds.). (1990). *Straight and deviant paths from childhood to adulthood.* Cambridge, England: Cambridge University Press.

Rowland, J. R. (1992). Statement to the hearings before the U.S. House of Representatives Select Committee on Children, Youth, and Families, April 28, 1992. In *The Profits of Misery: How psychiatric treatment bilks the system and betrays our trust.* Washington, DC: U.S. Government Printing Office.

Rutter, M. Cox, A., Tupling, C., Berger, M., & Yule, W. (1975). Attainment and adjustment in two geographical areas. I. The prevalence of psychiatric disorders. *British Journal of Psychiatry, 126,* 493–509.

Rutter, M., Tizard J., & Whitmore, E. (Eds.) (1970). *Education, health and behavior.* London: Longman.

Rutter, M., Yule, B., Quinton, D., Rowlands, O., Yule, W., & Berger, M. (1975). Attainment and adjustment in two geographical areas: III. Some factors accounting for area differences. *British Journal of Psychiatry, 126,* 520–533.

Schroeder, P. (1992). Statement to the hearings before the U.S. House of Representatives Select Committee on Children, Youth, and Families, April 28, 1992. In *The profits of misery: How psychiatric treatment bilks the system and betrays our trust.* Washington, DC: U.S. Government Printing Office.

Taylor, E., Sandberg, S., Thorley, G., & Giles S. (1991). *The epidemiology of childhood hyperactivity.* Oxford, England: Oxford University Press.

Webster-Stratton, C. (1991) Annotation: Strategies for helping families with conduct disordered children. *Journal of Child Psychology and Psychiatry, 32,* 1047–1062.

Appendix A. *Hourly Rates of Staff, 1991*

Hourly rates of clinical staff were calculated by taking their annual salary, including national insurance, dividing it by 1,450 hours, and then multiply the quotient by a factor to account for a combination of estate costs, operating costs, and staff support. To obtain average rates for "all doctors" or "all clinical staff" when a mixture of different individuals typically performed a task, these hourly rates were averaged. This summary is detailed in the table below.

The salaries in round numbers are believed to be accurate. They are divided by a 37.5-hour week and 43 weeks (52 minus 6 weeks of vacation, 2 for public holidays and sickness, 1 for training, minus 10% for nonspecifically attributable times) to arrive at 1,450 hours. The resulting hourly rates are then multiplied by 1.3556, an increase reflecting figures given us by the business office to reflect the proportion of the unit's budget devoted to estate costs, operating costs, and support staff. We had no way to verify these figures. Indeed, the unit business office and expanded management team has no budget for the unit, and despite repeated requests and weeks of efforts, none was produced. It seems appropriate to carry these calculations out to only two places.

Responsibility level	Salary	Rate per hour	Rate with overhead
	£	£	£
Consultant	63,500	44	59
Sr. registrar	30,000	21	28
{Either}		32	44
Registrar	25,000	17	23
{All Drs.}		27	37
Community Psych. Nurse		14	19
Clin. Psychol. Trainee	15,000	10	14
{All clin. staff}		23	28
{All staff except consultant}			22
Day unit staff		11	15

Appendix B. *Details of Diagnosis, Related Service Packages for Each Diagnosis*

DRSP: Service Package for Behavioral and Conduct Disorders

Service	Person hours	Rate per hour[a]	1991 Total costs
		£	£
1. Preschoolers: Mild/moderate, outpatient			
Assessment, treatment plan, and write-up	2.5	44	110
Parent/child therapy	6	22	132
Follow-up	3	22	66
Total package cost			308
2. Preschoolers: Severe, outpatient			
Assessment, treatment plan, and write-up	2.5	44	110
Psychological testing	3	22	66
Parent/child therapy			
1 hr/wk × 12	12	22	264
Reviews/meetings			
3 × 1.5 hrs × 2	7	28	196
Follow-up	3	22	66
Total package cost			702
3. PreSchool: Severe, day unit			
Assessment, as above	2.5	44	110
Psychological testing	3	22	66
Parent/child therapy			
1 hr/wk × 12	12	22	264
Preschool group			
2 hrs/wk × 30 × 1/2 staff[b]	30	15	450
Parents group			
2 hrs/wk × 30 × 1/4 staff	15	28	420
Reviews/meetings			
5 × 2 hrs × 2	20	28	560
Total day unit treatment costs			1,870
4. School age, preadolescents: Mild/ moderate			
Assessment, as above	2.5	44	110
Psychological testing	3	22	66
Family therapy			
1 hr/wk × 10	10	22	220
Follow-up	3	22	66
Total mild outpatient costs			462

Appendix B.   (continued)

Service	Person hours	Rate per hour[a]	1991 Total costs
		£	£
5. School Age, Preadolescents: Severe outpatient			
Assessment, as above	2.5	44	110
Psychological testing	3	22	66
Family therapy			
1 hr/wk × 12	12	22	264
Follow-up	5	22	110
Total severe outpatient costs			550
6. School Age, Preadolescents: Severe, day unit 1-year treatment			
Assessment as above	2.5	44	110
Psychological testing	3	22	66
Occupational therapy testing	3	22	66
Day unit			
9 hrs/wk × 30 × 1/6	45	15	675
Family therapy			
1 hr/wk × 25	25	22	550
Review meetings with family			
1.5 hrs × 3	9	22	198
Professionals' planning & treatment coordination meetings			
1 hr × 12 × 2	24	28	1,008
Follow-up	5	22	110
Total package cost			2,783
7. Adolescents: Mild/moderate, outpatient			
Same as preadolescent			462
8. Adolescents: Severe, outpatient			
Same as preadolescent			550

Appendix B.   (continued)

Service	Person hours	Rate per hour[a]	1991 Total costs
		£	£
9. Adolescents: Severe, day unit			
1-year treatment			
Assessment, as above	2.5	44	110
Extensive networking	6	37	222
Psychological testing	3	22	66
Day unit			
9 hrs/wk × 30 wks × 1/3	45	15	675
Parent training/counseling			
1 hr/wk × 6; 2 hr/mo × 4; 1 hr/mo × 12	20	22	440
Case review planning, coordination			
1 hr/mo × 12 × 2 staff	24	28	672
Review meetings with Child Protection, other agencies and institutions			
12 hrs.	6	37	222
Review meetings with Family			
1.5 hrs × 3 × 2 staff	9	28	252
Total package cost			2659
10. Adolescents: Severe, day unit			
2-years treatment			
Assessment as above	2.5	44	110
Extensive networking	6	37	222
Psychological testing	3	22	66
Day unit			
9 hrs/wk × 60 wks × 1/6	90	15	1,350
Parent training/counseling			
1 hr/wk × 6; 2 hrs /mo × 8; 1 hr/mo × 12	34	22	748
Case review, planning, coordination			
1 hr/mo × 24 × 2	48	28	1,344
Review meetings w/family			
1.5 hrs × 6 × 2 staff	18	28	504
Review meetings w/other agencies including Child Protection			
1.5 hrs × 4 × 2 staff	12	37	444
Total package cost			4,788

[a]Rates per hour are given in British pounds and are explained in Appendix A
[b]Health staff: index child = 2:4 (others are teaching or voluntary attachments.)

Appendix B.   (continued)

DRSP: Service Package for Emotional Disorders

Service	Hours	Rate per hour	Total costs
1. Preschool: Mild/moderate, outpatient Same as for mild/moderate behavioral problems			305
2. Preschool: Moderate/severe, outpatient			
Assessment, treatment plan, and write-up	2.5	44	110
Psychological testing	3	22	66
Family therapy			
6 sessions	12	22	264
Follow-up	3	22	66
Total package cost			506
3. Preschool: Severe, preschool group Same as for severe behavioral problems			1,870
4. School age: Preadolescent, mild/moderate Same as for mild/moderate behavioral disorders			462
5. School age, preadolescent, severe Same as for severe conduct & behavioral disorders			550
6. School age: Preadolescent, severe, day unit Same as for conduct disorders with day unit			2,783
7. School age: Adolescent, severe, day unit Same as above			2,783
8. School age: Adolescent, moderate/severe			
Assessment	2.5	44	110
Psychological testing	3	22	66
After-school psychotherapy group or social skills group			
2 hrs × 30 × 1/3 staff	20	15	300
Family therapy			
1 hr × 12	12	22	264
Follow-up	3	22	66
Total package cost			806

Appendix B.   (continued)

Service	Hours	Rate per hour	Total costs
9. Older adolescents: Moderate/severe			
Assessment	2.5	44	110
Behavioral & cognitive therapy			
1 hr × 20	20	22	440
Family therapy			
1 hr × 6	6	22	132
Follow-up	3	22	66
Total package cost			748

DRSP: Service Package for Handicapped or Epileptic with Psychiatric Problems

Same as for conduct and emotional disorders but may require further investigations, including specialized neuropsychological testing, and liason with pediatrician and pediatric neurologist.

DRSP: Service Package for Child Abuse (Physical, Sexual, Emotional, Neglect)

Service	Person hours	Rate per hour	Total costs
1. Preschoolers 2-year treatment			
Assessment, treatment plans, contracting, write-up	2.5	44	110
Extensive networking	6	37	222
Psychological & occupational therapy testing	6	22	132
Cognitive/behavioral counseling with parents			
1 hr/wk × 50 plus 2/mo × 12	74	28	2,072
Group for parents			
2 hrs/wk × 60 × 1/4 staff	30	28	840
Group for child			
2 hrs/wk × 60 × 1/2 staff	60	15	900
Staff case conference			
1 1/2 hr/mo × 12 × 3 staff	54	28	1,512
Review meetings, Child Protection case conferences, meetings with other agencies	18	37	666
Total package cost			6,454

Appendix B.   (continued)

Service	Person hours	Rate per hour	Total costs
2. School Age: Preadolescents & adolescents			
Assessment, as above	2.5	44	110
Psychological testing	3	22	66
Extensive networking	6	22	132
Day Unit for Child			
9 hrs/wk × 30 × 1/6^c	45	15	675
Monthly treatment management meeting			
1 hr/mo × 12 × 2 staff	24	37	888
Follow-up sessions	5	22	110
Total package cost			2,421
3. All ages: Sexual abuse cases			
Assessment, as above	2.5	44	110
Extensive networking			
10–15 hrs.	12	22	264
Group for child			
2 hrs/wk × 10 × 4/2 staff = 1/2 staff	10	22	220
Carers' group			
2 hrs/wk × 10 × 1/2 staff	10	22	220
Follow-up sessions & conferences	5	22	110
Total package cost			924

(If no day unit, may need individual sessions for a total of 1158 pounds, or group therapy for a total of 1298 pounds.)
^{c}Ratio is 1:3 but one of 2 staff members is a teacher.

DRSP: Service Package for Nonorganic Failure to Thrive

Service	Person hours	Rate	Total costs
Treatment similar to preschool abuse group			6,454

DRSP: Service Package for Anorexia Nervosa

Service	Person hours	Rate	Total costs
1. Mild cases			
Assessment, treatment plan and write-up	2.5	44	110
Therapy	8	22	176
2 hrs/wk × 4, 1 hr/wk × 50	50	22	1,100
Group treatment			
1 1/2 hrs/wk × 30 × 1/3	15	15	225
Follow-up	3	22	66
Total package cost			1,677

Appendix B.   (continued)

Service	Person hours	Rate	Total costs
2. Severe, complex cases			
Assessment, as above	2.5	44	110
Hospitalization			
1/4 hr/day × 90 Consult.	27.5	59	1,622
90 days bed rate @ 150			13,500
Liaison w/hospital staff			
1 hr/wk × 12	12	22	264
Therapy			
1 hr/wk × 12	12	22	264
Parents therapy			
1 × 12	12	22	264
Then easy care package, minus assessment			1,567
Total package cost			17,591

DRSP: Service Package for Bulimia

Service	Person hours	Rate	Total costs
Like package for mild anorexia, but with 25 weeks of follow-up. Thus 1677 pounds plus 484 pounds.			2,161

(Note: Sexual or substance abuse is often discovered during treatment. Then add appropriate service package.)

DRSP: Service Package for Psychosis

Service	Person hours	Rate per hour	Total costs
Assessment, treatment plan, write-up	2.5	44	110
Psychological testing	3	22	66
Testing, imaging			160
Day unit[d]			
9 hrs/wk × 25 × 1/6 staff	37.5	15	562
Drug therapy			
1/2 hr/wk × 10; 1/2 hr twice/mo. × 9	14	37	518
Cost of drugs (depends on case)			
Continuous assessment with school, family. Coordination of services with other agencies			
1 hr/wk × 50	50	37	1,850
Total package cost, with day unit			3,266
without day unit			2,704

[d]If appropriate.
Additional: Hospitalization in 15% of cases. Average cost is indeterminable.

Appendix B.   (continued)

DRSP: Service Package for Sleep Disorders

Service	Person hours	Rate	Total costs
Assessment	2.5	22	55
Sleep clinic			
1 staff × 1 hr × 5 wks	5	22	110
Total package cost			165

NOTE: Most can be treated by Health Visitors, if trained.

DRSP: Service Package for Encopresis (Soiling), Diurnal and Nocturnal Enuresis (Wetting)[e]

Service	Person hours	Rate per hour	Total costs
Assessment, write-up, and treatment plan	2.5	44	110
Behavioral modification			
1 hr. × 8	8	37	296
Pediatric liaison	1	37	37
Total package cost			443

[e]For those not treatable by doctors, nurses, health visitors, and others.

DRSP: Service Package for Maternal Depression

Service	Person hours	Rate per hour	Total costs
Assessment, treatment plan, and write-up	2.5	44	110
Behavioral/cog. therapy by staff			
1 hr/wk × 20 wks × 1 staff	20	37	740
May include group therapy/support			
2 hrs/wk × 30 wks × 1/4 staff	15	28	420
Total package cost, including group therapy			1,015
without group therapy			850

Appendix B.   (continued)

DRSP: Service package for School Phobia[f]

Service	Person hours	Rate per hour	Total costs
Assessment, plan, write-up	2.5	44	110
Treatment Group			
1 hr/wk × 6 wks	9	15	135
Family counseling			
1 hr/wk × 6 wks	6	22	132
Telephone arrangements, discussions, staff consult			
1 hr/wk × 6	6	22	132
Interdisciplinary meeting to plan return			
1.5 hr × 2 staff	3	28	84
Review meeting(s)			
1 hr × 3 × 2	6	22	132
Follow-up interventions (variable)	3	22	66
Total package cost			769

[f]Some children initially assessed as school phobic will turn out to have mixed disorders. Day unit program for preadolescent and adolescent conduct disorders should be added.

Service Package: Referrals for Opinion from Other Agencies and the Children Act of 1989

Service	Person hours	Rate per hour	Total costs
Paper/file review	.5	59	59
Calls to family, agencies, groups, for their records	1	44	44
Clinical, personal assessments	3	44	132
Court report	3	44	132
(supervision by consultant for senior registrar)	2	44	88
Network meeting			
1 × 1.5 hrs	1.5	44	66
Total package cost			521

THE UTILIZATION AND OUTCOMES OF CURRENT TREATMENTS FOR DEVELOPMENTAL PSYCHOPATHOLOGY

7

Survey of the Utilization of Psychiatric Services for Children and Adolescents in Germany

HELMUT REMSCHMIDT

MARTIN H. SCHMIDT

REINHARD WALTER

Two studies were undertaken to examine the utilization of psychiatric services for children and adolescents in a three-county region of Germany.

THE USE OF PSYCHIATRIC SERVICES FOR CHILDREN AND ADOLESCENTS IN THREE GERMAN COUNTIES: A STUDY OF A TOTAL POPULATION OF SERVICE USERS

Aims of the Study

The aims of the first study were to get an overview of the total population of consumers of psychiatric services for children and adolescents in three German counties, comprising a total of 574,000 inhabitants (the "model region"). A central question was how many children and adolescents up to the age of 18, or their parents on their behalf, were using the existing psychiatric services for children and adolescents. Further, the study was to investigate the differences between the three counties with respect to the use of the services and which variables were associated with service

Table 7.1 *Types of Clinical Services Included in the Study*

	Survey of all patients attending the following clinical services within one year:
P.C.	1. Early intervention centers 2. Child guidance clinics 3. Adolescent services at public health agencies 4. Psychological practices 5. Other psychological services
S.C.	6. Public consulting centers 7. Outpatient units in hospitals 8. Inpatient units in hospitals 9. Child psychiatric private practices 10. Mobile child psychiatric service

P.C.: Primary consultation services.
S.C.: Secondary consultation services.

use. The study was part of the German Federal Republic's model program "Psychiatry," which gave us the unique opportunity to conduct this comprehensive evaluation supported by the government.

Methodology

Included were the two child and youth psychiatric hospitals in Marburg as well as 62 outpatient services, 31 of which were located outside of the model region, two child and youth psychiatric hospitals outside of the model region, and four supplementary institutions (all within the model region). Complete participation of all supplementary and inpatient institutions in the model region was achieved. Only three outpatient clinical services specializing in children and youth within the model region refused cooperation, but all had small numbers of patients. Fortunately, the numbers of patients of these clinical services could be estimated. The three outpatient clinical services outside of the model region all took part. Thus, it was possible to include a complete consumer population in our documentation.

The different clinical services were grouped into nine types, according to their goals and areas of service, as shown in Table 7.1.

The mobile child psychiatric service was financed as part of the model program. The different clinical services can be summarized according to their function as so-called "clinical services for primary consultation" (items 1–5 in the table) and "core clinical services" (secondary and tertiary consultation) (items 6–9).

This division was based on the concepts of the Psychiatry Enquête as an intertwined system of psychosocial, psychotherapeutic, and psychiatric institutions. 5,000 patients were surveyed within the designated time period by the above-mentioned institutions. Of these, only the patient data for 1 year ($n = 3,280$) are reported here, including the clinical services within the model region and patients living outside of the model region.

Patient documentation consisted of personal and social data, as well as a diagnosis employing the multiaxial classification scheme for psychiatric diseases in children and adolescents according to Rutter, Shaffer, and Sturge (Remschmidt & Schmidt, 1977). These combined elements comprised the survey instrument used in this investigation.

To increase the motivation to cooperate, payment was given for each survey form filled out. All survey forms were checked for plausibility and consistency, and in doubtful cases, colleagues at the respective institutions were contacted prior to the data entry. The evaluation was based on 3,280 in- and outpatient survey forms, which included valid statements of the multiaxial diagnoses.

Results

Clinical Psychiatric Syndromes

Table 2 gives an overview of the diagnoses of 3,280 cases (inpatients and outpatients) on the first axis of the multiaxial classification system (MAS) who attended any of the services within the model region. The table also describes the influence of age in relation to the different diagnoses. As can be seen from the table, 38.8% did not suffer from any clinical psychiatric syndrome. This applies mainly to children with specific developmental disorders, somatic disorders, or intellectual deficits classified on other axes. Out of the total sample, 5.6% ($n = 180$) suffered from psychotic disorders, 6.7% ($n = 214$) from neurotic disorders, 3.5% ($n = 111$) from the hyperkinetic syndrome, etc. The small number of neurotic disorders has to be explained. With regard to the MAS, only those neurotic disorders are classified under this label that correspond to the prototype of neurotic disorders as known from adult psychiatry (e.g.,

phobic disorder, anxiety disorder, etc.), whereas all other comparable disorders in childhood and adolescence are subsumed under the
heading of "specific emotional disorder." This category comprises
16.4% of all patients ($n = 524$) in Table 7.2.

As far as *specific developmental disorders* are concerned (axis
2 of the MAS), the following results were obtained. No specific
developmental disorder could be diagnosed in 70.2% of all patients
($n = 2297$). A specific reading disorder was found in 6.3% ($n = 201$), a specific arithmetic disorder in 1.3% ($n = 42$), a specific
developmental disorder of speech and language in 10.4% ($n = 330$),
and a specific developmental disorder of motor functions in 10.3%
of all cases and over all ages ($n = 329$).

With regard to sex differences, a specific reading disorder (dyslexia) was significantly more frequent in boys (8.7% of all boys vs.
3.2% of all girls: $\chi^2 = 37.9$, $df = 1$, $p < 0.001$). The same applied
to the specific disorder of motor functions. With regard to social
class, there was a very clear preponderance of specific developmental disorders coming from the lower social classes as compared
to the upper social classes ($\chi^2 = 18.7$, $df = 3$, $p < 0.0003$). However,
this was not true for dyslexia (specific reading disorder), specific
arithmetic disorder, and multiple developmental disorders.

With regard to *intelligence* (axis 3), most of the patients (boys and
girls) belonged to the category "normal intelligence." The higher
intelligence scores were as frequent in boys and girls, whereas a
light preponderance of girls could be found with regard to the category "mild, moderate, and severe retardation." This is demonstrated in Table 7.3.

In relation *to somatic symptoms and disorders* (axis 4), it was
found that half of the patients had no somatic disorders. Among the
somatic disorders, epilepsy was the most frequent one (12.7%; $n = 383$), followed by minimal brain dysfunction (11.1%; $n = 334$), and
other neurological disorders (4.6%; $n = 140$).

With regard to *abnormal psychosocial circumstances* (axis 5),
the highest load was found for patients with conduct disorders and
adjustment reactions (more than 80%), followed by neurotic disorders, specific emotional disorders, psychoses, and hyperkinetic syndromes (more than 60%). The lowest rates of abnormal psychosocial
circumstances was found in those patients who had no psychiatric
diagnosis (25%).

Table 7.2 *First Axis Diagnoses for Inpatients and Outpatients* (*N* = 3204)

	0 to 2 years	3 to 5 years	6 to 8 years	9 to 12 years	12 to 15 years	15 to 17 years	Older than 17 years	All ages
Axis I								
No disorder	241	175	241	200	169	171	47	1244
	19.4%	14.1%	19.4%	16.1%	13.6%	13.7%	3.8%	38.8%
	87.3%	52.2%	41.8%	38.0%	29.1%	26.2%	18.2%	
Psychoses	2	11	13	7	14	72	61	180
	1.1%	6.1%	7.2%	3.9%	7.8%	40.0%	33.9%	5.6%
	0.7%	3.3%	2.3%	1.3%	2.4%	11.0%	23.6%	
Neuroses	0	5	21	22	45	73	48	214
	0.0%	2.3%	9.8%	10.3%	21.0%	34.1%	22.4%	6.7%
	0.0%	1.5%	3.6%	4.2%	7.7%	11.2%	18.6%	
Special syndromes	16	67	110	110	114	88	30	535
	3.0%	12.5%	20.6%	20.6%	21.3%	16.4%	5.6%	16.7%
	5.8%	20.0%	19.1%	20.9%	19.6%	13.5%	11.6%	
Adjustment reactions	1	17	20	22	37	53	7	157
	0.6%	10.8%	12.7%	14.0%	23.6%	33.8%	4.5%	4.9%
	0.4%	5.1%	3.5%	4.2%	6.4%	8.1%	2.7%	
Disorders following brain damage	0	5	7	19	13	19	14	77
	0.0%	6.5%	9.1%	24.7%	16.9%	24.7%	18.2%	2.4%
	0.0%	1.5%	1.2%	3.6%	2.2%	2.9%	5.4%	
Conduct disorders	1	11	42	57	114	140	29	394
	0.3%	2.8%	10.7%	14.5%	28.9%	35.5%	7.4%	12.3%
	0.4%	3.3%	7.3%	10.8%	19.6%	21.5%	11.2%	
Emotional disorders	9	45	130	117	112	90	21	524
	1.7%	8.6%	24.8%	22.3%	21.4%	17.2%	4.0%	16.4%
	3.3%	13.4%	22.6%	22.2%	19.3%	13.8%	8.1%	
Hyperkinetic syndrome	7	24	46	19	12	0	3	111
	6.3%	21.6%	41.4%	17.1%	10.8%	0.0%	2.7%	3.5%
	2.5%	7.2%	8.0%	3.6%	2.1%	0.0%	1.2%	
Others	2	5	12	16	36	59	33	163
	1.2%	3.1%	7.4%	9.8%	22.1%	36.2%	20.2%	5.1%
	0.7%	1.5%	2.1%	3.0%	6.2%	9.0%	12.8%	
Total	276	335	576	526	581	652	258	3204
percent	8.6%	10.5%	18.0%	16.4%	18.1%	20.3%	8.1%	100.0%
Number of entries	279	365	642	589	666	765	293	3599

Utilization of Services

One of the main aims of the study was to find out how the different services, especially the outpatient ones, were used by children and their families. We analyzed the proportion of patients from the respective three counties who used the in- and outpatient services

Table 7.3   *Intelligence Distribution of the Sample of Service Users* $(N = 2996)$

		Sex	
Axis III	Male	Female	Both
	163	124	287
High intelligence	56.8%	43.2%	9.6%
(IQ > 114)	9.3%	9.9%	
Normal intelligence	1270	883	2153
(IQ 85–114)	59.0%	41.0%	71.9%
	72.8%	70.5%	
Low intelligence	187	117	304
(IQ 70–84)	61.5%	38.5%	10.1%
	10.7%	9.3%	
Mild, moderate, and severe	124	128	252
retardation	49.2%	50.8%	8.4%
(IQ > 70)	7.1%	10.2%	
Total	1744	1252	2996
	58.2%	41.8%	100.0%

$\chi^2 = 10.5 \; df = 3 \; p \leq 0{,}015$

within the whole model region consisting of the three counties. As Table 7.4 demonstrates, the proportion of the service users is very different with regard to the three counties.

This result is interesting in two ways:

1. The most advanced county with the best equipped services shows the highest rate of service attenders (3.9%; $n = 1962$) among children and adolescents below 18 years of age. County III, with the lowest density of services, shows the lowest attendance rate (1.9%, $n = 749$).

Table 7.4   *Proportion of Children and Adolescents Under 18 Years of Age in the Three Counties Using In- and Outpatient Services of the Model Region*

	County I (Marburg) 238,000 inhabitants 50,393 < 18 years	County II (Frankenberg) 155,000 inhabitants 33,566 < 18 years	County III (Schwalm) 181,000 inhabitants 40,029 < 18 years
Inpatients and outpatients (Children and adolescents < 18 years)	3.9% ($n = 1962$)	2.6% ($n = 867$)	1.9% ($n = 749$)

2. Nevertheless, in the relatively well-equipped County I (Marburg), the total rate of attenders does not reach the rate of 5%, which is postulated as a minimal estimate of patients in need of treatment (Castell, Biener, Artner, Dilling, 1981; Weyerer, Castell, Biener, Artner, & Dilling 1988).

As far as *inpatient treatment* is concerned, three results emerged from our study:

• With increasing distance between place of residence and place of inpatient units, there was a decrease in the rate of inpatient treatment.
• Regions with a better-equipped outpatient service had a higher rate of inpatient treatments, but a significantly shorter duration of inpatient treatment.
• Patients from regions with fewer in- and outpatient facilities differed from those where more in- and outpatient facilities were available on three variables: On average, they were 1 year older (15.1 vs. 14.2 years), had a more severe psychiatric diagnosis, and their duration of treatment was significantly longer (median: 65.0 vs. 32.0 days).

Conclusions

Under the model program "Psychiatry" of the Federal Government of Germany, we had the unique opportunity to study a complete in- and outpatient user population of psychiatric services for children and adolescents in three German counties, comprising a total of 574,000 inhabitants, out of whom 123,988 were under 18 years of age. The total rate of users of in- and outpatient services differed between the three counties and was 3.9% for the most advanced County I (Marburg) and 1.9% for County III, which had the lowest density of all types of services. In all counties, the proportion of users was below the rate of 5% that has been postulated as a realistic figure for psychiatrically disturbed children and adolescents in need of some kind of treatment. As the distance between the place of residence and the place of services played an important role in service utilization, the conclusion could be drawn that more community-based services are necessary. In response to this conclusion, we developed a mobile service for psychiatrically disturbed children and adolescents for two of the three counties. This mobile service has existed for more than 10 years in the county of Marburg

(County I) and has worked very successfully (Remschmidt & Walter 1989; Remschmidt, Walter, & Kampart, 1986).

THE NEED FOR TREATMENT: A POPULATION-BASED STUDY IN A REPRESENTATIVE SAMPLE OF SCHOOLCHILDREN.

Aims of the Study

After the first study aiming at the review of a complete patient population who attended psychiatric services for children and adolescents in three counties, the aim of the second study was to investigate a *representative sample of schoolchildren* between 6 and 18 years of age in order to find out the rate of psychiatrically disturbed children and adolescents and also the rate of those children who attended the services within the same counties as described in the first study. It was also our intention to find out if the rate of treated patients would differ when compared to the rate of the first study, which was based on a consumer population.

Methodology

For the purpose of this study, a total sample of 1969 subjects (996 boys and 973 girls) was drawn which was representative of the entire population of schoolchildren in the same three counties as investigated in the first study. The sample comprised the age groups between 6 and 18 years. As instruments, we used the Parents' Form of the Child Behavior Checklist (Achenbach & Edelbrock, 1981, 1983), and, in addition, for children and adolescents over 10 years of age, the Youth Self-Report (YSR), also developed by Achenbach and Edelbrock (1987).

As a method for defining the degree of psychopathology and the necessity for treatment, we used an expert rating with 16 experienced doctors and psychologists from the Marburg child psychiatric university unit. These experts were asked to check a list of symptoms that would imply the necessity for treatment. According to the assessments of the experts, critical items were defined and the definition of a case included at least two of these critical items and the severity of the respective items on a three-point scale.

Table 7.5   *Prevalence Rates of Psychiatric Disturbances in Relation to Different Types of School*

Type of school	N	n	Disturbed (%)
Remedial school	64	15	23.4
Elementary school (grades 1–4)	567	94	16.6
Elementary school (Grades 5–9)	196	32	16.3
Elementary school (furtherance level)	195	30	15.4
High School (lower level)	271	23	8.5
High School (higher level)	449	32	7.1
Vocational school	227	25	11.0
	1969	251	12.7

Results

The overall prevalence rate of psychiatrically significant disturbances defined according to the experts' rating was 12.7%, which included 251 children and adolescents out of the total sample of 1,969. The prevalence rates varied remarkably with regard to type of school (Table 7.5). As can be seen from the table, the highest prevalence rates were found in special remedial schools and elementary schools, the lowest, in high schools. According to the parents' report, only 64 children out of 1,969 (3.3%) had received treatment because of a psychiatric disorder or a specific developmental disorder. That means that the majority of the patients who had been rated as needing some kind of psychiatric treatment (12.7%; $n = 251$) did not receive any treatment. By assuming a 5% rate of treatment necessity, one would expect that 98 children would have been treated, in contrast to the 64 who had actually received treatment. This means that a minimum of 34 children and adolescents (34.6%) in need of some kind of treatment remained untreated.

Conclusions

Our second, population-based study employed a representative sample of school children ($N = 1,969$). Only 64 (3.3%) who had been rated by means of the Child Behavior Checklist (parents' version), utilizing a threshold established by a panel of experts, and rated as needing treatment, had actually received treatment. This figure is approximately the same as that found in our first study, which utilized a total population of users of services for psychiatrically disturbed children and adolescents in three counties and found a rate of 3.9% of users in the county with the best-equipped facilities.

DISCUSSION

Surveys of services as part of quality assurance become more and more important in child and adolescent psychiatry. This paper deals with two aspects of service evaluation: The first study was a survey of services in three German counties comprising 574,000 inhabitants by the analysis of a *complete sample of service users*. With a few exceptions, all services for psychiatrically disturbed children and adolescents up to the age of 18 participated in the study. The number of service users differed between the three counties: The highest rate (3.9% of all children and adolescents below 18 years of age) was found in the most advanced county (Marburg), and the lowest rate (1.9%) in the county with the lowest density of services (Schwalm). The relationship of the distance between the location of residence and the location of services to a decrease in the rate of inpatient treatment provides a good argument for the need to organize community-based services. Such a community-based service was realized by the establishment of a mobile service nearly 10 years ago (Remschmidt et al., 1986). The availability of services was also responsible for the fact that children and adolescents from well-equipped counties (who were on average able to reach these services earlier) showed a significantly shorter duration of inpatient treatment.

The second study reported in this paper viewed service-users from a different perspective, namely, from a representative sample of schoolchildren of the same three counties. Using the Child Behavior Checklist of Achenbach and Edelbrock (1981, 1983), a rate of psychiatrically disturbed children and adolescents of 12.7% was found, while only 3.3% had received in- or outpatient treatment. It is interesting that this rate is not very different from the one (3.9%) found in the best-equipped county in the first study, which was based on a complete user population. Both rates, however, are below the 5% rate of treatment need which is accepted as a realistic estimation of the need for treatment in children and adolescents up to 18 years of age.

In conclusion, both studies, based on different samples and also different methods, led to a similar result concerning the estimation of the need for treatment in the investigated age group. The results can be looked upon as a realistic empirical basis for the number of children in need of treatment in community-based services for children and adolescents with psychiatric and specific developmental disorders.

ACKNOWLEDGMENTS

It is only seldom possible to register the sort of consumer population described in this paper so completely. We were able to accomplish this only with the help of a great number of people who viewed our investigation as an important step toward the improvement of child and youth psychiatric services. We would like to express our thanks to all involved. The completeness of this investigation was also made possible only through the official support of the Federal Republic of Germany and the State of Hessen, which requested that all institutions cooperate.

REFERENCES

Achenbach, T. M., & Edelbrock, C. S. (1981). Behavioral problems and competencies reported by parents of normal and disturbed children aged 4 through 16. *Monographs of the Society for Research in Child Development, 46* (Serial No. 188).

Achenbach, T. M., & Edelbrock, C. S. (1983). *Manual for the Child Behavior Checklist and Revised Child Behavior Profile*. Burlington, VT: Queen City Printers.

Achenbach, T. M., & Edelbrock, C. S. (1987). *Manual for the Youth-Self-Report and Profile*. Burlington, VT: University of Vermont, Department of Psychiatry.

Castell, R. A., Biener, K., Artner, K., & Dilling, H. (1981). Häufigkeit von psychischen Störungen und Verhaltensauffälligkeiten bei Kindern und ihre psychiatrische Versorgung. Ergebnisse einer repräsentativen Querschnitt-suntersuchung 3-bis 14jähriger. *Zeitschrift für Kinder- und Jugendpsychiatrie, 9,* 115–125.

Remschmidt, H., & Schmidt, M. H. (Eds.). (1977). Multiaxiales Klassifikationsschema für psychiatrische Erkrankungen im Kindes-: und Jugendalter nach Rutter, Shaffer und Sturge. Bern, Germany: Huber. (2nd ed., 1986; 3rd, rev. ed., 1994.)

Remschmidt, H., & Walter, R. (1989). *Evaluation kinder- und jugendpsychiatrischer Versorgung. Analysen und Erhebungen in drei hessischen Landkreisen.* Stuttgart, Germany: Enke.

Remschmidt, H., & Walter, R. (1990). Psychische Auffälligkeiten bei Schulkindern. Eine epidemiologische Untersuchung. Göttingen, Germany: Hogrefe.

Remschmidt, H., Walter, R., & Kampert, K. (1986). Der mobile kinder- und jugendpsychiatrische Dienst: Ein wirksames Versorgungsmodell für ländliche Regionen. *Zeitschrift für Kinder- und Jugendpsychiatrie, 14,* 63–80.

Weyerer, S., Castell, R., Biener, A., Artner, K., & Dilling, H. (1988). Prevalence and treatment of psychiatric disorders in 3 to 14-year-old children: Results of a representative field study in the small town rural region of Traunstein, Upper Bavaria. *Acta Psychiatrica Scandinavica, 77,* 290–296.

8

Issues in the Evaluation of Systems of Mental Health Services: A Perspective and Recent Developments

PHILIP J. LEAF

Providers and planners of mental health services must better utilize knowledge of the etiology of mental disorders to develop and deliver services that strengthen children, families, and communities (Costello, Burns, Angold, & Leaf, 1993). This is particularly true in the many countries attempting to "manage" healthcare and healthcare costs (Thornicroft, Brewin, & Wing, 1992). We have learned much about the etiology of mental disorders and behavioral problems in the past decade (e.g., Bernstein, Borchardt, & Perwein, 1996; Birmaher et al., 1996; Cicchetti and Cohen, 1995; Jensen et al., 1997). We have made great strides in identifying treatments that are effective when delivered by clinicians in nonresearch settings (e.g., Cantwell, 1996; Henggeler, Melton, Smith, Schoenwald, & Hanley, 1993).

Where data are available concerning the actual outcomes accruing from standard mental health services, however, outcomes for the youth served are frequently less positive than desired (Weisz, Weiss, & Donenberg, 1992). This research suggests that attention needs to be paid both to expanding services and to ensuring that the services provided achieve the maximum benefits possible. In this effort, greater attention needs to be placed on monitoring outcomes for children and families, on the qualifications of those providing the services, and on the constraints placed upon these service providers. In addition, greater emphasis needs to be placed on studying service outcomes in the settings where children with serious emotional disturbances and their families are likely to utilize these services: primary care settings, schools, and community programs (Leaf, Bogrov, & Webb, 1997), in addition to the office-based practices of clinicians.

The difficulties of improving clinical practice and access to effective mental health services must be substantial. How else can we explain the large numbers of children experiencing significant emotional and behavioral problems who are not receiving treatment for these problems (Leaf et al., 1996)? In few, if any, countries are children with significant behavioral or emotional problems given a high priority within the public mental health service systems. Most public and private attention on mental disorders continues to focus on adults. Indeed, in many countries, this attention on adults is focusing on a smaller and smaller subset of disorders. Despite the growing evidence of the high rates of mental disturbances in many communities, children experiencing significant impairment from their mental disorders continue to lack services (Leaf et al., 1996).

In many countries clinicians trained to deal with mental disorders in children and adolescents are in extremely short supply. Even where these clinicians exist, some treatments with demonstrated efficacy are ignored by or unavailable to the vast majority of providers. "Managed care," along with the growing awareness of the costs associated with mental disorders, makes it important that clinicians carefully examine the systems that exist for organizing and delivering mental health services and actively work to promote more effective services. These opportunities will frequently exist outside of the offices of individual clinicians (Henggeler & Santos, 1997). New strategies for training clinicians and supporting clinical services will be required if we are to bring together child-focused clinicians, children, and treatment opportunities. This could be an important role for future meetings of the International Association for Child and Adolescent Psychiatry and Allied Professions (IACAPAP) because there is a great need to disseminate treatment strategies proven effective in standard service settings.

Both policy makers and clinicians need to become more concerned with monitoring the outcomes of their efforts and determining the extent to which mental health services actually reduce the duration of illness episodes, prevent the recurrence of emotional and behavioral disorders, and/or reduce the disability accompanying emotional and behavioral problems. This is not the goal of most ongoing efforts related to "managed care." To date, most of these efforts in the United States and elsewhere have focused primarily on cost reduction. Other efforts have focused more on the quest for coordination rather than the linkage of children and adolescents with effective services. Administrative linkages are easily established, yet there is little evidence that coordination of services itself results in improved outcomes for children and their families.

If clinicians are not going to lead the efforts to provide effective services, there is a significant risk that efforts to develop services will continue to be driven more by economic factors than clinical outcomes. Few clinicians are engaged in systematic monitoring of the outcomes of their services. Few communities have a coherent strategy for determining when or whether services are effective. This, however, is not likely to continue. Purchasers of mental health services such as governments and employers are becoming concerned that their funds be used in as cost effective a manner as possible. Consumer advocacy groups are shifting from focusing only on the expansion of services to asking questions about the effectiveness of those services that are provided. Clinicians, therefore, can continue manifesting a lack of interest in monitoring outcomes only at their peril.

If clinicians do not develop ways of delivering services that are effective in the vast majority of communities in which they are used, and demonstrate the benefits of these services, governments and private purchasers of services are going to lose interest in supporting mental health service providers. There already is too little interest in the needs of children and adolescents. If the majority of clinicians remain uninterested in documenting the outcomes they achieve, someone else will do so. How likely is it that these efforts will be consistent with the best interests of children and adolescents experiencing emotional and behavioral problems?

If we are to stem the epidemic of childhood mental disorders encountered in many communities, it is critical that clinicians and those knowledgeable about developmental psychopathology increase their efforts to deliver preventive as well as remedial services. In the past, efforts to engage in discussions concerning the prevention of mental disorders may have promised much more than they were capable of delivering. Especially when talking about the needs of younger children, this is no longer the case.

With the expansion of managed care, mental health professionals are being held to a higher standard than that which they are accustomed. Decisions are being made concerning where and how to spend money. It is important that clinicians recognize that the effectiveness of their services will soon be evaluated by monitoring outcomes of treatment, not simply on the basis of the number of patients treated. In evaluating the impact of alternative financing arrangements and options for organizing mental health services for children and adolescents, we need to move beyond research that focuses only on treatments provided under ideal situations, i.e., efficacy studies.

Our current knowledge base consists almost entirely of the results of clinical trials that exclude children with co-occurring psychiatric disorders, that rely solely on highly motivated volunteers, and that use clinicians who are functioning under conditions that differ considerably from those likely to exist in all but the most richly funded research laboratories. If we are interested in increasing the effectiveness of the mental health services that are delivered in a nation, region, or city, we need evidence of how treatment works in standard treatment settings and the factors that improve outcomes in these settings. In a "managed care" environment, future studies also will have to have "population-based" service goals. Purchasers of preventive and remedial services are becoming increasingly concerned with whether the services they purchase reduce the dysfunction associated with disorders for the entire population for which they have responsibility. Programs that can meet the needs of only a small segment of the targeted population are not likely to receive long-term funding.

It is no longer adequate for evaluations to monitor only the quantity of clinician contacts. If we are serious about having an impact on the mental health status of a nation, region, or community, we need to evaluate organizations, systems of services, and programs of prevention in terms of the extent to which the actual risk of having a disorder and the level of disability associated with these disorders is reduced.

Thornicroft et al. (1992) and their colleagues in Great Britain have discussed a quality assurance model that has three components: optimal treatment and care, optimal social opportunities and environment, optimal self-attitudes and motivation. Each of these components is essential for the optimal social and personal functioning of the individual. An important aspect of this model is that it recognizes that optimal treatment and care is only one of three components necessary for optimal social and personal functioning. Optimal social opportunities and environment and optimal self-attitudes and motivation are also critical, and problems achieving positive long-term outcomes might be attributable to factors other than the quality of the care being provided.

Thus our evaluations of treatment outcomes must take into account factors in addition to the specific services being provided. Factors moderating or mediating the actual effectiveness of services cannot be ignored by clinicians, service providers, and policy makers. The context within which individual treatments are provided takes on great significance because family and community environments have important effects on the perceived outcomes of treatment. This also means that clinicians have to become more interested in factors outside of their offices if they are to ensure that their services are effective in reducing the disability associated with psychiatric disorders and the rates of these disorders in our communities.

Because emotional and behavioral problems can affect children and adolescents in many different ways, it is critical that future evaluations include multiple outcomes in their assessments of effectiveness. Although we have made great strides in identifying psychiatric disorder, our methods for monitoring the dysfunctions associated with these disorders is much less well developed. The importance of this problem cannot be overestimated because it is the dysfunction that is of great interest to policy makers and families.

In addition to judging the outcomes of services by monitoring the prevention of new cases of a disorder, the duration of a disorder, and the occurrence of comorbid disorders, greater attention needs to be paid to documenting the impact of services on morbidity and dysfunction. Our procedures for monitoring mental disorders focus primarily on symptoms. For future efforts at evaluation to be successful, greater attention will have to be paid to monitoring dysfunction and impairment. Of particular importance will be monitoring impairments that are related to poor school performance and engagement in high-risk behaviors with great cost to society. Because many disorders encountered by children and adolescents are chronic and persistent in nature, it is critical that future evaluation efforts focus on monitoring the reduction of disability, increasing the amount of time between illness episodes, and reducing the onset of disorders in adulthood.

I acknowledge that these evaluation criteria are quite broad and recognize that communities must establish priorities concerning their allocation of scarce fiscal and political resources. Likewise, clinicians must allocate their scarce intellectual resources in the face of a pandemic of mental disorders in our children and youth. The efforts of many nations in this area are far ahead of those being made in the United States. Unlike the United States, many countries already have the capacity to monitor the mental health status of their residents, the services used, and the effectiveness of these services. Countries should be encouraged to increase these efforts and to link the levels of need found with efforts to provide effective services—services that produce benefits when delivered within the contexts and constraints of real communities.

If we are going to evaluate the effectiveness of services based on their impact on the observed existence of psychiatric disorders and their associated disabilities, providers of mental health services need to become more concerned with the effects of public policies on the need for and use of mental health services, and the outcomes produced by these services. This suggests that we need to go beyond the evaluation of individual treatments and examine all the factors that mediate or moderate the impact of services on the prevalence and incidence of psychiatric disorders and their associated dysfunctions. Thus we need to focus on the full range of care needed by children with mental disorders or at high risk for these disorders. Here I use the term "care" as used by Wing and his colleagues.

> Care will be defined in terms of the medical, psychological, and social interventions that are used as "state of the art" by well trained mental health practitioners. It includes treatment, rehabilitation, counseling, training, supervision, resettlement, and welfare (Wing, Brewin & Thornicroft, 1992).

If we are serious about wishing to reduce the risk of mental disorders for children and the morbidity caused by mental disorders, we need to be concerned with the full range of services and care being used to affect the rates of these disorders, and the impairment associated with these disorders. The components of mental health services include: (a) all the specialists, generalists, and informal caregivers involved in services; (b) the settings in which these individuals work; and (c) the organization necessary to finance and deliver services (Wing et al., 1992).

Child psychiatrists constitute an important but relatively small component of the service system in most countries. Failure to disseminate the knowledge base of child psychiatry and to work with other professionals is done only at the risk of excluding child psychiatrists from many decisions that influence the status of their patients. For example, Leaf et al. (1996) found that more children aged 9–17 in the four communities studied were treated in school settings than were treated by child psychiatrists. Although the exact nature of the services provided was not monitored in this study, it is clear that in the United States, the school has become an important component of the de facto mental health service system. Efforts at planning and evaluation that limit their focus only to clinics and hospitals will produce data that is inconsistent with the actual treatments being received by youth.

One of the problems facing the evaluation of mental health services is that we do not yet have consensus on how to establish the need for and monitor the use of mental health services. Although many procedures exist for assessing need, for categorizing the services provided, and for monitoring changes in functioning related to the services, no consensus exists as to which procedures are best and which are not adequate for specific tasks. Until we achieve some consensus concerning how to assess need for and outcomes of mental health services, we will not be able to tell policy makers and purchasers of services how much these services contribute towards improving the mental health and social functioning of their communities.

Now, the most widely used strategy is the informal monitoring of complaints and the number of children receiving services, with the assumption that more services and fewer complaints is better. Some agencies utilize social indicators of need or risk to monitor need although these indicators are rather insensitive to the changes produced by treatment. Clearly, these methods leave much to be desired. A few agencies and providers are developing ''report cards'' for use by consumers or are undertaking population surveys.

None of these methods, with the possible exception of the report card, focuses on organizational or service-level variables. This is a major limitation for those trying to relate organizational structures and financing to the outcomes for children. It is a problem because we know from studies of adults with serious mental disorders that changes in the organization of mental health services do not necessarily translate into changes in the outcomes for patients.

It is likely that future efforts to establish the effectiveness of mental health services will require a wider range of assessment procedures. These should include randomized clinical trials in standard treatment settings, cohort studies, case control studies, ethnographic studies, and other qualitative approaches. In evaluating the need for services, future studies should focus on the multiple domains of functioning that are important for children and adolescents. These include role performance, thinking and thought disturbances, behavior towards others, mood/emotions, self-harmful behaviors, and substance abuse. Because children are not the sole targets for services, it will be important to monitor the basic needs of and outcomes for caregivers and community institutions such as schools and juvenile justice facilities.

Recent focus on healthcare markets, interorganizational networks, and the management of care has paid too little attention to the actual nature of the services being provided and the barriers to providing effective services. Efforts to monitor mental health services and outcomes are going to increase, not decrease. Without greater participation by clinicians and consumers in the evaluation process, it is clear that the interests of these two groups will not be well served by the solutions devised. If mental health specialists are going to maintain input into the services that are available, it is critical that they help set the criteria for evaluating services and participate in the design, implementation, and interpretation of evaluation efforts.

REFERENCES

Bernstein, G. A., Borchardt, C. M., & Perwien, A. R. (1996). Anxiety disorders in children and adolescents: A review of the past 10 years. *Journal of the American Academy of Child and Adolescent Psychiatry, 35,* 1110–1119.

Birmaher, B., Ryan, N. D., Williamson, D. E., Brent, D. A., Kaufman, J., Dahl, R. E., Perel, J., & Nelson B. (1996). Childhood and adolescent depression: A review of the past 10 years. Part I. *Journal of the American Academy of Child and Adolescent Psychiatry, 35,* 1427–1439.

Cantwell, D. P. (1996). Attention deficit disorder: A review of the past 10 years. *Journal of the American Academy of Child and Adolescent Psychiatry, 35,* 537–547.

Cicchetti, D., & Cohen, D. J. (Eds.). (1995). *Developmental psychopathology.* New York: Wiley.

Costello, E. J., Burns, B. J., Angold, A., & Leaf, P. J. (1993). How can epidemiology improve mental health services for children and adolescents? *Journal of the American Academy of Child and Adolescent Psychiatry, 32,* 1106–1114.

Henggeler, S. W., Melton, G. B., Smith, L. A., Schoenwald, S. K., & Hanley, J. H. (1993). Family preservation using multisystemic treatment: Long-term follow up to a clinical trial with serious juvenile offenders. *Journal of Child and Family Studies, 2,* 283–293.

Henggeler, S. W., & Santos, A. B. (Eds.). (1997). *Innovative approaches for difficult-to-treat populations.* Washington, DC: American Psychiatric Press.

Jensen, P. S., Mrazek, D., Knapp, P. K., Steinberg, L., Pfeffer, C., Scholwalter, J., & Shapiro, T. (1997). Evolution and revolution in child psychiatry: ADHD as a disorder of adaptation. *Journal of the American Academy of Child and Adolescent Psychiatry, 36,* 1672–1679.

Leaf, P. J., Bogrov, M., & Webb, M. B. (1997). The East Baltimore Mental Health Partnership. In S. N. Henggeler & A. B. Santos (Eds.), *Innovative approaches for difficult-to-treat populations (pp. 117–138). Washington, DC: American Psychiatric Press.*

Leaf, P. J., Cohen, P., Horwitz, S., Narrow, W. E., Regier, D. A., Alegria, M., Goodman, S. H., Hoven, C. W., & Vanden-Kiernan, M. (1996). Mental health services use in the community and schools: Results from the four community MECA study. *Journal of the American Academy of Child and Adolescent Psychiatry, 35,* 889–897.

Thornicroft, G., Brewin, C. R., & Wing, J. (Eds.). (1992). *Measuring mental health needs.* London: Gaskell.

Weisz, J. A., Weiss, B., & Donenberg, G. R. (1992). The lab versus the clinic. *American Psychologist, 47,* 997–1006.

Wing, J., Brewin, C. R., & Thornicroft, G. (1992). Defining mental health needs. In G. Thornicroft, C. R. Brewin, & J. Wing (Eds.), *Measuring mental health needs* (pp. 1–17). London: Gaskell.

9

Evaluating Community-Based Mental Health Services for Children with Serious Mental Illness: Toward a New Paradigm of Systems of Care

LEONARD SAXE

The United States prides itself on the sophistication of its healthcare system and its ability to harness research knowledge to improve the health and welfare of its citizens. Yet, particularly for children with serious mental disorders, there is a substantial gap between rhetoric and reality. Children with serious mental illness have not benefitted from our professed concern to make available the best services (cf. National Commission on Children, 1991; Saxe, 1986). Such a state of affairs has not gone unaddressed, however, and in recent years several important research-based efforts have been undertaken to develop systems of care for children with serious mental illness (Rog, 1995). The goal of these developmental efforts has been to develop effective community-based mental health services and to provide care that matches the needs of children and their families. The recent development of systems of care for children with mental disorders is described below, with a particular focus on evaluative research studies of new service systems.

Mental health services for children in the United States are undergoing substantial change, influenced by new understandings of treatment, by the increasingly effective activities of advocates for children (see Saxe & Cross, 1997), and by a host of changes in the nation's system of health and social services. Many of the developments seem contradictory and reflect the push and pull of different policies. On the one hand, health and social services have been decentralized and removed from government control; on the other hand, the United States has moved, particularly in the healthcare sector, from an individually focused to a managed care system. Research, although not consistently influential, has both documented the failures of the care system and provided an impetus to try new approaches to treatment.

Along with describing the overall development of systems of care for children, the discussion below considers two recently completed demonstration programs which were the focus of systematic evaluation study. The Mental Health Services Program for Youth (MHSPY) was an effort developed by the Robert Wood Johnson Foundation (RWJF), a private philanthropy, to develop systems of care in eight communities (England & Cole, 1992; Saxe, Cross, Lovas, & Gardner, 1995). The Fort Bragg Child and Adolescent Mental Health Demonstration was a sophisticated quasi-experiment, supported by the U.S. Department of Defense and designed to assess whether a system of care could provide better and more cost-effective care for children with serious mental disorders (Behar, 1996; Bickman et al., 1995). Both projects were designed to apply state-of-the-art knowledge about the needs of children and involved establishing new types of organizations to provide mental health and social services aid to children and their families.

The results of the MHSPY and Fort Bragg demonstrations have been the focus of contradictory interpretations and, although they support beliefs about the potential for providing community-based treatment, they do not provide unequivocal evidence for the superiority of managed mental healthcare. The findings of these large-scale studies suggest that the path to improved care for children with serious emotional disorders is complex. Their findings are interpreted here as suggesting a new paradigm for thinking about mental healthcare for children and the directions that future practice and research should take.

ORIGINS OF SYSTEMS OF CARE

The provision of more adequate care for children with serious emotional disorders has long been discussed in the United States (Joint Commission on Mental Health for Children, 1970; see also Saxe, Cross, Silverman, & Batchelor, 1987). Undoubtedly, we have failed to match our rhetoric with fully effective programs; nevertheless, there has been substantial progress since the 1960s when, absent effective treatment, large numbers of children were institutionalized. Recent efforts to develop more responsive services had their origins in the recognition that we were hospitalizing children or placing them in residential centers without effective treatment, and efforts were undertaken to shift services into community settings. By the early 1980s, however, it was clear that community services were not providing the level of services that children with emotional disorders needed and that our knowledge of treatment was being poorly applied.

An important catalyst for change was a 1982 report, developed under the sponsorship of a national advocacy organization, the Children's Defense Fund (CDF; see Knitzer, 1982). The CDF documented glaring deficiencies in the children's mental health system and found that, among the more than 2 million U.S. children with severe emotional disturbances, only a small number received adequate mental health services. The report concluded that services provided to children were fragmented and uncoordinated and recommended that services be provided to children in their homes and communities.

Child and Adolescent Service System Program

In part as a response to the CDF report, the federal government initiated efforts in the early 1980s to develop children's mental healthcare systems through the Child and Adolescent Service System Program (CASSP; Day & Roberts, 1991; Katz-Leavy, DeCarols, & Quinlan 1996). CASSP was established to help states reorganize agencies that serve children in need, including child welfare, juvenile justice, education, and mental health. The goal was to help them develop systems that could provide coordinated services. It was recognized that children with emotional problems faced difficulty functioning in school, were often involved with the social welfare and criminal justice systems, and, more often that not, were referred back and forth among these agencies. The result was that they failed to receive either effective or adequate care.

CASSP promoted a philosophy that viewed the child as the focus of mental health services, with professionals and families as partners in aiding these children (Stroul & Friedman, 1986, 1996). CASSP promoted individualized care and emphasized that such aid be provided in the least restrictive setting. The theory was that care provided in the community would promote the child's adaptation and would thus be more effective. Simultaneously, such community-based care would obviate the need for costly institutional services and free resources for provision of more services.

CASSP had a profound effect on how states organized care for children and families dealing with emotional disorders and has been at the forefront of efforts to reform mental health services. Not only did CASSP provide incentives for child-serving agencies to reorganize their activities, but, at a more profound level, the CASSP principles made clear that children's mental disorders need to be treated with the help of a broad array of family and community supports. Implementation of the CASSP principles transformed the way in which professionals interacted with children and their families and made them interdependent. In 1993, CASSP was extended and moved beyond being a demonstration program and provided a means for the federal government to assist communities in developing comprehensive care systems for children with serious emotional disorders. As part of this ongoing initiative, the government provides both technical assistance and support for systematic research on the effectiveness of services.

OTA Report

Shortly after the CDF study, and after the CASSP initiative was underway, the U.S. Congress took an interest in the problems of children's mental healthcare and requested a scientific study of the knowledge base. In a resulting study that colleagues and I developed for the Congress' Office of Technology Assessment (OTA; see Saxe et al., 1987; Saxe, Cross, & Silverman, 1988), we substantiated CDF's central conclusion about the lack of appropriate services. The OTA report documented the gap between the numbers of children in need of treatment and those children who received what current standards considered appropriate care. Epidemiological estimates indicated that more than 12% of children had a diagnosable mental disorder, and half of this group of children (6%) were conservatively estimated to have a serious mental disorder. Data from the treatment system made clear that the majority of these children received no services and that many of those who received treatment were inappropriately served. As was suspected, the available system of care concentrated its resources on a relatively small number of children placed in residential settings (e.g., psychiatric hospitals, residential treatment centers). The majority of children did not have access to resources for institutional care (such as private insurance), and, as a result, their needs were ignored.

The OTA report noted that our knowledge of children's mental healthcare had grown substantially. There was increasing evidence for the effectiveness of a variety of mental health treatments and, more importantly, considerable evidence that schools and families could provide important services. Although it was clear that the specificity of our knowledge about the effectiveness of particular treatments was limited—it's not clear what is the best treatment for a particular child with a set of individual problems—there was substantial evidence that most children in need were not getting the benefit of the knowledge we had available (see Saxe et al., 1988).

OTA also found that, while the CASSP initiative reflected the best current thinking, it was not structured to allow a test of the ideas. One problem was that the CASSP funds could only be used by states to restructure services; in many cases, what was necessary was the provision of new services. Children with serious mental disorders needed access to a variety of supportive services that the mental health system was not able to provide and that could not be easily financed under current rules. What was needed, clearly, were efforts to develop new ways of providing care.

MENTAL HEALTH SERVICES PROGRAM FOR YOUTH

Not long after the OTA report was released, MHSPY was conceived to extend CASSP's efforts and to test some of the assumptions about the breadth of needs of children with serious emotional disorders. MHSPY was born out of resolve to implement the reforms that had been widely discussed, but had not yet been implemented widely (Beachler, 1990). The RWJF, which designed and funded MHSPY, wanted to test the operationalization of coordinated community-based mental healthcare for children. The loose theory was that children, even those with the most serious mental disorders, could be treated within their community *provided* that a broad range of services were available and that the family, school, and other settings in which these children lived were made partners in developing supportive services. It was expected that coordinated community-based services could reduce reliance on out-of-home placements for children with serious mental disorders and could make more efficient use of limited mental health resources (England & Cole, 1992; Saxe et al., 1995).

MHSPY reflected the *Zeitgeist* of the 1980s that responsibility for health and social welfare programs should devolve from national and state agencies to local communities and was propelled by the parallel notion that the costs of health and social programs needed to be restrained. The underlying idea of MHSPY made sense to both those who had traditionally advocated for more spending and attention to children's programs and those who had advocated fiscal constraint and individual, rather than societal, responsibility. Perhaps because of this unusual confluence, even before the program was implemented, it become the accepted wisdom about care for children with serious emotional disturbances.

MHSPY was designed to demonstrate that fundamental change in the delivery of mental healthcare was feasible and could lead to more effective, and more widely available, services to those in need. The demonstration aimed explicitly to change the organization, financing, and responsibility for providing mental health services. Eight communities across the United States, representing diverse geographic and demographic areas, participated. The sites included portions of large cities such as Cleveland and San Francisco, the entire state of Vermont, and several rural and semi-urban counties of North Carolina. Each project was a joint endeavor between state agencies and local communities.

The Foundation provided nearly $20 million to help participating communities reorganize their care system and pay for new services. It also required that each site establish a state–local partnership that was expected to generate additional financing and to help develop the system of care and implement case management (see Cole, 1996; England & Cole, 1992). Communities were to focus their Foundation resources on the children with the most severe mental disorders, in part to determine if the costs of institutionalization could be reduced. All of the sites developed collaborations among public and private agencies that provided mental health, child welfare, education, and, with one exception, juvenile justice services.

Maintaining children in the community, rather than having them extruded to hospitals, was to be accomplished by providing case management and developing a continuum of care. The continuum of care was designed to provide a coordinated matrix of services, from identification and development of a treatment plan to implementation and follow-up. A key element of the MHSPY strategy was the development of financing schemes that would allow flexible use of treatment dollars; that is, treatment funds could be shifted easily from one type of service to another based on the child's needs. Projects had to create mechanisms for interagency coordination, find ways to involve parents and other caregivers, and expand community-based services. Expanded services often required development of services that were not well supported, such as therapeutic foster care, crisis intervention, independent living programs, and intensive home visiting. The emphasis was on services intended to provide flexible, intensive interventions in the community.

Evaluation

The development of each of the MHSPY projects was tracked over a 5-year period as part of a systematic evaluation (see Cross & Saxe, 1997; Saxe et al., 1995). Although the design was nonexperimental (i.e., no comparison communities were studied), the longitudinal nature of the design permits us to draw a number of inferences about the effect of the program. The data make clear that it is, indeed, feasible to develop a continuum of care and to coordinate children's services among traditionally separate child-serving agencies (e.g., social services, hospitals, schools). Although each of these agencies has a different mandate, different funding, and often a history of noncooperation, it was possible for them to collaborate to expand the rudimentary services for children which existed in most communities. The evaluation data support the hypothesis that systems of care were, indeed, feasible with the appropriate organizational and financial support (Cross & Saxe, 1997).

The changes over time were impressive: Each MHSPY site was able to implement elements of an organized continuum of care and establish links among agencies. Nevertheless, sites differed in their success and there were inevitable gaps in the systems. One of the gaps that seemed to appear most frequently was a strong linkage between the social welfare system (i.e., the public agency responsible for abused and neglected children) and other agencies with direct responsibility for children with emotional disorders (in particular, mental health and education). Such an outcome is, perhaps, not surprising, since social service agencies have to deal both with children's individual difficulties and, many times, with the lack of a family support system. They have more difficulty accepting the system of care philosophy that sees the family as a partner in the provision of care, and, thus, there were often strains and even legal barriers to their working with families.

By the end of the project (c. 1995), most communities had stable systems of care which were to survive the end of RWJF funding, although none of the systems was static. In virtually every community, the systems underwent almost constant evolution. Such change is probably healthy and necessary and reflects the need of the systems to adapt to changing circumstances, from changing community demographics to changes in the availability of funding.

A major question about MHSPY was the ability of sites to provide effective community-based care and whether it was possible to maintain children at risk of psychiatric hospitalization in the community. There is substantial evidence that the demonstration accomplished this goal and that these at-risk children were provided multiple, intensive services in their communities. Although most of the children received psychotherapeutic services, one of the most frequently used services was "respite." Respite enabled parents to have help caring for their children and was seen, anecdotally, as key to enabling parents of children with serious emotional disorders to keep them at home.

Data collected from a client information system indicated that hospitalization and residential treatment were rarely used and that the rates were significantly lower than one would expect with a population of children diagnosed with the most serious emotional disorders (for most sites, less than 5%; see Cross & Saxe, 1997). Low levels of hospitalization and residential treatment resulted despite the fact that many of the children became involved in the program at the point at which they were deemed at high risk for hospitalization (Cole, 1996; England & Cole, 1992). Furthermore, many of the children who were treated outside the community came from rural sites where, not surprisingly, developing a continuum of care is particularly difficult.

One reason that MHSPY sites were able to maintain children in their communities is that they were able to develop new means of financing services. Many of the new and expanded services developed by communities (e.g., respite care) were made possible by developing funding pools and by requesting waivers to provide so-called "wraparound funds" (money that could be used to supplement therapy and provide support for children and families). These funding mechanisms allowed clinicians to address the totality of the health, mental health, and educational and social needs of each child and family served. Explicit in this strategy is the assumption that children with serious mental disorders have changing needs for services and that flexibility is essential if children are to be maintained outside of hospitals.

A challenge in drawing conclusions from MHSPY is that each of the eight communities implemented the project somewhat differently and had a different organizational structure. Some of the differences had to do with which agency had overall responsibility for coordination. Thus, some programs were run by mental health agencies (e.g., a community mental health center), one by a social service agency, and several by new organizations created to integrate multiple agencies. There were a plethora of individual adaptations to varying environments and conditions that resulted in somewhat different program "models." Several communities were dealing with endemic poverty, others with a lack of trained professionals or a history of independence among those responsible for aiding children. Local culture also played a role, and some communities had stronger traditions of developing their own solutions to problems such as children with multiple needs.

What is clear is that no single model of care seemed better than any other. In part, this result reflects the need for each system to develop in synchrony with local needs and culture, but it also reflects our lack of knowledge of what specific treatments are linked with what kinds of success in outcome. The present study did not allow an objective assessment of treatment effectiveness. Efficiency may not be equivalent to effectiveness, and it is unclear, given the current knowledge base, whether even making available a set of desirable services is going to ameliorate the distress of children with serious emotional disorders. Some researchers have argued (see e.g., Weisz, Han, & Valeri, 1997; Weisz, Weiss, Han, Granger, & Morton, 1995) that there is scant data to support the real-world effectiveness of mental health treatments for children. If so, merely reorganizing systems so that services are available to children in need will have limited impact.

The Fort Bragg demonstration was begun subsequent to MHSPY (in 1990) and was explicitly developed as an experiment to test the effectiveness of the system of care services to children with emotional disorders (Behar, 1996; Bickman et al., 1995). Funded by the Department of Defense (Army), the Fort Bragg demonstration was conducted with children of military personnel. In some cases, these children were served directly by the military healthcare system; most, however, received a special form of health insurance to purchase their services. In collaboration with the State of North Carolina, the demonstration developed a full continuum of children's mental health services for military dependents. Independent of the program, an evaluation was conducted (see Bickman, 1996; Bickman et al., 1995) to assess the demonstration and the impact on the children served. The evaluation was designed as a quasi-experiment that compared outcomes in the Fort Bragg community with outcomes at two other comparable military sites.

There are, undoubtedly, differences in a sample of military dependents and the general population, and even more important differences in the availability of healthcare to those affiliated with the military and those in the general population. Nevertheless, the Fort Bragg demonstration provided an important test of the ideas underlying coordinated continua of care. Whatever existing external validity limitations there are, they are compensated for by the ability to test ideas about care in a closed system of health and social services. The underlying question was whether a continuum of care would be more responsive to the needs of children and families and avoid unnecessarily restrictive treatments, such as psychiatric hospitalization.

As implemented by the State of North Carolina, the site of the demonstration, and the agency that took responsibility for developing the continuum, the program emphasized intermediate services such as in-home crisis stabilization, after-school group treatment, therapeutic foster care, and crisis management, to help fill the gap between outpatient psychotherapy and institutional treatment. The program was put into place in 1990 and, throughout its multiple–year implementation, children's outcomes were carefully monitored. Parallel monitoring was conducted in the two comparison sites.

The results of the demonstration (see Bickman, 1996; Bickman et al., 1995) can be summarized succinctly, although their meaning is the subject of considerable ongoing debate (see, e.g., Behar, 1997; Bickman, 1997; Hoagwood, 1997; Saxe & Cross, 1997). Care provided at the demonstration expanded dramatically and, compared to baseline, three times the number of children were served. The demonstration site provided care for far more children than were served at the two comparison sites (13.6% in the demonstration site, compared to 6.8% in the comparison communities). An implementation analysis provided strong evidence that a continuum of care was made available and that individual children had access to a broad array of services. There was further evidence that these services were of high caliber.

In terms of outcomes, children in the demonstration were less likely to use hospital and residential treatment, but more likely to use intermediate services, as well as significantly more likely to have psychotherapy visits and to spend a longer time in treatment. What was surprising and has created considerable consternation, however, is that clinical outcomes were generally no different. Children who received services at both demonstration and comparison sites improved, although demonstration site children did have better scores on mental health measures. Moreover, the demonstration was far more expensive and spent 1.5 times more money per child than the comparisons (Behar, 1996; Behar, Macbeth, & Holland, 1993).

The Fort Bragg evaluation has attracted considerable attention (see the *American Psychologist* issue of May 1997) because it challenges the assumption that a continuum of care both improves access to care and enhances children's mental health outcomes. To the disappointment of those who advocate coordinated systems of care because they believe it is essential to make comprehensive services available to children with emotional disorders (see, e.g., Stroul & Friedman, 1996), the Fort Bragg results suggest that children are not better off being served by a continuum. Bickman (1996, 1997), the principal architect of the Fort Bragg evaluation, believes that the emphasis on how care is managed has been misplaced. In his judgement, we need to "return to basics" and develop more effective treatments.

Bickman's view is supported by a number of other researchers, most importantly Weisz and his colleagues (Weisz, Weiss, & Donenberg, 1992; Weisz et al., 1995). Weisz has conducted meta-analyses of the literature on children's mental health treatments and concludes that there is not evidence for the effectiveness of the services that are offered in actual community settings. He implies that there is a good reason why there has been an implementation gap in making these services available: We simply did not know enough about how to help children with serious emotional disorders.

Although our research knowledge lacks specificity, the Fort Bragg quasi-experiment and the nonexperimental MHSPY demonstration make clear that there are important methodological limits to our research. The limits of our methods may be as critical to overcome as the substance of the interventions themselves. In this view, the results of Fort Bragg are being overinterpreted (cf. Behar, 1997; Friedman & Burns, 1996; Saxe & Cross, 1997) and, while they do not show the superiority of a continuum care, they do not negate the underlying construct. A key methodological problem with Bickman's study was that the control group (i.e., the comparison military communities) actually received intensive and coordinated mental health services. Because children in these communities were covered by the military's dependant care insurance program (CHAMPUS), they had access to a broad array of high-quality services. Thus, the results may be a function of a diffusion of the treatment, rather than a lack of effectiveness for the experimental intervention.

The Fort Bragg findings, in fact, showed that a comprehensive continuum of care could be developed and increases access to services for children in need (Hoagwood, 1997; Saxe & Cross, 1997). Even more significantly, the study also showed important improvements in the functioning of children following receipt of services. Children in both the demonstration and comparison sites improved and their gains were relatively impressive. Eighty-four percent of demonstration-served children improved (based on the Reliable Change Index; Jacobson & Truax, 1991) on a key outcome measure. Although Bickman reports that 80% of the children still had at least one diagnosis after a year and that few were "free of mental health problems," complete absence of mental health problems is an unrealistic goal and was not the intent. The magnitude of children's gains was superior to other reports of care provided in community settings (without comprehensive services) and provides important evidence of the positive effects of mental health treatment for children.

The lack of superiority in clinical outcomes for children and the larger costs at the demonstration site suggest, however, that we are only at an early stage of understanding how to provide effective and cost-efficient mental healthcare. Clearly, there is a need to learn more about the conditions associated with positive outcomes and to understand better how the delivery of services affects outcome. If, in fact, the present assumption is correct—that the effectiveness of treatment is linked to how closely one can match treatments with children's and families' needs—it is essential that we develop a "continuum" of research. The continuum needs to include basic research studies, as well as efforts to test models of caregiving in actual communities.

NEW PARADIGM

Systems of care for providing services to children with mental disorders have been characterized as a "new paradigm" (Cole & Poe, 1993). There are many ways to describe this new perspective, but these systems of care seem to embody fundamental changes in how services are provided. The best characterization is, perhaps, as a patient-focused paradigm for restructuring health services, where clinical needs are placed at the fore and health professionals have to form a partnership with patients and families to make key decisions about care. The claim cannot be made that this paradigm will bring about more effective care, but it provides a way to think about developing and testing more effective care.

Patient-focused care should not be a revolutionary paradigm but, in the United States, where we have experienced several decades of rapid progress in health technology and concomitant institutionalization of health services, the recipient of healthcare has often been subordinated. Decision-making power has shifted both to those responsible to the institutions that provide health services and, in many cases, to those who provide financing. Particularly for children, who are assumed not to have the ability to make their own decisions, the transfer of authority has been notable. The new paradigm for children's mental health services takes back this authority and gives a central role to parents and, in some cases, children.

Development of a new paradigm has not happened *de novo,* and a great deal of discussion has concerned the need to reshape health and social systems to respond to the needs of those served (e.g., Schorr, 1989). For children, the guiding principles are that care must be community/family-based *and* that it must be comprehensive (cf. Children's Defense Fund, 1992; National Commission on Children, 1991). The necessity of both principles is that families have the responsibility for children, but it is clear that they cannot cope alone with problems such as serious mental illness. Professional help is needed, but professionals cannot alone have the responsibility, either.

Children have been victim to our society's inability to resolve fundamental problems with our health and social systems. They are more likely than adults to live in poverty and to lack health insurance, and they have the most difficult problems accessing appropriate healthcare. Improving children's health and their ability to function should be important in its own right, but practically, it makes sense because changing the course of a child's development has the longest-lasting impact. Children in the 1990s are, hopefully, what the elderly were to social and health reform in the United States during the 1930s and 1960s, when Social Security (retirement insurance) and Medicare (health insurance for the elderly) were flagship social programs that changed how the government dealt with its citizens. Developing "systems" of services for children may not only improve the care of vulnerable children but provide a model for the kinds of programs that are needed: those involving community collaboration but focused on the needs of individuals.

Whether the issue is how the education, juvenile justice, or mental or physical health systems treat children, the paradigmatic view of a child's integrated needs seems a useful way to reconsider how we aid children. Experience with both the MHSPY and Fort Bragg demonstrations does not provide unequivocal evidence to support this view, but the view of children as part of a family and a community seems so obvious that one wonders how it could have been ignored for so long. Children with serious mental illness have a set of needs that seem extraordinary, but how we treat them is symbolic of how we view all children. Our failures to provide effective and efficient services for these children make them more visible, but the underlying principles are universal. All children need both their homes and the support of those in the communities with whom they interact.

The development of demonstrations to improve care for children with serious emotional disorders perhaps proves the adage that with wisdom comes ignorance. Although the results of both demonstrations suggest that it is possible to improve care for children, the demonstrations also expose our lack of knowledge and the limits of our ability to learn from research how to provide effective services to children and families. This lack of knowledge should be an incentive to develop and test better systems. We have the paradigm that should allow us to structure these systems in ways that exploit our best knowledge and allow for our assumptions to be tested. It only remains for us to carry through on the promise represented by current advances.

ACKNOWLEDGMENTS

Appreciation is expressed to my colleagues who collaborated with me on the development of my ideas about children's mental health. Most importantly, I need to acknowledge the late Dr. Judith K. Gardner, who was a key inspiration and who loved and understood children. I would also like to thank IACACAP President Donald Cohen, who invited me to present this work, and my colleague at Brandeis University, Ted Cross. I may be contacted by email at saxe@binah.cc.brandeis.edu.

REFERENCES

Beachler, M. (1990). The mental health services program for youth. *Journal of Mental Health Administration, 17,* 115–121.

Behar, L. B. (1996). Policy implications of the evaluation of the Fort Bragg Child and Adolescent Mental Health Demonstration Project. *Journal of Mental Health Administration, 23*(1), 118–121.

Behar, L. B. (1997). The Fort Bragg evaluation: A snapshot in time. *American Psychologist, 52,* 557–559.

Behar, L. B., Macbeth, G., & Holland, J. M. (1993). Distribution and costs of mental health services within a system of care for children and adolescents. *Administration and Policy in Mental Health, 20,* 283–295.

Bickman, L. (1996). A continuum of care: More is not better. *American Psychologist, 51,* 689–701.

Bickman, L. (1997). Resolving issues raised by the Fort Bragg evaluation: New directions for mental health services research. *American Psychologist, 52,* 562–565.

Bickman, L., Guthrie, P. R., Foster, E. M., Lambert, E. W., Summerfelt, W. T., Breda, C. S., & Heflinger, C. A. (1995). *Evaluating managed mental health services: The Fort Bragg Experiment.* New York: Plenum.

Children's Defense Fund (1992). *The state of America's children: 1992* Washington, DC: Children's Defense Fund.

Cole, R. F. (1996). The Robert Wood Johnson Foundation's Mental Health Services Program for Youth. In B. A. Stroul (Ed.), *Children's mental health: Creating systems of care in a changing society* (pp. 235–248). Baltimore, MD: Paul H. Brookes Publishing.

Cole, R. F., & Poe, S. L. (1993). *Partnership for care: Systems of care for children with serious emotional disturbances and their families.* Washington, DC: WBGH.

Cross, T. P., & Saxe, L. (1997). Many hands make mental health systems of care a reality: Lessons from the Mental Health Services Program for Youth. In C. T. Nixon & D. A. Northrup (Eds.), *Children's mental health services: Research, policy, and evaluation* (pp. 45–72). Thousand Oaks, CA: Sage.

Day, C., & Roberts, M. C. (1991). Activities of the Child and Adolescent Service System Program for improving mental health services for children and families. *Journal of Clinical Child Psychology, 20*(4), 340–350.

England, M. J., & Cole, R. F. (1992). Building systems of care for youth with serious mental illness. *Hospital and Community Psychiatry, 43,* 630–633.

Friedman, R., & Burns, B. J. (1996). The evaluation of the Fort Bragg project: An alternative interpretation of the findings. *Journal of Mental Health Administration, 23*(1), 128–136.

Hoagwood, K. (1997). Interpreting nullity: The Fort Bragg experiment—a comparative success or failure? *American Psychologist, 52,* 546–550.

Jacobson, N. S., & Truax, P. (1991). Clinical significance: A statistical approach to defining meaningful change in psychotherapy research. *Journal of Consulting and Clinical Psychology, 59,* 12–19.

Joint Commission on Mental Health for Children (1970). *Crisis in child mental health: Challenge for the 1970s* (Foreword by Abraham A. Ribicoff). New York: Harper & Row.

Knitzer, J. (1982). *Unclaimed children.* Washington, DC: Children's Defense Fund.

Lourie, I. S., Katz-Leavy, J., DeCarolis, G., & Quinlan Jr., W. A. (1996). The role of the federal government. In B. A. Stroul (Ed.), *Children's Mental Health: Creating systems of care in a changing society* (pp. 99–114). Baltimore, MD: Paul H. Brookes Publishing.

National Commission on Children (1991). *Beyond rhetoric: A new American agenda for children and families.* Final report of the National Commission on Children. Washington, DC: U.S. Government Printing Office.

President's Commission on Mental Health (1978). *Report to the President from the President's Commission on Mental Health.* Washington, DC: U.S. Government Printing Office.

Rog, D. (1995). The status of children's mental health services: An overview. In L. Bickman and D. Rog (Eds.), *Creating a children's mental health service system: Policy, research and evaluation.* Thousand Oaks, CA: Sage.

Saxe, L. (1986). Policymakers' use of social science research: Technology assessment in the U.S. Congress. *Knowledge: Creation, diffusion, and utilization, 8,* 59–78.

Saxe, L., & Cross, T. P. (1997). Interpreting the Fort Bragg children's mental health demonstration project: The cup is half full. *American Psychologist, 52,* 553–556.

Saxe, L., Cross, T. P., Lovas, G. S., & Gardner, J. K. (1995). Evaluation of the Mental Health Services Program for Youth demonstration: Examining rhetoric in action. In L. Bickman and D. Rog (Eds.), *Creating a children's mental health service system: Policy, research and evaluation* (pp. 206–235). Beverly Hills, CA: Sage.

Saxe, L., Cross, T. P., & Silverman, N. (1988). Children's mental health: The gap between what we know and what we do. *American Psychologist, 43,* 800–807.

Saxe, L., Cross, T. P., Silverman, N., & Batchelor, W. F., with Dougherty, D. (1987). *Children's mental health: Problems and services.* Durham, NC: Duke University Press. [Originally published by the Office of Technology Assessment, U.S. Congress; OTA-BP-H-33; Washington, DC: U.S. Government Printing Office.]

Schorr, L. B. (1989). *Within our reach: Breaking the cycle of disadvantage.* New York: Anchor Books, Doubleday.

Stroul, B. A., & Friedman, R. M. (1996). The system of care concept and philosophy. In B. A. Stroul (Ed.), *Children's Mental Health: Creating systems of care in a changing society* (pp. 3–22), Baltimore, MD: Paul H. Brookes Publishing.

Stroul, B. A., & Friedman, R. M. (1996). The system of care concept and philosophy. In B. A. Stroul (Ed.), *Children's Mental Health: Creating systems of care in a changing society* (pp. 3–22). Baltimore, MD: Paul H. Brookes Publishing.

Weisz, J. R., Han, S. S., & Valeri, S. M. (1997). More of what? Issues raised by the Fort Bragg study. *American Psychologist, 52,*(5): 541–545.

Weisz, J. R., Weiss, B., & Donenberg, G. R. (1992). The lab versus the clinic: Effects of child and adolescent psychotherapy. *American Psychologist, 47,* 1578–1585.

Weisz, J. R., Weiss, B., Han, S. S., Granger, D. A., Morton, C. B. (1995), Effects of psychotherapy with children and adolescents revisited: A meta-analysis of treatment outcome studies. *Psychological Bulletin, 117*(3), 450–468.

MODELS OF TREATMENT AND PREVENTIVE INTERVENTIONS FOR DEVELOPMENTAL PSYCHOPATHOLOGY

10

The Mental Health System for Children and Adolescents: Issues in the Definition and Evaluation of Treatments and Services

Epidemiological, service utilization, educational, judiciary, and other types of data document the large and increasing numbers of children whose lives are burdened by developmental and psychiatric difficulties. They are found in every type of family and community context, in every social class, and among all ethnic groups. There are, however, some groups that are at particular risk, where multiple factors combine to make children and adolescents particularly vulnerable. Thus, at this moment, mental health clinicians are particularly aware of the cumulative trauma of multigenerational adversity and poverty in the inner city, the problems of the rural poor and of recent immigrants, the strains posed by homelessness and family breakup, and the impact of various toxins and infections (including HIV/AIDS, cocaine, alcohol, tobacco) on the development of children (National Commission on Children, 1991). As risk factors accumulate, the probability of disorders increases.

The rates of psychiatric illness are high among children living in adversity throughout the world. Even in the most economically advanced nations, 8% to 10% of children have some type of diagnosable mental disturbance, and up to 20% of children growing up in inner city poverty are impaired to some degree in their social, behavioral, and academic functioning (Costello, 1989; Institute of Medicine, 1989; Offord, Boyle & Szatmari, 1987; Rutter, 1989; Shaffer et al., 1996; Verhulst, Van der Ende, Ferdinand, & Kasius,

1997). The cost of these conditions—in suffering for the child and family, in the effects on community resources, in the loss of productivity, and in the need for long-term intervention—is staggering. Given this scope of difficulty, it is important to find and implement methods for reducing risk. Enhanced attention to children at risk probably will result in more "case finding." The number of identified children in need of treatment is thus likely to increase.

Child psychiatrists need to work towards improving treatments for children and families and helping to make effective treatments accessible and affordable. Clinical and basic research are clarifying types of disorders, causal pathways, and new psychological and biological treatments (Rutter, 1997). Yet, for many types of disturbances, there is little or no knowledge about what, if any, treatments definitely alter natural history. What do we know and what do we need to learn about the types of treatments which can be helpful for children and adolescents and their families? There are very useful methodologies for systematically answering these types of questions (Kazdin, 1987a,b, 1988, 1989). For those professionals who are also engaged in the education of the next generation of child psychiatrists, psychologists, social workers, and other mental health clinicians, the answers to these questions will define the ethical basis of the educational curriculum and the knowledge and uncertainties that should be transmitted to our students. A developmental psychopathology framework can help clarify the purposes and goals of treatment and the shape of future systems of intervention (Cicchetti and Cohen, 1995).

THE CONTEXT OF TREATMENT

Children come for care for diverse conditions and problems. While categorical diagnoses are useful landmarks, they are limited in conveying the pathways into care or the reasons for needing intervention as these might be presented in a diagnostic formulation. Internationally, child psychiatrists, psychologists, and others are generally familiar with the concepts of the diagnostic typology and nomenclature of the two major systems, the International Classification of Disease (ICD 10) and the Diagnostic and Statistical Manual of the American Psychiatric Association (DSM-IV). These systems provide an international language for research, treatment, and scientific and clinical communication. Yet, the categorical approach to diagnosis embodied in these systems may also be a burden for clinicians. In DSM, in particular, specific symptoms are used to specify discrete disorders (categories) with little concern for variability over time and among a group; history; concurrent strengths and difficulties; or personal or communal context. The categorical approach has obscured the real reasons for treatment as these are conveyed by an elaborate clinical formulation, with its implications for a range of interventions over time. In spite of the DSM and ICD classifications, most conditions that clinicians deal with are not circumscribed diseases with clear-cut treatments.

Children rarely are brought to mental health services or enter treatment, outside of some research protocols, for a single, definable reason. More generally, children are in treatment because of a confluence of vectors: a range of problems expressed in their behaviors and feelings, in their particular families, at particular moments in their lives, in particular school situations. It is unusual for there to be a single site of difficulty. And children typically earn more than one categorical diagnosis. On inpatient child psychiatric services, in particular, children may satisfy the criteria for four or five diagnoses (ADHD, conduct disorder, learning disability, a chronic medical condition), and their problems reflect many sources of strain: constitutional, familial, intrapsychic, and communal. Finally, the disorders and problems which bring children into therapy are often of very long duration, relative to the child's age.

These conditions are distinguishable from those of most adult patients, by various factors: (a) the central role of biological and constitutional influences in the childhood disorders, (b) the appearance of disorders during the course of development, (c) the close interplay with family and community, and (d) their persistence for large proportions of the child's lifetime before treatment is obtained. The recent, scientific interest in comorbidity reflects the fact that the edges of a disorder are not sharply defined in childhood and that underlying dysfunctions and external adversity may find expression in many different areas of functioning, including the rate of development, specific symptoms, and physical symptoms.

CONCEPTUALIZING DEVELOPMENTAL PSYCHIATRIC THERAPIES

Conceptualization of the context for intervention must take account of the nature of development and enormous transitions. The basic principle of developmental psychopathology, and the heuristic power of this new framework, is the attempt to bring psychopathology into closer relationship with developmental processes and to illuminate the multiple pathways that lead to dysfunction (Cicchetti & Richters, 1997). Even when one might be able to delineate a pattern of symptoms that satisfies the current sense of a categorical disorder, such as autism or depression, developmental factors and the emergence of new capacities, competencies, and tasks are salient in considering treatment and its goals. Even the diagnosis of disorders, such as attentional and overactive disorders, must be based on developmental assessment. And there is no metric—no thermometer or scale, no neuropsychological test, no structured interview, no neuroradiological procedure—that is independent of clinically guided, developmental assessment.

Developmental considerations include the child's phase and stage, developmental tasks being faced by the child, the relation between the disorder and developmental processes (does it affect a narrow sector or one developmental line or is there a broad disruption of development?), and biological issues relating to development (including constitution, maturational rate, and factors such as the onset of puberty). Changes in a child's environment are also linked with development. The child's family, community, and school change along with the child. Children experience different aspects of the world in different ways as they mature, and they confront different responsibilities, opportunities, and potential traumas. In child psychiatry and psychology, as in children's lives, nothing stands still and nothing is simple.

THE GOALS OF PSYCHOSOCIAL AND OTHER "ENVIRONMENTAL" TREATMENTS

Psychosocial therapies are so diverse it is difficult to speak of them as one type of treatment. On one side, therapies may consist of one or two meetings with parents or a child to provide comfort and support and help them cope with a specific difficult experience or situation (e.g. the death of a relative) or a normative crisis (such as the birth of a sibling). At such times, there may be relatively nonspecific indications of distress (e.g., sleep problems, worries, irritability) or more clear-cut symptoms (enuresis, temper tantrums, sadness). A good deal of useful caregiving of this type is provided by pediatricians, by mental health professionals such as school psychologists, nurses, and social workers, and by other caregivers, such as ministers, rabbis, and priests.

On the other side of the spectrum, psychosocial therapies may be introduced because of longstanding derailment of development and persistent behavioral and emotional symptoms (pervasive overactivity, depression, and recurrent aggression towards others). These psychosocial therapies are guided by explicit theories and are offered by individuals with specific training and expertise. The "classical" paradigm of such a therapy within child psychiatry is dynamically oriented psychotherapy in which a child and family are provided with the opportunity for engagement with a professional skilled in understanding children and trained in providing a treatment defined by specific psychological techniques. The goals of such treatments are broad: to help a child resolve internal conflicts and resume a normal process of development (Freud, 1965).

Between the quick and dirty one-shot "crisis interventions" aimed at helping healthy children navigate rocky periods of life, and many-year child psychoanalysis aimed at helping disturbed children function more adequately, there is every shade of therapeutic ambition and clinical intensity.

The different approaches to psychosocial treatment can be subdivided and distinguished along various dimensions, including:

1. theoretical emphases (e.g., behavioral, cognitive, or psychodynamic);
2. degree of definition of "the treatment" and how well defined the procedure is (e.g., structured approach with specific techniques that can be taught to practitioners without much training; semistructured approach; or more open-ended, interactive approach requiring and permitting a great deal of clinician judgment);
3. scope (e.g., emphasis on target symptoms or on providing new skills and improving overall functioning);

4. the "patient" being treated and the role of the institutional context (individual therapy; family therapy; or work with daycare providers, teachers, childcare workers, etc.);
5. duration of treatment (short-term treatment, lasting weeks or months, or long-term treatment, lasting six months to years);
6. frequency of contacts between therapist and patient (episodic or as needed, monthly, weekly, several times weekly).

Further dimensions could be added to this list, such as the combination of psychosocial therapies with other modalities, particularly the use of medication. But it is quickly apparent that there are very many possible combinations of these variables. This subdivision suggests the diversity of approaches that can be used and studied. For example, a child may receive a psychosocial treatment that is behaviorally oriented, attempts to provide new skills, involves the family in therapy, and continues for a few months of weekly visits. Any one of these variables can be altered. Or the child may receive a very different treatment that is dynamic, long term, and involves three or more clinical sessions a week. The parametric transformations are infinite. The typology is thus overly rich. In addition, these types of treatment can be placed in a matrix of other approaches that are used simultaneously.

In virtually all nations, all young children through early adolescence or later are within the domain of responsibility of a school system. In many nations, the government and society place substantial responsibilities on school systems for special educational services that are closely related to psychosocial therapies. In the United States, the largest single site of psychosocial intervention for children with behavioral difficulties occurs within schools or in close relation with the educational system. Again, using the United States as an example, the largest item on any American city's budget is for education, and special education accounts for a relatively high percentage of this budget. Up to 10% of all school children may be classified as in need of special educational services, at tremendous cost. In the city in which I work, about 20% to 25% of the school budget is used for 5% of the children: those with special needs. This funding includes children with severe, early-onset, serious emotional and developmental disorders and intellectual disabilities, as well as children with more common learning difficulties. For example, before children with disruptive disorders are seen for specifically psychiatric therapies within the mental health system, they have usually experienced a range of school-based interventions (such as discipline, retention in grade, formal attempts at behavior modification, suspension from classes, psychological evaluation, and special programming or classroom placement). Mental health professionals tend to see the "treatment failures." Many of the approaches within the school may be concurrent with psychiatric intervention. In addition, especially in the United States, children are likely to receive medication for behavioral difficulties; the vast majority of such medication is prescribed by family physicians and pediatricians, not mental health professionals. For children who are receiving care within the mental health system, psychosocial therapies, especially with the most difficult conditions, are generally integrated with, or provided alongside of, other treatments that the child may receive, including special education, tutoring, family guidance, and individual therapy for parents.

Today, mental health professionals and educators recognize that it is generally not enough to try to stop a child patient from doing something that is unwanted (e.g., oppositionality) or to get the child to do something that is desirable (e.g., to go to school). More often, we need to help the child develop new social, adaptive, and emotional competencies. Thus, children with conduct disorders require therapies to not only help them solve their disputes with less hostility but also to learn new social skills to help them form friendships and share in group activities. Similarly, depressed and anxious children need help in acquiring skills and interest that provide pleasure. Even when a child is seen as needing help because of focal difficulty or a single, traumatic experience (e.g., witnessing a violent episode), therapeutic engagement often elicits broader difficulties in need of intervention. For children and adolescents with developmental disorders, goals include helping the child in many sectors of life (social, communicative, adaptive, and emotional) and developing long-term supportive environments and opportunities (Cohen & Volkmar, 1997).

Many children with psychiatric disorders require different levels of intervention in relation to care, from work with families and other caregivers through major reorganization in the child's living situation (e.g., dealing with family placement, work with foster and social work agencies, or locating a suitable residential placement).

Thus, the scope of psychosocial therapies and psychiatric intervention is enormously broad. The systematic evaluation of structured approaches to treatment, as reported in the scientific literature on therapeutic trials, encompasses only a narrow sector of what actually is done in the "real world" of psychosocial intervention with psychiatrically disturbed children and families. For example, the children included in many research studies (e.g., trials of treatment for hyperactivity or classroom disruption) are identified on the basis of being within the top percentiles of overactivity as rated by teachers. They are not actual psychiatric patients. The study of such statistically defined groups and the artificial explication of "the therapy" from the broader clinical context of actual care may account, at least in part, for the difficulty in extending laboratory findings to clinical practice. In general, treatments work best in the hands of the developers and less well in the complex, muddled world of clinical reality. Far more research is needed on the ways in which treatment actually is provided, what types of treatments can be mounted in clinical practice, and what works and for whom (Brady & Kendall, 1992; Kendall, 1993; Kendall & Morris, 1991).

BIOLOGICAL CONTRIBUTIONS TO TREATMENT

With future advances in developmental psychopharmacology, it will become increasingly possible to use medications and other biological approaches based on the scientific understanding of the development of children and their nervous systems. The field is only in its infancy. Yet, the empirical psychopharmacology for various disorders (ADHD, tic syndromes, obsessive-compulsive disorder, self-injurious behavior, schizophrenia) has already dramatically influenced child psychiatry (Biederman, 1996). For some conditions, such as the use of stimulants for certain children with severe attentional disorders, the scientific data in support of drug efficacy are as solid as for any branch of medical therapeutics (Cantwell, 1997). In the design of effective and realistic treatment models, however, the best ways of staging and integrating biological and psychosocial approaches remains an important area of investigation.

The use of medication is not without concern. For good reasons, child psychiatrists and others are often uncertain if and how medication will affect a particular child's overall adaptation and long-term development. There are also continuing and important concerns about the potential side-effects that may emerge from the exposure of the developing nervous system, in which networks are being laid down and new genes are being expressed, to medications which affect multiple parameters of neuronal function. Also, there are real possibilities of abuse of medication by clinicians who prescribe medication too often, when other (and perhaps more expensive) treatments are indicated, or in various combinations that lack scientific basis. In the United States, in particular, there is an epidemic in the use of stimulant medications and in malignant polypharmacy, the use of four or five medications at the same time for various "symptoms."

Pharmacology is only one of many different new, biological influences in clinical child psychiatry. Advances in understanding brain formation and function from the perspective of genetics, molecular biology, and functional brain imaging are beginning to influence models for understanding disorders and designing therapeutic intervention. The elucidation of the pattern of genetic transmission of a disorder, such as Tourette's syndrome, and the possibility of prenatal diagnosis through chromosomal analysis, as with Fragile X syndrome, have brought child psychiatrists into the field of caring for individuals with genetic disorders. The discovery of additional genetic markers or loci will allow for early diagnosis of vulnerability to other conditions. With this power will come new clinical, educational, and ethical issues. We already are able to provide genetic counseling for disorders with clearly defined patterns of inheritance (such as Fragile X syndrome and tic syndromes), and we are at a sensitive moment in relation to genetic counseling for disorders such as Asperger's syndrome or manic-depressive illness, where familial contributions are apparent but data are far from certain about modes of inheritance. This genetic knowledge and associated clinical counseling will increasingly be integrated into multigenerational models of treatment.

Understanding pathogenesis from a molecular biological perspective will not only add precision to counseling, but will allow for the design of therapeutic interventions that are specifically targeted at biological roots of disorders. It is not science fiction to fantasize about gene therapies for major disorders; we may also be in the position, in the not too distant future, to consider new approaches to pharmacotherapy, e.g., the use of approaches for inhibiting gene

action, for affecting transcription factors, or for otherwise intervening in gene action, such as through hormonal manipulations that
influence gene function. Treatments for infants carrying specific vulnerability genes may start during gestation or in the very first days
of life.

Current child psychiatric neuropharmacology is generally constrained by medications that are borrowed from adult psychiatry, with
children as ''orphan indications.'' These drugs affect many neuronal
systems, operating at points in neurophysiology distal to the basic developmental dysfunction. Child and adolescent neuropsychopharma-
cology in the next decade or two will address specific neurobiological
substrates of vulnerability to disorder, including the action of genes
that govern development. Child psychiatrists and other clinicians
need to be prepared to capitalize on these advances in treatment models which will profoundly influence their practice, especially for the
most serious developmental, neuropsychiatric disorders.

Functional magnetic resonance imaging (fMRI) is now providing
new understanding of pathogenesis and may affect diagnosis and
classification. Functional MRI provides a dynamic portrait of the
brain's functioning during specific tasks, such as reading, thinking,
inhibiting a movement, or responding to an emotional stimulus. This
methodology allows child researchers and, increasingly, clinicians
to see the parts of the brain that are used when a child with a
disability engages in an important process, and the availability of
alternate pathways. For example, we can examine what parts of the
brain are used when normal and disabled children look at a familiar
or unfamiliar face (or a sad or happy emotion), code the stimulus,
feel an emotion suitable to the stimulus type, and then decide, on
the basis of the perception, whether the face is expressing delight
or fear. Individuals with serious disturbances in social development
(such as autism and associated pervasive developmental disorders)
appear to use different parts of the brain than normal individuals
during this essential, social process. Even when they are correct in
their decision, their brains treat human facial recognition as if the
face were a thing (like a chair or shape) and not a person. How to
translate such findings into treatment approaches, and to monitor
the impact of therapies, is a realistic goal for the next decade.

THE SOCIAL CONTEXT OF TREATMENT

Others who care about them, most often their parents, bring children to treatment. Sometimes, care is demanded of the parents by a social service agency or legal agency, or as a condition for the child's remaining in a school; in these cases, both child and parent may feel coerced into treatment. Most often, children do not really understand why they are coming for therapy. This is understandable for the youngest patients, who do not have a framework to understand why their behavior and feelings are deviant or their own roles in relation to their unhappiness, anger, and worries. This lack of "self–reflectiveness" may even be true for young adolescents, who may see themselves as normal or as victims, but not as in need of therapy. This realization may only slowly, or never, emerge during the course of therapy.

Clinical treatment of children is always in the context of the family and school. This contrasts sharply with clinical work with adults. Generally, psychologists and psychiatrists do not even see, yet alone speak with, an adult patient's spouse. It is quite rare for a therapist to discuss an adult patient with an employer, even if the patient wishes for such contact. Yet, for children, it is taken for granted that parents, teachers, and pediatricians will form some type of collaboration and may become cotherapists. Since the inception of child psychiatry, before World War II, multidisciplinary and multimodal approaches to treatment have been virtually the standard of practice.

CHOICE OF TREATMENT

The choice of clinical approach is based on many factors, in addition to the child's specific clinical presentation. These include:

- the clinician's expertise;
- the clinician's theoretical orientation in relation to different clinical situations and types of disorders;
- the availability of resources;
- the wishes of parents and other adults;
- the child's willingness to participate (including schedule and other demands on the child's time); and

• economic factors (what type of insurance the parents have, if any; the limits on length and intensity of treatment defined by the insurance; the family's ability to pay).

There is rarely a one-to-one correspondence between a categorical diagnosis and a treatment. The family may have to choose among alternatives; the clinician has the responsibility of providing information and guiding the selection of treatments. Researchers have preferred to study explicit, sharply defined treatments and to focus on one, well-defined disorder. But real clinical work is at the opposite end of the spectrum, as children have several disorders (or very broad-based conditions) and receive several therapies. As noted above, when research studies use clients (patients) who are not clinically referred and restrict other parameters for inclusion in research, the relevance of the research to clinical decision-making may be limited. There is a remarkable paucity of studies on economic factors in relation to the choice and availability of psychosocial therapy. As insurance providers become more active in defining the type and scope of treatments that will be covered, and as nations consider new approaches to the financing of mental healthcare, there is a greater need for data on short- and long-term clinical and financial implications of providing different types of treatment.

BASIC PREMISES OF PSYCHOSOCIAL TREATMENT

Regardless of differences, psychosocial treatments are premised on the concept that an adult with special training can mobilize a process of therapeutic change through interaction of one type or another with a child.

This premise embodies some of the most fascinating phenomena of life: that we are changed by the people with whom we interact, and that another person can make a difference not only in how we feel at the moment but in how we function later. A child takes in aspects of another person in such a way that this newly internalized, internal representation can serve as a new or renewed regulation of the child's behavior and affect. The process of therapeutic change involves not only changes in behavior but also a more persistent, generalized alteration of psychological structures and functions. These concepts seem intuitive. Their empirical validation has been arduous. There are friendly and intelligent skeptics, as well as hard-nosed insurance companies, that correctly demand documentation about these processes and assurances that clinicians know how they are proceeding with particular patients.

There is a second premise of many psychosocial approaches: the importance of *understanding*. Clinicians generally believe that changing an individual's understanding of himself or herself—his or her understanding of relations with others, the way he or she responds to situations, the meaning of events in his or her life, his or her goals, values, and ambitions—will affect the individual's life and how he or she feels about it. Indeed, a good deal of life is involved in trying to understand the lives that we are leading. Self-reflection and attempting to understand one's mind are major activities of mental life, and these activities may serve self-curative as well as self-regulatory functions. In spite of their many divergences, most psychosocial therapies, from Freud to cognitive and educational treatments, converge in this emphasis on understanding and cognitions within the therapeutic process. The premise is shared even by behavioral techniques that explicate and help the child and family understand the contingencies of reinforcement that shaped and continue to influence behavior. How do children with different types of difficulties begin to understand their lives during therapy? How does this understanding change feelings, behavior, and symptoms? Developmental psychology and neuroscience research, as well as the data from therapeutic interventions will help shape a general theory about self-understanding in the course of therapy as well as in the normal course of life.

Self-understanding both reflects and moves development forward, both in life and in treatment. Yet, surprisingly, when therapy has gone well for a child, the child will often remember very little of what has transpired. The understanding gained during treatment becomes a part of the self, rather than being experienced as a theory learned from outside. This transformation is a hallmark of successful internalization (Loewald, 1980).

SETTINGS, SITES, AND SYSTEMS

Inpatient hospitalization, residential treatment, day hospitalization, therapeutic foster care, outpatient/office-based therapy, home-based services: all of these are settings or sites or containers of treatment, but they are not treatments per se. Neither are wraparound services or family preservation programs treatments per se. (And managed care, as this term has become used, is not care at all: it is a method of administration of healthcare as a business to increase the profits of corporations.)

Psychosocial, educational, and biological therapies of various types, and in varied combinations, are delivered in diverse settings: in inpatient units, in day hospitals and special schools, and in offices. These categories are administrative, not psychological concepts; they do not tell us what the child is actually offered, experiences, and takes in. Further, for many critical purposes, such as the evaluation of treatment efficacy, defining standards, and calculating reimbursement rates, this bewildering diversity poses grave problems. We need far more research on the operational definition of settings, sites, and containers of treatment.

The definition of parameters of settings and sites—of variables to be included in models of treatment—is central not only to scientific research but also to the prescription of care and the organization of training. For example, in studies of institutions for the retarded, specific variables such as group size and stability of caregivers are more closely related to quality than the size of the institution as such. What variables are important in mental health settings? How can these be measured?

Psychiatric facilities which provide intensive, life-space treatments, which become "total institutions" for a child, for shorter or longer periods of time, are multifaceted environments populated by varied individuals and defined by varied forms of human encounters. Often, these are described from the provider's point of view (e.g., individual psychotherapy, recreational therapy) rather than from the child's experiences of them. Defining precisely what is delivered, to whom and by whom, and in what combinations, and how these are registered by the child, is essential for understanding the nature of the many different types of treatments that are provided. The study of therapeutic action requires a very fine dissection of therapeutic settings into operationally defined, experiential, and replicable modules. When child psychiatrists are asked about the advantages of inpatient vs. outpatient treatments for conduct disorders or other conditions, they need to be able to specify the ways in which settings crate, contain, and deliver particular treatments.

Hospitalization not only offers new experiences (new people with whom the child can relate and identify, new contingencies, and new opportunities). The removal of a child from home sometimes represents, in itself, both a loss and a benefit. It is a loss when relationships that are sustaining are disrupted. These relationships then require both preservation and repair. It is a gain when a child is freed from ongoing abuse, neglect, or traumatic relationships; when a family is in crisis and chaos and cannot care for its members; or when the child is dangerous to others and to the self. Assessment of treatment thus requires knowing what is provided that is new, and also where the child is coming from. What do children give up and gain when they enter the hospital? To know the meaning of hospitalization, the clinician must know the meaning for the child of home and family; of withdrawal from the familiar; of respite from adversity; of abandonment, escape and banishment; of safety and being cared for and about.

In any therapeutic setting, the therapeutic intervention is a process defined over time and with specific intentions in relation to progressively affecting the child's internal experiences and outer behavior. The process starts before the child is "admitted," in the course of clarifying the basis for intervention and defining goals. The process continues throughout the period of therapeutic engagement, in infinite numbers of transactions that are guided, as much as possible, by theories of therapeutic intent and interaction. The therapeutic process points towards the future, to the time when the treatment will terminate and the child will move into another clinical setting or return to family life. When therapeutic programs function well, this multistage, nuanced process is clearly understood by all the clinicians and is transmitted to the child, family and other professionals. It constitutes an ideology against which specific actions can be charted for conformity and consistency.

Settings and sites are part of larger systems that have evolved over the course of decades. This history has ben shaped by knowledge, by social policy, and by various forms of financing. Funding has come from insurance; federal, state and local government; charities, religious groups, and private fees. Theory, knowledge, and funding have influenced the creation of psychiatric facilities in general hospitals, the rise and fall of state mental hospitals, the founding of privately funded asylums, the enthusiasm for community-based programs, and the industry of psychotherapies. The patchwork of services, programs and institutions, and caregivers of every stripe is like the street plan of an ancient city. The mental health "system" has evolved in response to need, compassion, and the accidents of topography. The "system" of services has been shaped over time by many incremental and empirical decisions, as well as by powerful providers (such as hospitals), payers (such as insurance companies and government) and professional groups. In the United States, "clinicians" and "therapists" with many different types of professional education have set up their stalls and attracted their clientele, competitively bargaining for positions in the market. Families easily lose their way in the mental health "maze," or they are afraid to take the first steps into the bazaar.

Today, health service research is beginning to provide a road map of treatment processes. Such studies point a way towards more rational policy. Throughout the world, universities, foundations, and government bodies are mounting projects that can help in the design of new systems, such as the integration of care by case managers. The systematic national and regional planning for spectrums of care must occur in local communities, based on locally defined needs and available resources. In developing nations, such planning reveals the need to organize new services that are responsive to the needs of children and families, accessible, and affordable. In developed nations, many communities have the essential components of a rational system that can provide a range of integrated services, from acute family intervention through longer term intensive treatment. What tends to be missing is the matrix; the organizational system that can glue together the various components, allow for a child and family's smooth transition from one component to another, and monitor quality and effectiveness along the way.

Child psychiatry is at the beginning of rigorous, scientific study of child mental health service delivery. There are few, if any, evaluated replicable models for administrative arrangements that are time-tested. Alas, further changes in the system will not wait for all the data to be in. Child and adolescent psychiatrists are being forced to respond to alterations in the systems of service delivery which are driven by the ideology and economics of others. Mental health workers may lament the passing of the old professional world, but there are also consolations in envisioning new models that can be responsive to the demands of large numbers of children and adolescents who have not been adequately served.

A RESEARCH PROGRAM ON MODELS OF TREATMENT

Child mental health services are important and also costly. They are appreciated by patients and by society, but they are also being challenged by administrators and scientific critics. Available research and clinical knowledge provide a framework for shaping international, collaborative programs of research on child psychiatric therapies. In designing studies, clinicians and researchers should be sensitive to the complexity of children's disorders and development and of mental health interventions. No study can be perfect or include all variables. Yet, as a field, child mental health professionals should be engaged in studies that consider a range of variables and concerns, including the following:

1. The treatments should be grounded in a theory of child development as well as a theory of therapeutic action. That is, the therapies should reflect current understanding of the nature of children's development, developmental psychopathology, and potential approaches to altering behavior and facilitating development.
2. The psychosocial treatments should be well defined, currently practiced, and have a track record of implementation. There should be experts who believe in the effectiveness of the treatment. A treatment should not be evaluated until clinicians have used it for a long enough period of time to feel that it is practical and useful.
3. The therapeutic approach should be well documented and sufficiently "manualized" to permit training, replication, and systematic assessment. Concepts such as "hospitalization" and "psychotherapy" require greater specification so that they can be replicated, systematically assessed for effectiveness, and compared with alternate methods.
4. Treatments should be provided by expert clinicians who are trained in understanding children and families, not only one specific disorder or treatment. The clinicians should be experienced and recognized by peers as doing "good clinical work." It is important, especially in relation to third-party payers, to be certain that the methods being evaluated are in fact the types of treatment that experts provide to their patients.

5. Research on treatments should arise from realistic situations. The clients should be real patients, referred for care, and not simply "subjects" who are recruited for a study (such as the 10% of the children in ᵥ classroom who are judged by the teacher as being overactive).

6. There should be access to the raw data of treatment through methods such as videotaping, observation through one-way screens, and blind ratings of clinical status and change.

7. Initial, periodic, and final assessments should be broad-based and clinically relevant not only to specific symptoms but to the functioning of the child and family in varied contexts. This type of assessment should include varied methods with proven reliability and validity, including semistructured information from interviews, observations, and relevant testing (neuropsychological, projective, adaptive).

8. The full range of treatments must be documented and their effects considered. These include interventions with the family, school-based approaches, the use of medications, psychosocial therapies, recreational activities, etc.

9. The design and carrying out of research on psychosocial therapies will generally require and benefit from the skills, interests, and orientations of varying disciplines. It would be ideal to include the expertise of therapists from different orientations who could look at the same data from different perspectives, e.g.,. to include behavioral therapists in studies of dynamically oriented treatments, analysts in the study of cognitive therapies, and behavioral scientists (including dynamically oriented clinicians) in studies of the efficacy of medications. In addition, developmental psycholinguists, experts in cognitive development, social workers, anthropologists, and others would add considerably to understanding the nature of the child's difficulties, what the child can extract from interventions, and the familial and community context of treatment, which may have a great bearing on how disorders are presented and how treatment is experienced by the family and child.

10. For the immediate future, research programs on psychosocial treatments for children would perhaps be most wise to focus on the process of treatment and the nature of therapeutic action, rather than on demonstrating efficacy or the superiority of one treatment over another. This does not mean that summative

evaluations are not important. Indeed, there is a real need to know which children benefit from which types of treatment. However, a single-minded preoccupation with these questions would be premature. Before we reach this point, a great deal more work needs to be done in relation to assessing children and families and also defining treatments, mounting them in ways which can be studied, developing research groups, establishing valid and reliable measures, and conducting the studies in ways that exemplify clinical sensitivity and ethical rigor.

11. In the future, the study of psychosocial and biological therapies would be enriched by closer integration of the research and findings of this type with other aspects of developmental research. These associated fields of study include basic research on social, cognitive development and emotional development; the study of children's emerging theories of mind, the quality of peer relations, the modulation of aggression, and the impact of family dynamics; the influences of ethnicity, gender, social class, and family background on children's development; and the neurobiology of development.

12. Finally, treatments need to be studied within the overall context of research on the implementation and delivery of services. Research on service delivery, especially for children and adolescents with serious emotional disorders, is critical to understanding how to better provide treatments for children with psychiatric disorders. The study of systems of care includes a range of issues: who comes for care, what facilitates or reduces the likelihood of a family and child receiving treatment and remaining in care, what kinds of treatments can be provided in what types of settings, how treatments are disseminated and how professionals are instructed in their use, how much treatments cost, how the costs relate to immediate and longer term costs and benefits, etc. Research on innovations in service delivery, e.g., case-management techniques, methods for improving service integration and linkage, and the use of family support services, is closely related to understanding the potential benefits of psychosocial interventions and treatments, especially for the most burdened children and families.

The study of therapeutic methods has often been split off from other modes of developmental and biological inquiry, resulting in impoverishment of both the therapeutic research and the more fundamental studies. Yet, investigation of therapies may provide information available from no other source concerning the child's developing central nervous system and other neurobiological systems (e.g., those subserving attention and aggression), as well as the child's strongest emotions, unconscious processes, cognitive strategies, modes of psychological defense, styles of symbolizing and understanding experience, and capacity for forming and using intimate relations.

In summary, designing, implementing, and evaluating psychosocial and biological treatments raise numerous methodological and theoretical complexities. The design of studies requires sufficient sample sizes, rigorous methods, and suitable clinical settings; the execution of such studies is extraordinarily difficult in the real world. The demands of insurance companies make the tasks even more daunting. Yet, it is only through systematic research that we are likely to determine what treatments are most effective and where new knowledge is needed, and rigorous studies are required to test new models of care. Child and adolescent psychiatrists need to inform legislators, regulators, payers, as well as parent and colleagues, about the effectiveness of our treatments, as well as about the benefits of systematic investigation. Each child in treatment may be seen as a test of clinical hypotheses and as a potential source of new information to guide therapy. And there are virtually no treatment models that are so clearly supported by the data that they can remain unquestioned. Such research may seem to increase the cost of clinical care, for example, if the child psychiatrist insists that a child not start on medication before a thorough evaluation and the initiation of a multifaceted treatment program. Yet, research is ultimately the most useful investment for cost containment.

Clinicians are given privileged access to children because they offer hope for reducing distress and being helpful. Thus, the information that can be derived from well-conducted studies of important treatments may not only be useful in guiding clinical work; it may provide knowledge about children's inner life and thoughts that is available in no other way.

ACKNOWLEDGMENTS

This chapter reflects years of discussion about mental health services with colleagues in the Yale University Child Study

Center, including Drs. Solnit, Schowalter, Woolston, Schaefer, King, Leckman, and Volkmar and with Ms. Jean Adnopoz, who has a masterful understanding of clinical care and its delivery.

Portions of this presentation appeared in a paper by the author on psychosocial therapies in the *Journal of Abnormal Child Psychology* in 1994.

REFERENCES

Biederman, J. (Ed.). (1996). Contemporary perspectives on pediatric psychopharmacology [Special Section]. *Journal of the American Academy of Child and Adolescent Psychiatry, 35,* 1274–1321.

Brady, E. J., & Kendall, P. C. (1992). Comorbidity of anxiety and depression in children and adolescents. *Psychological Bulletin, 111,* 244–255.

Cantwell, D. (Ed.). (1997). The scientific study of child and adolescent psychopathology: The attention deficit disorder syndrome. *Journal of the American Academy of Child and Adolescent Psychiatry, 36,* 1033–1079.

Cicchetti, D., & Cohen, D. J. (Eds.). (1995). *Developmental psychopathology, Volume 1. Theory and methods. Volume 2. Risk, disorder, adaptation.* New York: Wiley.

Cicchetti, D., & Richters, J. (Eds.). (1997). Conceptual and scientific underpinnings of research in developmental psychopathology [Special issue]. *Development and psychopathology, 9*(2).

Cohen, D. J., & Volkmar, F. (Eds.). (1997). *Handbook of autism and pervasive developmental disorders.* New York: Wiley.

Costello, E. J. (1989). Developments in child psychiatric epidemiology. *Journal of the American Academy of Child and Adolescent Psychiatry, 28,* 836–841.

Freud, A. (1965). *Normality and pathology in childhood.* New York: International Universities Press.

Institute of Medicine. (1989). *Research on children and adolescents with mental, behavioral, and developmental disorders.* Washington, DC: Institute of Medicine.

Kazdin, A. E. (1987a). *Conduct disorders in childhood and adolescence.* Newbury Park, CA: Sage.

Kazdin, A. E. (1987b). Treatment of antisocial behavior in children: Current status and future directions. *Psychological Bulletin, 102,* 187–203.

Kazdin, A. E. (1988). *Child psychotherapy: Developing and identifying effective treatments.* New York: Pergamon Press.

Kazdin, A. E. (1989). Developmental differences in depression. In B. B. Lahey and A. E. Kazdin (Eds.), *Advances in clinical child psychology* (Volume 12, 193–220). New York: Plenum.

Kendall, P. C., & Morris, R. J. (1991). Child therapy: Issues and recommendations. *Journal of Consulting and Clinical Psychology, 59,* 777–784.

Kendall, P. C. (1993). Cognitive-behavioral therapies with youth: Guiding theory, current status, and emerging developments. *Journal of Consulting and Clinical Psychology, 61,* 235–247.

Loewald, H. (1980). *Papers on psychoanalysis.* New Haven, CT: Yale University Press.

National Commission on Children. (1991). *Beyond rhetoric: A new agenda for children and families.* The Final Report of the National Commission on Children. Washington, DC: U.S. Government Printing Office.

Offord, D. R., Boyle, M. H., Szatmari, P., Rae-Grant, N. I., Links, P. S., Cadman, D. T., Byles, J. A., Crawford, J. W., Blum, H. M., & Byrne, C. (1987). Ontario Child Health Study. II. Six month prevalence of disorder and rates of service utilization. *Archives of General Psychiatry, 44* 832–836.

Rutter, M. (1989). Isle of Wight Revisited: Twenty-five years of child psychiatric epidemiology. *The Journal of the American Academy of Child and Adolescent Psychiatry, 28,* 633–653.

Rutter, M. (Ed.). (1997). Child psychiatric disorder: Measures, causal mechanisms, and interventions [Special issue]. *Archives of General Psychiatry, 54,* 9.

Shaffer, D., Fisher, P., Dulcan, M. K., Davies, M., Piancetini, J., Schwab–Stone, M. E., Lahey, B., Bourdon, K., Jensen, P., Bird, H., Canino, G., Regier, D. A. (1996). The NIMH Diagnostic Interview Schedule for Children: Description, acceptability, prevalence rates, and performance in the MECA study. *Journal of the American Academy of Child and Adolescent Psychiatry, 35,* 865–877.

Verhulst, F. C., Van der Ende, J., Ferdinand, R. F., & Kasius, M. C. (1997). The Prevalence of DSM-III-R diagnoses in a national sample of Dutch adolescents. *Archives of General Psychiatry, 54,* 329–333.

11

Research Priorities for the Improvement of Mental Health Services for Children and Adolescents: A Social Work Perspective

R O N A L D   A .   F E L D M A N

The intervention and research efforts of the mental health professions can benefit from fruitful interchanges concerning the merits and liabilities of their respective theoretical frameworks, service delivery systems, and research paradigms and priorities. Toward this end, four key priorities are discussed in this chapter regarding contemporary social work research about mental health services for children and adolescents. These pertain, respectively, to research concerning risk status, the measurement of children's behavior, treatment contexts, and follow-up intervention systems.

Recent years have seen growing conceptual and operational linkages among allied mental health professions. Numerous benefits can result from such linkages, including the realization that shared theoretical orientations and intervention objectives affirm the fundamental utility of frameworks developed by differing professions. Yet, such linkages also highlight the fact that the remediation of children's behavior problems is a complex and demanding task which requires a wide range of resources that seldom can be supplied by a single profession.

As interprofessional linkages emerge, they also generate new kinds of problems. The boundaries and domains of allied professions become increasingly blurred, where once they were insular and clearly delineated. Ambiguities regarding domain or control sometimes lead to purposeful or inadvertent struggles for professional dominance. These can be averted only through vigorous efforts to keep abreast of incipient difficulties and through ongoing collegial efforts that address them proactively. Before important commonalities can be forged among helping professions, however, the frameworks and perspectives that characterize one profession often challenge those of another. Yet, it is essentially through challenge and response that professions better prepare themselves to address shared concerns. Accordingly, this chapter discusses four priorities in social work research that may help to inform those that obtain in child and adolescent psychiatry. They pertain, respectively, to research about children's risk status, the measurement of behavior change, treatment contexts, and follow-up intervention systems.

Child and adolescent psychiatry typically employs research paradigms and methodologies that focus upon the individual client as the primary unit of analysis. In contrast, social work usually employs research paradigms and methodologies that are based upon an eco-systems perspective and that seek to examine the "person-in-environment" (Meyer & Mattaini, 1995). That is, social workers endeavor to understand the critical interactions between at-risk children and their social surroundings. Referring to the four topics mentioned above, the following discussion brings a social work perspective to bear upon research concerning child and adolescent mental health.

MEASUREMENT OF RISK STATUS

Myriad factors determine whether or not an at-risk child will experience a behavior disorder at some point in the life-course. It is commonly believed that the key factors that enable a child to withstand mental illness are personal capabilities or traits termed variously as coping skills, behavioral competencies, or stress-resistance. In brief, proponents of this view invoke a *trait model* of childhood disorder that is deeply grounded in the discipline of psychology. Until recent years, the trait model has dominated theoretical, practice, and research conceptions of mental health and mental illness. In contrast, other observers posit that environmental stressors are the key variables that determine whether or not a child will become mentally ill. They employ a situational or *environmental model* of childhood disorder that is grounded essentially in the discipline of sociology. The environmental model has gained numerous adherents in the last three decades.

Social work research is predicated fundamentally upon the assumption that both perspectives must be considered in order to formulate a realistic model of risk for childhood mental illness and, in turn, to generate the most efficacious intervention strategies. By itself, neither model is sufficiently inclusive to explain the complexities of childhood vulnerability and/or resistance to mental illness. Rather, childhood behavior disorders are a consequence of the interactions and relative balance between stressful or protective environments and strong or weak personal coping skills. In brief, such a model posits that all environments can vary along a continuum that ranges from decidedly protective, on the one hand, to decidedly stressful, on the other; likewise, it is posited that personal coping skills can range along a continuum that varies from decidedly strong to decidedly weak. Hence, from this perspective, one can formulate a *social interaction* model of children's risk for mental illness.

To date, clinicians and researchers have tended to define and to measure risk status primarily in terms of a given child's coping skills. Thus, for example, some deem the stress-resistant child to be merely a "healthy child in an unhealthy setting" (Garmezy, 1974). Yet, most children who reside in stressful settings are, in fact, free of observable mental disorders. Some environments appear to be at high risk only when they are contrasted with others that pose less severe challenges for children. In absolute terms, however, they entail only low or modest risks for the children who reside in them.

Neither a trait model nor an environmental model enables the researcher or the practitioner to fully comprehend the real dynamics of childhood risk. Even though they are the dominant models in practice and research, they are relatively sterile for predictive or clinical purposes. Instead, contemporary social work research is predicated upon the assumption that childhood risk status ought to be defined primarily on the basis of the mutual interaction and relative balance between environmental stressors or protectors and a child's ability to cope. In terms of this social interaction model, children who are exposed to stressful environments, are not necessarily considered at high risk so as long as they have exceptionally strong coping skills. Likewise, children with weak coping skills are

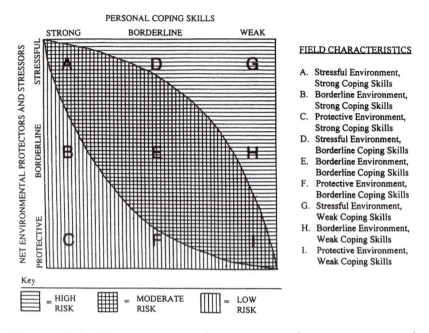

Figure 11.1   *Net environmental protectors and stressors, personal coping skills, and childhood risk status for mental illness (adapted from Feldman, Stiffman, & Jung, 1987, p. 59).*

not necessarily at high risk so long as their environments are protective ones where the extant environmental protectors are stronger than the extant environmental stressors. Such a model is relative and interactive rather than absolute and static.

Three sets of variables are of central importance for this model of childhood risk status: children's behavior, environmental stressors and protectors, and personal coping skills. The interplay among the two latter sets of variables determines the nature of the first, that is, whether a particular child will be at high, moderate, or low risk for a behavior disorder. Figure 11.1 succinctly summarizes a social interaction model that can guide research concerning children's mental health. Issues pertinent to the measurement of children's behavior are discussed in a later section of this manuscript. At this juncture, attention is devoted to environmental stressors and protectors and, then, to personal coping skills.

Environmental Stressors and Protectors

Numerous environmental stressors have been identified as key risk factors for children. These include the death of a parent, sibling, or pet, parental unemployment, low socioeconomic status, frequent geographic mobility, marital discord on the part of parents, and large family size. Children are exposed to risk factors that can vary along a continuum in terms of their number and/or the stress they engender. Moreover, such factors can vary over time, being at high levels during acute crises and at lower levels after crises have subsided.

Conversely, a child can be buffered by environmental protectors that provide insulation or relief from factors that can adversely affect mental health. These, too, can vary along a continuum in terms of their quantity and/or the amount of protection afforded. Examples include parental employment, high socioeconomic status, marital harmony, supportive peer groups, and accessible social services.

In concert with a child's coping skills, it is the net balance between key environmental stressors and environmental protectors that essentially determines whether or not a child will be at high risk for a behavior disorder (for a detailed discussion, see Feldman, Stiffman, & Jung, 1983, pp. 56–74). Importantly, this conception suggests that an environment characterized by strong protectors need not necessarily be a "protective" environment. Likewise, an environment characterized by formidable environmental stressors is not necessarily a "stressful" environment. Rather, it is the net balance between stressors and protectors that determines whether a particular environment will be regarded as healthy or unhealthy or, more specifically, as protective or stressful. Accordingly, a stressful environment is one in which the extant stressors clearly exceed the extant protectors; conversely, a protective environment is one in which the extant protectors exceed the extant stressors. And a borderline environment is one in which the pertinent stressors and protectors are approximately equal in strength; that is, because neither set of factors clearly exceeds the other in strength, a fluid situation obtains.

In terms of this conception, environments can be arrayed along a continuum which, for heuristic purposes, varies from "protective"

to "borderline" to "stressful." All other things being equal, a decided surfeit of environmental stressors (vis-a-vis protectors) results
in a high likelihood of behavior disorder on the part of an at-risk
child. Likewise, a relatively equal balance between environmental
stressors and protectors presupposes a moderate likelihood of disorder, while a decided surfeit of environmental protectors (vis-a-vis
stressors) suggests a low likelihood of disorder.

Personal Coping Skills

Most researchers define low-risk youngsters solely in
terms of their personal stress-resistance, suggesting thereby that
these children possess unique skills or competencies that enable
them to cope with the environmental stressors impinging upon them.
Hence, their definitions of children's risk status are based solely
upon the child's coping skills. Relatively little attention is paid to
the extent of environmental stress and protection that affects the at-
risk child or, in turn, to the resultant demands placed on the child's
coping skills.

Among the personal abilities that enable a child to resist significant environmental stressors are the child's cognitive and problem-
solving abilities, perceptual acuity, persistence, assertiveness, ability
to make and sustain friendships, and related social competencies.
Like environmental stressors and protectors, these skills can
strengthen or deteriorate over time. Coping skills, too, can be arrayed along a continuum which, for heuristic purposes, varies from
strong to borderline to weak. All things being equal, it is posited
that children with weak coping skills will have a relatively high
likelihood of disordered behavior, whereas children with borderline
coping skills will have a moderate likelihood of behavior disorder.
Children with strong coping skills will have a comparatively low
likelihood of behavior disorder.

Environmental Protectors and Stressors, Personal
Coping Skills, and Children's Risk Status

The main features of the social interaction model of childhood risk are set forth in Figure 11.1. As indicated, coping skills are
arrayed here along a continuum ranging from strong to borderline to
weak. Likewise, the social environments that potentially confront
any child are arrayed along a continuum ranging from stressful to

borderline to protective. Analogously, a child's potential risk for a behavior disorder or mental illness is deemed to vary along a continuum that ranges, respectively, from high risk to moderate risk to low risk.

In brief, this model posits that children are likely to be at high risk for a behavior disorder when their coping skills are significantly weaker than the net environmental stressors and protectors to which they are exposed. Conversely, children are likely to be at low risk for a behavior disorder if their coping skills are significantly stronger than the net environmental stressors and protectors. Children are likely to be at moderate risk, in contrast, if their coping skills are neither significantly stronger nor significantly weaker than the net environmental stressors and protectors. In such instances, it is neither evident that the children have sufficient coping skills to prevail against the extant stressors and protectors nor that the latter will overwhelm the children's coping abilities.

The research and intervention implications of this model of childhood risk status are manifold. For example, various combinations of the relevant factors can differentially affect a child's vulnerability (see Figure 11.1). Risk can be determined on the basis of the mutual interactions among stressful, borderline, or protective environments and strong, borderline, or weak coping skills. The distribution of risk statuses (that is, high risk, moderate risk, or low risk) follows from the fact that the two main predictors (personal coping skills and net environmental protectors and stressors) are conceptualized as continuums. For illustrative purposes, these distributions can be arrayed in terms of nine overlapping "fields" that portray the juxtaposition of the two main predictors. In three of these fields, the net environmental stress clearly exceeds the child's coping skills; therefore, children located within these fields are likely to be at high risk for a behavior disorder. In three other fields, the child's coping skills clearly exceed the net environmental stress; these children are likely to be at low risk. And, in the three remaining fields, the child's coping skills and net environmental stressors and protectors are approximately equal in strength; such children are at moderate risk. Nonetheless, unique differences among the moderate-risk, high-risk, and low-risk children in each of these fields are relevant for research and practice.

Moderate-Risk Children

In Figure 11.1, the children depicted by fields A, E, and I of the model (the cross-hatched areas) tend to be quite similar to one another in one important respect: they are all sufficiently susceptible to behavior disorders to be designated as moderate-risk subjects. However, these children differ markedly from each other when one examines the interrelationships among their respective coping skills and net environmental stressors and protectors. Thus, perhaps contrary to popular expectation, the children in field A exhibit strong coping skills. Yet, they are at moderate risk because, on balance, they are also exposed to a highly stressful environment that can neutralize their available coping skills. When a child encounters extreme stress, even superior coping skills cannot assure that a behavior disorder will be averted.

The children depicted by field I are also considered to be at moderate risk. Here, however, the at-risk child is faced with a relatively protective environment. While most children are likely to remain healthy in such circumstances, the youngsters in field I are vulnerable because they possess weak coping skills. Indeed, as suggested by fields G and H, these children are likely to become victims of a behavior disorder if they are subsequently confronted with either a borderline environment or a stressful environment.

The model also postulates a third genre of moderate-risk child: one whose borderline coping skills are threatened by a borderline environment (that is, an environment in which the pertinent stressors and protectors are equipotent). This probably represents one of the more common childhood conditions, albeit one that may be less prevalent than those depicted in fields B, C, or F. Because of the unstable situation entailed by their circumstances, the children in field E are likely to drift toward low-risk status if there is either a slight improvement in their coping skills (field B) or a slight reduction in net environmental stress (field F). Conversely, they are likely to drift toward high-risk status if there is an increment in net environmental stress (field D) or if their coping skills should deteriorate (field H).

Systematic research eventually needs to determine which of these three sets of presenting conditions is most prevalent among children of varying ages and social backgrounds. Is it possible, for instance, that the majority of moderate-risk youngsters have strong coping skills that are neutralized by stressful environments? Or, alternatively, are they confronted by borderline environments that nonetheless are problematic given borderline coping skills on their part? The model suggests even further that the kinds of moderate-risk children depicted in field A can be helped best—and, perhaps, only—when mental health interventions are directed toward key environmental stressors and protectors rather than toward their personal coping skills. Traditional clinical therapies are likely to be of little use for such youngsters because their coping skills already are strong. Instead, it would seem more productive for intervention agents to weaken the environmental stressors that impinge upon such youngsters or to strengthen key environmental protectors. For the children depicted in field I, conversely, the preferred modes of intervention would be more traditional since these children's environmental protectors are relatively strong. In contrast, the moderate-risk children depicted by field E would benefit most readily from a multipronged intervention strategy that aims to reduce environmental stressors and strengthen environmental protectors while concurrently enhancing personal coping skills. If successful, such a strategy would enable these youngsters to progress from moderate risk to low risk.

High-Risk Children

Figure 11.1 also illustrates the plight of children who are likely to be at high risk for behavior problems. While three different sets of high-risk conditions are postulated in the model, a common feature characterizes all of them: the environmental stressors to which these children are exposed significantly outweigh the coping skills and environmental protectors that are brought to bear against them. Popular conceptions of the mentally ill child often exemplify the situation depicted in field G. Here the child with weak coping skills is confronted by a decidedly stressful environment. Because these children are severely disadvantaged in two major respects (namely, weak coping skills and a stressful environment), it is probable that they will be victimized to a much greater extent than the children depicted by either field D or field H. Their high-risk status is likely to be far more stable and irremediable than that of other children. To the extent possible, professional interventions should aim to help these children by reducing their environmental stressors, strengthening their environmental protectors, and enhancing their personal coping skills.

In fields D and H, the gap between the child's coping skills and net environmental stressors is smaller than in the preceding case. Nevertheless, several key distinctions characterize the two former situations. In field D, the children's borderline coping skills are inadequate when they are confronted by a decidedly stressful environment. In field H, the children's net environmental stressors are merely borderline, but they are likely to succumb to them because of deficient coping skills.

In fields D and H, the child's plight is not as intractable as in field G, and the probability of developing a behavior disorder is lower. Nevertheless, interventions should be directed concurrently toward reducing environmental stressors, strengthening environmental protectors, and enhancing personal coping skills. Given the relatively great environmental stress depicted in field D, however, somewhat more attention should be directed toward its diminution than toward the enhancement of coping skills. Conversely, perhaps, intervention efforts directed toward children in field H ought to concentrate more on the enhancement of coping skills than on the reduction of environmental stressors or the strengthening of environmental protectors.

Low-Risk Children

The model in Figure 11.1 also identifies three different sets of conditions that enable some children to remain at low risk for behavior problems. Such children are at risk only in the sense that they are subject to certain environmental stressors which influence their behavior. In each instance, however, these children are deemed to be at low risk because their personal coping skills substantially exceed the net environmental stress to which they are exposed. As long as the relative balance among environmental stressors, environmental protectors, and personal coping skills remains constant, these children are likely to be affected little, if at all, by the pertinent stressors. Indeed, if their coping skills should improve even marginally, they are likely to become even less vulnerable.

The most stable and desirable conditions exist when children with strong coping skills live in an environment that is decidedly protective (field C). Such youngsters are likely to remain at low risk even if their coping skills should deteriorate to a borderline level or, as is more likely, if the net environmental stressors should rise to a borderline level. Mental health policy makers, administrators, and practitioners need to attempt to stabilize the conditions in field C when they appear and to establish them when they do not.

Field B, in contrast, depicts a situation in which a child with strong coping skills lives in a borderline environment. Here, too, the child is at relatively low risk, although not as markedly so as in field C. Because the child has strong coping skills, relatively few efforts at preventive intervention need to be directed toward the child. However, if the child's coping skills should deteriorate to a borderline level, or if the environment should become decidedly stressful, the child's risk status would shift from low to moderate. Unlike formulations of risk status framed essentially in terms of a target child's personal competencies, the social interaction model assumes that one's status can be altered by a variety of means. If the relative balance between a child's coping skills and net environmental stressors and protectors remains relatively constant, the child's risk status will be stable. But, if their relationship should change for one reason or another, including treatment interventions, the child's mental health and corresponding behaviors are likely to change accordingly.

A third genre of risk status is depicted by field F. Here, a child with only borderline coping skills encounters readily manageable, low-level environmental stressors; that is, on balance, the environment is protective. In these circumstances, children's low-risk status can be strengthened only by improving their coping skills. The net environmental stress already is extremely low and, therefore, unlikely to shift for the better. In contrast, either a deterioration in the child's coping skills, an increment in environmental stressors, or a decrement in environmental protectors could shift the child toward moderate risk. This would occur, for instance, if the net environmental stress progresses from a protective level to a borderline level or, alternatively, if the child's coping skills should deteriorate from a borderline level to a low level. Since environmental changes occur rapidly during childhood and adolescence, the former likelihood is far more probable than the latter.

Environment, Personal Coping, and Childhood Behavior Disorder: An Illustration

Empirical support for a social interaction model of childhood risk status is found in part from a field study of 264 children who were raised in families with one or more mentally ill parents (Feldman, Stiffman, & Jung, 1987). One relevant finding from this study is depicted succinctly in Figure 11.2. This figure shows how a child's risk status is associated with the interactions between a major personal coping skill (activity competence) and a major environmental stressor (the proportion of family members who are mentally ill). Respectively, risk status, activity competence, and family mental illness were operationalized in terms of high scores (that is, above the clinical cutting-point) on the Child Behavior Checklist (CBCL; Achenbach and Edelbrock, 1981), high scores on the Activity Competence Scale of the CBCL, and the total proportion of the at-risk child's family members (namely, parents and siblings) who were diagnosed as mentally ill.

Figure 11.2 reveals a significant interaction ($t = -3.20, p < .001$) between activity competence and the proportion of mentally ill persons in the at-risk child's family. This interaction, in which activity competence and the proportion of mentally ill family members predicts the CBCL scores of at-risk children, indicates that the relationship between activity competence and behavior problems depends upon the proportion of mentally ill persons in the child's family. As pictured in Figure 11.2, the interaction between the environmental stressor (the proportion of mentally ill family members) and the coping skill (the child's activity competence) reveals how these variables moderate each other's effects as they predict children's behavior problems. Respectively, the slopes depict how activity competence differentially predicts behavior problems for subjects with either high, medium, or low proportions of mentally ill persons in their family. The regression lines converge toward the high end of scores on the activity competence scale.

Thus, for instance, when an at-risk child has high activity competence, the proportion of mentally ill persons in his or her family does not seem to affect the extent to which behavior problems are manifested. However, if the child has low activity competence, the proportion of mentally ill family members exerts a strong influence on the extent of his or her behavior problems. In cases of low activity competence, the proportion of mentally ill persons in the family is strongly linked with behavior problems on the child's part. The difference between the right side of the figure, in which children's competence is high, and the left side, in which it is low, attests to the behavior discrepancy. On the right side there is a clustering of

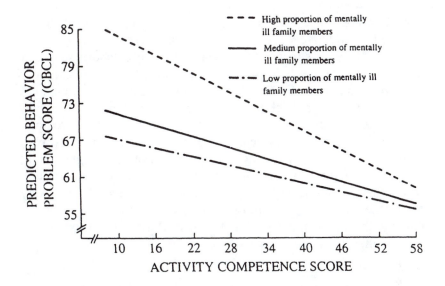

Figure 11.2 *Behavior problem scores as a function of activity competence scores for subjects (n = 264) with high, medium, or low proportions of mentally ill family members (from Feldman, Stiffman, & Jung, 1987, p. 209).*

subjects from families with either high, moderate, or low proportions of mentally ill persons. Subjects with high activity competence register very similar scores on the CBCL. But, as depicted on the left side of the figure, if the child's activity competence is low, the extent of his or her behavior problems varies tremendously in accord with the proportion of mentally ill family members. At-risk children who live in a family with a low or moderate proportion of mentally ill persons exhibit considerably lower behavior problem scores than at-risk children who have high proportions of mentally ill persons in their family.

The left side of Figure 11.2 also shows that the behavior problem scores of subjects with low activity competence and low proportions of mentally ill family members are similar to those for children with high activity competence and moderate to high proportions of mentally ill family members. This finding is consistent with the social interaction model of childhood risk: children with low activity competence and high proportions of family mental illness tend to have high behavior problem scores. In contrast, children with low activity competence and low proportions of family mental illness tend to have relatively few behavior problems.

These findings support the social interaction model set forth above. Thus, children with strong coping skills have excellent prospects for remaining at low risk, regardless of extant environmental forces. But, as at-risk children's coping skills diminish, they are increasingly likely to become victims of environmental stressors. To remain healthy, at-risk children with weak coping skills must reside in an environment where the extant protectors significantly outweigh the extant stressors. Regardless of environmental stress, in contrast, children with strong coping skills are far more likely than other youngsters to remain at low risk for mental illness. Clearly, then, risk status is a function of children's environments as well as their personal coping skills.

MEASUREMENT OF CHILDREN'S BEHAVIOR

Like the above-cited perspective regarding risk status, social work research often tends to approach behavior measurement in ways that differ from those which prevail in allied mental health professions. Thus, for example, while psychiatry typically employs nominal-order categorizations, such as the DSM-IV (Diagnostic and Statistical Manual) system, to classify a person's mental health status, social work researchers have criticized the validity and reliability of such systems (see, for instance, Kirk & Kutchins, 1992). Rather, they tend to view a subject's aberrant behavior in the context of his or her overall behavior pattern, including observable behavioral strengths. This is best accomplished through the elaboration of ordinal or interval measurement scales that yield advantages not afforded by nominal or dichotomous classification schemes.

Delinquency, Conduct Disorder, and Antisocial Behavior

Accurate measurements of behavior change are essential for research concerning clinical interventions. Yet, investigators' undue reliance on rudimentary systems of clinical assessment can often hinder and, even, predetermine their research findings. Nowhere is this more evident than in the research literature on juvenile delinquency, conduct disorders, and antisocial behavior.

Intervention and research programs in these realms often classify youths simply as "delinquent" or "nondelinquent" or, alternatively, as manifesting a "conduct disorder" or not. Yet, the dichotomous nature of such categorizations leaves considerable room for measurement error. More problematic, from a research perspective, is that such classification systems can transform disparate "high-frequency" forms of maladaptive behavior into low-base-rate "either-or" phenomena, e.g., either delinquent or nondelinquent. As a result, it is difficult, if not impossible, to ascertain the extent of actual behavior change that occurs on the part of subjects due to treatment interventions.

To avert such difficulties, outcome measures in child mental health research should be conceptualized as continuous interval scales. Thus, rather than attempt to determine whether one is delinquent or nondelinquent, or classifiable as having a conduct disorder or not, it is more useful to ascertain the extent of a child's maladaptive behavior by determining the rate or proportionate frequency of a given behavior.

Most field studies of juvenile delinquency focus on serious misbehaviors that are manifested on a relatively infrequent basis by any given child. Even though the mean incidences of some antisocial behaviors, such as rape and robbery, are distressingly high for certain subsamples of subjects, few children exhibit these behaviors frequently. They are low-base-rate behaviors. It is unlikely that they constitute even one tenth of 1% of any child's total behavioral profile. Their extremely low frequency poses serious problems for measuring behavior change and for the prediction of future antisocial behavior on the part of a child.

Accordingly, research should strive to examine a child's antisocial behavior from the perspective of his or her overall behavioral profile. This is especially germane in the case of high-base-rate behaviors. Yet, most mental health research seems to ignore this fundamental principle. A delinquent/nondelinquent dichotomy is not particularly useful for purposes of diagnosis, service delivery, or research. Rather, delinquency, conduct disorder, and similar behaviors are a matter of degree. Virtually all children fall somewhere between the extremes of a continuum that ranges from no delinquency to continuous delinquency. Therefore, patterns of antisocial activity and similar behaviors can best be understood by measuring them in terms of *rate* and *proportion*. Typically, clinicians need not be as concerned about youths who commit an antisocial act only once as about youths who manifest a repeated pattern of deviance over a sustained period of time. While nearly every child commits an antisocial or delinquent act at one time or another, only a small segment of the population assumes a stable delinquent role.

By examining the proportionate distributions of prosocial, nonsocial, and antisocial behavior that are exhibited by a child, "delinquent" behavior also is not viewed merely as an attribute or trait. Rather, it is judged according to the extent of a youth's deviant behavior and, more specifically, with regard to the extent that it constitutes a significant proportion of the child's overall behavior profile. The fact that delinquency and conduct disorder are not all-or-none dichotomous phenomena requires that traditional ways of viewing erstwhile delinquents be modified. That is, children need not be deemed either delinquent or nondelinquent; rather, they are more or less delinquent.

Such distinctions can best be advanced by measuring subjects' mean proportionate incidences of prosocial, nonsocial, and antisocial behavior. Attainment of this research goal entails the elaboration of comprehensive but mutually exclusive classification categories that can be arrayed in terms of an interval scale. One such method has been employed in a large-scale field experiment of group-based treatment interventions for delinquent youths (for a detailed discussion, see Feldman et al., 1983, pp. 78–86). This study was based upon time-series observational samplings of youths' behavior in three kinds of treatment groups. The data were recorded by highly trained nonparticipant observers.

The observation system was designed to measure the relative frequencies of prosocial, nonsocial, and antisocial behavior exhibited by each subject in a treatment group. The tabulation of prosocial, nonsocial, and antisocial behavior was accomplished through the use of a checklist that yielded highly reliable data. Behavioral observations were made in a fixed order every 10 seconds for 1 subject, then for another, and so on until all of the children had been observed. This procedure was reiterated for the full duration of each group session, and it continued for nearly 9 months. After the observational data were collected, they were tabulated in order to calculate the proportion of each youth's behavior that was recorded as either prosocial, nonsocial, or antisocial. This was done by dividing the total number of prosocial behaviors recorded for an individual by the grand total of all three types of observed behavior. Likewise, when nonsocial or antisocial behaviors were calculated, the cumulative totals for those particular behaviors were entered as the numerator of the equation.

This approach toward the measurement of children's behavior yields a number of important benefits for research. First, one can ascertain not only the absolute frequency with which targeted behaviors are manifested but, more important, their proportionate frequencies. This is particularly advantageous when the target behavior is a low-base-rate phenomenon, that is, one which occurs infrequently. The procedure averts the necessity of labeling a child as "delinquent" on the basis of merely one antisocial act. Instead, it enables both the researcher and the clinician to estimate the extent to which a child is delinquent or antisocial by viewing his or her actions in the context of the child's overall behavior profile. It permits the researcher to determine the extent to which the child's antisocial behavior is offset by prosocial and nonsocial behaviors.

Second, such an approach also is of great utility for measuring changes in behavior that derive from treatment interventions. It is especially advantageous for the measurement of high-base-rate behaviors. Via-a-vis approaches that employ dichotomous categories of classification, this method permits discrete and comparable calibrations of the extent of a subject's behavior change. For example, it is hazardous to infer that a child's behavior has improved significantly when his or her tantrum behaviors decline merely from 20 per week to 18 per week. But the meaning of such figures can vary substantially depending on the total number of prosocial, nonsocial, and antisocial behaviors exhibited by the child in identical time frames. Thus, if a child manifests 50 behaviors in the first week of time-sampling behavioral observations, the 20 antisocial behaviors observed would constitute 40% of the child's behavior profile. In contrast, if the child becomes much more active in the second week of observations and manifests, for example, 100 behaviors, the 18 antisocial acts observed would represent only 18% of the child's overall behavior profile. This would represent a discrete, measurable, and marked decline in antisocial behavior; in effect, the proportion of antisocial behavior in the child's total behavioral profile will have declined by more than half from week 1 to week 2.

TREATMENT CONTEXTS

Group treatments are a major intervention modality for children with behavior disorders. Typically, treatment groups bring together children who exhibit similar forms of dysfunction. Thus, for example, treatment groups are formed for substance abusers, assaultive children, and other discrete categories of youths. However, emerging research suggests that desired behavior changes are most likely to be realized when antisocial youths are treated in peer groups that are constituted largely of prosocial peers rather than in groups constituted entirely of antisocial peers. In one such study (Feldman et al., 1983, pp. 137–147), 91% of 23 antisocial youths who were treated in small groups of prosocial peers showed a posttreatment decline in antisocial behavior. The subjects' proportionate antisocial behavior declined from 5.4% of their total behavioral profile to 3.2%, that is, by more than 40%.

In contrast, antisocial youths who were treated in traditional groups (that is, in groups comprised entirely of peers who had been referred to treatment for their own antisocial behavior) fared measurably worse as a result of group intervention. Only 51% of 175 such youths showed a decline in antisocial behavior. More important was the fact that, on average, these youths exhibited a slight increment in antisocial behavior ($M = + 0.3\%$). In the course of treatment, their antisocial behavior increased from 5.4% of their total behavioral profile to 5.7%). Compared with similar youths who were treated among prosocial peers (for whom 3.2% of posttreatment behavior was antisocial), their behavioral profiles were considerably more antisocial. Hence, group-based interventions can benefit from conceptual and research designs that attend more readily to the differential peer composition of treatment groups.

FOLLOW-UP INTERVENTION SYSTEMS

A related issue is of central concern for social work research and practice, namely, the realization that long-term behavioral gains from treatment depend essentially on the extent and quality of follow-up services for the original intervention. For example, numerous intervention programs for juvenile delinquents report marked behavioral gains at the termination of treatment. Yet, follow-up studies several years afterward report very high rates of recidivism. Consequently, it often is concluded that the intervention program was a failure (see, for example, Bailey, 1966; Lipton, Martinson & Wilks, 1975; Romig, 1978).

Such conclusions disregard the fact that innumerable mediating events occur after the termination of treatment. Many, if not most, militate against the retention of hard-earned treatment gains. Others, however, can reinforce or sustain treatment gains. To better understand the actual effects of an intervention program, it is essential to conduct continuous long-term follow-up studies of the youths who have been treated. It is probable that such studies will demonstrate that treatment gains are best sustained by follow-up, or "booster," interventions that aim to reinforce the gains derived from earlier treatments. Studies that document such findings are essential if more effective mental health services are to be devised for at-risk children and youths.

SUMMARY

Four social work research priorities can inform and facilitate the efforts of allied mental health professionals to develop more effective mental health services for children and adolescents. Respectively, they pertain to the identification of children's risk status, measurement of behavior change, composition of treatment contexts, and elaboration of follow-up intervention systems.

REFERENCES

Achenbach, T. M., & Edelbrock, C. S. (1981). Behavioral problems and competencies reported by parents of normal and disturbed children aged 4 through 16. *Monographs of the Society for Research in Child Development, 46*:188.

Bailey, W. G. (1966). Correctional outcome: An evaluation of 100 reports. *Journal of Criminal Law, Criminology and Police Science, 57,* 153–160.

Feldman, R. A., Caplinger, T. E., & Wodarski, J. S. (1983). *The St. Louis conundrum: The effective treatment of antisocial youths.* Englewood Cliffs, NJ: Prentice-Hall.

Feldman, R. A., Stiffman, A. R., & Jung, K. G. (1987). *Children at risk: In the web of parental mental illness.* New Brunswick, NJ: Rutgers University Press.

Garmezy, N. (1974). The study of competence in children at risk for severe psychopathology. In C. Koupernik & E. J. Anthony (Eds.), *The child in his family: Children at psychiatric risk.* New York: Wiley Interscience.

Kirk, S. A., & Kutchins, H. (1992). *The selling of DSM: The rhetoric of science in psychiatry.* New York: Aldine de Gruyter.

Lipton, D., Martinson, R., & Wilks, J. (1975). *The effectiveness of correctional treatment: A survey of treatment.* New York: Praeger.

Meyer, C. H., & Mattaini, M. A. (Eds.). (1995). *The foundations of social work practice.* Washington, DC: National Association of Social Workers Press.

Romig, D. A. (1978). *Justice for our children: An examination of juvenile delinquency rehabilitation programs.* Lexington, MA: Lexington Books.

12

Treatment Outcomes: Psychoanalytic Psychotherapy

MARIO BERTOLINI

FRANCESCA NERI

SUMMARY

In the last 20 years, evaluation of psychotherapeutic outcome has become more sophisticated. In this paper we present data from a child and adolescent psychotherapeutic service in a public institution. Sixty cases were collected from 1987 until 1995, and all of them have come to termination. We discuss the efficacy, costs, and benefits of a public psychotherapeutic service.

INTRODUCTION

All psychotherapists attempt to evaluate and describe the progress achieved in their patients with their own techniques. The possible measures they might use can be, for example, the development of symptoms and the transference relationship, and evaluation of the changes that involve integration of the different parts of the patient's personality.

Such clinical impressions, on the one hand, are of utmost importance in evaluating therapeutic improvement, but on the other hand, they are not objective and thus present numerous challenges in their application. For example, therapist and patient, as noted by Cramer (1993), can concur in a collusive but artificial positive evaluation of changes. Moreover, the amplitude and the nature of such changes are difficult to evaluate objectively.

Nevertheless, in the last 20 years it has been necessary to find a way to present the results of the theory and technique of psychoanalysis to health organizations. This has prompted studies to evaluate the efficacy of treatment, specifying the changes occurring in psychotherapy and improving our comprehension of the processes of change. However, in countries in which there is no public health system, the need for outcome assessment was already manifested in the 1960s in order to demonstrate the efficiency of the treatments, so that they would continue to be included among reimbursable services. This has played an important role in propelling the development of studies on the results of psychotherapy.

It belongs to the field of process research, which essentially addresses the validation and refinement of the psychoanalytic theoretical model using appropriate research instruments, and to the field of outcome research to verify the results of treatment for a group of patients.

The research we present here belongs to the latter field and represents the last stage of a voyage of reflection within the Service for Psychoanalytic Psychotherapy of the Child and Adolescent (Bertolini, Ferri, & Fornari, 1994) of the National Health Service District n. 29 of the Lombardia Region (USSL n. 29). Since 1987, within the Child and Adolescent Neuropsychiatric Working Group of USSL 29, a psychotherapy service for children and adolescents has been operating with a psychoanalytic orientation.

External consultants, physicians, and psychologists employed by the regional health service of the Working Group work in the psychotherapy service. They have personal training requirements (personal psychoanalytic treatment completed) and adhere to a program of weekly group and individual supervision of cases by a didactic member of the IPA (Italian Society of Psychoanalysis).

The service thus established offers the possibility of psychotherapy to the public and maintains control of the quality of the treatments. At the moment, there are 11 therapists, each providing a total of about 30 hours per month.

The work environment (public-institutional), the homogeneity of personal training, the stable presence of supervision, the fact that some therapists have been in the group for many years (some began to work together before 1987), and the theoretical-clinical discussion of cases have resulted in particular attention being dedicated to specific phenomena. These include verification of the quality of the work performed and conceptualization of the institutional aspects of the psychotherapeutic work, in particular, the efficacy and maintenance of psychotherapeutic work in children and adolescents in relation to other forms of intervention. We have consequently directed attention, whose form has evolved in response to our results, to the psychotherapeutic work of the service since 1987.

In response to continuing questions in this field, we made choices that assure methodological correctness and reliability of results rather than providing simple responses to complex questions related to the data and available instruments.

In fact, classification problems are often cited in reviews when defining disorders and treatments, or when discussing difficulties explaining mechanisms of action of treatments and controversies due to the different etiopathogenic hypotheses in this field of research. All these factors make the definition of measures and criteria for results quite complex, and the nature of the measures makes assessment equivocal and debatable. In fact, "soft" endpoints and "soft" measures (called "soft" because of the methodological problems that their use poses) must be used, and these are nonetheless necessary to accurately describe what one intends to measure in a way that is sensitive and pertinent to the objective of the study.

The appropriate training of psychotherapists consists of personal analysis, supervision, and theoretical education. Such a requirement guarantees the quality of the services and their conformity to a certified treatment according to a high standard, which is difficult to find in routine public services.

The definition of health proposed by the World Health Organization implicitly defines the efficacy of a health treatment as the capacity of the intervention to maintain an individual in, or return (completely or partially) an individual to, a condition of physical, psychic, or social well-being, considering his or her overall functioning. Accordingly, we chose to evaluate several areas to define the psychic health of the subjects in psychotherapeutic treatment. Those identified were areas that, consensually in the literature, are considered to indicate the results of a treatment: symptom remission, hospital recoveries, discontinuation of drugs, social functioning, and interpersonal relations.

Objectives

The aim of the study was to describe the current condition of patients treated by psychoanalytic psychotherapy in the period from 1987 to 1994 and who had been discharged from the Service for at least 1 year by June 1995.

Methods

The design is a cross-sectional study in the final month of a longitudinal follow-up of patients. Evaluation of the condition of the patients, i.e., of the results, was carried out on the basis of the following parameters:

- overall psychopathologic condition, evaluated by a Global Assessment of Functioning (GAF) scale score;
- number of hospitalizations since discharge;
- personal independence in daily activities in relation to age;
- familial functioning and social network (the instrument used to attribute a score in these two areas utilized the scale of Morosini, for measurement of social and familial functioning; the original version was modified for application in the developmental period);[1,2]
- educational and work functioning;
- evaluation of relations with the internal/external world;
- evaluation formulated by the therapist on the basis of the interview;
- later treatment provided by another health service.

The information was collected with the aid of a clinical schedule. In addition to a section relative to the previous parameters, it collected sociodemographic data and information on the history of therapeutic interventions for the patient from the time of discharge until the study month.

All therapists invited their patients to individual interviews during which information relative to the aforementioned parameters was collected. The purpose of the interview, as described to the patient, was for the therapist and patient to evaluate together the usefulness of the work done.[3] In case it was not possible for the patient to participate in the interview, a meeting was held with the parents (only in the case of underage patients). In two cases the interview

Table 12.1   *Sources of Information About Patients*

	N	%
Interview with patient	35	74.4
Interview with parents	6	12.8
Interview with patient and parents	4	8.5
Interview by telephone	2	4.2

was completed by telephone because of the patient's relocation to another region.

RESULTS

Characteristics of the Sample

The overall sample, made up of all patients treated since 1987 by the Psychotherapy Service and discharged for at least one year (in June 1995), consisted of 60 subjects. Information was not obtained for 13 (20%) patients: 3 subjects refused to participate in an interview, and 10 cases were lost due to change of residence. The study sample is thus of 47 subjects. The period between the discharge date and the day of the interview in June 1995 varied from 1 year to 6 years, with a mean of 2.9 years. Information was collected, by the therapist who had previously treated the patient, during an interview with the patient in 74.4% of the cases, during an interview with the parents in 6 cases (12.8%), during an interview with the patient and the parents in 4 cases (8.5%), and by telephone in 2 cases (4.2%); see Table 12.1. There were 27 males (57%) and 20 females (43%). The mean age of the sample at follow-up was 18.2 years (range: 8–28 years). Owing to the wide age range, the subjects were grouped according to age (Table 12.2). The largest age group was 15–20 years (49%), followed by older than 20 years (34%). Therefore, we dealt with a follow-up sample formed mainly

Table 12.2   *Distribution of Patients' Age at Follow-up*

Age range	N	%	Mean age
8–14 years	8	17	11
15–20 years	24	49	17.4
Over 20 years	15	34	23

of adolescents and young adults. Almost all of the patients lived with their parents, as expected given their age. Only 2 patients had married and lived on their own with a spouse. Most of the patients were students ($n = 29$, 62%), whereas 38% were working (in 3 cases, the work was ''protected''). None of the patients were unemployed or inactive.

Therapy was concluded by 75% ($n = 35$) of the patients and interrupted by 25% ($n = 12$) of the patients. The mean duration of the therapy for the overall sample was 3.5 years (range: 1–8 years). The mean duration of the therapy was 3.8 years for patients who had concluded therapy and 2.5 years for those who had interrupted therapy. It should be noted that interruption of the psychotherapy by the patient never occurred in a period of less than 1 year from the beginning of therapy. This means that all the patients who entered the Psychotherapy Service (whether they eventually interrupted or concluded the therapy) maintained contact with the therapist for a significant period (even more so if we consider that the treatment consisted of an average of 2 sessions a week). Other types of intervention, in collaboration with other agencies or services of the USSL district, were given to the patients during the period of psychotherapeutic treatment in 53% of the cases ($n = 25$): 14 patients received educational support (3 of them also had an additional teacher); 3 patients received socioeducational rehabilitation; and 8 patients received drug therapy, but only during the first 2–3 months of treatment. Meetings with patients and parents were planned in all cases.

As regards the therapeutic interventions following discharge of the patients (Table 12.3), it should first be noted that no patient was hospitalized for psychiatric reasons. Moreover, it should be emphasized that patients who found themselves in stressful conditions after termination of therapy (in most cases related to moderate-to-severe stressful events like the death of a loved one or severe organic diseases) had requested assistance from their own therapist or another therapist, thereby maintaining an overall equilibrium. A small number of patients ($n = 11$, 22%) received other types of intervention following discharge, some beginning during the psychotherapeutic treatment: 5 patients received brief psychotherapeutic treatment, with their own therapist or with another; 3 patients were registered in socioeducational rehabilitation centers and were placed in work programs; 1 patient was seen by a specialist (neurologist);

Table 12.3 *Therapeutic Interventions Following Discharge*

Therapeutic Intervention	N
Hospitalizations	None
Psychotherapy with previous therapist in case of difficulties	3 patients
Psychotherapy with another therapist	2 patients
Assistance from other specialist (neurologist)	1 patient
Placement in special schools	2 patients
In the care of other services	
In socioeducational & rehabilitation centers/work programs	2 patients
In care of social services	1 patient
In special schools	1 patient

2 patients (one with a diagnosis of autism, and the other of severe psychosis) were placed in special schools. Only 4 patients (8%) were being cared for by other services.

From a diagnostic point of view, the population was distributed as follows (Figure 12.1): neurosis (*n* = 17, 36%), borderline personality disorder (*n* = 15, 32%), psychosis (*n* = 6, 13%), autism (*n* = 2, 4.5%), anorexia (*n* = 4, 8.5%), and other (*n* = 3, 6%: 1 psychosomatic disorder, 1 severe social deprivation, 1 organic psychosis).

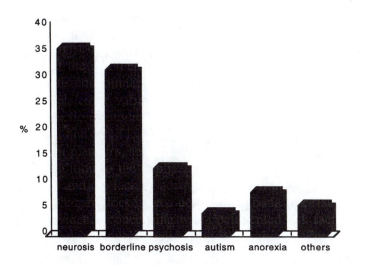

Figure 12.1. *Diagnostic categories*

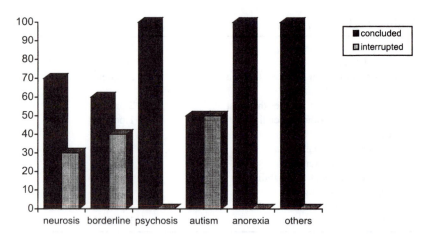

Figure 12.2   *Interrupted vs. concluded therapies according to diagnosis*

Analysis of the completion of therapy (concluded vs. interrupted) for each diagnostic group (Figure 12.2) showed that there were more interruptions (60% concluded vs. 40% interrupted) among the patients with a borderline diagnosis. This data is in line with literature reports, yet the percentage of therapy interruptions in our study was lower than those reported in the literature. In the other diagnostic groups the percentage of therapy concluded vs. interrupted was as follows: neurosis, 70% concluded vs. 30% interrupted; borderline, 60% concluded vs. 40% interrupted; psychosis, 100% concluded; autism, 50% concluded (1 case) vs. 50% interrupted (1 case, but followed for 5 years and semiconcluded as judged by the therapist); anorexia, 100% concluded; other, 100% concluded.

FOLLOW-UP CONDITIONS OF THE PATIENTS BASED ON OUTCOME PARAMETERS

First, we will present the results of the different measures for the overall sample and then the results for the same parameters per diagnostic group and per therapeutic status (interrupted vs. concluded). The mean follow-up score on the GAF scale (which goes from 0 to 90) for the overall sample was 69, which corresponds to good clinical, social, scholastic/work functioning, in spite of the

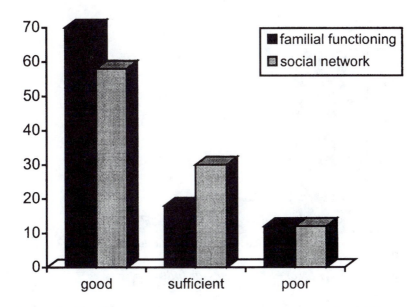

Figure 12.3 *Familial functioning and social network at followup*

presence of some difficulties or slight symptoms (for example, depression and anxiety). However, it should be noted that the score
ranged from 10 (for an autistic patient) to 85.

As regards familial functioning during the month before the interview, the scores for this outcome parameter were distributed as
follows (Figure 12.3): 68% (*n* = 32) of the patients showed good,
19% (*n* = 9) sufficient, and 13% (*n* = 6) poor familial functioning.
The scores indicating social networks (the quantity and quality of
significant social relations in the life of the patient) during the month
before the interview were slightly lower (Figure 12.3): 57% (*n* =
27) of the patients had a good social network or a good integration
into the social environment and/or group of peers; 30% (*n* = 14)
had a sufficient social network, although with some difficulty in
interpersonal relations, and 13% (*n* = 6) had a poor social network,
few social relationships, and significant difficulty with interactions.

Evaluation of the degree of personal autonomy in daily activities
(in relation to developmental expectations) showed a therapeutically
favorable distribution (Figure 12.4): almost all the patients (*n* = 6,
87%) demonstrated adequate autonomy; only 5 patients (11%)
showed partial autonomy; and only 1 patient (2%) showed an inadequate degree of autonomy.

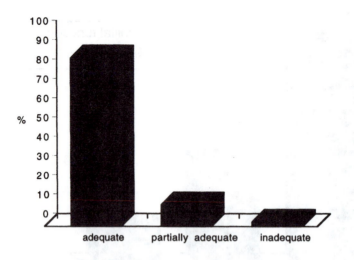

Figure 12.4   *Personal autonomy at followup*

Educational and work functioning was good for almost all the patients: in only 2 cases did the therapist indicate difficulty in both areas. As noted before, no patient was unemployed. The patients unable to work in an unprotected work situation were placed in work projects (through a work grant) and were performing their tasks regularly.

Analysis of the mean GAF scores by diagnostic group showed the expected differences. The score was lowest (corresponding to poor psychological and social functioning) in patients with a diagnosis of psychosis (mean GAF = 55) and autism (mean GAF = 30). Nonetheless, the therapists who followed such patients for years (therapy was concluded in 100% of cases) reported, in the comments accompanying the evaluation, some considerations that emphasize how the conditions of these patients, although overall more unfavorable than those of the patients of the other diagnostic groups, are characterized by more than appreciable results. The outcome obtained in such patients must be related to the basic impairment, which remains in spite of the therapy. The mean GAF score was similar among the other diagnostic groups: borderline, 68; neurosis, 73; anorexia, 80; other, 70. There were no significant differences in the GAF scores between interrupted and concluded therapies.

Analysis of familial functioning by diagnostic group showed that almost all the patients with a diagnosis of neurosis or anorexia had good familial functioning characterized by stable and supportive relations (only 2 patients with a diagnosis of neurosis showed only "sufficient" familial functioning, or one characterized by some difficulty). For the other diagnoses, the number of patients with slight or significant difficulty in familial functioning was larger: among borderline patients, 40% had familial functioning characterized by slight ($n = 4$) or significant ($n = 2$) difficulty; in the group of psychotic patients, 50% ($n = 3$) presented sufficient or poor familial functioning; and 100% of the autistic patients ($n = 2$) had familial functioning characterized by moderate to severe difficulty. However, the difficulty in familial functioning of psychotic patients cannot be unequivocally taken as a consequence of the disorder of the subject. In fact, it may be linked to the difficult dynamics of family groups of this type, independent of the relational capacity of the subject. The number of patients in this group was in any case too small to allow any further conclusions.

As regards the score for social network by diagnostic group, it was similar to that observed for familial functioning: the patients who presented the greatest difficulty in this area of outcome belonged to the diagnostic categories psychosis, autism, and borderline disorder. However, as regards the last diagnosis, it should be noted that a significant number of patients maintained good results in social relations: 53% of the borderline patients ($n = 8$) had a good social network. As regards all of these outcome parameters, there were no significant differences between patients who interrupted and those who concluded the therapy.

Analysis of the scores assigned by the therapist showed that there were significant variations among diagnoses. The patients with a diagnosis of psychosis or autism again had the most unfavorable or problematic outcomes.

CONCLUSIONS

We arrived at three conclusions. First, all patients, to differing degrees according to the diagnosis upon admission to the service, presented symptomatic improvement, as revealed by the follow-up measures, and were stable with time after termination of the treatment.

The GAF and Morosini scales (for familial functioning and social network) indicated that more than 75% of the patients examined in the study had follow-up scores within the normal range. The fact that no patient had to be hospitalized in a psychiatric setting after termination of the psychotherapeutic treatment confirms this. Such an outcome is even more important if we consider that 49.5% of our patients had personality disorders and psychoses and were in adolescent and childhood age groups (characteristics indicated in the literature as indices of risk for repeated psychiatric hospitalization). The psychoanalytic psychotherapeutic treatment might therefore give better results than could be obtained with other psychiatric treatments; these included avoidance of hospitalization, reduction or elimination of symptoms, and facilitation of stable life activities and relations. This is possible even in the childhood and adolescent periods, during which the dynamics of developmental processes can render less stable and definitive the emotional equilibrium reached.

In contrast, psychotherapists know the differences between the benefits of intrapsychic understanding that a person derives from an analytic treatment and the simultaneous improvement in behavioral and social adaptation. Such differences are observable at the end of the patient's treatment, in the judgment of the therapist, who refers to the type of transference relation developed, the quality of the objective relationship, the presence of anxiety of integration in relation to the capacity for insight, the types of defensive adjustments, as well as to the distinction described by the same therapist between therapy concluded and therapy interrupted.

Nevertheless, this study shows (by means of the scores obtained on the various scales and the lack of need to hospitalize patients) that psychotherapy, even before its conclusion, can produce beneficial effects which emerge from follow-up psychiatric assessment.

Our second conclusion is that there was no significant difference in our series between the scores of patients who terminated and those who interrupted treatment. Such a finding caused us to reflect on the inability of some patients to confront their anguish, related to the process of individualization and reduction of omnipotence. Symptom modification, adhesion to adaptive processes, and normalization can be an expression of defensive renunciation in order to stabilize a transference dependence felt as excessively destabilizing. It is a process of escape to normality, whose quality may be recognized in the confrontation and reading of transference and countertransference characteristics in the therapeutic relationship.

The training of therapists (by means of supervision and group discussions), and their capacity to reflect on the characteristics and progress of the therapeutic relationship, allow them to understand the distinct significance for the individual of behavioral and work changes and, in this way, to construct an environment that will sufficiently benefit their patients.

That psychotherapy has included the creation of a facilitating environment is demonstrated by the high number of positive responses at follow-up (only 3 of 60 patients replied negatively to the request for an interview to verify the results obtained), by the return of patients to the Service in the event of traumatic episodes, and by the duration of treatment before an eventual interruption. Such findings are noteworthy when compared with literature data concerning patients of the same age undergoing therapy at psychiatric services, which cite a distinctly greater number of interrupted therapies, a shorter duration of treatment with the service, and a high turnover of patients in the service due to early interruptions.

The same studies indicate that, among other factors that can affect psychotherapeutic results, the training and professional competence of the therapist can influence the duration of therapy, the incidence of interruption, etc.

Finally, we come to the following conclusion regarding the problem of cost vs. benefits: the USSL currently pays 35,000 Italian lire for each session, for a mean cost per therapy of about 5 million Italian lire. It should be remembered that the cost of one day of hospitalization for diagnosis and psychiatric care is about 400,000 Italian lire and that therefore, in a simplified way, we can say that the entire course of psychotherapy costs the same as 13 days of hospitalization. In addition, a study on the costs of a pilot center for childhood psychoses in the Lombardy Region calculated a mean cost per year for a psychotic patient to be 65 million Italian lire.

Psychoanalytic psychotherapy in a child and adolescent psychiatric setting that provides access to trained therapists thus appears to be an effective means to obtain results, even in the presence of complex and severe clinical profiles, that other psychiatric treatments reach in a less stable way.

NOTES

1. The score assigned to the different items of the scale for evaluation of familial functioning has been recodified in an overall

score that reapportions the different scores relative to single items. It is thus necessary to designate these classes of scores: 1, good familial functioning; 2, sufficient familial functioning (presence of some difficulties); 3, poor familial functioning (presence of some moderate to severe difficulties in the family interaction).

2. The score assigned to the different items of the scale for evaluation of social network has been recodified in an overall score that reapportions the different scores relative to single items. It is thus necessary to designate these classes of scores: 1, good social network; 2, sufficient social network (some difficulty with interpersonal interactions); 3, poor social network (poor interpersonal context characterized by significant difficulty).

3. The judgments of the therapist were indicated in the classes: 1 = adequate; 2 = partially adequate; 3 = inadequate.

REFERENCES

Ambrosi, P., Berlincioni, V., Pansini, L., Risaro, P., & Petrella, F., (1993). L'interruzione del trattamento nel servizio pubblico: Entità del fenomeno e criteri valutazione. *Rivista Sperimentale di Freniatria, 67,* 65–79.

Andrews, G. (1993). The benefits of psychotherapy. In N. Sartorius, G. De-Girolamo, G. Andrews, A. German, L. Eisenberg (Eds.), *Treatment of mental disorders. A review of effectiveness.* Washington, D.C.: World Health Organization.

Andrews, G. (1993). The essential psychotherapies. *British Journal of Psychiatry, 162,* 447–451.

Andrew, G., & Harvey, R. (1984). Does psychotherapy benefit neurotic patients? A reanalysis of the Smith, Glass and Miller data. *Archives of General Psychiatry, 38,* 1203–1208.

Aulas, J. J. (1991). Evaluation de la psychothérapie dans la dépression. *La Revue Prescrire, 11,* 319–320.

Bachrach, H. M., Galatzer-Levy, R. Skolinoff, A., & Waldron, S. (1991). On the efficacy of psychoanalysis. *Journal of the American Psychoanalytic Association, 39,* 871–916.

Balestrieri, A. (1990). Sui fattori specifici e aspecifici nelle psicoterapie. *Psicoterapia e Scienze Umane, 2,* 78-86.

Beitman, B. D., Goldfried, M. R., & Norcorss, J. C. (1989). The movement toward integrating the psychotherapies: An overview. *American Journal of Psychiatry, 146,* 138–147.

Bergin, A. E. (1963). The effects of psychotherapy: Negative results revisited. *Journal of Consulting Psychology, 10,* 244–250.

Bergin, A. E., & Lambert, M. J. (1978). The evaluation of therapeutic outcomes. In A. E. Bergin, & S. L. Garfield (Eds.), *Handbook of psychotherapy and behavior change. An empirical analysis* (2nd ed. pp. 130–190). New York: Wiley.

Bertolini, M., Ferri, P., & Fornari, S. (1994). Riflessioni catamnestiche su un servizio di psicoterapia dell'etá evolutiva e adolescenziale in instituzione pubblica. *Imago, 2,* 123–131.

Bertolini, M., Ferrari, P., Neri, F., & Tassan, M. (1996). Efficacia della psicoterapia psicoanalitica in un servizio pubblico di neuropsichiatria infantile: Esiti a distanza e costi/benefici. *Imago, 3,* 125–137.

Cramer, B. (1993). Peut-on évaluer les effets des psychothérapies? *Psychothérapies, 4,* 217–224.

Crits-Cristoph, P. (1992). The efficacy of brief dynamic psychotherapy: A meta analysis. *American Journal of Psychiatry, 149,* 151–157.

Glass, L. L., Katz, H. M., Schnitzer, R. D., Knapp, P. H., Frank, A. F., & Gunderson, J. G. (1989). Psychotherapy of schizophrenia: An empirical investigation of the relationship of process to outcome. *American Journal of Psychiatry, 146,* 603–608.

Goldfried, M. R., Greenberg, L. S., & Marmar, C. (1990). Individual psychotherapy: Process and outcome. *Annual Review of Psychology, 41,* 659–688.

Hoglend, P., Sorlie, T., Sorbye, O., Heyerdahl, O., & Amlo, S. (1992) Long-term changes after brief dynamic psychotherapy: Symptomatic versus dynamic assessments. *Acta Psychiatrica Scandinavica, 86,* 165–171.

Hillis, G., Alexander, D., & Eagles, J. (1993). Premature termination of psychiatric contact. *International Journal of Social Psychiatry, 39,* 100–107.

Howard, K. I., Davidson, C. V., O'Mahoney, M. T., Orlinsky, D. E., & Brown, K. P. (1989). Patterns of psychotherapy utilization. *American Journal of Psychiatry, 146,* 775–778.

Krupnick, J. L., & Pincus, H. A. (1992). The cost-effectiveness of psychotherapy: A plan for research. *American Journal of Psychiatry, 149,* 1295–1305.

Liberati, A. (1986). Guida alla letteratura crititca di un articolo sulla efficacia di un trattamento. *Nuovi Argomenti di Medicina, 2,* 341–351.

Luborsky, L., Crits-Cristoph, P., McLellan, T., Woody, G., Piper, W. Liberman, B., Imber, S., & Pilkonis, P. (1986). Do therapists vary much in their success? Findings from four outcome studies. *American Journal of Orthopsychiatry, 56,* 501–512.

Luborsky L., Crits-Cristoph P., Mintz J., & Auerbach A. (1988). *Who will benefit from psychotherapy?* New York: Basic Books.

Luborsky, L., McLellan, A. T., Woody, G. E. et al. (1985). Therapist success and its determinants. *Archives of General Psychiatry, 42,* 602–611.

Luborsky, L., Mintz, J., Auerback, A., Crits-Cristoph, P. et al. (1980). Predicting the outcome of psychotherapy: findings of the Penn Psychotherapy Project. *Archives of General Psychiatry, 37,* 471–481.

Nishizono, M., Docherty, J. P., & Butler, S. F. (1993). Evaluation of psychodynamic psychotherapy. In N. Sartorius, G. De Girolamo, G. Andrews, A. German, & L. Eisenberg, (Eds.), *Treatment of mental disorders. A review of effectiveness* (pp. 147–169). Washington, D. C.: World Health Organization.

Sparr, L., Meffitt, M., & Word, M. (1993). Missed psychiatric appointments: Who returns and who stays away. *American Journal of Psychiatry, 150,* 801–805.

13

Prevention Research in Child and Adolescent Psychiatry

PETER S. JENSEN

Because of the relative lack of progress in developing effective models and methods for preventing mental illnesses in children and adolescents and adults, the National Institute of Mental Health (NIMH) asked the Institute of Medicine (IOM) to survey the existing research base, examining the current research infrastructure and progress of the field, and to make recommendations concerning a comprehensive prevention research agenda for the next decade. This report, entitled "Reducing Risks for Mental Disorders: Frontiers for Preventive Intervention Research" was released in 1994, and provides a blueprint for NIMH's current prevention research efforts for the foreseeable future. In the area of children and adolescents, such a blueprint has been urgently needed, both to stimulate the research efforts in this regard, as well as to address the growing mental health problems that are faced by children and adolescents, even during a time of diminishing resources. For example, recent studies have reported prevalence rates of 15% to 28% (Anderson, Williams, & McGee, 1987; Bird, Canino, Rubio-Stipec, et al., 1988; Costello, Costello, Edelbrock, et al., 1988; Jensen, Watanabe, Richters, et al., 1995; Offord et al., 1987; Shaffer et al., in press), with rates varying depending upon the levels of impairment required to meet cut-off criteria for a diagnosis, and other authors have reported that rates of psychopathology appear to be on the rise (Achenbach & Howell, 1993, Ryan et al., 1992).

The following comments summarize a number of the important recommendations emerging from the IOM report to guide researchers as they develop and test methods and models for preventing child and adolescent mental disorders. As noted in the report, while prevention of mental disorders is a laudable goal, the field currently falls far short of a substantial knowledge base, apart from the well-documented evidence for the benefits of early childhood nutrition on children's health and development, the effects of intensive early interventions (e.g., Head Start) on children's school readiness and short-term outcomes, and the immediate benefits of novel school-based approaches in involving parents, educators, and mental health professionals in creating more safe and productive school environments. Thus, the federal research agenda outlined in the IOM report identifies three major areas of focus: (a) developing an infrastructure to coordinate research and service delivery programs and to train new researchers; (b) increasing the knowledge base concerning effective preventive interventions, and (c) conducting well-evaluated preventive interventions.

Among clinicians, older models of prevention have discussed the concepts of primary, secondary, and tertiary prevention. While these models have proved valuable, they have blurred the boundaries between prevention and treatment, and these older conceptualizations have been replaced by newer approaches. Generally, prevention can be defined as those measures adopted by or practiced upon persons who are not currently suffering from an illness, designed to reduce the likelihood that the disease will affect them some time in the future. Within this definition, three models of preventive interventions have been proposed: First, universal preventive interventions for mental disorders are targeted to the general public or a whole population that has not been identified on the basis of individual risk. Second, selective preventive interventions for mental disorders are targeted to individuals or a subgroup of the population whose risk of developing mental disorders is significantly higher than average. The risk groups may be identified on the basis of biological, psychological, or social risk factors that are known to be associated with the onset of a mental disorder. Last, indicated preventive interventions for mental disorders are targeted to high-risk individuals who are identified as having minimal but detectable signs or symptoms foreshadowing mental disorder, but who do not meet diagnostic criteria at the current time.

Like prevention, the concept of risk factors also needs careful specification. Risk factors are those characteristics, variables, or hazards that, if present for a given individual, make it more likely in terms of statistical prediction that this individual rather than someone selected randomly from the general population will develop the disorder. In this context, it should be noted that the risk factor must be shown and/or known to precede the actual development of the disorder; otherwise it is more appropriate to term it a correlate, concomitant, or consequence. Too often, researchers refer to correlates or variables associated with psychopathology within cross-sectional studies as "risk factors." This is incorrect and misleading, and often leads to confusion among clinicians, researchers, program planners, and policy makers (see Kraemer et al., 1997).

In addition to the haphazard, problematic use of the term "risk factor" and the lack of adequate research that a purported psychological hazard does indeed constitute a bona fide risk factor, all too often evidence concerning well-documented risk factors fails to be translated into public policy and new programs and practices. All new preventive intervention research findings are useless without the process of *knowledge exchange*. The success of the preventive intervention research efforts lies in how effectively knowledge can be exchanged among researchers, community practitioners, and policy makers to successfully implement a program in real-life settings and ultimately, with widespread societal application, to reduce the incidence of mental disorders. This series of steps, from (A) identifying a problem or disorder and determining its extent, (B) scientifically establishing the risk factors that clearly antedate the onset of the disorder and that might be altered in order to reduce the onset of the disorder, (C) designing and carrying out pilot and confirmatory trials of a theoretically sound preventive intervention, (D) designing and conducting large-scale field trials of the preventive interventions, to (E) facilitating large-scale implementation and ongoing evaluation of the preventive intervention in the community constitute a sound "preventive intervention research cycle" (Mrazek and Haggerty, 1994).

The preventive intervention research cycle parallels the body of knowledge that has grown over the last 15 years, as the field of risk assessment, evaluation, and management and associated methodologies have grown rapidly. Though relatively new, this field is concerned with the critical process of linking science with decision-making and public policy. Despite its relative newcomer status, its importance cannot be overstated, since many governments have agencies with regulatory responsibilities (e.g., within the United

States, the Occupational Safety and Health Administration [OSHA], the Environmental Protection Agency [EPA], the National Institute of Occupational Safety and Health, various institutes of the National Institutes of Health, and the Food and Drug Administration [FDA]). Such agencies are usually intimately involved in the science, methods, and technologies of risk assessment.

Risk assessment includes the area of *risk estimation,* i.e., the estimation of probabilities of identified adverse outcomes in specific populations or subpopulations, and the identification of the magnitude of the association between identified risk factors and such outcomes. Risk outcomes estimation may include both *individual* outcomes (e.g., one person's likelihood of developing lung cancer after exposure to asbestos) and *societal* outcomes (the likelihood of these adverse impacts upon the larger population). Societal risk takes into account the prevalence of the disorder, as well as its impact on the specific individual.

Risk assessment also includes *risk evaluation,* the complex process of determining the significance, meaning, or value of the identified hazards and other estimated risks to those exposed to the purported hazard or otherwise affected by decisions about exposure to the hazard. Risk evaluation includes the study of *risk perception* and the trade-offs between costs and benefits associated with exposure to risk factors. While some commentators have suggested that public opinions regarding risks are capricious and cannot be reliably ascertained for purposes of risk evaluation, U.S. federal law requires openness and public participation in this process. Some technologies have been developed to address these and related issues, such as cost–benefit analyses, other forms of economic analyses, and, in the medical sciences areas, single numerical figures designed to integrate qualitative and quantitative constructs, e.g., quality-adjusted life years.

Risk management consists of the process of developing, implementing, and monitoring policy decisions concerning identified risk factors (termed hazards in much of the biomedical hazards/risk factor literature). Ideally, risk management flows from risk estimation and risk evaluation. In the social and behavioral sciences in particular, risk management is an iterative process and is informed by public input, perception, and ongoing studies of the relationship between hazards, perceptions of hazards, and policy. But a somewhat unique problem for the social and behavioral sciences in risk estimation and management is that interventions to manage risk may affect perceptions/estimations of hazards. Further, psychological processes set in motion through such management efforts may also increase risk perception and even the nature of the hazards themselves. Thus, the relationships between risk estimation, evaluation, and management are particularly intertwined and not easily separable in the social and behavioral sciences. From this perspective, risk and risk reduction (prevention) are in part group and social-psychological phenomena, and because of the degree of societal concerns about various hazards, they can be conceptualized in some circumstances as both causes and effects.

In the area of psychological hazards or risk factors, the relationships among risk, risk definition, human behavior, and personal freedoms are complex and interconnected. As a result, risk management-related policies and prevention programs can be controversial. Strategies to change the culture of risk can be seen as meddling, interfering with constitutional freedoms, or otherwise inappropriate. In the social and behavioral sciences in particular, risk estimation, risk evaluation, and risk management are not distinct processes; rather, they are quite interconnected and have the potential to inform each other in an iterative fashion.

How does one establish acceptable levels of risk, such that public policy decisions can be made to regulate public exposure to a purported hazard? Risk is a relative concept. To fully understand the magnitude of risk in a given situation, its context must be known. For example, the degree of voluntariness with which the public allows itself to be exposed to a hazard is critical to assessing its impact and to understanding the public acceptability (risk evaluation) of that potential hazard. In addition, the base rate of the adverse outcome, the potency or certainty of the relationship between the hazard and adverse health outcomes, the severity of the health outcomes, and their reversibility are also important factors in determining the public's perceptions and the acceptability of the health hazard exposure. Likewise, the public's knowledge of and familiarity with the health hazard, factors such as compensation for exposure to the hazard, potential advantages of the activity or hazard exposure, and the advantages and disadvantages of available alternatives, all shape public attitudes toward health hazards. Based on this combination of factors, the public's perceptions of the degree of danger that a given hazard poses (perceived likelihood of personally experiencing an adverse health outcome as the result of a health hazard—a subjective probability—vs. the actual degree of risk imposed by that hazard—an objective probability) may vary by a factor of as much as 100 to 1 or its inverse (objective risk vs. subjective risk).

Risk assessment methodologies, while critical to guiding risk management decisions, cannot replace the process of risk evaluation. Certainly, scientists must provide input for measuring the cost–benefit ratio and determining the adequacy of cost–benefit assessments. Yet, if risk assessments are to adequately inform the decision-making process, scientists must obtain citizens' input concerning the risk–benefit trade-offs and the public's attitudes towards the relative hazards. As a consequence, risk–benefits assessments that incorporate public attitudes and values will often produce estimates of a variety of consequences, both good and bad, and as noted above, they may range over many orders of magnitude, often surrounded by a good deal of uncertainty.

For all of these reasons (problems with the definition of risk factors; varying public perceptions and acceptance of risks; public acceptance and impact of risk management procedures, e.g., prevention programs, that may in themselves have untoward effects), mental health prevention workers would be well advised to draw upon the fields of biomedical and toxic risk factor and hazards research to develop and conduct risk factor research, and (when such research identifies successful and feasible prevention strategies) to facilitate knowledge exchange of these findings with communities, practitioners, and policy makers. Mrazek and Haggerty (1994) have summarized these following principles.

First, preventive interventions are specifically developed through a series of phases, each step building upon its predecessor and supporting its successor.

Second, preventive interventions need not always wait for complete scientific knowledge about etiology and treatment. For example, knowledge of vitamin C was not needed to identify a strategy to prevent scurvy among shipbound sailors. Instead, awareness that eating citrus fruits prevented scurvy was sufficient. Similarly, handwashing and forceps sterilization was found to prevent puerperal fever and death among newly delivered mothers on maternity wards, far prior to the discovery of the responsible bacterial pathogens.

Third, given the complex web of interacting, multideterminant "causes" likely to lead to the development of mental disorders, preventive interventions typically are most effective when they consider multiple domains of intervention.

Fourth, preventive intervention programs should be rigorously designed, and the programs and their components should be evaluated extensively. Thus, when designing or evaluating a preventive intervention program, one should identify the risk and protective factors addressed by the intervention, the nature of the targeted population group, the exact components of the intervention program (including robust psychometric strategies and employment of controls), careful explication of the steps employed to ensure the fidelity of program implementation, and sound evidence of outcomes across all relevant domains. These outcomes include not just clinical outcomes (e.g., symptoms and disorders), but possibly also positive child functioning (social and cognitive skills, school performance), consumer-based outcomes (e.g., consumer satisfaction, measures of family burden), environmental outcomes (potential beneficial impact of the preventive intervention upon others, e.g., family members, peers, classroom, neighborhood), and services and service system outcomes (cost effectiveness, changes in placements, decreased service utilization, etc.)

Fifth, preventive interventions should focus on the community, in both planning and implementation. Particularly in the mental health arena, where mental illness is laden with public misperceptions and stigma, the public's understanding, awareness, involvement in, and commitment to all stages of a preventive program are crucial. Within the U.S. federal government, public health efforts to increase research and service programs to reduce the level of violence within society ran aground when public misperceptions circulated that the federal government was presumably instead planning to forcibly medicate children in schools without parental knowledge. While this notion appeared to be a mischievous and likely deliberately concocted rumor circulated to serve ignoble purposes, great alarm spread widely through many affected communities who had no knowledge, understanding, or prior involvement with the well-intentioned federal effort. Needless to say, the effort was quietly abandoned, but not before community members of a blue ribbon panel noted that such efforts in the future had to begin with clear community involvement and partnerships if they were to succeed.

Finally, prevention efforts require significant and sustained commitment on the part of national, regional, and local governments and coordination across disciplines and agencies. The commitments must include resources to train potential researchers how to conduct scientifically rigorous prevention research, the resources to actually carry out such work, and public and policy initiatives to implement successful preventive intervention programs in real-world community settings.

Conduct disorder, depression, and substance abuse might be cited as possible examples of disorders affecting children and adolescents for which substantial knowledge of risk factors has been developed, and where preventive interventions might be considered. Within conduct disorder, scientifically established risk factors include early aggression, early noncompliance, poor social skills, inadequate cognitive skills, school failure, exposure to delinquent peers, inadequate parental monitoring, and coercive parenting. While much remains to be learned about the risk and protective factors for conduct disorder, it is clear that the accumulation of risk factors as the child develops is more important than any specific risk factor. Quite possibly, a sensible prevention program might be developed that targeted several of these factors within a sound developmental framework, given careful attention to the timing and onset of particular risk factors and the optimal points, types, and targets of the intervention.

Risk factors that have been associated with the onset of depressive disorders include having a parent or other close biological relative with a mood disorder, having a severe stressor such as a physical illness, or death of a parent, having low self-esteem and/or a sense of low self-efficacy, being female, and living in poverty. Factors associated with the onset of alcohol problems include having a parent or other close biological relative with alcohol abuse or dependence problems, having a biological marker that is associated with later onset of alcohol dependence including decreased sensitivity to alcohol, demonstrating antisocial behaviors or a combination of aggressiveness and shy behavior during childhood, being exposed to group norms that foster alcohol use and abuse, and having easy access to alcohol. While evidence continues to mount concerning specific risk factors for various disorders, investigators should ideally posit a plausible, developmentally sensible model concerning malleable risk factors when designing prevention research programs.

In summary, prevention research is difficult to do and requires rigorous knowledge and scientific training by the potential investigator. Yet it is a worthy goal, not to be shyed away from, and child psychiatrists and allied professionals are encouraged to obtain the necessary training and or assistance in addressing these critical issues for populations in need. Prevention research is a critical cornerstone of public policy and risk management, all the more needed in times of shrinking public resources. Unfortunately, the mental health fields lag behind other disciplines and biomedical sciences in this area, and if they are to make the necessary progress, partnerships with parents and families, services system organizers and policy makers, and clinicians will be needed. Difficult though this process is, we must ask: if not now, when? And if not child psychiatrists allied with other mental health disciplines, who?

NOTES

1. Text based upon remarks delivered in Rome, Italy on April 18, 1996, and in Venice, Italy on April 22, 1996.
2. The opinions and assertions contained in this paper are the private views of the authors and are not to be construed as official or as reflecting the views of the Department of Health and Human Services or the National Institute of Mental Health.

REFERENCES

Achenbach, T. M., & Howell, C. T. (1993). Are American children's problems getting worse? A 13-year comparison. *Journal of the American Academy of Child and Adolescent Psychiatry, 32,* 1145–1154.

Anderson, J. C., Williams, S., McGee, R., et al. (1987). DSM-III disorders in preadolescent children. *Archives of General Psychiatry, 44,* 69–76.

Bird, H., Canino, G., Rubio-Stipec, M., Silva, P. A. (1988). Estimates of the prevalence of childhood maladjustment in a community survey in Puerto Rico. *Archives of General Psychiatry, 45,* 1120–1126.

Costello, E. J., Costello, A. J., Edelbrock, C., et al. (1988). Psychiatric disorders in pediatric primary care. *Archives of General Psychiatry, 45,* 1107–1116.

Jensen, P. S., Watanabe, H., Richters, J., Cortes, R., Roper, M., & Liu, S. (1995). Prevalence of mental disorder in military children and adolescents: Findings from a two-stage community survey. *Journal of the American Academy of Child and Adolescent Psychiatry, 34,* 1514–1524.

Kraemer, H. C., Kazdin, A. E., Offord, D. R., Kessler, R. C., Jensen, P. S., & Kupfer, D. J. (1997). Coming to terms with the terms of risk. *Archives of General Psychiatry, 54,* 337–343.

Mrazek, P. J., & Haggerty, R. J. (1994). *Reducing risks for mental disorders: Frontiers for preventive intervention research.* Washington, DC: National Academy Press.

Offord, D. R., Boyle, N. H., Szatmari, P., et al. (1987). Ontario Child Health Study: II. Six-month prevalence of disorder and rates of service utilization. *Archives of General Psychiatry, 44,* 832–836.

Ryan, N. D., Williamson, D. E., Iyengar, S., et al. (1992). A secular increase in child and adolescent onset affective disorder. *Journal of the American Academy of Child and Adolescent Psychiatry, 31,* 600–605.

Shaffer, D., Fisher, P., Dulcan, M., Davies, M., Piacentini, J., Schwab-Stone, M., Lahey, B., Bourdon, K., Jensen, P., Bird, H., Canino, G., & Regier, D. (1996). The second version of the NIMH Diagnostic Interview Schedule for Children (DISC-2. 3). *Journal of the American Academy of Child and Adolescent Psychiatry, 35,* 960–969.

14

A Framework for Preventive Intervention: Parental Awareness of Developmental Problems and Early Diagnosis in Child and Adolescent Psychopathology

G . L E V I

R . P E N G E

HEALTH SERVICES IN ITALY: THE SITUATION

In Italy, as in all countries of the Western World, a small number of children and adolescents with psychopathological disturbances are referred to the Mental Health Services for Children and Adolescents — 4% to 6% of all children are evaluated, compared with 15% to 20% revealed through epidemiological research (Costello, Burns, Angold, & Leaf, 1993; Boyle, et al.,1987; Rutter, 1989).

Presently in Italy, the Mental Health Services for Children and Adolescents directly monitor between 2% and 3% of the child population, apart from another 2% composed of disabled subjects (Levi & Meledandri, 1994). About 6% to 7% of the child population is tutored by other services (social welfare, the justice system, and the schools).

In Italy, as in other countries, many children are still referred to Mental Health Services for Children and Adolescents 2 or 3 years after the onset of disturbances, when the problem is already established and, often, when secondary disturbances are beginning to be noted. Widened clinical and etiological knowledge and increased social and cultural awareness of problems in childhood and adolescence have increased the number of referred subjects, but there remain many areas of disturbance which are misunderstood or denied.

FROM EXISTENCE OF A NEED TO REQUEST FOR HEALTH SERVICE GUIDANCE: THE ROLE OF THE PARENT

Knowledge of all the phenomena which lead to referral to the Health Services must guide the research and organization of projects intended to improve mental health in children and adolescents (Verhulst & Koot, 1992).

In which phase of a disturbance can we distinguish with certainty between cases and noncases? When are we able to form precise and concrete diagnoses and prognoses? What do we know about the mechanisms which lead from risk to disturbance? What kind of prevention are we really capable of effecting for psychopathological disturbances?

How can we translate scientific knowledge into "cultural" and social awareness? What should our first objectives be in this?

Among the many aspects which bear on the referral of a patient to the Health Services, in this paper we deal with those inherent in the adult conception of a child's world.

What are the behavioral problems or symptoms which parents see, but are not able to recognize as such? In other words: what is the model (the stereotype) of a child needing psychological or psychiatric help? Which signs of suffering in children and adolescents are perceived from an educational or social perspective and therefore dealt with only within the family or school? And, lastly, what is the relationship among the typology and severity of the disturbance, family dynamics, and access to Health Services?

TWO RESEARCH PROJECTS

In two parallel projects we have tried to analyze these questions exploring, in the general population, parental perception of a psychopathological problem and the correlation between such perceptions and the real presence of a disturbance.

The goal of this research is not an epidemiological survey of the phenomenon, but rather a better understanding of the mechanisms

Table 14.1 *First Research Project: Sample Description and Percentage of Subjects Scoring in the Clinical Range (+) for Each Age Group*

	6 yrs.	7 yrs.	8 yrs.	9 yrs.	10 yrs.	11 yrs.	12 yrs.	13 yrs.	14 yrs.	Totals
Number of subjects	326	452	562	453	521	461	406	401	45	3628
CBCL +	9.2	13.1	8.7	17	15.7	9.1	10.1	16.5	24.4	12.8
Total Scale +	6.13	10.2	5.5	12.6	10.9	12.3	6.1	11.9	22.2	8.7
Internalizing +	3.98	5.5	4.1	11.9	9.4	5.2	4.6	8.2	20.0	6.8
Externalizing +	5.52	6.4	4.4	7.0	6.1	3.7	6.9	10.7	17.7	6.4

that govern it. Only through such increased knowledge will it be possible to instigate educational policies in the population that generate parental awareness of suffering hidden in certain child behaviors and to diminish preconceptions regarding the Mental Health Services.

Among the different instruments used for research, we deemed the Child Behavior Checklist (CBCL, Achenbach 1991, the Parents Form) to be sufficiently reliable for identifying problems, easy to administer, and able to cover a wide range of problems and disturbances.

We adopted as a criterion indicative of a psychopathological problem the presence of scores in the clinical range within the Total Scale and/or within one of the main Groups of Syndromes (Internalizing and Externalizing).

PREVALENCE OF PSYCHOPATHOLOGICAL PROBLEMS, AS PERCEIVED BY PARENTS

The first research project, in collaboration with a parents association with branches all over Italy, asked parents to "answer a questionnaire about typical child behavior today and possible signs of the presence of a psychological disturbance."

There was an 80% response within the selected sample, well distributed among the different regions and social classes in the country.

The data collected refer to 3,628 children aged 6–14 (Table 14.1). Questionnaires relating to subjects with known psychological disturbances were excluded from the analysis.

Analysis of the CBCL data showed that 12.8% of cases scored in the clinical range in at least one of the three main scales; 8.7%

of cases scored in the clinical range in the Total Scale, while the percentage of subjects positive on the Internalizing and Externalizing Scales was lower (around 6.5%).

Comparison of different age groups showed a slight oscillation in the frequency of subjects scoring within the clinical range (from 8.7% in 8-year-olds to 16.5% in 13-year-olds), with a sharp peak in subjects 14 years old.

The cross-sectional structure of the study and the technique used are not conducive to establishing a coherent relationship between the different age ranges: the oscillations noted could in reality be related both to a variation in prevailing psychopathological disturbances during development and to variations in the intensity of their symptomatological manifestations. In every case, however, during the middle childhood and early adolescent phases, a significant percentage of the population, oscillating between 8% and 24%, showed the presence of some psychological problem.

During development, symptomatic phases seem to alternate with periods of "remission." In this sense adolescence is the last, as well as the largest, in a series of oscillations.

The data obtained confirmed the presence of a significant percentage of subjects during middle childhood and early adolescence who are described by parents as "atypical" when compared with subjects of the same age, but who are not referred to the Health Services. The number identified in this survey was approximately 4 times as many as those who were referred to the Health Services.

FROM PARENTAL PERCEPTION TO RECOGNITION OF THE SIGNIFICANCE OF A PSYCHIATRIC DISTURBANCE

Who are these children who, even though seen to have problems, are not referred to the Mental Health Services for Children and Adolescents? How much does the type of disturbance count in such nonreferral? What are the signs of strain which parents see, but do not recognize as a significant disturbance?

Together with the Association for Health Assistance of a large company, we are conducting a Campaign for Mental Health in Children and Adolescents, offering parents the possibility of consultations with a psychologist to "deal with small problems in order to avoid serious problems."

Table 14.2 *Second Research Project: Sample Composition and CBCL Score Distribution for Each Age Group*

	<6 yrs.	6–8 yrs.	9–10 yrs.	11–12 yrs.	13–14 yrs.	>14 yrs.	Totals
Number of subjects	490	364	258	241	278	70	1702
Normal range scores	369	274	174	159	193	48	1217
Clinical range scores	121	90	84	82	85	22	485
% clinical range scores	24.7	24.7	32.5	19.7	30.6	31.4	28.5

In this second research project, compilation of the parental CBCL results was followed by direct observation and examination, by means of semistructured clinical interviews with both parents and children, as well as by a series of projective, psychodiagnostic tests for the latter. All subjects shown by CBCL to be positive, together with a corresponding number of control cases, were included in this second project.

During the first two years of the research project, 1,711 CBCL results were collected (equal to 30% of the total sample of 5,000 families; see Table 14.2) including ages ranging from 4 to 15 years old.[1]

The percentage of positive CBCLs was 28.5% of the sample who returned the questionnaire and 8.5% of the entire target population, and therefore covers about two-thirds of the total "clinical" group defined by the previous research project.

Results for different age groups also are comparable to what was described above. With due caution, we feel it is therefore possible to use the data arising from a clinical observation of this sample (not, in itself, representative of the target population) to understand what happens in the general population.[2]

We present here data for the first 258 of 486 cases with CBCL results in the clinical range. Given that our interest lies in the relationship between parental perception of clinical problems and the actual presence of psychopathological disturbances, we do not take into account false negative scores for which such a perception of clinical problems seems to be absent.

Clinical examination (Table 14.3) led to a clinical diagnosis in 146 subjects (56.6% of cases with CBCL scores in the clinical range). At the time of this observation only about 5% of diagnosed cases were already referred to the Health Services.

Distribution by age group shows a lower percentage of clinical diagnoses in the under-6 years age group and in the 13–14 years

Table 14.3 *Second Research Project: Clinical Status of the Sample for Each Age Group*

	No problems		At risk		Pathology		Total
	n	*%*	*n*	*%*	*n*	*%*	*n*
< 6 yrs.	14	32.5	23	41.1	19	33.9	56
6–8 yrs.	5	11.6	9	18.7	34	70.8	48
9–10 yrs.	6	13.9	10	21.7	30	65.2	46
11–12 yrs.	4	9.3	13	27.1	31	64.6	48
13–14 yrs.	14	32.5	14	27.4	23	45.1	51
14 yrs.	0	0	0	0	9	100	9
Total	43		69		146		258

age group, while in the small group above the age of 14, all positive CBCLs correspond to a real psychopathological disturbance. Another 69 subjects (26.3% of observed cases) demonstrate problematical features not classifiable or putting them at high developmental risk. This percentage of children at risk exceeds 40% in subjects under the age of 6 years.

An analysis of the distribution of clinical diagnoses according to DSM-IV (American Psychiatric Association, 1994) criteria (Table 14.4) shows a large group of neuropsychological or cognitive disturbances (language and learning disabilities, in which the behavior described by parents appears secondary to a nonrecognition of the fundamental disturbance). These are followed by depression (major depression and dysthymic syndromes) and anxiety disorders.

Table 14.4 *Second Research Project: Clinical Diagnoses of the Sample with CBCL in the Clinical Range*

	number	%
No problems	43	16.6
At risk	69	26.3
Depression	34	13.2
Anxiety	23	8.9
Language or learning disability	48	18.6
Tic, stuttering, enuresis	10	3.8
ADD/conduct disorder	4	1.5
PDD	3	1.2
Personality disorder	24	9.3
Total	258	100

The presence of pervasive developmental disorders and personality disorders[3] is significant, given their low prevalence rate epidemiologically, while attention deficit disorders and conduct disorders are practically absent.

The parent's ability to identify a child's problems "correctly" as a psychiatric disorder increases with the child's age, which corresponds to the following age-related clinical diagnostic pattern: at a younger age, a positive CBCL more often corresponds to developing problems or to family-risk situations rather than to clearly definable disturbances. In the early phase of adolescence, the capacity of parents to perceive real pathological disturbances is again seen to diminish, given that many behavioral patterns typical of this age group are viewed as reflecting transient developmental problems.

On the whole, nonrecognition of a psychopathological disorder seems more frequent in disturbances with internalizing symptomatology, while problems causing major disturbance that have an impact on social groups seem, more commonly, to lead to a consultation.

FACTORS AFFECTING RECOGNITION OF A PSYCHIATRIC DISTURBANCE

We will now analyze in more detail some of the data relating to the more frequently seen psychopathological diagnoses (anxiety, depression, and personality disorders).

For each group, apart from the characteristics of the disorder, consideration was given to factors that might influence whether or not a parent would refer the child for evaluation: (a) parameters relative to parental perception of the disturbance; (b) the possible presence of stressful events, such as other severe illnesses or disturbances in the family unit; and (c) earlier clinical case-histories predating the survey (Table 14.5). These elements seem to be the most pertinent in the psychological process which leads from identification of problematic behavior to the recognition of a psychiatric disturbance and referral to the Health Services.

A qualitative analysis of the typology of individual disturbances has shown a notable symptomatological similarity with cases normally to be found in clinics, with a tendency towards an increased number, in our sample, of cases with low symptom severity and

Table 14.5   *Second Research Project: Factors Influencing the Referral Process*

		Depression		Anxiety		Personality disorder	
		n	%	n	%	n	%
Parental awareness	None	13	38.2	6	26.1	12	50.0
	Confused	15	44.1	11	47.8	7	29.1
	Focused	6	17.6	6	26.1	5	20.8
	Total	34		23		24	
Stressful events	None	10	29.4	4	17.4	0	0
	Psychiatric	11	32.3	9	39.1	19	79.1
	Organic	5	14.7	6	26.1	0	0
	Divorce	8	23.5	4	17.4	5	20.8
	Total	34		23		24	
Previous psychiatric consultations	None	26	76.5	19	82.6	10	41.6
	Isolated	8	23.5	2	8.7	12	50
	Continuous	0	0	2	8.7	2	8.3
	Total	34		23		24	

with less interference in interpersonal relationships and academic achievement.

With regard to the frequency of these disturbances in a clinical population (i.e., people referred to the Health Services), attention must be drawn to the high frequency, in the sample, of personality disorders, which are less often noted in children and adolescents as part of a clinical population.

Stressful situations within the family (Table 14.5), apart from constituting incidental factors, can also hinder adequate parental attention to children and their problems. These stressful situations are present in differing forms throughout each different diagnostic group. A psychiatric problem in one parent is present in most cases of personality disorders and in approximately a third of other disturbances. Serious organic illnesses in the family unit are more frequently associated with anxiety disorders, while the absence of a parent seems to characterize cases of depression.

Even though problematic situations were reported by the parent in the questionnaire (note that we examined only subjects with a CBCL in the clinical range on at least one of the scales), during clinical consultation only one third of the parents (Table 14.5) seemed able to identify their child's problem area correctly. For the most part, parental awareness appeared confused (focusing on noncrucial problems), and in a significant percentage (up to 50% in personality disorders) the described behavior was attributed to factors pertaining to temper, upbringing, and environment, with a total lack of recognition of the strain and suffering in the child.

This altered perception of disturbance is associated, in most cases, with little or no use of a suitable Health Service (Table 14.5). Among less serious cases there is a prevailing lack of any form of consultation, while in cases of personality disorders half of the subjects had isolated contact with various specialists not resulting in a specific diagnosis or course of treatment.

With regard to the relationship between parents and children or adolescents, we can distinguish two opposing tendencies: In anxiety disorders and some dysthymic cases, child behavior is seen as a personality trait, often in common with one of the parents, and not as a manifestation of strain or suffering. In cases of open conflict between parents, the child and his or her behavior are used as part of the conflict. In this way the disturbance is not questioned, but rather contained (and sometimes cultivated) within the family circle and family history, eventually becoming an integral part of them.

In other cases, predominantly in personality disorders, the child's psychic strain is perceived by a parent, but often confused with his or her own. The child's behavior is interpreted in terms of upbringing or is read as action against the parents. Child and disturbance are therefore identified and experienced as a threat and are both contested and rejected as a whole: they are seen as fastidious and disturbing. In this way, eventually, the very existence of the problem is negated.

DISCUSSION

The lack of referral to the Health Services among many children and adolescents with psychopathological disturbances (even when diagnosed as such) is a phenomenon present in a significant percentage of the child population and seems to be the consequence of several factors, potentially linked in a causal chain. Disturbances of low clinical significance, above all when connected with stressful family situations, form an interpretative context in which observed behavior is explained in terms of family relationships and events, and so rejected or masked and therefore protected. Even when parents' worries reach such a level that they seek professional help, confused objectives and low levels of family compliance (together with Health Service difficulties) result in diagnostic and therapeutic failure.

The confirmed presence of a significant percentage of children and adolescents with a structured psychiatric disorder that is unrecognized and untreated gives rise to reflection not only on the need to put information and awareness programs focused on psychopathological disturbances in children and adolescents into action, but also on the necessity of modifying Health Service structures in order to respond to this kind of problem. This is in addition to the need for further examination of theoretical observations about the path from the presence of a psychological problem to its definition as a case requiring referral to the Health Services.

NOTES

1. The percentage of participants in the campaign seems comparable to those in other undertakings by the same company with regard to nonpsychiatric illness.
2. The "clinical" group of research subjects identified seems to be a sample predominantly extending the number of "worried parents" who respond. In contrast, parents of children and adolescents with disturbances who were already referred and diagnosed did not generally participate in the program.
3. We use the term *personality disorder* to indicate those psychopathological disturbances not classifiable on axis I which, under clinical observation, manifest distortion in the process of personality formation accompanied by behavioral disturbances.

REFERENCES

Achenbach, T. M. (1991). *Manual for the Child Behavior Checklist/4–18 and 1991 Profile*. Burlington, VT: University of Vermont, Dept. of Psychiatry.
American Psychiatric Association (1994). *Diagnostic and Statistical Manual of Mental Disorders*, IV ed., Washington, DC.

Boyle, M. H., Offord, D. R., Hofman, H. G., Catlin, G. P., Byles, J. A., Cadman D. T., Crawford, J. W., Links, P. S., Rae-Grant, N. I., & Szatmari, P. (1987). Ontario Child Health Study, *Archives of General Psychiatry*, *44*, 826–836.

Costello, E. J., Burns, B. J., Angold, A., & Leaf, P.J. (1993). How can epidemiology improve mental heath services for children and adolescents?, *Journal of the American Academy of Child and Adolescent Psychiatry*, *32*(6), 1106–1117.

Levi, G., & Meledandri, G. (1994). Epidemiologia dei disturbi psicopatologici nell'età evolutiva. Rapporto preliminare. Parte I-II. *Federazione Medica*, *2–3*, 11–18.

Rutter, M. (1989). Isle of Wight revisited: Twenty-five years of child psychiatric epidemiology, *Journal of the American Academy of Child and Adolescent Psychiatry*, *28*, 633–653.

Verhulst, F. C., & Koot, H. M. (1992). *Child Psychiatric Epidemiology*, Newbury Park, CA: Sage.

15

The Mental Health Team in the Daycare Center: The Role of the Child and Adolescent Psychiatrist

MIGUEL CHERRO-AGUERRE

The present communication reports the experience of 7 years of work accomplished in daycare centers, during which we explored the role of a mental health team, and particularly that of a child and adolescent psychiatrist, in such institutions. Furthermore, as a consequence of the knowledge gathered during that work, we present a model of multidisciplinary and integrated work.

Goals

Through this work we will: (a) describe the experience of our university clinic during the last 7 years in daycare centers in poor neighborhoods; (b) discuss the role of the child and adolescent psychiatrist in that work; and (c) propose a model of multidisciplinary and integrated work that emerged from that experience.

Background

During the past 7 years a team from the Child and Adolescent Psychiatric Clinic of the Pereira Rossell Hospital in Montevideo, Uruguay, worked continuously in two places, a daycare center and a "day home," both located in poor areas. The different denominations, daycare center vs. day home, is due only to administrative-institutional reasons, since both institutions offer practically identical services. One of them is supported by the government of Montevideo, and the other by the national government of Uruguay. It is interesting to consider that those governments correspond to different political and ideological orientations. From now on, I will refer to both daycare centers and day homes simply as daycare centers (DCCs).

DCCs provide assistance to children 0 to 5 years of age, both of whose parents work. These children attend the center daily from 9:00 AM to 4:00 PM.

The presence of our team in the DCCs responds to a developmental model that considers the individual as a biopsychosocial being and that emphasizes the generation of health in the milieu of the daycare. In that conceptual framework, we understand mental health as one of the major components of general health. Our interventions in DCCs are community programs, since we leave the hospital and move into the community, specifically two neighborhoods of Montevideo, Cerro and Jardines. We will describe two phases in our work: one from 1989 to 1993, and the other from 1994 to early 1996.

During the first period, our presence in the two centers was established and consolidated. We integrated our team into that of the DCCs through the continuity of our work. The population assisted annually during that period comprised 135 children.

After 1994 our work expanded, and we covered up to 14 DCCs. This was made possible by a work contract signed between our clinic and the government of Montevideo. The population assisted annually in this period was estimated as 800 children (Figure 15.1).

Our work will be expanded even further if the plan we submitted to the National Institute of Childhood (a state agency) is accepted. If this happens, it would mean initiating a pilot project at four new DCCs run by the Institute. The intention is to utilize the plan for this pilot project as a model that would later encompass the entire country. The present paper summarizes, then, our 7 years of community work in DCCs and proposes a model of integrated work based on the experience and knowledge that we acquired through it.

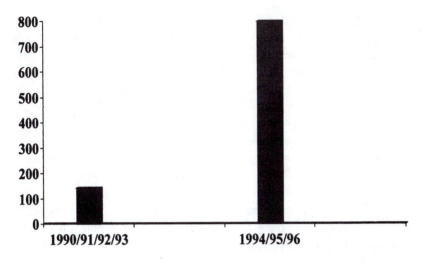

Figure 15.1   *Number of children in daycare centers in Montevideo assisted by mental health team in two phases of the program*

DESCRIPTION OF THE FUNCTIONS AND ROLE OF A MENTAL HEALTH TEAM IN A DCC

Our hospital clinic is part of the Medical School of the University of the Republic, but due to an agreement, it is located in a hospital of the Ministry of Public Health. The Director of the clinic leads and orients the staffs of both institutions. The clinic staff, especially psychiatrists and psychologists, are organized in medical-psychological teams and see patients together most of the time.

Our clinic undertakes clinical care, teaching, and research tasks. One of the basic concerns is the Graduate Training Program for Child and Adolescent Psychiatrists. One of the curricular assignments in our graduate program is attending DCCs at two different levels of training. Two mornings a week, our team, formed by residents of the third rotation and graduate students of the first and fourth levels, goes to the community DCC accompanied by teacher supervisors. First-level students observe normal development and learn to detect risk factors. Fourth-level students and residents confirm the presence or absence of risk in the cases presented by first-level students and handle clinical problems, either providing supervision or making the proper recommendation.

The team as a whole participates regularly in a meeting with the DCC staff to give advice about normal development and offer management hints for complex cases. The team also deals with staff in relation to demands referring to conflict situations in the team, proposals of activities such as workshops for personnel or parents or both, and administrative issues that need to be discussed by the mental health professionals. When we attend a DCC, our attitude is that of giving maximum respect to the unique contextual characteristics of each DCC, avoiding imposed recipes, and trying to accomplish work plans that meet both our needs and those of the DCC staff.

The aims of a mental health team in a DCC involve the children, the staff, the parents, the graduate students and residents, and multidisciplinary approaches to the work of the DCC.

The Children

Our goal is to promote the adequate development of children, fostering their integration in both the group of peers and the DCC, and offering them creative potential and ethical values. An integrated record for each child is kept. Behavior and development are assessed through observation in group interactions. Eventually, in specific cases, diagnostic interviews can be initiated in order to elaborate a therapeutic strategy.

The Staff

One of the greatest concerns of our team is to increase the staff members' self-esteem and to acknowledge the social impact of the service they provide. We try to rescue the staff from the disappointment and demoralization generated by the lack of recognition and appreciation in our society towards those who work in the education or health fields. We offer support and guidance concerning adequate management of children according to the different stages of development. We help staff members develop skills that allow them to recognize the stages of development, the conflicting needs that each stage brings about, and the best ways to cope with them. There are regular meetings with all the staff in order to recognize and discuss the tensions generated during the group work. Periodic meetings also are held with the neighborhood committee that administers the DCC.

The Parents

The main goal is to integrate parents into the tasks of the center, engaging them in collaborative management. When we first joined the DCC 7 years ago we found that one of the worst problems was the lack of parent presence and participation in the center's program.

We tried to solve the problem through different actions. For example, we organized educational-recreational workshops leading to sensitization and reflection. In these workshops, there were activities that facilitated communication between parents or between the parents and the center's team. In some situations parents empathically had to take their children's place. Likewise, topics of interest for parents were brought up in order to think together about them. Moreover, we held regular meetings with parents so that we could obtain information about the children or give assistance with the management of problems the parents found troublesome. A distinct feature of our DCC program is that it develops plans that take into account not only the children but also their caregivers (either their parents or whoever else takes that role) and the caregivers on the center's staff.

Residents and Graduate Students

Residents of the third rotation and first- and fourth-level graduate students work at the DCC. There are nine residents in our clinic, divided into three rotations of three residents each. Residents are graduates who obtain the position through a competitive examination. They work for 3 years, 8 hours a day, and receive a salary. Graduate students who have chosen our field receive their degree after a 4–year course that demands 4 hours of clinical work every morning. The educational aim of this clinical work varies according to the level of the graduate student.

In the case of first-level graduate students, the goal is the acquisition of observational skills regarding the different stages of development. Through observation, they learn about normal development and about risk factors and how to detect risks that may affect normal development.

For fourth-level students and residents, the aim is the promotion of clinical knowledge and abilities in the management of specific situations. They are also involved in teaching, since they must supervise the management of risk situations detected by first-level students.

For all graduate students and residents, the intention is for them to acquire the necessary skills to manage group situations, to form coordinated multidisciplinary teams, and to participate in workshops and in administrative coordination.

Multidisciplinary Team

By multidisciplinary, we mean a group of professionals from different fields that work together in a DCC. In our case, those fields are: education, pediatrics, psychiatry, psychology, physical therapy, music, art, social work, and dentistry.

Our goal for multidisciplinary work is cooperative effort in order to offer the center's staff members an integrated model that supports and sustains their work and gives relevance to their activities.

It was this concern, based on evaluations carried out at different stages of our work, that led us to conceive the "Model of Multidisciplinary Integrated Work" which we describe in the following section.

MODEL OF MULTIDISCIPLINARY INTEGRATED WORK

This model was developed, first, as a consequence of our frequent verification that in schools there is a summation of disciplines rather than an integration of them, and, second, in recognition of the need to return to educators the leading role that they deserve. In order to offer children stimuli of a diverse nature, schools and DCCs frequently expose them to, for example, bodily experience through psychomotor or physical education, together with musical, artistic, and mental health experiences. This exposure comes through the different disciplines, each of which generally has its own program, without any prior coordination among them. Thus, the program is neither integrated nor coordinated. It is as if the musicians of an orchestra played without accepting the direction of the conductor's baton. By working without coordination and/or integration, the DCC can expose the child to a disjointed and even chaotic world.

On the one hand, we consider that the modern world, through its different features, exposes the child to unsettling and turbulent stimuli that are in opposition to the humanitarian and altruistic goals that promote mental health. On the other hand, we have to take into account that human beings from a very early age have the natural capacity to transfer an experience felt through a specific sensory modality to all the other sensory modes, even though they have not had direct experience in them. That capacity of the human infant is known as amodal perception.

Daniel Stern (1985) referred to experiments to illustrate amodal perception, which he describes as the innate general capacity that infants possess to take information received in one sensory modality and transfer it to another sensory modality. This relatively new knowledge, discovered by research examining young babies' behavior, has great value for understanding the incredible programming that allows the human baby to face the world with a great integrating and generalizing capacity.

It is interesting to note the similarity between the structure of metaphor, one of the cornerstones of the symbolic world as well as poetic art, and the characteristics of amodal perception.

It seems, then, logical and rational that the models of work we offer the child agree with these inborn characteristics. In our model, children would discover their bodies through the discovery of the world and its colors, smells, and shapes, in a harmonious, coordinated, and integrated way. This presupposes a great amount of humility, creativity, respect, imagination, tolerance, and engagement from all the members of the multidisciplinary team, as well as in the disciplines themselves. It also presupposes that our teaching adequately encompasses the knowledge arrived at by scientific research.

In relation to the plan we have submitted to the National Institute of Childhood, and the suggestions we have given for the DCCs run by municipal authorities, concerning the project "Our Children" for 1996, the Model of Multidisciplinary Integrated Work involves the coordination of the following disciplines: mental health, psychomotor development, music, physical education, and the arts. As we mentioned above, this model was previously discussed and agreed upon among all disciplines. It must meet the needs of educators and the context of each center, so that in the future it can be implemented by them. At the same time, we try to coordinate the other disciplines involved: pediatrics, dentistry, social work, nutrition, etc. Nevertheless, this coordination does not mean the level of shared, interactive management implied by the Model of Multidisciplinary Integrated Work.

It is our belief that the model that we are proposing, developed from a rich field experience, is genuinely beneficial for the education of children aged 0–5. That conviction would lack scientific rigor if it were not accompanied by evaluation guidelines that verify whether the impact of the model is positive or not and, if we find it positive, that reliably determine its magnitude. The length of this paper does not permit a detailed description of these evaluation guidelines.

To finish, I should say that the Model of Multidisciplinary Integrated Work is but the natural response to the knowledge and the challenge that we perceived in the community, once we became receptive to its needs and concerns.

ACKNOWLEDGMENTS

I want to thank the authorities of the Medical School of the University of the Republic, the Ministry of Public Health, the National Institute of Childhood, and the government of the city of Montevideo, for making the work in daycare centers possible. I would also like to thank the children, parents, staff, and commissioners of the daycare centers, and the residents, teachers and colleagues of our clinic, who carried out this work.

REFERENCE

Stern, D. (1984). *The interpersonal world of the infant* (p. 51) New York: Basic Books.

16

Can Home Treatment Replace Inpatient Treatment of Child and Adolescent Psychiatric Disorders?

M. H. SCHMIDT

B. BLANZ

C. GÖPEL

B. LAY

INTRODUCTION

When planning for the needs for community-based treatment of children and adolescents with severe psychiatric disorders, besides the traditional treatment in inpatient or day care units, alternative therapeutic concepts have to be taken into account. Treatment in the home environment of a child (home treatment) is one alternative concept with the following advantages:

- Affected children or youth remain in the environments to which they are accustomed. Thus, disturbed behavior impairing everyday functioning can be influenced directly in the surroundings familiar to them. In addition, separation from the family, which often is experienced as a trauma (especially in younger children), can be avoided. Furthermore, nursery school or school are continued and social contacts are kept up.
- Patients with strong resistance against inpatient treatment (e.g., eating-disordered adolescents) become more compliant.
- Automatically, the contact between the therapist and the significant people around the child becomes closer. The child's caregivers are

directly involved in the therapeutic process, improving their understanding and parenting competence. Thus, modification of the behavior of the significant individuals influencing the psychosocial
environment can be achieved more easily. This is often more difficult
to change than the behavior of the child or youth.

- Apart from symptom reduction, treatment of severe child and adolescent psychiatric disorders includes improvement of everyday functioning. But the transfer of such positive changes from an inpatient
setting to the natural living conditions of the child, in many cases,
either fails to succeed to the required degree or requires special
interventions. In home treatment, such transitional problems do
not arise.
- Home treatment is cost-efficient. The costs are reckoned to amount
to less than half of the costs for treatment in inpatient or day care
units. This aspect of economical management of financial resources
is an important argument, and not only in times of limited financial resources.

But home treatment cannot be applied to all children or youths
with psychiatric disorders. There are the following contraindica-
tions: self–endangering behavior, especially the danger of suicide;
behavior distinctly endangering other persons, such as aggressive
outbursts or maltreatment of parents; extremely severe disorders
requiring continuous control and supervision; child maltreatment or
sexual abuse by a member of the family; and marked psychiatric
disorder of the child's caregiving individual. Furthermore, if the
caregiving individuals urgently need to be relieved of the strain
caused by the child's disturbed behavior, if the child has to be removed from the caregiving individual's influence, or if coping with
separating from the caregiving individuals is an aim of therapy, then
home treatment is unsuitable for the child or youth.

The presence and cooperation of at least one significant caregiving individual is an important requirement for home treatment.
For practical reasons, the child's home must lie within a radius of
30 kilometers from the institution offering home treatment. Home
treatment can only serve as an alternative to inpatient treatment if
the disorders show a minimum severity comparable to disorders
treated in inpatient units. To our present knowledge, only about
10% to 15% of inpatients meet all these requirements for home
treatment (Remschmidt & Schmidt, 1988).

In studies evaluating the effectiveness of home treatment in children and adolescents with psychiatric disorders, no difference could be found compared to the effectiveness of inpatient or day care treatment (Remschmidt & Schmidt, 1988; Winsberg, 1980). In the present study a modified question is examined: whether home treatment carried out by an experienced nurse supervised by a clinician is as effective as inpatient treatment (Blanz & Schmidt, 1996).

METHODS

The study included patients aged 6–16 years with at least average cognitive abilities (IQ ≥ 85), whose severity of psychiatric symptomatology would have required inpatient treatment. For reasons of comparability with the effects of inpatient treatment, diagnoses occurring in less than 4% of the inpatients were excluded. Inpatients matched for age, gender, diagnosis, and degree of impairment served as a control group.

The patients meeting inclusion criteria and their parents were given detailed information about home treatment, including what it means, offers, and requires. Both parents had to give their consent, and the presence of at least one parent during treatment was required. These families were admitted to the treatment program. Therefore, assignment to the home treatment group was not randomized but optional. It was considered that motivation and compliance might be better in a self-chosen than in an assigned treatment modality.

The instruments used for diagnostic assessment included general and specific features of disorders. In particular, they included assessment of symptomatology, diagnosis, severity of disorder, various aspects of social functioning, and overall impairment (for a detailed description of instruments, see Göpel, Schmidt, Blanc, & Rettig, 1996). The instruments were applied to both the home treatment group and the inpatient control group prior to and at the end of treatment. Additionally, in both groups, the treated child, the parents, and the therapist were asked to judge the subjectively perceived therapeutic effects in 4 week intervals. One year after the end of treatment, both groups were to be followed up; this is still in progress.

Compared to the previous study, in which child and adolescent psychiatrists treated the patients at home (Remschmidt & Schmidt, 1988), the actual treatment in the present study was carried out by nurses specializing in child and adolescent psychiatry. They were instructed and supervised by a child and adolescent psychiatrist once a week, analogous to inpatient practice, in which therapy is planned by clinicians and the child's behavior is mainly modified by the nursing and educational staff. Besides, from an economical viewpoint this simplification could justify future implementation of the home treatment concept to the service sector of healthcare. Basic elements of therapy were behavior therapy-oriented interventions and counseling for the caregiving individuals which aimed at improving their parenting competence. Within the first month of treatment, there were approximately two direct therapeutic contacts per week, each lasting several hours. At the beginning of the second month they were reduced to one direct contact per week, and, depending on the need, substituted for by a weekly intensive telephone consultation within the second or, at the latest, the third month of therapy.

RESULTS

To date, 42 patients (25 males, 17 females; mean age, 11.4 years, $SD = 3.1$) have been treated by home treatment with the diagnoses of phobic anxiety disorders ($n = 2$), obsessive-compulsive disorders ($n = 3$), eating disorders ($n = 5$), Asperger's syndrome ($n = 3$), hyperkinetic disorders ($n = 20$), conduct disorders ($n = 5$), and mixed disorders of conduct and emotions ($n = 4$).

Mean duration of treatment was 3.5 months ($SD = 1.0$), comprising 38 hours ($SD = 11.0$) of direct contact with the patient or the caregivers. On average, the therapist had 20 hours ($SD = 5.0$) of personal contact with the patient, 19 hours ($SD = 4.0$) with the parents, and 3 hours with the grandparents or teachers, and gave on average 8 ($SD = 5.0$) telephone consultations. Furthermore, a mean time of 5.7 hours ($SD = 1.0$) in direct contact with the family was expended for scientific evaluation.

Data analysis shows a highly significant result: home treatment improved all outcome variables investigated, in particular, symptomatology, severity of disorder, degree of impairment, and various levels of functioning (family relations, school performance, social interactions, leisure interests, independence, school behavior). Moreover, the patients, parents, and therapists each reported at least a 90% improvement in the overall problems.

At this point, 20 patients treated by home treatment have been compared with 20 inpatients matched for age, gender, diagnosis, and degree of impairment (15 males and 5 females in each group; mean age 11.2 years, $SD = 3.1$). The corresponding pairs had an ICD-10 diagnosis of obsessive-compulsive disorders ($n = 1$), eating disorders ($n = 2$), Asperger's syndrome ($n = 2$), hyperkinetic disorders ($n = 9$), conduct disorders ($n = 3$), or mixed disorders of conduct and emotions ($n = 3$). In examining the effects of therapy, no difference could be found between home treatment and inpatient treatment. The 1-year follow-up of the initial 12 home treatment patients also showed that the improvements achieved remained stable over the year.

DISCUSSION

To date, 42 children and adolescents with severe psychiatric disorders conventionally requiring inpatient treatment have been treated by home treatment. Highly significant improvements were found in symptomatology, severity of disorder, degree of impairment, and deficits in various fields of functioning. Based on the results of the initial 20 patient-control pairs investigated, the therapeutic effects of home treatment were comparable to those of inpatient treatment (Blanz & Schmidt, 1996; Göpel et al., 1996). The incomplete 1-year follow-up shows that the improvements achieved by home treatment remain stable.

High motivation and compliance of the child's significant caregivers are required for the success of home treatment. Our present experience is that both are promoted if the specialized nurse is, in general, familiar with the living conditions of families with children. Even if the initial conditions are optimal, the home treatment patient cannot be structured and monitored as comprehensively as the inpatient. In difficult situations, parents have to rely on their acquired cotherapeutic competencies. In this context telephone consultation proved to be an essential support.

According to these results, home treatment is as effective as inpatient treatment regarding improvement in symptomatology, as well as severity of disorder and social adjustment. It was also shown that home treatment can be carried out successfully by experienced specialized nurses, provided that they are instructed and regularly supervised by a child and adolescent psychiatrist. Therefore, home treatment does not necessarily have to be performed directly by a child psychiatrist or clinical psychologist.

Our experience suggests that one experienced therapist can treat 4 patients simultaneously by the above-described procedure. Despite the time and costs required for preparation of therapy, for traveling, and for supervision, home treatment is distinctly more cost-efficient than inpatient treatment.

The future aim of this study is to compare, in total, 120 courses of treatment (home treatment group, $n = 60$; inpatient control group, $n = 60$), using for example, the judgement of experts who are blind to the applied treatment modality. In the same way, diagnosis-specific evaluation of the achieved therapeutic effects is planned. The evaluation will aim at several specific questions, such as (a) under which circumstances certain psychiatric disorders can be improved by home treatment, and (b) which psychiatric disorders (or the child's environmental conditions) can be influenced less successfully by home treatment and therefore will require other treatment modalities. In this manner, the basis for differentiated indicators for home treatment will be developed.

REFERENCES

Blanz, B., & Schmidt, M. H. (1996, July). *The outcome of home treatment compared to inpatient treatment of children with psychiatric disorders.* Paper presented at the 8th Congress of the Association of European Psychiatrists, London, England.

Göpel, C., Schmidt, M. H., Blanz, B., & Rettig, B. (1996). Behandlung hyperkinetischer Kinder im häuslichen Milieu. *Zeitschrift für Kinder- und Jugendpsychiatrie, 24,* 192–202.

Remschmidt, H., & Schmidt, M. H. (1988). Therapieevaluation in der Kinder- und Jugendpsychiatrie: stationäre Behandlung, tagesklinische Behandlung und Home-Treatment im Vergleich. *Zeitschrift für Kinder- und Jugendpsychiatrie, 16,* 124–134.

Winsberg, B. H. (1980). Home vs. Hospital care of children with behavior disorders. *Archives of General Psychiatry, 37,* 413–418.

17

Mental Health Services for Infants and Young Children

LINDA C. MAYES

The subspecialty of child psychiatry that focuses on the mental health needs of infants and preschool-aged children is itself a young field. Only within the last two to three decades has it been appreciated that very young children may have unique and sometimes severe mental health and developmental problems that require special developmentally tailored interventions. The mental health needs of preschool-aged children raise several issues that warrant considerations above and beyond those concerns about mental health needs for children and adolescents in general. This chapter will highlight these special considerations, point to different service delivery models, and outline a broad research agenda for the mental health needs of infants and preschool children. First we turn to those nosological issues that make considerations of mental health services for very young children a special area.

DEFINITIONAL BOUNDARIES

Models of mental health services for young children vary according to the discipline evaluating and treating the child, the prevailing theoretical emphasis within that discipline or that individual practitioner, the explicit goals of the intervention, the diagnostic nosology relied upon, and the characteristics of a particular community or culture vis-à-vis work with young children and families. These five areas are clearly interrelated and influence one another.

As to variations among disciplines, in the first years of life there is a less clear distinction among psychological or psychiatric, educational, or neurologic interventions. For very young children, each approach is relevant to considerations of the child's "mental health" or mental development. Educational interventions may focus more on the child's adaptation to a given environment or set of developmental tasks and in particular on enhancing the child's adaptive behaviors so as to maximize opportunities for social-cognitive development. Neurological interventions may emphasize remediation and improving physical/motor skills as an adjunct to enhancing adaptive and cognitive skills. Child psychiatric or psychological interventions may focus on those areas of development in which there are delays or apparent maladaptive behaviors as well as on the place of the child in the family and the parents' actions and feelings toward the child. Each focus captures an essential element of development in very young children and none is mutually exclusive of the other. Indeed, this is why, for very young children, mental health services are often conceptualized, if not delivered, by a team of professionals, each consulting with one another and with the family. As we will discuss under alternative models for mental health services with young children, this team may function as a unit or as individual clinicians with whom the family interacts individually. These two models of multidisciplinary services (and the variations in between) present different advantages and disadvantages for parents as consumers.

The prevailing theoretical emphasis both within and between disciplines also shapes the nature of the mental health services for infants and very young children. For example, an educational approach to a 4-year-old with behavioral difficulties may be quite different from a child psychiatric approach based on a psychodynamic model of anxiety and activity regulation. The ultimate goals of both interventions may be the same: to help the child develop a repertoire of behaviors and strategies for more successful and adaptive adjustment to peers, school, and home. But the underlying theoretical emphases that guide the interventions are quite different. One may be based primarily on notions of behavioral management, while the other is grounded in a biologic-environment interaction model in which the emergence of central nervous system–based emotional regulatory capacities is shaped by environmental input and activity. For work with infants and young children, very little conceptual work has been done to make explicit the various theoretical foundations for different mental health interventions and how, despite different technical languages, there may be theoretical similarities among educational, psychological, and neurological intervention models.

The explicit goals of the intervention vary not only according to the discipline and the prevailing theoretical emphasis but also according to whom the intervention is directed. For infants and very young children, interventions are frequently directed toward the child's parents, other adult caregivers, or even a daycare or early childhood education classroom. Particularly with younger children, the goal of an intervention may be, for example, to improve the quality of relatedness between parent and child, so-called dyadic work. Intervention goals cannot be discussed in isolation from theoretical underpinnings, though quite often, in clinical settings working with younger children, therapeutic goals as stated may be relatively atheoretical. For example, even the goal of improving dyadic relatedness implicitly involves several different theories. One might be based on notions of early attachment and the creation of early internal working models on which later templates for relationships are founded. Another less dynamic theoretical grounding for an intervention goal, such as improving the quality of dyadic relatedness, might be to facilitate the adults' abilities to recognize and interpret the infant's needs, a social cognition approach.

The particular nosologic approach to diagnosis also lends to variation to definitions and implementation of mental health services. Particularly for infants and young children, categorical diagnoses as defined by DSM-IV (the Diagnostic and Statistical Manual of the American Psychiatric Association) are less defined and phenomenologically less clear. Complex problems such as failure to thrive, sleeping and feeding difficulties, and even language delays are more often symptoms rather than specific diagnoses and usually reflect interactions between biological vulnerabilities and environmental circumstances. Even disorders that are more specific in older children (e.g., anxiety or conduct disorders) are less well demarcated in the preschool age group where increased activity, worries, and rituals may be developmentally normative. Several classification schemas have been proposed for infants and younger children that focus on developmental function and needs (e.g., the regulatory disorder category of the Zero to Three Classification System). Other systems rely on measures of impairment such as degree of developmental delay or severity of delay in adaptive behavior. The diagnostic system used to guide the intervention also reflects, as stated above, the profession evaluating the child and family and providing the services. However, the eclectic and non-uniform approaches to diagnostic nosology for mental health problems in infants and young children limit the ability to compare responses to different intervention modalities among diagnostic profiles.

The fifth area of special consideration regarding mental health services for infants and young children is the impact of community and cultural standards and expectations. That mental health interventions for young children is a relatively recent field reflects an important shift in understanding the importance of early development, as well as the need for intervening early in order to maximize intervention impact. On a more specific level, however, certain goals of an intervention program that are applicable to young children in one culture may not be appropriate for another. For example, an educational intervention designed to promote greater independence and ability to tolerate separation from home for school may not be acceptable in cultures where children more traditionally spend their preschool years at home. In these instances, mental health interventions need to be conducted in the theoretical and social context of a given culture or community. In turn, the range of mental health services for younger children will vary in both emphasis and implementation according to the prevailing social and cultural milieu in which these are offered.

MODELS OF MENTAL HEALTH INTERVENTION FOR INFANTS AND YOUNG CHILDREN

In this section, we review four different models of mental health services for infants and young children. These are parent-focused interventions, interventions working with parents and children together, school-based consultation and intervention, and individual work with the child. These models are neither pure nor exclusive. Individual work with a child is often combined with consultation with schools and parent-focused interventions. We review these in their general and more common forms to highlight the variety and special nature of mental health interventions for very young children.

In the last couple of decades, particularly in the United States, where federal legislation (Public Law 99–457, 1986) encouraged it, there has been a renewed recognition of the importance of early development in setting the stage for later social and cognitive adaptation. With the mandating of services for children with special developmental needs comes the parallel requirement for detection and assessment. It should be emphasized that all early detection and assessment programs, whether based in educational or well-child-care systems, do not as a rule access emotional or psychological health in very young children. Rather, the primary emphasis is usually on motor, intellectual, language, and social development. This means that children with, for example, problems in anxiety regulation may not meet eligibility criteria for educational interventions even though their emotional difficulties may interfere in the long run with their adjustment to school.

While there are actually very few epidemiologic studies of the mental health needs of populations of infants and young children, a few studies from pediatricians' practices in the United States suggest that between 5% to 15% of preschool-age children have developmental and/or psychological problems warranting at least an evaluation (Starfield, 1982; Starfield et al., 1980). Of these, approximately a quarter may have serious enough problems to warrant psychological and/or educational interventions. Again, as suggested in the preceeding section, the definition of mental health needs varies according to a number of parameters, so these percentages may be difficult to generalize without greater specificity and agreement across disciplines and theoretical perspectives as to what constitute psychological/mental health needs in young children. Nonetheless, by most criteria, these estimates point to a significant number of young children that would benefit from mental health and/or psychoeducational intervention in the preschool years. When populations at increased risk are examined (e.g., premature infants, children of substance-abusing parents), the proportion that would benefit from mental health interventions increases dramatically. For example, as many as half of young children from substance-abusing families may have significant problems with attention, anxiety, and disruptive behavior before the age of 5.

Parent-Focused Interventions

Interventions for infants and younger children that function primarily through work with parents are based on the quasi-theoretical principal that helping parents indirectly affects their young children. These changes are mediated directly, through changes in parental attitude and behavior and indirectly through improved parental confidence, decreased stress, and increased social support (Meisels, Dichtelmiller, & Liaw, 1993). Familiar models include early interventions for maternal postpartum depression in which the parent is so psychologically compromised as to be unable to care for the infant (Zahn-Waxler, Cummings, Iannotti, Radke-Yarrow, 1984). Other approaches include working directly with parents about such problems as sleep disturbances, feeding difficulties, or conduct/behavioral problems in their infants or toddlers. With any one of these issues, the intervention with parents focuses on one or more of the following areas: (a) understanding how adults view their role as parents and the meaning of the baby to them; (b) instruction regarding basic information about child development; (c) behavioral guidance (e.g., specific behavioral approaches to repeated night waking or temper tantrums); (d) instruction and modeling of developmentally appropriate ways to communicate with infants and young children; (e) individual interventions for parents regarding their own psychological concerns. Certain of these interventions may be delivered either one-on-one or as a group, the latter affording parents the opportunity to learn from one another and develop a support network among themselves.

Affecting the infant and young child through work with parents is a technique also contained in the family support model. In the mid-1970s in the United States, changing socioeconomic conditions and the failure of existing social service systems to address the needs of a growing number of families in poverty led to the development of the family resource/support movement (Weissbourd & Kagan, 1989). Individual programs in the family support model are quite different from one another, but all are united by a focus on enhancing parental competency by providing a community resource addressing a range of family needs. Some family support programs provide direct services to parents, while others offer a range of educational, social, and recreational activities. There may be parent-child classes, in-home support workers, and access to telephone support lines. Programs may be geared toward specific life situations such as a family crisis precipitated by child abuse or neglect or family violence. Staffing includes mixtures of professionals, paraprofessionals, and volunteers. Programs may be free-standing or integrated within a school, hospital or mental health clinic.

Interventions for Parents and Children Together

While no mental health intervention for young children can be accomplished without the participation of parents or caring adults, there is an increasingly practiced model of delivering mental health services to a parent-child dyad. In some cases, these forms of intervention are simply a sum of individual work with a child and individual work with parents performed by the same or different clinicians. Joint work of this nature often consists of direct enrichment or psychotherapeutic work with the child and accompanying education and support for parents. In other forms of parent-child work, parents are seen in the actual presence of their child and helped to read their child's cues and to provide interventions specifically suited to the child's needs. Growing out of interventions that focused primarily on disturbances in attachment between a parent and child, work with the dyad is now applied in a number of different circumstances, including that of toddlers with conduct problems.

Parent-child, or dyadic, interventions are particularly well suited for parents and their infants or preverbal children. The so-called "interaction guidance" (Cramer, 1995; Lieberman, 1985; McDonough, 1993) assists families in understanding their child's behavior and their own responses to that behavior. The model also seeks to foster the development of adults as parents. The central tenet is that efforts to work with parent-child problems take place within the context of the parent-child relationship rather than focusing solely on problems in the child or in the parent. Families are engaged in a therapeutic process by working first with strengths in the parent-child relationship before focusing on the problematic areas. Observations of play between parent and child and using videotapes of the parent-child play as well as other examples of dyadic interactions are among the several techniques used in this particular intervention model. Sessions may be conducted in the home as well as in a clinic. Mental health clinicians from a range of disciplines including child psychiatry, social work, psychology, and nursing practice this model of mental health services for very young children.

School-Based Consultation

Increasingly, a model of mental health service delivery for very young children (as well as for the school-age child) is to see children where they spend much of their day—in daycare, nursery, and kindergarten programs and in special intervention services such as those that provide a comprehensive program of special education, physical and occupational therapy, and language intervention. School-based consultation is a particular challenge for child psychiatrists or neurologists who may not have been sufficiently trained in educational intervention approaches or in observing and evaluating children in the context of a group. Successful consultation to early childhood educational programs requires a common technical language and an evaluative approach that speaks to both the child's strengths and the problems and concerns for which the consultation has been requested. Consultations are sought for a number of reasons, including: (a) advice on whether or not a referral for more extensive evaluation should be considered; (b) questions of classroom behavioral management; and (c) questions regarding normalcy or age adequacy of specific behaviors and capacities. In some models, consultation is provided to the educational staff regarding child developmental issues in general, while in others, consultation is usually about a specific child or family. Combinations of both often work quite well inasmuch as closer working relations with staff through group consultation improve the working alliance between the teachers and the consultants. Depending on the working environment and policy of the program, consultants may also meet directly with parents or participate in parent-teacher meetings.

A much less common model, though one that is familiar in therapeutic nursery programs, is one in which individual psychotherapeutic interventions are offered to the children at the site of their educational program. A room is set aside for the child and therapist to work together; and, just as children often leave their group for speech and language or physical therapy, they also leave for individual work with their psychotherapists. Most applicable to children 4 years old and older, this approach makes psychotherapeutic interventions more readily available to children from families where both parents work and may also cause less disruption in the child's usual day. The therapist usually arranges to meet with the parents, sometimes at the school after hours or in another setting, to keep the parents involved in the treatment and to follow closely the child's development and behavior outside the school and therapeutic session. The particular theoretical approach to the psychotherapy varies according to the theoretical background of the clinician, and the success of such a model requires not only the practical but also psychological acceptance by the school. Therapists may be called upon to provide in-service sessions about the nature of psychotherapy with young children, and to make distinctions between play as used therapeutically and play as used in an educational setting. Issues of confidentiality, what other children know, and what is discussed with teachers require explicit consideration.

Individual Work with Children

It is probably incorrect to single out individual therapeutic work with young children as a model of mental health services in and of itself, for there is no one approach to individual services for infants and preschool children. We single it out to make the point that for very young children, individual mental health services are more broadly defined than for school-aged children and adolescents. These include, in addition to psychotherapy, speech and language therapy, physical and occupational therapy, and work with a child developmentalist or special educator. And very young children, more often than not, are receiving these kinds of individual services simultaneously. For example, psychotherapy with a 4-year-old may also be accompanied by individual speech and language services, and the psychotherapist and speech and language therapist at least consult with one another, if not work in close collaboration. Similarly, as has already been stated, for infants and very young children, never is a psychotherapeutic intervention offered without also working with parents. That work may be as little as regular meetings to report on the progress in the treatment and to gather information or as intensive as a parallel therapeutic intervention with the parents.

Psychotherapeutic work with young children is accomplished by professionals from a number of disciplines in addition to child psychiatry or psychology. Early childhood educators, social workers, and sometimes pediatricians work psychotherapeutically with children 3 years old and older. Theoretical approaches run the gamut for psychodynamic to behavioral management and supportive. There is no consensus or standard set of guidelines for psychotherapeutic work with young children, but there are, in different mental health communities, sets of experiential guidelines often shared by practitioners that cover, for example, preferred frequency of sessions or standard length of treatment.

RESEARCH AGENDA FOR MENTAL HEALTH
SERVICES FOR INFANTS AND YOUNG CHILDREN

A suggested research agenda for mental health services
for this age group has been implied in the preceding paragraphs.
Five areas are among those most pressing:

- Establishment of a theoretically based, diagnostic nosology for behavioral, developmental, and psychological problems among infants
and young children. Such a nosologic classification needs to take
into account what may be developmentally normative for an 18-
month-old (e.g., rituals) and not for a preschool- or kindergarten-
age child. Similarly, recognizing generally the inherent problems
with categorical diagnoses for mental health disorders in children, a
diagnostic nosology for infants and young children needs to be examined in terms of its relation to those diagnostic approaches most
commonly used for older children and adolescents.
- Population-based studies of the prevalence of developmental and
behavioral problems in infants and young children across different
communities and countries, an agenda made feasible by a commonly
available diagnostic nosology for this age group.
- Efforts to codify, or "manualize" the more frequently practiced
models of mental health intervention with young children. The aim
of such an endeavor is not necessarily to insure uniformity of practice
across clinical settings—an impossibility even with the most detailed
of manualized approaches—but rather to make explicit the many
variations in a given therapeutic approach and to permit process and
outcome studies across different clinical settings. A secondary aim
of codification of mental health interventions is also to make explicit
the underlying theoretical principles that guide the intervention.
- Outcome studies, using the first and third agendas as a foundation,
examining, for example, the differential efficacy of working with
parents alone and parent and child together on problems of conduct
and behavior.
- An examination across communities and models of mental health
services of the barriers to accessing such services for the families of
infants and young children. Changing patterns of third party payment
and healthcare reimbursement in countries such as the United States
will have both positive and negative impacts on the ease of access
and availability of mental health services for very young children.
The shape of this impact is yet to be studied.

CONCLUSIONS

In the last three decades, there has been a remarkable increase in knowledge about the first years of life. Most recently, understanding about early brain development and the complex interactions among biology, environment, and experience in shaping early development has highlighted the critical nature of psychological interventions in the first years of life. Mental health services for very young children require a multidisciplinary approach, and the field has evolved simultaneously in the disciplines of child psychiatry, pediatrics, psychology, social work, neurology, early childhood education, and nursing. With that range of theoretical and professional backgrounds, the resulting services are also quite diverse. The agenda for the next decade of work in this area is to bring together these multiple viewpoints around critical areas for the development of the field, including improved diagnostic nosology, a better understanding of the number of young children needing services, pathways for accessing those services, and more explicit descriptions of the important features of a mental health intervention for very young children and their families.

REFERENCES

Cramer, B. (1995). Short-term dynamic psychotherapy for infants and their parents. *Child and Adolescent Psychiatric Clinics of North America, 4,* 649–660.

Lieberman, A. (1985). Infant mental health: A model for service delivery. *Journal of Clinical Child Psychology, 14,* 196–201.

McDonough, S. C. (1993). Interaction guidance: Understanding and treating early infant-caregiver relationship disturbances. In C. Zeanah (Ed.), *Handbook of Infant Mental Health* (pp. 414–426). New York: Guilford Press.

Meisels, S. J., Dichtelmiller, M., & Liaw, F. (1993). A multidimensional analysis of early childhood intervention programs. In C. Zeanah (Ed.), *Handbook of Infant Mental Health* (pp. 361–385). New York: Guilford Press.

Starfield, B. (1982). Behavioral pediatrics and primary health care. *Pediatric Clinics of North America, 29,* 337–390.

Starfield, B., Gross, E., Wood, M., Pantell, R., Allen, C., Gordon, I. B., Moffatt, P., Drachman, R., & Katz, H. (1980). Psychosocial and psychosomatic diagnoses in primary care of children. *Pediatrics, 66,* 159–167.

Weissbourd, B., & Kagan, S. (1989). Family support programs: Catalysts for change. *American Journal of Orthopsychiatry, 59,* 20–31.

Zahn-Waxler, C., Cummings, E. M., Iannotti, R. M., & Radke-Yarrow, M. (1994). Young offspring of depressed parents: A population at risk for affective problems. In D. Cicchetti & K. Schneider-Rosen (Eds.), *New directions for child development: No. 26. Childhood depression* (pp. 81–105). San Francisco: Jossey-Bass.

18

Designing Mental Health Services for Adolescents

ROBERT A. KING

Adolescence marks the age of onset for many forms of psychopathology. Epidemiological studies in North America and Western Europe suggest prevalence rates of diagnosable mental disorders approaching 20% in adolescents (Offord & Fleming, 1996). Some difficulties, such as schizophrenia, appear to be near-universal across cultures and reflect the interplay of neuromaturational changes of the second decade of life with early congenital deficits and the psychosocial stresses of adolescence. The prevalence and phenomenology of other pathologies, such as eating disorders, substance abuse, and attempted suicide, vary tremendously across cultures and epochs and appear highly susceptible to social influences. Beyond the clear-cut forms of psychopathology diagnosable under the DSM (Diagnostic and Statistical Manual of the American Psychiatric Association) and ICD (International Classification of Disease) schemas, adolescence also marks the onset of significant health- and life-endangering behaviors, including recklessness; tobacco, alcohol, and substance use; risky sexual activity; physical fighting and weapon carrying; and noncompliance with medical care (Dryfoos, 1990). These behaviors are major sources of morbidity and mortality, with accidents (especially motor vehicle accidents), homicide, suicide, and increasingly, HIV, constituting the principal, and, ironically, the most potentially preventable, causes of death in young people in many regions of the world.

Designing developmentally appropriate mental health services for adolescents poses a challenge both within the walls of the traditional mental health clinic and beyond. Selma Fraiberg once remarked that the aims of psychotherapy and the aims of adolescence are diametrically opposed. In large measure, adolescents seek autonomy, resist acknowledging vulnerability or anxiety, resist the claims of adult authority, and prefer action or altering their environment to the hard work of internal change. The wider use of group interventions and time-defined cognitive behavioral treatments (with their emphasis on skill building and bolstering competency) limit the perceived regressive dangers of treatment and hence render it more palatable for some adolescents. (At the same time, such modalities are also much favored by insurance companies because of perceived savings in professional labor costs.) Unfortunately, such approaches may deprive some youngsters of what they need the most, a longer term therapeutic relationship with a concerned and empathic adult.

In the United States and other parts of the world, the same exigencies of healthcare financing have led to comparable changes in adolescent inpatient psychiatric care: dramatically shortened lengths of stay, increased emphasis on milieu groups, and heavy use of psychotropic medication. One positive result of shortened hospital stays, however, has been the development of a spectrum of ''step-down'' services (day or partial hospitalization programs, therapeutic day schools, and in-home therapeutic services) to continue the work begun in hospitals with a greater level of intensity than is possible in outpatient clinic visits alone. The benefits and limitations of these various clinical approaches urgently need to be studied empirically, including their long-term psychological and economic consequences. Although these shorter term modalities may prevent institutionalization and be appropriate for adolescents with more transient and reactive difficulties, the potential for disrupting continuity of care is great and especially problematic for more severely disturbed adolescents, as often reflected in the ''revolving door'' of frequent discharge and readmission.

To be effective in reaching the largest number of adolescents, prevention, case-finding, and therapeutic interventions must be available outside the confines of traditional mental health facilities. For example, innovative projects have demonstrated the feasibility and efficacy of school-based programs that include prevention (with an emphasis on social skills development), in-school counseling, and close collaboration between school personnel and mental health teams assigned to the school (Weissberg, Gullotta, Adams, Hampton, Ryan, 1997; Zigler, Kagan, & Hall, 1996; Comer, Haynes, Joyner, & Ben-Avie, in press). This collaboration facilities identification of students in need of services, developing appropriate classroom modifications for such students, and easy access to treatment for adolescents (and families) unwilling or unable to utilize clinic-based services. These programs have been especially effective when linked to school-based primary healthcare clinics and comprehensive social services.

The integration of comprehensive social, medical, and mental health services in the school setting is also rational from the etiological and preventive perspective. In general, the risk factors for psychopathology do not constitute a unique set of hazards, distinct from other forms of social adversity. For example, although depression is arguably the greatest risk factor for adolescent suicidality, substance use (even in modest amounts), early onset of sexual activity, physical fighting, family adversity, and lack of parental monitoring all constitute risk factors for suicidality in their own right as well as via their contribution to the vulnerability to depression. Hence, prevention, case-finding, and interventions addressed to these risk factors may be expected to have both health and broader social benefits.

Although in many parts of the world the school system is the community institution most in contact with adolescents, there are numerous countries, and indeed American neighborhoods, where fewer than half of adolescents complete a high-school education, leaving many youngsters beyond the reach of school-based programming. To reach these youth, mental health services need to be linked to other resources working with out-of-school youth, such as teen drop-in centers, runaway shelters, and street health clinics.

One unsettled controversial issue such services highlight is the extent to which adolescents have the right to seek mental health services without their parents' knowledge or consent. Advocates of considering adolescents "emancipated" for the purposes of seeking mental health services argue that such confidentiality is essential to reach adolescents struggling with issues related to abuse, substance use, or gender orientation. Opponents argue that such provisions undermine parental authority and deprive parents of the right and ability to be involved in crucial decisions regarding their children.

As noted above, mental health difficulties rarely occur in isolation from other behavioral and family difficulties. Hence, the youth most in need of mental health interventions are also frequently well known to the police, juvenile justice, and child welfare agencies. Increasing the coordination of these agencies with mental health services can have powerfully synergistic effects in improving services for troubled youth. For example, the Yale Child Study Center Community Police/Child Development model program provides training of police officers in work with adolescents and their families; regular and emergency mental health consultation, as well as direct clinical services, for youth in contact with the juvenile justice system; and coordinated follow-up for high-risk youth (Marans, 1995).

Since they are often testing the limits of existing social institutions, adolescents are especially vulnerable to periods of abrupt social change when the authority of parents, school, and other community institutions are absent or disrupted. While immigration or rapid urbanization or industrialization may stimulate the adaptive capacities of some adolescents and their families, such changes may overwhelm others. Under extreme conditions of civil war or social upheaval, barely adolescent boys may end up as the armed foot-soldiers of partisan armies or drug gangs, and teens of both genders may become exploited sex industry workers (Apfel & Simon, 1996). Such examples remind us that the concept of "adolescence" as a sheltered transitional period is less than a century old and is predicated on a requisite level of family, educational, and economic supports. These extreme examples underline the fact that mental health services for adolescents cannot be divorced from the broader issues of providing economic and educational opportunity, supporting families, and helping to maintain or restore meaningful positive contacts between adolescents on the one hand and adults and community institutions on the other.

REFERENCES

Apfel, R. J., & Simon, B. (Eds.). (1996). *Minefields in their hearts: The mental health of children in war and communal violence.* New Haven, CT: Yale University Press.

Comer, J. P., Haynes, N. M., Joyner, E., Ben-Avie, M. (in press). *Child by child, school by school: Educating for the 21st century.* New York: Teachers College Press.

Dryfoos, J. G. (1990). *Adolescents at risk.* New York: Oxford University Press.

Marans, S. (1995). *The police-mental health partnership: A community-based response to urban violence.* New Haven, CT: Yale University Press.

Offord, D. R., & Fleming, J. E. (1996). Epidemiology. In M. Lewis (Ed.), *Child and adolescent psychiatry: A comprehensive textbook* (2nd ed.), pp. 1166–1178). Baltimore, MD: Williams & Wilkins.

Weissberg, R. P., Gullotta, T. P., Adams, D. R., Hampton, R. L., Ryan, B. A. (Eds.). (1997). *Healthy Children 2010. Establishing preventive services.* Thousand Oaks, CA: Sage.

Zigler, E., Kagan, S. L., & Hall, N. W. (Eds.). (1996). *Children, families, and government: Preparing for the twenty-first century.* New York: Cambridge University Press.

19

Designing Mental Healthcare Systems: Implications for the Training of Future Clinicians

PETER S. JENSEN

It is useful to consider what principles might constitute a "wish list" of what we would do if we could redesign mental health systems, and within those systems, a role for child and adolescent psychiatrists. In doing so, we also are effectively redesigning the principles guiding the training of future clinicians.

EVIDENCE-BASED MEDICINE

First, the central guiding principle is that child psychiatry and mental health practices must be derived from "evidence-based medicine." While some worry about the ethics of research with children, I would suggest (as have others) that to not do research with children and adolescents is unethical, given our lack of knowledge concerning the effectiveness of our procedures and the clear evidence of their costs and burdens upon society. This requires that we establish standards for our therapeutic processes (e.g., practice parameters and guidelines), and that we measure these therapeutic processes and their results. Do we do what we say we do or think we do? How do we know, and what would other, "blind" and objective observers say about, what our procedures appear to be? What do our patients think about what we are doing, and/or about why we are doing it? Likewise, evidence-based medicine requires the measurement of outcomes. These outcomes include not just clinical outcomes (e.g., symptoms and disorders), but also child functioning (social and cognitive skills, school performance), consumer-based outcomes (e.g., consumer satisfaction, measures of family burden), environmental outcomes (potential beneficial impact of the child's treatments upon others, e.g., family members, peers, classroom, neighborhood), and services and service system outcomes (cost-effectiveness, changes in placements, service utilization, etc.) These measurements of processes and outcomes should ideally be built into quality assurance programs, and lead to a formal requirement in residency review criteria and board certification exams for stipulations for training child psychiatrists in methods for better assessing what they do and the outcomes they achieve. It is time that we dispel the notion that what we do is an "art." We are not artists, but humane and humanistic science-based practitioners.

THE ROLE OF THE CHILD PSYCHIATRIST

What should be the appropriate role for the child psychiatrist in today's rapidly changing healthcare systems? First, at least within the United States, I believe that we need to consider that we are first and foremost physicians, and we must work with the medical model. If not, we denied someone else a place in medical school, and we should have chosen something else. What should be our focus? Our expertise rests on the understanding of brain–behavior relationships, within a developmental context. In many ways, our profession may be mislabeled, and we might be more appropriately considered developmental neurobehaviorists, or perhaps neurobehavioral pediatricians. Should these child psychiatrists be "the team leader"? Child psychiatrists may not be particularly trained to act as such, and probably should not be, except in biomedical settings. Leadership is often a personal characteristic, and leaders come from all disciplines. Yet in some settings, professionals from certain disciplines have particular expertise and might be more naturally able to consider the broad range of issues involved and to obtain the cooperation of multiple disciplines. For example, a psychiatrist might be ideal for this role in biomedical settings like a hospital or specialty clinic. But in other settings, (e.g., schools, courts, day treatment settings, administrative agencies) quite possibly a person from another discipline would have the requisite skills. Exceptions to this rule (like all rules) abound, however, and always will.

COORDINATION AND INTEGRATION OF MENTAL HEALTH TREATMENT SYSTEMS WITH OTHER CHILD SERVICE SECTORS

Mental healthcare should be integrated with other pediatric medical health services, as well as education, social services (foster care, child abuse) and juvenile justice. Funds for providing care should follow children, not bureaucratic structures or system hierarchies. Furthermore, planning and coordination to provide these linked, one-stop-shopping mental health services should be required at the state, county, and local levels, for both public and private systems. This requires that child psychiatrists and other mental healthcare workers be trained in such models and in such systems. In addition, such systems should have ''consumers'' (family members) involved in their design and evaluation so that obstacles to good healthcare and to family use of services are reduced.

LOCATION OF SERVICES

Child psychiatrists need to work where the sickest children are. This will require increased affiliations with pediatrics and tertiary care settings, and more extensive use of triage capabilities (so that the child psychiatrists' expertise is reserved for more severe cases). In addition, other settings for the more optimal location of child psychiatrists are schools, inpatient settings, and juvenile justice settings.

IMPLICATIONS FOR CLINICAL TRAINING

Because of the above considerations, a number of questions, outlined below, should be considered. Some apply specifically to the training of child and adolescent psychiatrists, and others apply more generally to the training of all mental health professionals who are trained to deliver some components of mental healthcare to children and adolescents. These considerations are not meant to reflect problems or even solutions for all countries, and may only apply to training clinicians in the United States.

1. Given the current status of a lack of knowledge about the efficacy of many of our "standard treatments," should research be a required part of the training of child and adolescent psychiatrists? In fact, in view of our lack of knowledge concerning what works and what does not, is it even ethical to train child and adolescent psychiatrists who are not also trained in research, i.e., trained to evaluate the effectiveness of what they do in the course of their clinical work? It should be noted that Dr. Feldman (Chapter 11) indicates that social work programs in the United States have successfully built into their training and accreditation criteria that social workers must be trained to evaluate the effectiveness of their own treatments, including as a minimum, single case designs, quasi-experimental designs, or other appropriate approaches.

2. What should be the most appropriate clinical focus and role of child and adolescent psychiatrists, and should the training of child and adolescent psychiatrists be based upon their roles first as physicians? Should their focus be as experts in brain and behavior, within a developmental framework? Should professionals from this specialty require a different name, rather than "child and adolescent psychiatrists?" Alternative terms might be "developmental neurobehaviorists," or perhaps "neurobehavioral pediatricians."

3. When, if ever, should the child and adolescent psychiatrist function as the team leader of the multidisciplinary team? Within biomedical settings, and in the context of the evaluation and treatment of children with brain–behavior disturbances, there is an appropriate role for the child and adolescent psychiatrist as "leader," but in many other settings (e.g., schools, ambulatory clinics, etc.) it is quite possible that other professionals are equally or better skilled to address certain clinical and treatment issues concerning the child. For example, psychological testing is the relatively undisputed area of expertise of psychologists, and certainly, many social workers and psychologists are as skilled as or even more skilled than many child and adolescent psychiatrists in group and family therapies. Should child and adolescent psychiatrists abandon all attempts to be experts in all clinical and treatment areas, and focus first on their roles as physicians? Their training should reflect the influence of answers to these questions.

4. Given the radical shifts in healthcare delivery systems, and the need to conserve and use mental health resources in the most appropriate manner, should child and adolescent psychiatrists be trained in organizational and medical economic issues?
5. Should training in cross-cultural issues be a more central, required component of current training programs?

To address these questions, and to bring about the necessary changes outlined above, will take enormous efforts and changes in the organization and reimbursement schemes of current systems. Such reorganizational tasks are not easily undertaken and, as we know from the aborted attempt at healthcare reform at the national level in the United States, it seems likely that powerful forces remain invested in the status quo. Ironically, market forces have themselves actually been responsible for a good deal of reorganization already, and the same forces may well bring about a number of the changes outlined above, e.g., evidence-based medicine, consumer input and involvement in systems, etc. Nonetheless, it seems preferable for child and adolescent psychiatrists and other mental health professionals to take an active role in shaping our fates, rather than to passively wait while systems are restructured without our input or focused efforts to ensure that these changes benefit children.

NOTES

1. The opinions and assertions contained in this paper are the private views of the author and are not to be construed as official or as reflecting the views of the Department of Health and Human Services or the National Institute of Mental Health.

INTERNATIONAL MODELS OF MENTAL HEALTH SYSTEMS FOR CHILDREN AND ADOLESCENTS: WHAT IS THE REALITY WHEN WE PUT PRINCIPLES INTO PRACTICE?

20

Child and Adolescent Psychiatry in France

COLETTE   CHILAND

PIERRE   FERRARI

SYLVIE   TORDJMAN

In this chapter, we address questions concerning the training of child and adolescent psychiatrists and of practitioners in related professions. Then, we present the diverse types of public and private practice in child psychiatry, as well as the theoretical orientations prevailing in France. Finally, we give some indications regarding research in child psychiatry.

TRAINING OF PSYCHIATRISTS

In France, psychiatry separated from neurology after the events in May 1968. Prior to this, both fields belonged to "neuropsychiatry."

Child psychiatry represents a specialization of general psychiatry. It is taught through an additional option in the psychiatry curriculum.

Generally, it is therefore impossible to practice child and adolescent psychiatry unless one has acquired the qualification to be a psychiatrist. Yet, recently it has become possible for pediatricians to obtain a degree in child psychiatry (which does not involve becoming a child psychiatrist) if they have completed certain courses and internship requirements during their internat (residency).

Access to training in psychiatry is through the internat at the Centres Hospitaliers Universitaires (C.H.U., University Hospital

Centers). The internship begins with a competitive examination at the end of the medical curriculum, which can be taken only twice. It gives access for 4 years to positions of responsibility in specialized services in which the intern can acquire the qualification of psychiatrist. The child psychiatry option can be granted to interns who have the qualification in psychiatry if they have also spent four semesters of their internship in services qualifying for child psychiatry and regularly attended a certain number of seminars which fulfill the child psychiatry requirements.

Thus, recruitment of psychiatrists as child psychiatrists in France is carried out through a competitive examination (considered as both democratic and very selective).

This examination evaluates candidates more for their abilities to learn and to memorize a great amount of information than for their clinical abilities, their creativity, and their motivation to get involved in the field of psychiatry.

For a period of time, long ago, there was a specialized internship in psychiatry that one could enter if one had an inclination toward psychiatry. This is not the case today, and it can happen that candidates choose psychiatry based on their rank for the internship, regardless of personal interest in psychiatry.

Because child psychiatry is not in itself considered as a specialty, theoretically, any medical doctor specialized in psychiatry can practice child and adolescent psychiatry. Actually, in most high-ranking positions offered in child and adolescent psychiatry, it is generally required that candidates have completed the additional option for the title of child psychiatrist. Yet the majority of French psychiatrists support more versatility in psychiatric practice to avoid compartmentalization between general and child psychiatry.

TRAINING OF ALLIED PROFESSIONALS

Besides private practice, work in child psychiatry is the result of a multidisciplinary team. Associated with psychiatrists, we find psychologists, speech therapists, diverse educators, psychomotor specialists, social workers, and nurses.

All these professionals, except psychologists, are trained outside of universities, in specialized schools into which candidates can enter after their high-school degree. Currently, these short training periods tend to be 1 or 2 years longer than before, for a total of 3–4 years of schooling. The training acquired in these schools is most often multipurpose. It occurs mainly through daily work in child and adolescent psychiatry departments so that these professionals become competent in child psychiatric disorders.

Psychologists are trained in universities for 5 years. During their final year, they can specialize in child and adolescent psychology. Only a psychology degree with training in clinical and abnormal psychology theoretically allows one to work in child and adolescent departments.

In France, these allied professions have a lower economic status than in other European countries (United Kingdom, Scandinavia, etc.) or in the United States.

CHILD PSYCHIATRY CLINICAL PRACTICE

A number of practitioners work in both the public and private domains. Some of them practice in only one domain. Public sector care in child psychiatry is well developed in France. In 1972, the government created child and adolescent psychiatry sectors. The main goal of the child psychiatry sectors was to carry out, in their geographical areas, the entirety of the preventive and treatment activities concerning child and adolescent mental health.

Thus, the child and adolescent psychiatry sector is in charge of:

1. A complete psychiatric examination of the child, if necessary, psychological, speech, and psychomotor evaluations, and even a school assessment. This examination includes a thorough interview with the parents.
2. The treatment of the child, if necessary. Theoretically, every type of therapeutic action can be carried out within each sector: therapeutic consultations, family guidance consultation, or more frequent and more regular therapy (psychotherapy, speech therapy, psychomotor or educational therapy) individually or in groups.

All the therapies proposed within the sector are free and are performed as close as possible to the families' homes.

Psychiatry sectors are in close contact with the other agencies dealing with childhood: mother and child protection agencies, public healthcare centers, day-care centers, schools, child social work family court, and childcare services in hospitals. Concurrently, the psychiatry sector is developing a series of training, teaching and research programs that will contribute to setting up primary prevention. The team in charge of these preventive actions is multidisciplinary. The multidisciplinarity is based on significant work done during clinical and administrative meetings.

Sectors may have at their disposal five types of facilities for performing treatments. However, not every sector has all the existing facilities available. The five types of facilities are listed below.

Centres Médico-Psychologiques (Medical Psychological Centers). Outpatient consultation and treatment centers, which are the bases of operation of the coordinated activities.

Daycare Hospitals. Institutions in charge of children with serious mental disorders during the day, providing intensive treatments as well as the necessary educational programs (the latter are carried out by special education teachers from the public education system).

Part-time Therapeutic Centers. Institutions in charge of therapeutic treatments for a number of hours each day, while allowing the child to stay in the regular school system; this facility is for less serious cases.

Full-Time Residential Treatment Centers. For long-lasting psychotic pathologies, residential treatment is justified by the seriousness of the illness or by family disorganization. For more acute pathologies, particularly with adolescents (depression, suicide attempt, anorexia nervosa), shorter confinements are possible, allowing the implementation of a therapy that can be continued after leaving the hospital.

Therapeutic Family Placement. The patient is placed in a family setting for children with psychiatric disorders through assistance paid for by the hospital and supervised by a sector's specialized team.

Some public or semipublic healthcare units working in the field of child psychiatry are nevertheless independent from child psychiatry administrative structures. These are mainly:

The Centres Médico-Psycho-Pédagogiques (CMP: Medical-Psychological-Educational Centers). These are managed by nonprofit, private associations. The CMPs have done pioneering work in ambulatory treatment of children with psychological disorders and difficulties in school. They function within the same framework as the child psychiatry structures and represent an important part of the child psychiatry care system.

The Centres d'Action Médico-Sociale Précoce (CAMSP: Early Intervention Medical-Social Centers). These aim at taking care, very early on, of the special education and treatment of preschool children with somatic disorders, and motor, sensory or mental handicaps. The CAMSPs can be multipurpose or specialize in treating a specific handicap. They propose the treatment and remediation required by the child's condition/state which can be performed in groups or individually, at the center or at home.

The Instituts Médico-Éducatifs or Médico-Pédagogiques (Medical-educational Institutions). Managed by nonprofit private associations, they provide, under medical supervision, educational and pedagogical activities with children who generally have a mental deficiency, sometimes associated with psychotic disorders or a physical handicap.

THEORY

Psychodynamic approaches (from psychoanalytic theories) continues to have a large influence on the majority of child and adolescent psychiatrists. Hence, this influence can be found on the psychological approach, remediation, institutional work, individual or group therapy, or work with the family, all of which are favored in child therapy. Pharmacological treatments have only a limited use. For example, the use of Ritalin today remains rare.

The classification used to fill out the diagnostic forms is the Classification Française des Troubles Mentaux de l'Enfant et de l'Adolescent (French classification system). However, the OMS ICD CIM 10 classification and sometimes the DSM (Diagnostic and Statistical Manual) are also used for international publications.

RESEARCH

The sectors' budget does not mention research funding. Funding has to be found from other sources, such as the Institut

National de la Santé et de la Recherche Médicale, the Centre National de la Recherche Scientifique, or organizations that can support research or lead research networks in child psychiatry.

OFFICIAL ORGANIZATIONS

The Société Française de Psychiatrie de l'Enfant et de l'Adolescent et des Professions Associées publishes a journal, Neuropsychiatrie de l'Enfance et de l'Adolescence. In addition, there are other publications concerning child psychiatry such as *Psychiatrie de L'Enfant, Journal de la Psychanalyse de l'Enfant,* and *Revue adolescence.*

CONCLUSION

French child psychiatry is characterized by (a) its sectored network of care structures implemented in the whole country since the 1970s, (b) with its completely free healthcare, which can therefore be available to the most underprivileged (these public services are financed by Social Security), as well as (c) its psychodynamic approach, which supports understanding and treatment of the psychiatric disorders of children and adolescents.

21

Approaches to the Development of Mental Health Systems for Children in the Nordic Countries

HELGA HANNESDÓTTIR

OVERVIEW OF CHILD AND ADOLESCENT PSYCHIATRY IN THE NORDIC COUNTRIES

The Status of Children

The history and roots of child psychiatry go back almost 250 years, yet the development of specific services for child psychiatry is much more recent, beginning only about 27 years ago in Iceland. The European Union of Medical Specialists (EUMS) has recently acknowledged child and adolescent psychiatry/psychotherapy as a main specialty in medicine. For decades, the main emphasis in the development of child psychiatry in the Nordic countries has been on promoting clinical services.

All the Nordic countries are divided into healthcare districts. Except for Iceland, in each district there is a central hospital for specialized healthcare with a child psychiatric service for in- or outpatients or a child psychiatrist who sees children on a consultative basis. In most districts there are child guidance clinics that belong to either the social service or healthcare sectors. Due to the current economic recession, profound changes are taking place in Sweden, Norway, and Finland to decrease the cost of services in child psychiatry. One day in the hospital for child psychiatric care can cost around four times the amount for adult psychiatric services, which has aroused interest among clinicians in the effectiveness of child mental health services.

Table 21.1 *Total Community and State Budgets for Child and Adolescent Psychiatry in 1995 in Gothenburg, Norway, and Iceland*

Gothenburg, Sweden	500,000 individ.	9,000,000 U.S.D.
Iceland, child psychiatry	260,000 individ.	1,693,388 U.S.D.
Iceland, adult psychiatry[a]	260,000 individ.	27,351,830 U.S.D.
Norway, child psychiatry	4,370,000 individ.	90,000,000 U.S.D. (11%)
Norway, adult psychiatry	4,370,000 individ.	700,000,000 U.S.D. (89%)

[a]Child and Adolescent psychiatry is administered by Adult Psychiatry in Iceland.

There are many similarities in the five Nordic countries, yet many differences exist as well. Total budgets for child psychiatric services vary greatly within and between the countries (Table 21.1). In all countries, medical treatment is socialized and care at hospitals is free for children and adults. Taxes are high: 35% to 63% depending on income, with Denmark presently having the highest rate. Acute medical care is excellent, the infant mortality rate is low, and longevity is high. But many of the needs of children and adolescents with mental problems have not been met, especially in Iceland. Child psychiatry must utilize its knowledge of the etiology of mental disorders to promote the health of children and must strengthen the capacity of families and communities to reduce the incidence and prevalence of substance abuse and mental health disorders in later life. Linkages of mental health specialists with schools, the police, social service agencies, and the juvenile courts has begun to provide an important contribution toward improving the interorganizational networks.

Family life has changed during the past two decades in all Nordic countries. Live births have decreased. Legal abortions, the divorce rate, and the urban population have increased. The number of children living with one adult and the number of women who work outside the home have increased markedly. The accident rate among children in Iceland is very high, and there is an increase in the suicide rate for adolescent boys between 15 and 24 years in both Finland and Iceland. Immigration into Sweden has been the highest among the Nordic countries in recent decades, and over 70 languages are spoken in some Swedish public schools.

Clinical Services

All countries have general service programs in child and adolescent psychiatry, but recently there has been much discussion

Table 21.2 *The Status of Child and Adolescent Psychiatry in the Nordic Countries*

	First clinical service	Specialists	University chairs	Dissertations since 1985	Clinical orientation
Denmark	1935	85	3[a]	2	Multidisciplinary[d]
Finland	1920	193	6[b]	14	Multidisciplinary
Iceland	1970	10	0	0	Multidisciplinary
Norway	1951	100	5[c]	5	Multidisciplinary
Sweden	1956	350	4	14	Multidisciplinary

[a]One associate professor, one visiting professor (University of Odense) and one emeritus professor.
[b]One associate professor.
[c]One visiting professor (University of Oslo).
[d]Child psychiatrists, pediatricians psychologists, social workers, occupational therapists, nurses.

about the coordination of services. The need for child psychiatric beds has been estimated to be about 4 beds per 10,000 children. There is an increased tendency to look at prevention and treatment of mental disorders of children as an issue of general public health.

The university chairs were established in the late 1950s and early 1960s. The number of specialists (Table 21.2) in the discipline varies, according to the population in each country, which is from 5 to 7 million, except in Iceland (population: 260,000). Clinical child psychiatry is relatively well established in all Nordic countries, except for Iceland, Greenland, and the Faroe Islands, with consultative work being done in pediatric wards and in the social sector. Clinicians are careful not to overlook important biophysical factors in the evaluation and treatment process, by not focusing solely on socioeducational factors. In crisis situations, intervention through support is often enough, together with family therapy in the outpatient department. The main focus is on service to children within their families and to communities and schools through work with the family. The philosophy of work has been to consider individual needs and current problems: biophysical, intrapsychic, and within the family. Individual psychotherapy is administered in conjunction with family therapy, psychoeducational treatment, and art and music therapy. The role of psychoactive medication is explored if there seem to be indications for this, especially in cases of attention-deficit hyperactivity disorder (ADHD).

Table 21.3   *Service Utilization Rate in Child and Adolescent Psychiatry in Four Nordic Countries*

Denmark	0.1%
Iceland	0.2%
Norway	1.95%
Sweden	5% to 25%[a]

[a]Percentage of adult population who have been in contact with child or adolescent psychiatric services.

An important turning point was reached in research at the beginning of the 1980s, when the first Nordic child psychiatry research meeting was organized in Finland in 1982; since then, meetings have been organized in all five countries every 2–3 years.

The connection between hospitals (run at the state level) and the healthcare sector (run at the community level) is currently being challenged in Denmark and Norway. Academic structure is weakest in child and adolescent psychiatry in Iceland and Denmark, in spite of the recent growth in research and publications. Except in Sweden, there is a low service utilization rate (Table 21.3), which, when compared with prevalence rates from epidemiological studies, indicates that great clinical needs are not being met.

Infant psychiatry is a new and rapidly developing clinical and scientific field within child psychiatry and is most developed in Finland. The main future goals cover four different areas, all aiming at better treatment for patients: (a) to improve quality in the daily clinical work for patients and professionals; (b) to develop methods for measuring the quality of treatment; (c) to improve education for students and specialists; and (d) to promote basic and clinical research and development.

The Nordic countries need new models for administering clinical work and rethinking mental health services for children and adolescents. We talk about ''healthcare without limits,'' while at the same time the service utilization rate is very low and adolescent addiction disorders are drastically underrecognized in all the Nordic countries. Healthcare administrators are missing the fact that adolescents are suffering from serious addictive disorders, probably the most common unmet mental health problem, with various comorbidities (Stefánsson, Hannesdóttir, & Lindal, 1994). We need to break down the walls between ministries, communities and states, institutions, and professionals to build up new services where professional people put their knowledge and experience together to give children with mental health disorders, including drug and alcohol abuse, unlimited care. It is important and necessary to follow closely and strengthen the relations between child psychiatry and neuropediatrics due to new research in the latter field. We must prevent isolation of the child psychiatry specialty, possibly through more collaboration between professors of child psychiatry and by planning joint education, training, and clinical services in child and adolescent psychiatry among all the Nordic countries, which is plausible because of their small populations and fairly similar cultures and problem types, approaches, and attitudes within the specialty.

DENMARK

History

Child psychiatry developed in Denmark from three main specialties: medicine, educational knowledge developed in the school system, and social psychiatry attached to the social welfare system. The first department of child psychiatry was established for outpatients in 1935 in Copenhagen at the State Hospital. Since the 1940s, the services have advanced, and in the 1970s, outpatient departments for treatment were developed in most communities. In the 1960s, services were developed within the social and educational system for children with psychotic symptoms. Later came child psychologists and social workers, who worked to improve services for children who needed special education in the schools. The U.S. child guidance clinics were models for many of the services that developed later (Smedegaard, Hansen, & Isager, 1993). Child psychiatry now provides services for children between the ages of 0 and 15.

Adolescent psychiatry has recently been associated with child psychiatry, but earlier belonged to both child and adult psychiatry. Financing during the last 20 years has come from the communities, both for hospital care and outpatient care. The number of hospital beds has decreased over the past two decades.

Structure of Services

Both child/adolescent and adult psychiatry are divided into healthcare districts in the counties. The services are divided into (a) daycare hospitals, available in seven counties, (b) overnight hospital care, available in nine counties, and (c) outpatient care, available in all the counties. Outpatient care has been on the increase, mainly since 1970, and in some counties it is the primary mode of service.

Policies and Procedures

There has been an increased focus on genetic-biological perspectives in recent years, but earlier treatment was more oriented to psychodynamic psychotherapy. Family and systemic theory have also been popular as treatment orientations in past years, but individual therapy or play therapy is on the decrease. The relationship with adult psychiatry has been limited and is mainly connected to children of psychotic parents.

Teamwork between child psychiatrists and educators, physical and occupational therapists, social workers, nurses, and psychologists has been emphasized. Only four to six new child psychiatrists graduate each year in Denmark. There are many positions open and increased worries about long waiting lists for service. Political forces have been advocating for child psychiatric services with the social administration in recent years, and in a few communities they exist already.

FINLAND

History

Child psychiatry has, since the 1960s, been included in the training of all medical students. The trainee must have 80 hours of theoretical seminars (of which 20 hours must be in health administration, management, and economics) in addition to the daily and weekly clinical and theoretical training and supervision provided by the training department. The theoretical seminars are arranged by the Finnish Child Psychiatry Association and other societies and organizations. In recent years the university child psychiatry departments have jointly organized theoretical seminars for trainees who attend psychotherapy training for at least 3 years. The status of formal psychotherapy training in the context of the university program will be strengthened due to the EUMS decision to recognize the specialty of child and adolescent psychiatry/psychotherapy.

Scientific Training and Research

The first Nordic child psychiatry research meeting was organized in Finland in 1982, and planning of a systematic scientific training program in child and adolescent psychiatry began in 1984 and was realized between 1985 and 1987 by the combined efforts of the five child psychiatry university departments, with the main financial support coming from the Ministry of Education. This program was, in fact, the first nationwide research training program in the medical sciences in Finland.

The training program consisted of six biannual 3–day seminars totalling 80 hours of theoretical lectures and 54 hours of research presentations. The program produced more than 20 research reports on child psychiatric epidemiology and promoted the development of a child psychiatric scientific community at the national and local levels. After the training program, research seminars and personal supervision were arranged on a regular basis in the university child psychiatry departments. In addition, the tradition of the Annual Postgraduate Research Meeting in Child Psychiatry was created and arranged by each university department in turn. Internationally recognized researchers were invited to give lectures and to supervise the presentation of research projects at the meetings (Piha & Almqvist, 1994).

At present, the main focus of research is child psychiatric epidemiology. A multicenter study, which grew out of the research training program, is being carried out collaboratively among all five university departments. It has had a continuous connection with the London School of Child Psychiatric Epidemiology. Other major ongoing research projects involving international collaboration are focused on the development of twins, early mother-infant interactions, identity and self-esteem, depression, and child psychiatric inpatient treatment.

Infant psychiatry is a new and rapidly developing clinical and scientific domain within child psychiatry. Finnish achievements in infant psychiatry are well acknowledged, and the Sixth Congress of the World Association of Infant Mental Health was held in Tampere, Finland in 1996.

Structure of Services

Finland is divided into 20 healthcare districts. In each district, there is a central hospital for specialized medicine with a child psychiatric outpatient unit, and most have an inpatient unit too. In all districts there are child guidance clinics belonging to the social sector, and in some districts, there are child and adolescent mental health centers that were formerly part of the adult mental hospital districts.

Before the Act on Child Guidance Clinics in 1972, there were 37 different units. In the 10 years after the Act, the number more than doubled, to 89 clinics. Currently, about 110 child guidance clinics are operating, and the network covers the whole child and adolescent population. This network forms the basis of child and adolescent psychiatric outpatient services. The staff of child guidance clinics consists principally of clinical psychologists and social workers. Many units have suffered from the absence of a child and adolescent psychiatrist.

Within the organization of adult psychiatric care, there exist about 30 small child and adolescent mental health centers. Adult psychiatrists have not shown much interest in the psychiatric problems of children and adolescents because they have been satisfied with and relied on the services provided by the social sector. According to instructions given by the National Board of Health, every central hospital had to establish at least one child psychiatric outpatient unit before 1982. Outpatient care child psychiatry and psychosocial work has for decades been very individually oriented. The main treatment method has been supportive rather than analytic psychotherapy, owing to the lack of adequate training. The psychotherapy of the child has been accompanied by parental guidance. Since the beginning of the 1980s, the family therapy approach has increasingly prevailed. In the 1990s, different forms of network therapy have emerged in the child psychiatric field.

Inpatient Treatment

The first beds for child psychiatric inpatient treatment were reserved in an adult mental hospital in Helsinki in 1924, and the first true child psychiatric ward was opened in 1927 in Tampere. This ward may have been the first child psychiatric ward in Europe. Most of the child psychiatric inpatient treatment facilities in central hospitals were established at the beginning of the 1980s in accordance with the instructions of the National Board of Health. At present, there are about 280 beds for child psychiatric inpatient treatment in 20 different hospitals. Only one family ward exists. The number of professionals is, on average, 15 staff members for 8 beds. There are 114 beds for adolescent psychiatry, while the estimated need is about 265.

The length of treatment in child psychiatric wards averages 11 months. The therapeutic approach is mostly individually oriented. Individual psychotherapy and family therapy are applied in about one third, and medication in one fifth, of the cases. There are only a few beds for child psychiatric emergency treatment.

Organization

The Finnish Child Psychiatry Association was founded in 1956 and has very actively offered opportunities for further training and emphasized the importance of international contacts. Currently, the Association concentrates more on the promotion of the professional interests of child psychiatrists. In 1985 the Association established the Finnish Child Psychiatry Research Foundation. The following year, in connection with the 30th anniversary of the Association, the first grants for child psychiatric research were awarded.

ICELAND

Organization

Child psychiatry was established in 1970 and developed from pediatrics, psychology, and psychiatry. It is a department within the adult psychiatric division of the National University Hospital. Child psychiatry has not been given high priority in the university hospital administration. In 1987, adolescent psychiatry was established in the same hospital. During the past 20 years there has been a family therapy orientation in the specialty. The outpatient unit determines the primary mode of treatment. Those hospitalized are only a small number: on average, 14.6% of the patients (Hannesdóttir & Stefánsson, 1995). Budgets from the state and the communities vary greatly between the Nordic countries and within them, as seen in Table 21.1.

The specialty has never had a chair at the Medical Faculty in spite of 23 years of teaching medical students, and has therefore not been established as an academic specialty in Iceland. New research work has not been presented to medical students in their teaching at the university or used in other ways to promote the development of the specialty in the country. The teaching runs parallel to the teaching of adult psychiatry. The need to integrate teaching in child and adolescent psychiatry into various other fields of study has been advocated, but is in no way fulfilled at present in Iceland.

Within the Government Agency of Child Protection and the Ministry of Social Affairs, for the past 30 years a service has been given to adolescents between 12 and 15 years of age with behavioral and delinquency problems. The program is provided by teachers, educators, social workers, and psychologists and currently consists of residential treatment homes for 45 adolescents. The service is primarily in charge of the day-to-day administration of 80 child protection committees in the country. At the city hospital in Reykjavík, there is in the department of adult psychiatry an inpatient unit for school children with behavioral problems, directed by a social worker. Recently, two communities developed a service for families with young problem children in Reykjavík run by a social worker. These three programs have suffered from the absence of child or adolescent psychiatrists.

One child psychiatrist is developing a program for children in the north of Iceland within the district hospital on the initiative of the inhabitants of the district. The National Center for Addiction Medicine is building a program for adolescents with alcohol and drug abuse disorders, with a child and adolescent psychiatrist on the staff. A few child psychiatrists working part time in the private sector have played an important role in the program in past years.

The Ministry of Health has not yet decided upon a national policy for supporting mental health for children and adolescents. This has caused serious difficulties in the administration of child and adolescent psychiatry in Iceland for many years, with a resulting lack of ambition and stifling of the independence of the discipline and the autonomy of the services given.

RESEARCH

Research has been carried out since the 1960s, mostly as individual projects in both clinical and epidemiologic research. The first international research project in epidemiology is being carried out at present and is the largest project. This project focuses on the mental health of children from 2 to 18 years, selected at random from the general population, using the Child Behaviour Check List of Achenbach and Edenbrocks (1983) as a screening instrument (Hannesdóttir & Einarsdóttir, 1995).

THE FUTURE

The future goals are first and foremost to exert a stronger influence on the government to gain a chair at the university, in order to integrate teaching, training, and clinical work and to do more research work, especially in the field of genetics. More coordinated community work is needed among all specialties taking care of children and adolescents. This, along with more integration of services, can be achieved through improved laws and legislation and by breaking down the walls between the ministries and child psychiatry professionals. There is a considerable shortage of mental health programs for guidance of children and parents, which in other countries are connected to outpatient services in the communities, pediatric departments, and primary care physicians.

The future of child and adolescent psychiatry in Iceland is uncertain in many ways, mainly due to a lack of academic leadership and limited interest from the government and communities, a shortage of organized services for the whole country, and the budgetary crisis faced by the Medical Faculty and the University Hospital.

NORWAY

History

The first department of child psychiatry in Norway was opened in 1950. Since 1951, child psychiatry has been an independent medical specialty. The specialty requirements (in all five Nordic countries) consist of 5–6 years of training: 3 years of general training in child and adolescent psychiatry, and an additional 2–3 years of training distributed among (a) pediatrics (6 months), (b) adult psychiatry (1 year), (c) neurology or mental retardation or training at other institutions (1 year), and (d) outpatient care. These program requirements are in accordance with rules and regulations for specialty training in medicine. There are no formal exams as yet (Spurkland, 1993).

Norway is divided into 19 counties, and in each county there are one or more multiprofessional outpatient services in child and adolescent psychiatry. One third of them have inpatient units for brief assessments of families and children. A computerized program for registration of clinical work has been developed in recent years. In Oslo, child psychiatry does not belong to the health ministry, but to the social ministry, against the wishes of most child and adolescent psychiatrists.

Four regional university centers combining clinical practice with teaching and research have now been developed (Vanvik & Spurkland, 1992). In 1963, the Department of Adolescent Psychiatry was developed at the University Hospital. In 1953 the Nic Waals Institute was established. These institutions have been responsible for multiprofessional training in child and adolescent psychiatry in Norway.

Organization and Staff

There are 19 health districts, and the organization of the outpatient work in these districts was finished in 1986. In addition to the outpatient clinics in the communities, there are also inpatient units attached to the hospitals within the districts. Therapeutic homes are available for psychotic/autistic children aged 7–12 years old and for adolescents aged 13–18 years old with psychiatric problems. There are emergency units for adolescents and family units that admit the whole family, both for overnight and day hospital stays. One third of the districts have family treatment units, but two thirds of the districts have treatment units for children. Only one third of the districts have treatment available for adolescents. Within the Nordic countries, Norway has led in the practice of hospitalizing families with psychiatric disorders.

During the last few years there has been an increased political interest in joining the service of child and family protection with child psychiatry, against the recommendation of child psychiatrists.

Norway is divided into five health districts for child psychiatry, and the plan is to develop four regional centers for child and adolescent psychiatry, attached to the four University Hospitals in Tromsö,

Trondheim, Bergen, and Oslo, with the Nic Waals Institute playing the central role. These regional centers are intended to have both clinical and teaching responsibilities and to organize research projects.

During the last 15 years there has been a marked increase in research in child psychiatry in Norway. The National Medical Research Council, during the years 1982–1990, reorganized a research program in psychiatry. There is now a program supporting three years of training in research. In 1992 there were nine candidates working on their doctoral theses in child and adolescent psychiatry. This program emphasizes integrating neuropsychobiology and psychiatric research.

SWEDEN

History

Sweden was the first country in the world to have a university chair in pediatrics. This was located at the Karolinska Institute in Stockholm in 1845, where the first chair of child and adolescent psychiatry in Sweden was also established in 1958.

In 1951 child and adolescent psychiatry in Sweden became a medical specialty and a discipline of its own. A course for medical students, included in the course in pediatrics, and an examination became obligatory. Professorships were established in Stockholm in 1958, at the University of Uppsala in 1963, and in Umea in 1966. In the 1980s, professorships were also created in Lund and Gothenburg. Since 1986, training in psychotherapy has also been obligatory.

A common interest in children's mental health and in the prevention of deviant behavior already existed among pediatricians, psychiatrists, psychologists, educators, and social workers in the first decades of the 1900s. Child and adolescent psychiatry has its roots more in pediatrics than in general psychiatry. These roots within pediatrics may have a specific influence on the education of medical students, the nature of the clinical training to become a specialist, and the scientific tradition that developed: during the late 1800s early pediatricians already showed an interest in (and investigated) not only questions covering the somatic status of children, but also the relationship between environmental social factors and the somatic and mental health and development of children. The pamphlet

"Broken Minds" (Jundell, 1915) in which the need for knowledge about the development of delinquent behavior is explained, can also be considered the starting point for the establishment of Swedish child and adolescent psychiatry as a medical discipline. At the Karolinska Institute, there is an "academic link" between the disciplines of pediatrics and child and adolescent psychiatry going back to the beginning of the century. The university departments at Uppsala and Lund developed within general psychiatry, also giving Swedish child and adolescent psychiatry an academic link to adult psychiatry (Rydelius, 1993).

At the beginning of the 1900s, an interest in child mental health developed in the compulsory public schools. In 1928, a special therapeutic home for psychopathic children was started, the "Mellansjö." A prospective longitudinal study of the children who were admitted to the therapeutic home was initiated describing more than 600 children. Follow-ups were carried out from the time of their admittance (1928–1956), during their stay, and including their later adjustment as adults, until 1969. The results indicate that genetic, psychosocial, and behavioral factors are necessary to explain future delinquency, including violent behavior (Fried, 1992). In 1934, Hanna Bratt established Erica Stiftelsen, a foundation to train teachers, psychologists, physicians, and social workers in diagnosing and treating children with school and psychiatric problems. Today, Erica Stiftelsen educates professionals in psychotherapy and is also open for patients in need of psychotherapy.

In 1924, the Swedish Parliament passed the Child Social Welfare Act. This Act forced communities in Sweden to have a child social welfare board and to develop programs supporting the social needs of children. The aim was to prevent delinquency. To do this, the Stockholm Child Social Welfare Board, inspired by the child guidance clinics and youth courts in the United States and the mental health movement, also started child guidance clinics in Stockholm in 1933. One of these child guidance clinics was established at the "KLB" in 1951. Thus, at the time, this hospital was both a child guidance clinic and a department of child and adolescent psychiatry, with in- and outpatient capacities. Today there are more than 30 child guidance clinics in the Stockholm County Council. In 1947 the Stockholm Child Welfare Board opened the "Children's Village of Ska," a treatment home for deviant children and their families.

At the beginning of this century Swedish professors of adult psychiatry showed interest in developing specific knowledge in child psychiatry. There was especially a scientific interest in recognizing the early symptoms of psychotic diseases, such as schizophrenia and manic-depressive psychosis. In 1947, the decisions and influences from within adult psychiatry at the universities at Uppsala and Lund resulted in the opening of child and adolescent psychiatric wards within these departments of psychiatry.

The next important step in its history was the 1957 government enquiry and Parliamentary decision concerning "Psychiatric Health Services for Children and Adolescents." This decision led to the development of the child and adolescent psychiatric health services in all Swedish counties, including inpatient units, outpatient departments, and therapeutic homes of three different kinds: for neurotic, psychotic, and antisocial children and teenagers.

Clinical Policies

All county councils developed clinics with in- and outpatient departments from the 1960s onward, developing therapeutic homes when a change in the Social Welfare Law in 1981 gave the responsibilities for such homes to the communities. Today there is a nationwide child and adolescent psychiatric healthcare organization for the whole population. However, in the Stockholm County Council, the Child Guidance Clinics Organization (the PBU) still exists but has developed into an organization more focused on psychotherapeutic treatment than on child and adolescent psychiatric outpatient care.

The Parliamentary decision in 1957 also established mental hospitals for children and adolescents, to be built at five places in Sweden and run by the state. Three of these were built by 1968 (located in Uppsala, Stockholm, and Lund) when the responsibility for the mental hospitals was transferred from the national government to the county councils. The hospitals for children and adolescents were all changed into ordinary clinics in the following years. Today they exist as the university clinics in Uppsala and Lund and as one of the five clinics in Stockholm.

Scientific Discipline and a Scientific Pioneer

The development of current knowledge in Swedish child and adolescent psychiatry was mainly achieved by two different methods, the retrospective "anamnestic" method of psychiatry and psychoanalysis, and the prospective "descriptive" method of pediatrics and the behavioral sciences. The origin of child psychiatry within pediatrics gave researchers in the discipline prospective approaches to the study of development and maturation from birth to adulthood. For example, the results from the Lundby study in Sweden (Hagnell, Essen-Möller, Lanke, & Öjesjö, 1990) indicate that an observation time of around 40 years is needed to study such events as the occurrence of criminality and alcohol abuse in the general population.

The late professor Sven Ahnsjö (1906–1992) became the first professor and chairman of child and adolescent psychiatry in Sweden. In 1941 he defended his thesis "Delinquency in Girls and Its Prognosis" (Ahnsjö, 1941) and was the most important proponent of child and adolescent psychiatry becoming a discipline of its own. Although his scientific training was in genetics, the results of his thesis showed that a multidisciplinary view and a social-psychiatric perspective concerning child psychiatric research were urgently needed. These opinions have greatly influenced research activities up to the present.

From 1960 to 1993, 33 theses were defended for Doctoral degrees as well as for one Master's thesis. This activity was enhanced in 1981 when the Swedish Medical Research Council gave economic support for a Research Planning Group in child and adolescent psychiatric and social pediatrics, giving the senior researchers in the discipline a possibility to meet regularly and discuss strategies to stimulate young child and adolescent psychiatrists to enter research programs.

Perspective for the Future

Since the first thesis in child and adolescent psychiatry in 1960 (Nylander, 1960), there has been increasing research activity.

This research activity has often focused on the development of longitudinal prospective methods using multidisciplinary cooperation and observation periods that cover the time span from conception to adulthood. Therefore, the Swedish Society of Medicine arranged the XXVIth Berzelius Symposium on "Mental and Psycho-Social Adaptation in Children—A Longitudinal and Prospective

Approach." The participants emphasized the need to improve research methods, to have more interdisciplinary cooperation in research, and to develop research on the borders between the medical disciplines and the behavioral sciences.

REFERENCES

Achenbach, T. M., & Edelbrock, C. S. (1983). *Manual for the child behaviour checklist and revised child behaviour profile.* Burlington, VT: University of Vermont.
Ahnsjö, S. (1941). Delinquency in girls and its prognosis. Uppsala Universitet. *Acta Paediatrica Scandinavica* (Suppl. 3).
Barn-och ungdomspsykiatri under 90–talet. (1993). Kristianstad, Denmark: Boktryckeri AB.
Direktoratet for Köbenhavns Hospitalsvæsen. *Psykiatriplan for Köbenhavsn Kommune 1988–2000.* Köbenhavn, Denmark, 1987.
European Union of Medical Specialists. (1992). *Compendium of medical specialist training in the E.C.* Brussels, Belgium
Fossen, A., & Diseth T. (1991). *Korttidsterapi med barn. En fokusert psykodynamisk tilnærming.* Oslo, Norway: Universitetsforlaget.
Fried, I. (1992). *The Mellansjö school- and treatment-home. Karolinska Insitutet, Stockholm.* Stockholm: Gotab (in Swedish).
Frisk, M. (1968). *Tonårsproblem. En studie av läroverksungdom* (thesis). Helsingfors Universitet, Finland. Helsinki: Samfundet Folkhälsen.
Hagnell, O., Essen-Möller, E., Lanke, J., Öjesjö, L., & Rorsman, B. (1990). *The incidence of mental illness over a quarter of a century.* Stockholm: Almqvist & Wiksell International.
Hannesdóttir, H. (1993). Child and adolescent psychiatry in Iceland. The state of the art, past, present and future. *Nordic Journal of Psychiatry, 47,* 9–13.
Hannesdóttir, H., & Einarsdóttir, S. (1995). The Icelandic child mental health study. An epidemiological study of Icelandic children 2–18 years of age using the Child Behavior Checklist as a screening instrument. *European Child & Adolescent Psychiatry 4*(4), 237–248.
Hannesdóttir, H., & Stefánsson, J. G. (1995). Child and adolescent psychiatric outpatients in Iceland. Demographic data and diagnosis. *Nordic Journal of Psychiatry, 49,* 169–174.
Jundell, I. (1915). *Broken minds.* Stockholm: Barnens Dagblad (in Swedish).
Key, E. (1909). *The century of the child.* London: Putnam.
Lask, B. (1987). Family therapy. *British Medical Journal, 294,* 203–204.
Lask, B., & Fosson, A. (1989). *Childhood illness. The psychosomatic approach.* Chichester, England, and New York: Wiley.

Nylander, I. (1960). Children of alcoholic fathers. *Acta Paediatrica Scandinavica* (Suppl. 121).

Nylander, I. (1979). A 20–year prospective follow-up study of 2164 cases at the child guidance clinics in Stockholm. *Acta Paediatrica Scandinavica* (Suppl 276).

Piha, J. (1991). Lastenpsykiatria ja psykiatria. *Suom Laakaril, 46,* 1142.

Piha, J., & Almqvist, F. (1994). Child psychiatry as an academic and clinical discipline in Finland. *Nordic Journal of Psychiatry, 48,* 3–8.

Psykisk barna- och ungdomsvård. (1957). Stockholm, SOU, 40.

Ringstad, T., & Spurkland, I. (1978). *Familier med nervose barn. Behandling ved innleggelse.* Oslo-Bergen Tromso: Universitetsforlaget.

Rydelius, P.-A. (1993). Child and adolescent psychiatry in Sweden—from yesterday until today. *Nordic Journal of Psychiatry, 47,* 395–404.

Sommerschild, H. (1987). Prevention in child psychiatry. *Acta Psychiatrica Scandinavica, 76* (Suppl.), 59–63

Spurkland, I. (1993). Training in Europe Series—Child and Adolescent Psychiatry in Norway. *ACPP Review & Newsletter,* 15(2), 1993.

Smedegaard, N., Hansen, N., & Isager, T. (1993). Danish child psychiatry. Past, present, future. *Nordic Journal of Psychiatry, 47,* 75–79.

Statistics in Iceland, Reykjavik, Iceland: Hagstofa Islands, 1991.

Stefánsson, J. G., Hannesdóttir, H., & Líndal, E. (1994). A note on an Increasing suicide rate in Iceland. *Arctic Medical Research, 53* (Suppl.2), 576–579.

Sundhedsstyrelsen. (1991). *90'ernes psykiatri. Omstilling på psykiatriområdet. Delrapport.* Köbenhavn, Denmark.

Sundhedsstyrelsen. (1991). *90'ernes psykiatri. Planlægning af psykiatrien. Hovedrapport.* Köbenhavn, Denmark.

Sundhedsstyrelsen. (1991). *90 érnes psychiatri. Indsatsen for psykisk syge. En faglig redegorelse.* Delarapport, Denmark.

The University Hospitals Annual Reports, 1970–1991. (1992) Reykjavík, Iceland: The University Hospital, Skrifstofur Rikisspitala.

Tyrfingsson, Th. (1996). *Annual Report from the National Center for Addiction Medicine,* Vogur Hospital, Iceland.

Vanvik, I. H., & Spurkland, I. (1993). Child and adolescent psychiatry in Norway. Today and tomorrow. *Nordic Journal of Psychiatry, 47,* 155–160.

22

Structure and Organization of Services for Children and Adolescents with Psychiatric Disorders in Germany

HELMUT REMSCHMIDT

INTRODUCTION

In Germany, the treatment of psychiatrically disturbed children and adolescents is funded by insurance for acute disorders, by the youth welfare organization, and by the social security system after the acute phase for rehabilitation and reintegration. The social security system is responsible only for physically handicapped and severely mentally handicapped children and adolescents, whereas the youth welfare organization is responsible for psychiatrically handicapped children and adolescents up to the age of 18.

With regard to the progress of child and adolescent psychiatry in Germany in general, four developments during the last 20 years have been decisive:

1. the Psychiatry Enquête of the Federal Government of Germany (report, 1975);
2. the model program, "Psychiatry," of the Federal Government of Germany (1980–1985);
3. the Psychiatry Personnel Equipment Act (stepwise introduction between 1991 and 1995), and
4. the inclusion of psychotherapy in the training curriculum and in the name of the specialty which has been since 1992, "child and adolescent psychiatry and psychotherapy."

These four developments have influenced current child and adolescent psychiatry and psychotherapy in a remarkable way. The Psychiatry Enquête, inaugurated by two members of the parliament, opened up the possibility for a broad inquiry about the situation of psychiatry and child and adolescent psychiatry all over what was then West Germany. After the report of the commission (1975), a model program, "Psychiatry," was created, which was carried out in 14 regions of the Federal Republic of Germany and which evaluated different types of services and created new ones. One region (Marburg) was devoted exclusively to the evaluation and establishment of child and adolescent psychiatric services. Many of these newly created services were continued. The Psychiatry Personnel Equipment Act was responsible for more satisfactory staffing of psychiatric hospitals and services, which led to a remarkable improvement of everyday work. The inclusion of psychotherapy in the curriculum for child psychiatrists and for general psychiatrists was not only important for the individual professional training of each child and adolescent psychiatrist, but also improved the status of child and adolescent psychiatry.

GUIDELINES FOR SERVICES FOR CHILDREN AND ADOLESCENTS WITH PSYCHIATRIC DISORDERS

The Expert Commission of the Federal Government of Germany proposed guidelines for services based on the following general principles (Report of the Expert Commission, 1988, pp. 383–385):

1. Services for psychiatrically disturbed children and adolescents should be equalized with services for children with other disorders or diseases. Ideally, children with psychological disturbances and their parents should pass through the same door as children suffering from an infectious disease, or a broken leg or those who need surgery.
2. This equality requires an integration of the relevant services into the field of medicine, though there is a broad overlap with other nonmedical services.
3. The services should be community-based, avoiding too long distances and too high thresholds for consultation. It was proposed

to define a region of approximately 250,000 inhabitants for out-patient services and a region between 500,000 and 750,000 in-habitants for inpatient and complementary services. It should be the aim of service planning to treat most of the children and adolescents within their home region. However, there are some disorders or diseases that need special services and that do not occur frequently enough to require a center for them in every region. These disorders involve: (a) children with chronic epilepsy and severe psychiatric problems, (b) children and adolescents with severe head injuries, (c) psychiatrically disturbed delinquent children and adolescents who cannot be held responsible for their delinquent acts for psychiatric reasons, and (d) severely mentally handicapped children and adolescents with a high load of psychopathological disorders.

4. The services should be qualified and respect age and developmental stage, the peculiarities of each child and his or her family, as well as risk factors and protective factors in the patient and his or her environment.

TYPES OF SERVICES

Table 22.1 gives an overview of the different types of child and adolescent psychiatric services in Germany. On the whole, there are enough inpatient beds, but they are not well distributed over the whole country. There are not enough outpatient services. This applies to outpatient services associated with hospitals as well as to private practice. Child psychiatry is one of the few medical disciplines in Germany in which private practice still offers good prospects and is not restricted.

There is also a shortage of daypatient facilities and a paucity of complementary services (rehabilitation programs, programs for chronic patients, and programs for special groups, such as drug-dependent children and adolescents and delinquent adolescents).

Outpatient Services

The majority of outpatient consultations are carried out by child psychiatrists in private practice ($n = 311$) and by outpatient

Table 22.1   *Services for Psychiatrically Disturbed Children and Adolescents in Germany*

I.   Outpatient services
  1. Child and adolescent psychiatrists in private practice
  2. Psychoanalytic child and adolescent psychotherapists in private practice
  3. Outpatient departments at hospitals
  4. Child psychiatric services at public health agencies
  5. Child guidance clinics and family counseling services
  6. Early intervention centers, pediatric social services

II.   Daypatient services
  1. Daypatient clinics. Two types: Integrated into or associated with inpatient settings, or independent
  2. Night clinic treatment possibilities

III.   Inpatient services
  1. Inpatient services at university hospitals
  2. Inpatient services at psychiatric state hospitals
  3. Inpatient services at general community hospitals or pediatric hospitals

IV.   Complementary services
  1. Rehabilitation services for special groups of patients (e.g., children with severe head injuries, epilepsy, etc.)
  2. Different types of homes for children
  3. Residential groups for adolescents

units of child psychiatric state hospitals and in university departments ($n = 25$). Outside the medical field, more than 1,000 child guidance clinics and also more than 1,000 psychoanalytic child and adolescent psychotherapists (most of them in private practice) participate in outpatient consultation and treatment. In 1988, the Expert Commission for the model program "Psychiatry" of the Federal Government of Germany proposed a ratio of one child psychiatrist per 200,000 inhabitants. But from the current point of view, this is an underestimation of actual need. With regard to child guidance clinics, the World Health Organization proposed a ratio of one child guidance clinic per 50,000 inhabitants. This figure has not yet been reached in any of the 16 states in Germany. For young children in the first 3 years of life, there are centers for early detection and intervention. There is an obligation for the counties of every state to provide those services that have mainly an educational orientation, though not all of them have a physician as a consultant.

Daypatient Services

Daypatient services are important and, if well organized, are effective and efficient services for the treatment of psychiatrically disturbed children and adolescents. There are three types of daypatient services: *associated* ones working in close relationship with inpatient departments, *integrated* ones carrying out their daypatient work on inpatient wards, together with inpatients, and *independent* daypatient services without any connection to an inpatient unit, most of them being associated with an outpatient department. The Expert Commission did not support the model of an independent and more or less isolated day hospital, because of a lack of flexibility between inpatient and daypatient treatment modalities. Instead, the Expert Commission proposed a triadic service system consisting of outpatient, daypatient, and inpatient services responsible for a circumscribed region. No proposal was made with regard to a certain ratio of day hospitals to number of inhabitants.

Inpatient Services

Currently, there exist 114 inpatient services, including 25 university departments. On the whole, there are enough inpatient treatment beds. However, they are distributed inadequately across the country. Thus, the Expert Commission proposed to provide a better distribution of services in the future, to provide more community-based inpatient services, to provide adequate buildings and personnel equipment, to provide the possibility that mothers be admitted to hospital together with young children needing inpatient treatment (rooming-in), and to respect a minimal size of an inpatient department (not less than 30 beds) in order to take care of different groups of patients who have to be separated on different wards.

In 1988, the Expert Commission proposed seven beds per 100,000 inhabitants in rural areas and up to 11 per 100,000 for an inner-city population. The current recommendation is 5–7 beds: 100,000 inhabitants, depending on the kind of population to be served.

Complementary Services and Rehabilitation

The task of complementary and rehabilitative services is to provide care for children and adolescents with long-lasting and chronic psychiatric disorders. There is a great need for these types of services, especially for those patients who cannot be reintegrated into normal life and their former environment after inpatient treatment. There are special laws regulating the financial support of these services (Bundessozialhilfegesetz). There are different types of services that are summarized under the headline of *complementary services:*

1. *Transitional homes (Übergangswohnheime)* that provide educational and vocational help after inpatient treatment for those patients who are not able to return to their former environment (family, school, professional field). There should be approximately 15 places per 500,000–750,000 inhabitants.
2. *Group homes* for adolescents, preparing them for their next step into independence while providing guidance and counseling through adult professionals. The proposal is to have two group homes with 6–8 places per 500,000–750,000 inhabitants.
3. *Youth Centers*: In contrast to the two institutions above, the adolescents are quite independent in these centers, as only meals and some leisure activities are provided. These institutions provide support for those adolescents who cannot return to their families and who are preparing themselves for their professional work or are already continuously working.
4. *Foster homes/family nursing* offer an effective alternative to youth centers, especially for children and adolescents with a chronic psychiatric illness or for handicapped children and adolescents. The advantage is that this type of institution provides a kind of family framework for patients that can take into account their special needs and/or peculiarities.
5. *Rehabilitation services* concentrate their activities on three fields: medical rehabilitation, scholastic and vocational rehabilitation, and social rehabilitation. There exist special workshops for adolescents with chronic psychiatric disorders that provide professional training, education, and continuous work under flexible conditions that take into account the abilities and handicaps of the patients.

PERSONNEL

Great progress for all psychiatric services, and particularly for child and adolescent psychiatric services, occurred with the

Psychiatry Personnel Equipment Act, which was realized stepwise between 1991 and 1995. The main advantage of this new personnel act is that the personnel needed for a certain ward or institution is no longer calculated in relation to the number but to the specific needs and requirements of the patients. Therefore, the patients are subdivided into several groups according to the amount of care, support, supervision, and treatment they need. The time required for every activity of the personnel with regard to different patient groups is registered, and on this basis an adequate number of staff members (doctors, psychologists, nurses, etc.), is calculated.

FUNDING OF SERVICES

In Germany, inpatient, outpatient, and daypatient facilities are paid for in one form or the other by the state. Germany has a compulsory insurance system. All patients and families are insured, and the insurance usually pays the costs for outpatient, daypatient, or inpatient treatment directly to the hospitals. This applies to all acute treatment needs. The responsibility for chronically psychiatrically ill children and adolescents is taken over by the youth welfare system and the social security system, depending on the kind and severity of the disorder. For example, for multiply handicapped children and adolescents (in the sense of a combination of somatic and psychiatric disorders) the social security system usually is responsible. For children and adolescents suffering from chronic psychiatric disorders, however, the youth welfare system has been responsible since 1991. This change in responsibility has imposed a heavy burden on the youth agencies, who were not prepared to handle these problems.

As far as the complementary services are concerned, the same funding agencies are responsible (youth welfare system and social security system). Several of these responsibilities are in the hands of nongovernmental welfare organizations and charities, who get their financial support from different sources, mainly the youth welfare system and the social security system.

Rehabilitation services are paid partly by insurance and partly by the social security system.

EVALUATION

Few studies have evaluated psychiatric services for children and adolescents in Germany so far. In the region of Marburg, which was the only region for the evaluation of child and adolescent psychiatric services within the model program "Psychiatry" of the Federal Government, we had the unique opportunity to do a comprehensive evaluation study of all services of three counties within a certain time span (Remschmidt & Walter, 1989; Remschmidt, Walter, Kampert, & Hennighausen, 1990; Walter, Kampert, & Remschmidt, 1988). The results of these evaluation studies are described in chapter 7 of this book (Remschmidt, Schmidt, & Walker).

REFERENCES

Remschmidt, H., & Walter, R. (1987). *Evaluation kinder- und jugendpsychiatrischer Versorgung. Analysen und Erhebungen in drei hessischen Landkreisen.* Stuttgart, Germany: Enke.

Remschmidt, H., Walter, R., Kampert, K.,. & Hennighausen, K. (1990). Evaluation der Versorgung psychisch auffälligr und kranker kinder und Jugendlicher in drei Landkreisen. *Nervenarzt, 61,* 34–45.

Walter, R., Kampert, K., & Remschmidt, H. (1988). Evaluation der kinder- und jugendpsychiatrischen Versorgung in drei hessischen Landkreisen. *Praxis der Kinderpsychologie und Kinderpsychiatrie, 37,* 2–11.

23

Mental Health Services for Children and Adolescents in the United Kingdom

IAN M. GOODYER

BACKGROUND

Mental health service delivery systems in the United Kingdom are, as with all medical services, embedded within the National Health Service. This means that both capital and revenue is obtained via a block grant through a centrally administered government system, the National Health Service. The funds themselves are raised from direct taxation of the population of the United Kingdom. As a result of recent reorganization of this service, we have a model where central planning shapes healthcare policy for the nation, but government passes the responsibility for detailed decision making down to local levels, where significant differences in population demographics (e.g., in cities, rural areas, industrialized vs. agricultural populations, elderly vs. children) need to be taken into account. The aim is to ensure an equitable distribution of finance to all areas of the country and to monitor the performance of health authorities charged with planning responsibilities. The government has certain health-of-the-nation targets that it expects to be incorporated into local healthcare planning. In practice, this public health model aims to help in the making of difficult local decisions by providing national data and policy advice on how to prioritize within a healthcare budget. As part of the previous government reorganizations, the local services were split into *purchasing authorities,* who have responsibilities for the organization, planning, and funding of healthcare for a given location, and *providing organizations,* who have specific responsibilities for healthcare delivery and for ensuring that, as much as current funds allow, services are "needs-led" rather than "demand-led."

In recent years there has been an increasing emphasis on "value-for-money services" and the need for cost effectiveness. This has resulted in (among other things) a recognition of the need for greater attention to the processes and mechanisms of healthcare delivery services, i.e., getting the most out of what we have, and undertaking quantitative economic evaluations to develop a new series of healthcare outcome indicators that will determine the costs and benefits of treatments. Such economic evaluations in the United Kingdom (and indeed elsewhere in the developed world) are comparatively rare. Five generic questions are generally considered core to such studies: What treatments should be provided? When? Where? To whom? and How?

Because of a central planning process, the current UK government is able to order reviews of the nation's healthcare needs relatively easily. In 1969, the National Health Advisory Service (HAS) was founded to advise on services provided for mental illness. The initial brief was confined to the elderly and learning disabled in recognition of the fact that those were populations often "lost" in the planning process of mental illness services for adults. The importance of the HAS is that it operates independently of government ministers and of the civil service branch of government, the Department of Health and Social Security. The HAS operates by sending teams of inspectors out into the country to undertake reviews of existing service facilities and current practice. Between 1969 and 1982 HAS inspectors repeatedly heard concerns about the lack of services in hospitals for young people with mental illness. A report was commissioned, and in 1986 the HAS published the first document on services for disturbed adolescents between the ages of 12 and 19. It is important to note that the HAS included in their report those adolescents who are disturbed within themselves and those perceived as disturbed by others (HAS, 1986). This report provided the impetus for local discussions to determine how to implement the principles outlined in the report, upon which a good service must be based. However, it was recognized that the findings were confined to a specific age range. Accordingly, a more in-depth and wide-ranging HAS report was commissioned to review the role and management of child and adolescent mental health services in the 1990s. This review surveyed the current national pattern of child and adolescent mental health provision (HAS, 1995). This seminal report has recently been summarized and key points published for a general readership (Williams, Richardson, & Emerson, 1996). The report had many positive things to say about service delivery across the United Kingdom, but noted gaps, duplications, and the lack of a national mechanism for joint effort and collaboration both within health systems and between the health system and other areas, such as social services, education, and the police. The report noted that joint efforts and collaboration are largely dependent on local informal networks. The HAS panel was multidisciplinary and included representatives from mental health nursing, economics, health service management, psychiatric social work with children and adolescents, pediatric epidemiology, law, and child and adolescent psychiatry.

The report was drawn up following the use of the Thematic Review Methodology. This procedure involves a series of steps: First, a background review of the literature related to service principles is undertaken. Second, position statements are developed from the review, or practical services principles prepared by the steering committee. Third, these are used to develop a hypothetical guide for the purchasing of child and adolescent mental health services. In other words, a set of theoretical ''gold standards'' are derived from what we know. Fourth, a series of service sites in the United Kingdom were selected for detailed visits, where face-to-face interviews were carried out with the personnel who organized and delivered services. Fifth, this fieldwork information was ''mapped'' onto the derived hypothetical standard.

The primary focus is on the current strategy and operational management of Child and Adolescent Mental Health Services (CAMHS). The fieldwork included health, educational social services, nonstatutory organizations, the police, and the judiciary. The overarching aim was to look at how CAMHS services could be made durable and workable yet be kept flexible enough to respond to changes that may come from new knowledge, alterations in government policy, or a change in public demand and needs.

Before proceeding into the details and influences of this report, it is worth reflecting on one of its core assumptions, namely, that there should be a central national mechanism for regulating the purchasing and provision of CAMHS. Of course, the assumption that this is a ''good thing'' is derived from the value system embodied within the National Heath Service, namely, that there is benefit to the nation in exercising a degree of central control by government on behalf of the public in the organization and delivery of healthcare services. There is considerable merit in some level of central planning and advice. First, it provides guidelines for standards of professional practice, training and education, and delivery of services. Second, it ensures a channel for information between localities and thereby comparisons of resource availability and need. Third, it allows government to redress imbalances in the health service provision that individual members of the public could not fix on their own and that local providers may not wish to fix, such as to disinvest in one area of the country on behalf of the population in another. These are but a few of the advantages of a flexible planning approach in which central and local governments may cooperate on behalf of the public good.

However, there are also risks: a burgeoning bureaucracy and a lack of connection between government planning, fiscal policy, and clinical needs are perhaps the largest dilemmas that face a national system with ever-increasing demands and, at least recently, higher expectations by both the public and the professionals seeking to implement clinical advances. It is against this background of the need for greater fiscal controls, while at the same time seeking to meet public need, that the restructuring of the National Health Service took place in the early 1990s. *Service providers,* i.e., those managing and delivering healthcare in hospitals and community settings, were reconstituted into *Health Care Trusts.* Trusts vary in size and in their constituent parts: some are focused on acute hospital care; others are focused on community services for the chronically ill, elderly, and other specialized services, with strong links with general practice and social services; yet others consist of a single large specialty such as all of mental illness and related community services. Whatever the ''organic'' constituent part, it is the job of Trusts to set prices for their services, ensure their efficient delivery, and manage the health needs of the population for whom they provide.

For example, the Child and Adolescent Psychiatry Services in Cambridge in the United Kingdom are part of Lifespan Healthcare NHS Trust, and are university affiliated. The Trust is responsible for the provision of a range of community services for the Cambridge arm of the Cambridge and Huntingdon Health Authority (the purchaser) and employs some 2,500 people involved in the care of the elderly, learning disabled, and children and adults with chronic medical difficulties and disabilities. The Trust serves 250,000 people; the Authority has purchasing responsibility for around 500,000. As well as Lifespan, there are two other Trusts within the Authority: One is focused entirely on acute hospital services, is the site of the University of Cambridge Clinical Medical School, and includes many highly specialized units; the other combines acute general services on a hospital site and a range of community services in the town of Huntingdon and its surrounding vicinity.

Providers obtain annual budgets for their services from healthcare purchasers. Purchasers are rightly concerned with providing healthcare to their immediate locality. Some specialist services may not, however, be locally available, and some services may need to be purchased from further afield.

Purchasing authorities have a responsibility to ensure that the Trusts' delivery of services is in the public interest and is cost effective. Purchasing authorities contract with Trusts for the provision of a range of healthcare needs and expect Trusts to meet performance targets, such as a given number of patient episodes of treatment, or to regulate the number of episodes prior to a spending year, e.g., the total number of hip operations allowable or the number of inpatient patient bed days. The responsibilities of purchasers are to ensure that government priorities are adhered to as much as possible and that Trusts carry out their clinical responsibilities within fiscal limits. Purchasers can change their priorities and can disinvest in one service to reinvest in another. Trusts and purchasers are in constant dialogue on these and many other related matters relating to health delivery systems and their accountability, fiscal efficiency, and clinical adequacy. It is within this purchaser-provider framework that CAMHS was reviewed and recommendations provided in the HAS (1995) report.

RECONFIGURING CAMHS IN THE UNITED KINGDOM

Mental Health and Disorder

A first task is to be clear about the terms *mental health, mental health problems, and mental disorder.* Mental well-being is considered to be an ideal state that can be helped or hindered by internal and external circumstances and events.

Mental health problems are operationally defined as impairments in personal and/or social function that could arise from a number of congenital, constitutional, environmental, family, or illness factors. Making the distinction between idiosyncracies of normal development and mild to moderate emotional and behavioral disorders that require intervention can be difficult. Disorders are best considered as a constellation of signs and symptoms that meet one or more sets of diagnostic criteria and impair current functioning in personal, family, social, or school circumstances. It is increasingly apparent that determining specific areas of functional impairment in the child or adolescent is a crucial step in evaluating the need for mental healthcare (Costello et al., 1996).

For the purposes of a child mental healthcare system, a four-tier structural organization has been proposed which takes into account the nature and characteristics, signs and symptoms of problems and disorders using a multiple respondent method of ascertaining mental health status. Thus, taking into account information from the child or adolescent, parent, teacher, and school staff and/or caregivers, a structure of healthcare delivery has been devised to service children according to (a) the degree of personal and social impairment within the child, the family, and/or other social environments, as well as (b) more nosologically based information, such as prevalence and diagnosis.

The proposal is for four tiers, each representing a distinct level of service ranging from community services, which will have direct and frequent contact with the public, to highly specialized services with minimal contact with the general population. Entry into the tiers and through the structure is determined by a set of filters. The structure is shown in Figure 23.1.

The first filter is between community and primary healthcare services of tier 1. The latter is made up of professionals who are not specifically trained in child development or psychopathology, but will also include some individuals designated as primary child mental health workers, who are. This implies that the community's first contact is with nonspecialists who will, however, be able to seek some specialist advice within this tier of care delivery. In practical terms, this may mean a child psychiatric nurse undertaking consultations with other tier-1 personnel about service delivery or individual

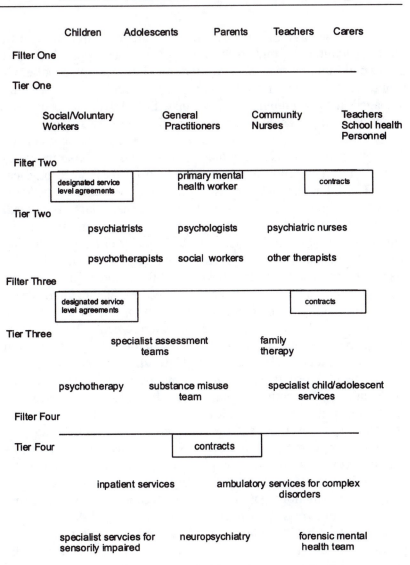

Figure 23.1

patients or undertaking specific work (such as behavioral management of preschool feeding or sleeping difficulties) directly. The exact process of healthcare delivery within a tier is not prescribed, but will be left to the providers to configure based on local resources. However, it will be expected that in all areas of the United Kingdom tier-1 services would be firmly in place within a designated provider unit and funded as a priority by the local purchaser. In other words, the high volume of mild to moderate mental health problems that afflict children and their families and may impinge on school environments, relatives, and other caregivers should be assessed and managed at the community level, but with a degree of specialized professional input as an adjunct within that delivery system.

As Figure 23.1 shows, the tier-2 services consist of specialist CAMHS professionals and voluntary sector staff working individually or in collaboration and, very likely, from designated physical sites. The filter into tier 2 consists of three components, the most clinically important of which is the established classical clinical procedure that tier-1 professionals refer children to the specialists. This procedure should be made more clinically efficient by having a CAMHS specialist in tier 1 and improving the sensitivity (false negative) and specificity (true positive) of the nature of the referrals. The filter also shows two financial processes in the filter. These reflect the ability of purchasing health authorities to commission from providers a designated service level agreement. This is a problematic area because purchasers require patient data information about the population they represent. Currently, service-level agreements are obtained by examining previous years' (often the last three) numbers of patient contacts, i.e., the number of face-to-face episodes per annum, the duration of a contact, length of treatment, and treatment specifics, e.g., psychometric assessment, drug prescribed, or psychological treatment. Negotiations between purchasers and providers are often lengthy and currently occur annually. As is well acknowledged, the reliability and validity of much of the essential information required for the agreements is variable and not consistent across the United Kingdom (Knapp, 1997).

Invariably, a health authority purchaser will contract with its local provider for tier-1 services which are an important and essential part of public health and provide funds to cover a given number of patient contracts for the coming 12 months. Providers publish monthly data, making a check on patient flow possible. Providers will use this ongoing data to determine the variance of Trust performance against the contract. At present, purchasers are uncomfortable if Trusts over- or underperform (i.e., see too many or too few cases), as there is generally very little flexibility in the contract arrangements and purchasers are accountable to central government for their spending plans.

In theory, there should be an equilibrium between costs and revenue for each of the 12 months. In practice, clinical activity is highly variable, whereas funding is broadly invariate within contracts; i.e., once purchasers and providers fix a contract, it remains for 12 months. If Trusts underperform, purchasers may fix a lower contract for the next year. If they overperform, there is, however, no guarantee funds will go up.

The majority of child psychiatry ambulatory cases will be managed in tier-2 services with CAMHS. These services are located in a geographical district serving a total population (adults and children) ranging in size from approximately 140,000 to 500,000, with the mode being around 250,000. The personnel mix within these services has varied enormously from one part of the United Kingdom to another, depending on local rather than central factors. These local factors are, in the main, more qualitative than quantitative. Thus the degree to which child mental health services are perceived as important or credible has often been a major determinant in service provision. The value of a centrally driven policy is that it sets minimum standards, which, by law, local Trusts must adhere to. While the national picture remains variable, the current policy places responsibility on both purchasers and providers to fund, manage, and evaluate a district CAMHS that contains both tier-1 and tier-2 services. Currently, child psychiatrists are accepting the responsibility for devising ''model services'' in terms of professional mix, service delivery systems, and evaluation procedures. It is hoped that, at least for the general outline of tier-2 services, it will be possible to provide most purchasers and providers with these model service provision plans upon which specific local needs can be mapped. For example, service units are unlikely to be the same in detail in inner-city areas with high rates of unemployment, family breakdown, and school nonattendance as in rural areas with a more homogeneous culture, rural poverty, and a widely dispersed population with family disharmony but less parental separation.

Figure 23.1 shows that tier-3 services are internal constructions derived from tier-2 personnel and structures. Tier 3 is important because it puts responsibilities on purchasers and providers to establish multidisciplinary teams with specialist functions within identifiable child mental health services.

Tier 4 comprises very specialized interventions and services that are unlikely to be provided in all units but are deemed necessary for a wider population base for uncommon or rare conditions.

These latter, tier-4 services provide difficulties for purchasers and providers. They represent low-volume, high-cost services. Invariably, purchasers (who represent populations, on average, of 280,000) only want 2–3 beds/annum for severe adolescent psychiatric disorders with median stays of 4–8 weeks (i.e., between 6–12 patients in a 52–week, 7–day unit). The planning of such services on a systematic basis is very difficult because knowledge of incidence, severity, relapse, and service utilization is often not available. Even when it is, there are no explicit mechanisms that require purchasing authorities to pool resources to provide such services. Services such as child inpatient units, specialized services for the learning-disabled child, or forensic services for adolescents, which require planning across wider areas and populations (say, between 1 and 2 million people) are at risk of being "lost" and must depend very much on goodwill and flexibility within the structure, as well as on a purchasing consortium approach whereby two or three purchasers agree to share costs and a trust accepts the responsibility for providing the service.

Provider units have generally recognized that units of between 10 and 14 beds are required for inpatient services if they are to cover capital and revenue costs on an annual basis and provide a viable service. Therefore, providers look to more than purchasers to find tier-4 units. For example, the intensive care inpatient unit for seriously ill adolescents in East Anglia (population: 2.5 million) is based in Cambridge within Lifespan Healthcare Trust. This 12 bed facility has 2 or 3 beds purchased by three different authorities and 3 beds available for flexible purchase from anywhere within the United Kingdom as needs arise. Central policy makes clear that tier-4 services are required, but has not indicated whose responsibility it is to provide them. There are, therefore, considerable variations in the distribution and provision of tier-4 services in the United Kingdom.

Unlike tier 3, there are also some variations in perceptions on child psychiatry and in advice on who inpatient units should be for and when and how they should be used. While agreed-upon formal policy is lacking, the increasing trend across the country is for shorter-term admission for assessment diagnosis and stabilizing treatments of acute psychiatric disorder. Previous models for the longer-term management and treatment of conduct disorders is currently seen as less viable except for severe challenging behaviors

Table 23.1   *Components of a Successful Service*

- Assessment services
- Specialist reporting services, including for the courts
- Advice and short–term interventions on welfare, education, and health
- A range of case management services and treatment options, including those for individuals, groups, parents, and families
- Knowledge of other sources of expertise for complex conditions
- Collaborative work with other agencies, including case conferences and statutory proceedings
- Liaison and consultation services
- Training
- Research

requiring secure accommodation. However, there is considerable debate about who should accept responsibility for the latter: health services, social services, or the prison-related services. These are far from new debates, but have been thrown into relief by the reconstruction of health services.

In each of the tiers, the filters contain designated service level agreements and contracts, with the exception of tier 4, where, as already indicated, local service level agreements cannot be sufficient to contract for these.

The hypothesized components of a successful service are summarized in Table 23.1.

Health and local authority purchasers (the latter refer to social services agencies, who often wish to purchase elements of a tier-2 and-3 service, particularly child protection services and family therapy teams) can set their own pace in choosing services that fit local needs. Active dialogues between purchasers and providers has resulted in a much greater understanding of needs and how these needs can be met. While the total budget available to purchasers is set by the government and is itself obtained via direct taxation, providers are able to be creative in their search for service agreements by working with more than one purchaser, and are able to determine the best fit their finances allow between needs and resource availability. In addition, providers can obtain payment for seeing patients via an additional system known as "extra contractual referrals" (ECRs). These ECRs were specifically put into place to retain the ability to refer through the system when clinical needs arise. Purchasing authorities must retain an ECR budget and are

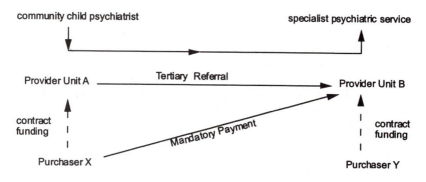

Figure 23.2

required to automatically pay providers (wherever they are in the country) when a clinician from one provider unit refers to a clinician in another, as is illustrated in Figure 23.2.

As can be seen, a community child psychiatrist in provider unit A and from purchaser X requires admission to the only inpatient unit run by provider B and in purchaser unit Y. This is called a tertiary referral (i.e., consultant to consultant) and is likely to occur only when the patient has received services from provider A, up to and including tier 3, but problems in diagnosis, assessment, or treatment remain. Purchaser X is required by law to pay provider B for this tertiary service.

This is an important open channel for consultant-to-consultant referrals, and it is accepted that it is essential to retain this needs-based access to tier-4 specialist services. However, it creates financial tensions for purchasers. First, they are unable to control these costs because it is not possible to determine the ECR flow rate, which depends entirely on consultant decisions. Second, ECR costs are invariably higher than designated service level agreements with a local provider. Third, ECR costs can reflect negatively on a purchaser's overall service purchasing policy. High ECRs can be interpreted as a poor service level base in the local provider, i.e., low quality of service and dissatisfaction with local services by family practitioners or the public demanding to be referred outside the local provider.

Interestingly, ECRs are also a potential source of difficulty for the receiving provider. In Figure 23.2, provider B is not obliged to tell purchaser Y, their local purchaser, about their ECR income; they are only obliged to provide returns to this or any other provider on

Table 23.2   *Tier-1 Child Mental Health Skills*

- Basic assessment of family function
- Basic–level interview skills with children
- Advise families on common child–rearing problems
- Recognize potentially clinically significant problems early
- Resolve simple parenting difficulties
- Intervene with simple anxious and behavioral symptoms
- Know when and where to ask for specialist assessment
- Have access to professional training and supervision

their local service level agreements. Tensions may arise if the local purchaser suspects that there is a "preference" for treating ECR patients who generate extra income for the provider unit.

Accusations of two-track services and financial rather than clinical needs being met may then arise. Overall, however, the attempts to bring about a better value-for-money service combined with retaining the NHS philosophy of meeting the needs of the public remain intact. The more explicit provision of information for both financial aspects of healthcare and the difficulties of controlling and forecasting clinical need and service utilization is viewed by managers and clinicians alike as beneficial to all. The difficulties in retaining an equitable health service on a restricted budget from central taxation is well known to many countries. The more open and reorganized NHS is a direct attempt to tackle these issues. The purpose is to retain and improve a patient-centered service within an efficient fiscal framework. It is argued that tier-1 services must be expounded and supported because this is where the highest volume of common emotional and behavioral difficulties can be managed. Improved training and education of primary medical teams is an important goal for the future. Research has shown that a high proportion of children who are recurrent attendees to family practitioners have mental disorders (Bowman & Garralda, 1993). It is suggested that the staff of tier-1 services should be trained on the mental health tasks shown in Table 23.2.

Many CAMHS use child psychiatry nurses and, to a lesser extent, community clinical child psychologists to provide these services. The need for improved leadership, communication, management, and performance monitoring is emphasized in the new structures. If the system is to achieve its aims, however, there is a fundamental need to retain systematic work records and to research service processes (including treatment effectiveness, sorely lacking in child psychiatry, and outcome evaluations). In this regard, many purchasers and providers find themselves at a disadvantage, as financial priorities emphasize current services rather than research and development. As a result, the central government has set a special research and development budget to encourage research into the NHS.

REFERENCES

Bowman, F. M., & Garralda, M. E. (1993). Psychiatric morbidity among children who are frequent attenders in general practice. *British Journal of General Practice, 46,* 6–9

Costello, E. J., Angold, A., Burns, B., Erkanli, A., Stangl, D. J., & Tweed, D.L. (1996). The Great Smokey Mountains study of youth: Functional impairment and serious emotional disturbance. *Archives of General Psychiatry, 53,* 1137–1143.

Health Advisory Service. (1995). *Child and adolescent mental health services: Together we stand.* London: Her Majesty's Stationery Office.

Health Advisory Service. (1986). *Bridges over troubled waters: A report from the NHS Advisory Service on services for disturbed adolescents.* London: Her Majesty's Stationery Office.

Williams, R., Richardson, G., & Emerson, G. (1996). Improving mental health services for young people. *Psychiatry in Practice, 15*(2), 15–19.

24

International Perspectives on the Economics of Mental Healthcare for Children and Adolescents: Economic Policies and the Swedish Experience

KARI SCHLEIMER

In the 1970s and 1980s, Sweden developed a social system that came to be well known all over the world. Today we know, as some did already in those days, that this social system was not based on Swedish money but on very substantial loans from abroad: a problem we Swedes must deal with today.

A whole generation of Swedes has grown up with the belief that the government would always provide money for children, housing, healthcare, sick-leave, and so on. Private loans were obtained easily, sometimes almost thrown at people! Older teenagers would get money to start their own life and to own a house quite independent of the income of their parents.

Today the situation is different. Social subsidies have been reduced and restricted considerably. Teenagers are told to stay at home with their parents until they are self-supporting in some way. The first day of sick-leave must be paid by patients themselves and they receive less compensation for the following days. The Swedish population has suddenly become healthier and well! Child allowances also have been reduced, as have many other subsidies.

The most dramatic change can be seen within healthcare where there are higher fees for medical consultations and for medication. Some groups within society find themselves having to reconsider their real need for consultation. Therefore, all disciplines in health-care have had severe cutbacks. Generally, this has resulted in a clear reduction of beds for inpatient care in practically all clinics. More treatment has been turned into day care, and most care is given on an outpatient basis.

Child and adolescent psychiatry has also been affected. Our specialty, at least in Sweden, is very much exposed to seasonal variations. Summer is a low activity season, as is Christmas, compared to the school-term period in autumn and spring, where there is high activity. The need for beds is calculated on a low-season basis. In Malmö, we have 6 beds for a population of 240,000 inhabitants, of which about 50,000 are under the age of 18. Each of our outpatient teams has a day care unit.

Our budget cut was about 15% over a period of 3 years, and at the same time we have had an increase in new referrals of almost 60%. The budget cut has resulted in several outcomes:

1. Markedly shorter periods of inpatient care.
2. Decidedly shorter periods of outpatient care with new methods utilizing short-term therapies. Treatment programs no longer continuing for years. It is not known whether this is for the better or the worse. We have to find methods to support faculty members in investigating this question.
3. More intense collaboration with other "caregiving neighbors," such as
   • the somatic healthcare system, especially pediatrics, child plastic surgery, and primary health care;
   • the child welfare system;
   • the social welfare system;
   • the school system.
   This is in order to prevent double work and expenses. Since the social welfare system must also work with a reduced budget, the inclination to "psychiatrize" problems of a child or an adolescent has clearly increased.
4. A list of diagnostic considerations of high priority that has been established for child and adolescent psychiatry. The national Association of Child and Adolescent Psychiatry in Sweden has been involved with this prioritization. The priorities imposed by this list are as follows.

The first priority is to decide if there is an immediate risk to the child or the adolescent due to: suicide, acute psychotic state, other acute emergency state of a psychological/psychiatric nature, the need for acute assessment of possible physical or sexual abuse, an acute status of an eating disorder, or a need for crisis intervention in situations of severe violence, disasters, or a death within the family.

Second priority is given to conditions for which lack of intervention would facilitate the development of a chronic condition leading to severe suffering and/or handicaps and reduction of functions in the child.

Third priority is given to conditions and/or symptoms of a less severe type, but that still make the child or adolescent suffer or endure a reduced quality of life.

Fourth priority is given to evaluations requested by court systems, families, schools, and others, for which in some cases other factors may intervene as well.

These new priorities may make it more and more difficult to keep up with what child psychiatrists have been doing for many years in Sweden: acting as counselors to parents, children, and adolescents.

5. A new organization of the "on-call system" together with our sister department in Lund, only 20 km away. The child psychiatrist on duty (on call) at night and on holidays will serve all clinics where children may be cared for in both hospitals, in addition to the departments of child and adolescent psychiatry (CAP) in both hospitals (with both inpatient care and emergency out patient care).

6. In order not to carry out "double work" in the two nearby CAP departments in Malmö and Lund, an agreement has been made to take care of psychotic teenagers in Lund, and to take care of depressive and suicidal teenagers in Malmö, independent of where they live. This agreement will affect the training experiences for residents and house officers in both departments, and this problem still has to be solved.

7. Quality assurance will be emphasized, not the least with respect to waiting lists, which exist for the first time in 20 years. Not all child psychiatric problems can wait for assessment without complications, so we will have to screen every new patient immediately to make this assessment. Afterwards it is difficult to tell

the patient that he or she will have to wait for some time. How-ever, in my experience the use of quality assurance techniques has enhanced the understanding of classification and diagnosis, slowly accepted by all mental health professionals, as a tool for accurate assessment of the patient.

When examining the reasons for which children and adolescents are referred to child and adolescent psychiatrists, it must be recognized that other organizations must also take care of their problems:

• schools for learning disabilities and behaviour problems;
• social welfare agencies for conduct disorders and substance and alcohol abuse;
• other medical specialties for nonpsychiatric medical disorders.

However, only child and adolescent psychiatry with its multidisciplinary approach, has the competence and experience to assess, diagnose, and treat the child from many different points of view.

In Sweden all mental health services for children and adolescents and their families are based on no fee, which means that they are free, no matter how often the child comes for consultation. Some counties have tried to have consultations with child and adolescent psychiatrists paid for by the patient, but they have returned to free consultations due to administrative problems and costs, which they decided were not worth pursuing.

25

Mental Health Reform: The Israeli Experience

SAM TYANO

TAMAR MOZES

On the brink of the third millennium, there is occurring a process of change in the economy and organization of health services worldwide. We are experiencing a trend towards change from centralized managed systems to autonomous ones, and the establishment of mechanisms for evaluation and control in order to achieve quality, equity, and appropriateness for each service in times of limited resources.

The Israeli mental health services are also in the process of reform. The major changes being attempted are: (a) to integrate mental health into the basket of general medical services provided by health maintenance organizations; (b) to convert state psychiatric hospitals to autonomous public trusts; (c) to relocate the focus of mental healthcare from hospitals run by the Ministry of Health to the community; (d) to subject mental healthcare to market forces, with the aim of containing costs and generating more cost-effective care; (e) for the Ministry of Health to divest itself of direct service provision by giving operational autonomy to its hospitals and outpatient clinics; (f) to strengthen the Ministry of Health's planning and oversight function; (g) to divest the district psychiatrist of all hospital administration functions and to restructure the psychiatrist's role into the head of integrated regional mental health services.

BACKGROUND

Part of the worldwide process of change occurring in the economy and organization of healthcare is a reconsideration of roles of the public and private sectors in healthcare financing and delivery. This process of change is rooted in both political-cultural changes and a significant restriction of economic resources.

Although healthcare costs in Israel are low by international standards, they are rising rapidly. Healthcare costs in Israel in 1971 were 5.4% of gross domestic product and rose to 7.8% in 1979. During the 1980s, the share stood at about 7.3%. Since 1986 it has been on the rise, and in 1990 it was 7.9%, which is the highest that it has been over the last 30 years. This share is higher than in Finland, Japan, and the United Kingdom, but considerably lower than in the United States, Sweden, Canada, France, Holland, and Germany (Organization for Economic Corporation and Development, 1991).

The health insurance system before 1995 was such that every citizen could purchase health insurance coverage from one of several HMOs. Not all citizens were insured, because it was not obligatory. The HMOs provided free medical care except for mental health. Prior to 1978, care for mental health patients was partially covered by HMOs, but in 1978 there was a change in the mental healthcare delivery system that removed responsibility for mental health from HMOs. Almost all community health clinics and psychiatric hospitals became state managed and paid for by the state. Mental health services were developed and operated in accordance with budgetary allotments which were made available by the Ministry of Health. Like elsewhere in the west, there has been growing discontent in Israel about increased health costs without improved quality of care. In response to this, in 1988, the Israeli government established the Netanyahu Commission, to study healthcare and recommend changes. The problems particularly relevant to mental healthcare in the commission report were (State of Israel, 1990):

1. Mental healthcare is not formally provided for by health maintenance organizations (HMO)s.
2. There are regional differences in availability of services between the center of the country and the periphery, where there is an acute shortage of services in general, and particularly for children and adolescents.
3. There is a conflict of interest between the Ministry of Health's dual functions as provider of services and overseer of healthcare.

4. Hospitals' budgets are based only on occupancy of beds, which encourages the use of hospitalization.
5. Most psychiatric services are hospital-based, with little investment in outpatient services.

In 1995 a new national health insurance law was enacted which provided free health services. All citizens were required to be insured through an HMO of their choice. Those who were not were allocated to any of the HMOs according to a capitation formula. A healthcare tax of 4.8% of gross income was levied to cover the services provided by the new law. This total amount of money was collected by the National Insurance System, and redistributed to the four HMOs according to a weighted formula. Mental healthcare was supposed to go into effect only 3 years thereafter.

MENTAL HEALTH SERVICES IN ISRAEL: BASIC DATA

The healthcare system was established before the founding of the state of Israel in 1948. This health system, in general, was concerned with meeting the immediate needs of the early settlers, with little emphasis on mental health. Over the course of 50 years the number of psychiatric hospital beds increased from 1,200 for a population of 650,000 residents in 1948 to 8,500 in 1980, and then decreased to 6,700 beds for about 6 million residents in 1996 (see Figure 25.1). Today the hospitalization rate is 1.2 per 1,000 residents (see Figure 25.2). The distribution of beds by patient category is (see Figure 25.3): 1%: short-term observation; 25%: acute patients; 10%: rehabilitation; 40%: long-term care; 15%: psychogeriatric; 3%: in general hospitals; and 6%: children and adolescents. Involuntary hospitalization amounted to 18% of total admissions.

There are about 100 community mental health clinics, 60 of them run by the Ministry of Health. Treatment in these clinics is free except for a $3.00 copayment. In a single year, some 19 persons per 1,000 make use of outpatient mental health clinics, of whom 9 are new cases. The annual ambulatory service visits are 180 per 1,000 residents.

The approximately 380,000 visits to government-owned mental health clinics during 1995 were distributed as follows by type of

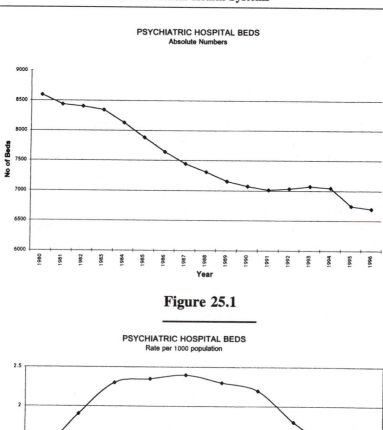

Figure 25.1

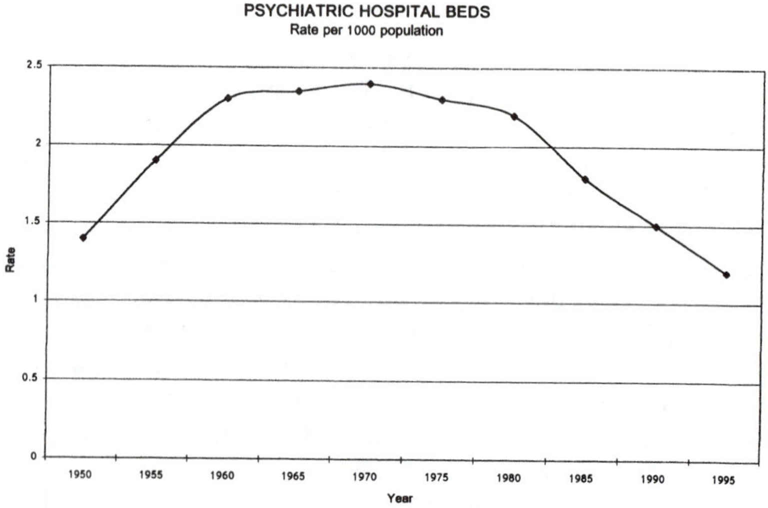

Figure 25.2

treatment received (see Figure 25.4): 41%: individual therapy; 28%: medication and follow-up; 7%: intake; 8%: group therapy; 4%: couple and family therapy; 12%: composite therapy. (Israel Ministry of Health, 1993, 1996).

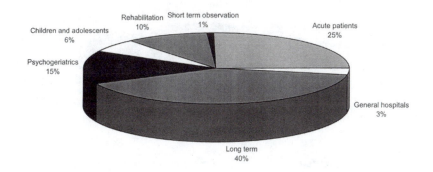

Figure 25.3 *Distribution of beds by patients category*

The Ministry of Health mental health budget breaks down as follows (see Figure 25.5): 65%: psychiatric hospitals; 11%: psychiatric wards in general hospitals; 8%: hospital-based day care; 13%: community care; 3%: other non-hospital-based care (Israel Ministry of Health, 1994).

DISCUSSION

There are different concepts concerning the place of psychiatry, in general, and child psychiatry, in particular, in the

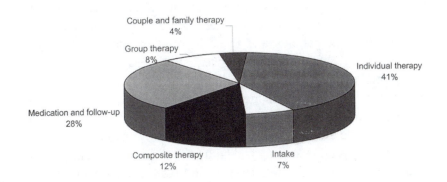

Figure 25.4 *Ambulatory care*

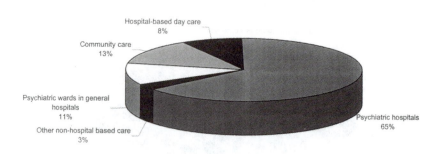

Figure 25.5   *Ministry of health mental health budget*

healthcare system. One approach is in favor of including the mental healthcare package within general healthcare coverage, which means directing the healthcare tax revenue to the HMOs which will provide mental health coverage. Another approach is concordant with the old arrangement, by which mental healthcare is under the government budget. Although the discussion seems to be about economic issues, there is an ideological agenda behind it. Based on the Netanyahu Commission, the Ministry of Health set up a reform program for the mental healthcare system in Israel. The guiding principles of mental healthcare policy are:

1. To fully integrate the mental healthcare system into the general healthcare system. The new law makes mental health services part of the HMOs. This legislation endorses and enacts the conception that mentally ill patients and those in need of supportive mental care have a right to freedom and equality of care; it provides a budget and sources of financing, defines the insurers' obligations to their clients in the area of mental health, as it does in the area of general medicine, and sets out the State's ultimate responsibility for provision. The HMOs' previous exemption from mental healthcare restricted preventive activity and held back the development of community-based mental health services and facilities. Each element of the network of mental health services was separately budgeted, the size of its funding governed by historical consideration alone; there was no mechanism for channeling patients to the type of care best

suited to their needs; and patient preferences played no part in the system.

As a result of the reform process, all mental healthcare services (primary, secondary, and tertiary) will be provided by the medical care system, which will significantly improve the spread, availability, and accessibility of the services and will minimize the stigma attached to them. Patients now have the right to choose their insurers and service providers and, via client advocacy associations, to be involved in decision-making on the nature, distribution and quality of services.

Expanding the role of the HMOs and the primary care physicians to include mental healthcare is expected to increase their awareness and motivation to detect and appropriately treat mental health problems in the primary healthcare setting. This is particularly important, since over one fourth of general practitioner visits are for psychological problems, many of which go unrecognized and untreated (Sartorius, Ustun, Costa e Silva, Goldberg, Lucrubier, Ormel, & Von Korff, 1993). Another theme of the reform process has been to end the role of the Ministry of Health as a direct provider of services and to delegate operational autonomy to the new providers. One of the purposes of this grant of autonomy was to introduce and stimulate interprovider competition.

2. To transfer the center of gravity of treatment from psychiatric hospitals to community-sited facilities. Prior to enactment of the health insurance law, psychiatric hospitals in Israel could admit patients without having to justify the decision to any regulatory body or insurer. In addition, there was no priori limit to length of inpatient stay and duration did not usually have to be justified for reimbursement. This led to overuse of inpatient care (Ginsberg, Penchas, & Israel, 1991). Mean length of stay in Israel acute psychiatric hospitals is, at present, about 60 days, which is longer than in New Zealand, Canada, or the United States.

In the new reality of a market-based healthcare system, HMOs will control the use of inpatient care through economically driven policies, and hospitals will be forced to develop an attractive billing system based on units of care. Various proposals have been made to move away from the per-diem method of reimbursing hospitals.

Ginsberg and colleagues (Ginsberg et al., 1991), after studying data from general hospitals in Israel, recommended a combination of capitation and/or diagnostic related groups (DRGs) linked with some form of payment via physician gatekeepers. DRGs are problematic in psychiatry, so we instead recommend differential reimbursement based on a combination of fee-for-service and regional capitation, similar to the "mixed" system proposed in the United States (Frank, Goldman, & McGuire, 1992). The consumer would be entitled to receive all needed services, and the provider would be encouraged to provide these services in the most efficient way. Treatment plans would have to be submitted to the insurer at regular intervals. Reimbursement would be based, in part, on capitation and, in part, on semi-per-diem payment, with differential care, for open and closed units, and for different age groups and levels of comorbidity. To minimize the number of "heavy user" patients, it is hoped that the per-diem payment will be adjusted for hospitals that lengthen mean time between admissions and shorten lengths of stay. This should help contain costs, better distribute risk between hospital and insurer, and promote the tailoring of patient-specific care plans. Similar work is being done on developing a fee schedule for outpatient mental health care. The fee for out-patient care will be based mainly on the fee for psychiatric services provided by hospitals, supplemented by fees for a day of clinic care, for rehabilitation care, for care in a hospital-substitute setting, etc. The pricing code adopted, and hence the wages of the workers in the different care settings, is structured 2 to 1 in favor of community-sited facilities over hospital services.

Service facilities are undergoing a transition to the status of autonomous operational units. The new conception is that funding, previously allocated according to historical consideration, will now be supplied by payment for the treatments that comprise the basket of mental health services and so push facility policy to become client centered. The different categories of facility (psychiatric hospitals, outpatient clinics) will begin to combine into comprehensive mental healthcare centers, and these centers and the HMOs have agreed on the operational procedures that will govern provider–insurer relations. Access to hospital services by consumers has been improved by allowing treatment to begin before the insurer's commitment to pay for hospital care has been submitted.

Should a mentally ill person require inpatient care, preference is now given to community-based hospital substitutes. Should inpatient care in a psychiatric hospital be unavoidable, preference is given to short-term stays in open units. The emphasis of treatment is on rehabilitation and avoiding chronification, at the same time minimizing the curtailment of the patient's freedom. Overall, the tendency of the system now is to accord predominance to outpatient care over inpatient care. In the light of this reorientation, from 1993 to 1995, all long-term hospital inpatients were reassessed. As a result of the assessment team's findings, some 250 patients are now awaiting a transfer to an old age home, about 184 to sheltered housing, about 65 to their own home or to their family, and some 200 to hostels. This transfer from hospitals to the community and/or to hospital substitutes will be effected, in our estimate, gradually over a number of years. The mix of psychiatric hospital beds is changing in response to enhanced availability of community facilities and minimally restrictive care.

3. To promote quality of service, placing the emphasis on a client-centered therapeutic approach, based on equality of provision in all regions of the country. There is an unequal distribution of mental health services. In the center of the country there is a disproportionate amount of care as compared to the North and South of Israel, where there is a particular shortage of community-based mental healthcare and all types of care for children and adolescents. To deal with the gaps in services, there was a restructuring of the Ministry of Health's Mental Health Division by decentralizing many of its powers to regional management boards. In June 1995, the District Psychiatrists, who have the legal mandate for compulsory commitment to mental healthcare, assumed their new function as Regional Psychiatrists, who are charged with heading Regional Mental Health Boards that supervise and coordinate, plan and develop all mental health services in the region, and play a part in information collection. Each Board works with a Regional Coordination Committee comprising representatives of the central government, insurers, voluntary agencies, providers, and service clients/consumers. The Boards' multidisciplinary staffs comprise: a planning and coordination assistant, a quality assurance inspector, an addiction therapy inspector, and a longterm care inspector. The Board also supervises compliance with staff performance standards and oversees the services provided by insurers. They are the entity for public inquiries and complaints.

Transforming patients from passive to active consumers aware of their positions and their rights under the National Health Insurance Act will certainly be neither easy nor short. Freedom to choose is hardly compatible with severe mental illness, but in fact only a minority of the mental health patients are so impaired as to not know their own interests, and with their families' help, these too will receive proper service.

In 1995 the National Mental Health Advisory Council was created. This important Council, comprising health economists and representatives of the mental health and family medicine professions, advises the Director-General of the Ministry of Health on policy and standards in the field of mental health and is a significant force in the enactment and assimilation of the reforms in the mental health system. The Council proposed standards for both inpatient and ambulatory services. These standards deal with basic structural issues and optimal staff planning, together with therapy planning milestones, and supervision. The therapy criteria are based on the basket of services. The main focus in the development of these standards has been to promise both quality and equality of caregiving. In all financial arrangements, these basic standards must be taken into account.

REFERENCES

Frank, R. G., Goldman, H. H., & McGuire, T. G. (1992). A model mental health benefit in private insurance. *Health Affairs, 10,* 116–123.

Ginsberg, G., Penchas, S., & Israel, A. (1991). Alternative methods of hospital reimbursement in Israel. *Israel Journal of Medical Sciences, 27,* 583–589.

Israel Ministry of Health. (1993). *Health in Israel: Selected data.* Jerusalem: Information and Computerization Services.

Israel Ministry of Health. (1994). *Overview of 1993: Activities of the Ministry of Health, Fiscal Year 1993.* Jerusalem: Israel Ministry of Health.

Israel Ministry of Health. (1996). *Mental health care services in Israel—Basic information.* Jerusalem: Information and Computerization Services.

Organization for Economic Co-Operation and Development. (1991). Data file.

Satorius, T. B., Ustun, J. A., Costa e Silva, J. A., Goldberg, D., Lecrubier, Y., Ormel, H., Von Korff, M. (1993). An International Study of Psychological Problems in Primary Care. Preliminary report from the World Health Organization collaborative project on *Psychological Problems in General Health Care.*

State of Israel. (1990). *The State Commission of Inquiry into the Operation and Efficiency of the Healthcare System in Israel. The Majority Opinion (Netanyahu Commission).* Jerusalem: Government Printing House.

26

Managed Care: How Is It Managing in the United States?

J . GERALD YOUNG

DIANA KAPLAN

Managed care swept into the world of healthcare services in the United States like a tornado, with new concepts, vocabulary, regulations, controversies, and dollars flying in the wind. So much change suggests that so much was wrong. How is managed care viewed by consumers, providers, payors, and interested others?

The following consists of brief comments describing issues arising in the wake of managed care's arrival. It is too early to provide a full assessment, yet selected observations depict the emerging reality of this new organization of healthcare services. It is followed by specific remarks about mental health services for children and adolescents, concerning both their relationship to managed care and the larger questions about their organizational challenges in a competitive environment.

COST CONTAINMENT

The development of managed care strategies (see Chapter 3) has occurred in response to various economic and clinical care objectives, leading to variations in the meaning of the term. While the essence of managed care is to achieve cost containment, it is also true that care can be managed to assure effective patient treatments or good patient management for patients with complicated conditions (such as those who need patient advocates to integrate their care, assure continuity of care and communication among clinicians, and enable access to necessary healthcare resources). These differing meanings depend in part on the perspective of the healthcare planning. A regional planning administrator manages care through determining the specific resources to provide, such as the types of services, number and nature of hospital beds or hospital equipment to purchase. A financial manager assesses resources use and devises strategies to keep costs low. An executive of a for profit managed care organization is attentive to all of these goals, and additionally must sustain profits and stock prices, as in any industry. An executive of a nonprofit hospital also aims at making a profit, which will be applied to capital construction, care of the poor, training, research, and similar social goals. A clinician manages care in order to bring the patient's health to the best possible level while not overutilizing resources and maintains records for quality assurance and patient care needs. There is much tension between these perspectives. For example, as for profit managed care organizations achieve profits, the financial resources of nonprofit organizations available for "subsidizing" socially significant activities are diminished.

For nations assessing the utility of privatization for their own healthcare systems, their examination of the outcomes in the United States must focus on these tensions. In an era of multinational corporations and an emerging international style of corporate administration, it will be attractive for other nations to join managed care systems seeking a global reach in what is already a global marketplace (wealthy patients fly to other countries for care). All nations need to consider both the successes and failures of manage care.

The Benefits of Managed Care

While many dispute the tactics through which managed care achieved its increasing control of healthcare delivery (see Young, Chapter 3), it has achieved some undeniably useful results. "These include attempts to eliminate waste and redundancy, a greater focus on health promotion and disease prevention, more attention to the management of chronic diseases, a focus on the accountability of physicians and health plans and on the quality of care, lower hospitalization rates without an obvious decline in the quality of care, heavy investment in patient-information systems, and—at least for the present—control of employers' health care costs'' (Kassirer, 1997). It is important to note, however, that its major advertised benefit, cost containment, might elude it as an achievement.

The Reduction of Healthcare Costs and the Challenge of Sustaining It

There is agreement that there have been remarkable reductions in healthcare costs in the United States; by the mid-1990s the rate of their increase became less than that of consumer prices in general. There is significant doubt, however, about whether this can be sustained after inefficiencies in the system have been eliminated and other sources of cost increases continue to be active; this is the next challenge to be confronted. Is it likely that recruitment of patients into more efficient managed care organizations supplied a one-time cost reduction and that expenses in the healthcare industry will once again soar? This, of course, is the haunting question at this point in the rapid development of managed care. It must be recognized that, while managed care has slowed increases in healthcare costs, it has definitely not stopped them. During the period from 1980 to 1995, managed care grew rapidly, and so did overall healthcare expenditures, quadrupling from $250 billion to almost $1 trillion. Moreover, total expenditures for healthcare in 1995 increased by 5.4% over the prior year, to $988 billion (Ginzberg & Ostow, 1997).

Not surprisingly, some of the "expenses" of obtaining cost reductions stimulate controversy. One study found that for-profit hospitals spend 23% more on administration than do comparable private, not-for-profit hospitals, and 34% more than public institutions (Woolhandler & Himmelstein, 1997). In particular, the for-profit hospitals spend more on marketing, lobbying, and executive compensation. The latter has been a special target for criticism, as very large salaries, bonuses, and stock options for some executives have fueled the fires of dispute. In response, some have said that more administrative expenses may have generated better administration, which increases the efficiency of the hospitals. The higher administrative costs are acceptable if efficiency is increased according to this reasoning. Some highly regarded corporations also have high administrative expenses, and this is accepted as part of the basis for their success: you need good administrators to run highly complex businesses. It is also hoped that the administrative costs associated with too many competing health insurance companies and healthcare programs will be reduced with progress in the market in the future, and that the early costs of mergers and acquisitions will lead to increased efficiency in the healthcare system.

The Problem of Imprudent Tactics for Attaining Apparent Cost Containment and Profits

Some methods leading to success in cost containment by managed care organizations raise fears about their purposes and the methods utilized to achieve their goals. Two examples indicate the nature of the dilemma.

Biases in Clinical Service Usage by Managed Care Patients

One of the persistent questions about cost containment in managed care systems is whether all of the reduction in cost is a true reduction. For example, one study examined enrollment in Medicare HMOs (health maintenance organizations); the expectation that HMOs can aid in the arrest of the growth of Medicare costs is the basis for active encouragement of enrollment in Medicare HMOs. Some critics, however, suggest that the HMOs are enrolling healthier Medicare patients. This study found several important biases in Medicare enrollment. First, those Medicare patients who use fewer services than average were more likely to enroll in HMOs. Second, those Medicare patients who leave HMOs subsequently use more services than average. These results persist when analyzed in subgroups of patients according to age, race, and income level. Moreover, the group of patients who move from HMOs to the fee-for-service system and then back to HMOs was examined. It was found that reenrollment in HMOs takes place *after* their hospital admission rates drop. They also found that in the group of patients disenrolled from HMOs for less than a year there was an association between the hospital admission rate within the first three months following disenrollment and the length of time before reenrollment, and a suggestion that those who remain ouside the HMO system for one year or longer might be more likely to need long-term care (Morgan, Virnig, DeVito, & Persily, 1997). It appears that patients disenroll from HMOs and obtain needed services through the fee-for-service medical care system, returning to Medicare HMOs after receiving the services. These patterns of usage make it very difficult for the Medicare system to achieve the cost reductions anticipated through fostering HMO enrollment of its beneficiaries. Moreover, it agrees with the observations of many physicians that managed care concentrates its services on the healthiest patients, leaving high service usage patients for other sectors of the healthcare system to manage, which refutes the heavily advertised assertions of cost containment and superior management techniques.

Accusations that For-Profit Healthcare Organizations Utilize Unethical Policies and Tactics

The Columbia/HCA Healthcare Corporation was rapidly built into the biggest for-profit hospital chain in the United States. Their aggressive tactics pulled together 340 hospitals and 570 home healthcare centers (the largest home health network in the nation), while provoking a frustrated backlash among hospital executives, physicians, and state attorneys general across the country. Eventually, these tactics led to a near collapse, however, as the government began an array of fraud investigations. The investigations involved 50 or more Columbia hospitals in questions concerning Medicare billings for physician services, laboratory blood work, physician recruitment, and referrals to home health agencies. They led to 35 search warrants served in seven states. Columbia's stock price dropped, which led to merger negotiations, initiated in 1997, with the second largest hospital chain in the country (less than half the size of Columbia/HCA), Tenet Healthcare.

Ironically, Tenet itself had a history of fraud investigation 4 years earlier. Tenet was originally National Medical Enterprises, a smaller hospital chain that settled Federal and state charges against it by paying $379 million in 1994, as well as several hundred million dollars more to individuals and insurance companies. The charges of fraud and abuses toward psychiatric patients stated that its psychiatric hospitals had bribed doctors to send patients to them, admitted patients to their care who did not need treatment, and subsequently kept them against their will until their insurance ran out. National Medical Enterprises was raided by 600 FBI agents. Tenet was formed as a new corporation, new management was brought in, the company was restructured, more hospitals were acquired, and the stock price again went up rapidly. In the meantime, Tenet had established a thorough system to prevent any further fraudulent practices.

By early March of 1998 the Columbia/HCA earnings exceeded Wall Street expectations and its stock price went up, suggesting that it would weather the storm. It was spinning off almost one-third of its 340 hospitals. Simultaneously, the Federal investigation of its business practices continued.

Determining the Cost-Effectiveness of Treatments

These disappointments leave clinicians searching for answers, in great part through examining the development of improved treatments that will reduce morbidity and restrain costs. Ultimately there must be some improved measures of cost-effectiveness of treatments, because a principle on which many medical and psychiatric treatments are offered in this current maelstrom of economic competition is that they *are* cost effective. This supplies the tie between the administrator who is concerned about cost containment and the physician who is concerned about optimal patient care. Such clinical studies are becoming much more common, and the difficulties encountered when conducting them is also now apparent. Measures and methodological decisions can make cost-effectiveness analyses either illuminating or uninterpretable (Ubel, DeKay, Baron, & Asch, 1996; Wolff, Helminiak, & Tebes, 1997). While these studies will be central to cost-containment efforts by clinicians in the future, full realization of their potential awaits an initial period of development of adequate measures and methodological refinements.

THE ORGANIZATION AND MANAGEMENT OF MANAGED CARE ORGANIZATIONS

Management Competencies in Managed Care Organizations: Is It Illusory?

Management problems in hospitals and in physician practices suggested that one of the most significant advantages of managed care would be its superior administrative capabilities, increasing income substantially on this basis. While there is reason to believe that this is true in many instances, it is also undeniably true that some managed care organizations have had significant problems in fundamental management activities.

A recent example has been the Oxford Health Plan, an east coast managed care organization with many customers in New York City. In the autumn of 1997, Oxford was said to be experiencing financial problems. Oxford had been remarkably successful, growing rapidly by gaining an identity as a managed care company that offered affordable coverage while allowing customers unusual flexibility when selecting a physician. This strategy led to a rapid increase in new customers, but the continuing large influx of new premiums masked emerging financial problems. These problems initially were revealed through increasing tardiness in paying physicians and hospitals and were explained as computer problems, but it eventually became known that Oxford had been unable to effectively track its accounts. It did not know how much it was receiving from members or paying out to physicians, and it overestimated revenues and underestimated costs. Its after-tax loss in 1997 ($291.3 million) exceeded by $78.6 million the total of all of its previous profits over 7 years. An infusion of $350 million from an outside investor was required to keep it afloat.

It continues to appear that Oxford's problems stemmed from providing high-quality service at a price that was well below its true cost. These problems are likely to lead to changes in the complexion of the company, so that it will begin to look like other managed care companies: it will raise premiums and begin to limit the choice of doctors. Before its sudden financial collapse, this transition was already being planned, along with the adoption of another strategy common in California, in which teams of physician specialists compete against one another for Oxford's members while remaining under Oxford's management umbrella. The advantage of this system is that it utilizes small networks that tightly monitor both healthcare costs and quality.

It does not take long for customers to feel the effects of such financial mismanagement and losses. Within months, one self-insured customer reported a premium increase of 69% by Oxford. Another customer said that his premium increase meant that it would become 1/3 of his monthly income. Other insurers and managed care companies were increasing rates in the New York region also, for unrelated reasons, causing alarm about another round of increases in healthcare expenses after a quiescent period.

Self-insured customers are the most vulnerable customers, presumably because they include a higher proportion of patients who require long-term and costly treatments. Oxford became very popular among such patients with individual coverage in New York: 65,000 of them, half of the total in the state, joined Oxford. Oxford lost $17 million on these customers in 1997. At the same time, it must be recalled that state law requires that it provide insurance to individuals.

These are for-profit companies, so we must examine profits when describing the history of problem companies in an otherwise growing industry. The stock prices for Oxford reflect the dramatic turn in its history. Investors paid $1.88 per share in the 1991 public offering. The share price peaked at $89 per share in July 1997, and had fallen to around $16 per share in the spring of 1998.

QUALITY OF CARE

The rapid transition to managed care would not have been possible without substantial unhappiness among Americans about soaring healthcare costs in the 1980s. However, having favored this transition, a large number of Americans became angry and dissatisfied with the managed care organizations who halted the rising costs of healthcare. A Harris poll in September 1997 determined that 54% of Americans believed that the trend toward managed care was harmful for them, an increase from 43% over the prior year. Physicians appear to be as dissatisfied as consumers, because another study indicated that 55% of 2,000 physicians surveyed thought that the healthcare system was deteriorating; these opinions were most prevalent in locations with well-established managed care organizations. Similar results in other surveys led to a firestorm of advocacy, as well as activity in Congress and in state legislatures aimed at regulating the healthcare industry, particularly its practices related to holding down costs to increase profits. Healthcare organizations understand the significance of the trend, and some are joining consumers in supporting regulation. In 1995, a Harris poll showed that 59% of adults interviewed liked the trend toward managed care and thought that it was a good thing, while 28% did not; by 1997 the comparable figures were 44% and 44%. Other polls show that the percentage of people judging that for-profit health plans provide better quality of care has dropped significantly, as has the percentage of people who perceive that for-profit health plans are more efficient. Nevertheless, other polls show continuing satisfaction with both not-for-profit and for-profit plans among most people, and it should be recognized that the short-term influence of events like the uncovering of fraudulent practices can have strong but transient effects on the results of surveys.

One of the tangible results of these events was that three large HMOs with a total of more than 10 million members (Kaiser Permanente, HIP Health Insurance Plans in New York, and the Group Health Cooperative of Puget Sound) joined two consumer groups in requesting more regulation of managed healthcare. They called for "legally enforceable national standards." One of the by-products of all of this activity is the inevitable focus on patients' rights and how they are to be asserted. While such issues have been in the background until now, legal and practical means for asserting patient rights are now being developed and utilized (Annas, 1997).

Perhaps most surprisingly, the state of California, the pioneer in managed care, began an extensive review of managed care activities in 1997. Its managed care systems cover more than half of the state's 32 million people, but the number of consumer complaints in 1996 was 18% more than in 1995. The concept that healthcare costs are reduced by rejecting treatment determined to be "not medically necessary" has become a particular focus, due to many stories of dramatic mismanagement of individual cases as part of these policies. Supporters of managed care, however, warn that it is an error to be caught in emotions concerning individual cases, which should not condemn the entire system; such problems occur in any healthcare system.

Inevitably, some small companies are using this new focus on quality of care as a route to success, offering programs for patients with specific chronic illnesses. While they continue to monitor costs to keep them low, they attempt to enhance quality of care not only to aid patients, but to improve the motivation and satisfaction of employees and avoid additional intrusive government regulations.

EQUITY AND THE CARE OF INDIGENT PATIENTS

When troubles occur, the first locus of cost-cutting is the coverage of poor patients. When Oxford fell upon hard times, it quickly determined that it would leave the Medicaid program in Connecticut, and the 33,000 poor people it had covered would be divided among other insurers in the state. This step raised fears that the same thing would happen in New York. Not surprisingly, this again raised questions about the fate of the poor in an era of privatization of healthcare. Advocates and government administrators question the commitment that managed care plans have to this population and worry not only that moving them from plan to plan disrupts their healthcare, but also that poor people appear to be treated as a commodity by being moved among plans who move in and out of the market according to financial needs.

On the other hand, increasing efficiency in single hospitals can have surprisingly good results, enabling them to make profits while caring for the poor. An example is St. Barnabas Hospital in the Bronx, New York, which gained two huge city contracts worth almost $450 million. The hospital has greatly increased revenues from an unlikely source, Medicaid. At the same time, critics of their methods raise familiar worries, in particular, that the stringent cost-cutting measures are at the expense of a high quality of patient care. For example, many physicians have felt that clinics were crowded and understaffed and that resident physicians were poorly supervised. The hospital answers that it has saved money through efficiencies like automated laboratories, computers for billing and records, avoidance of multiple tests, and using fewer workers while maintaining quality of care.

THE FUTURE OF MANAGED CARE

Is it useful to discuss a few for-profit healthcare corporations who have had notorious problems? This does not condemn all healthcare plans. However, the examples sited were leaders in the industry nationally or regionally, and, most significantly, the types of problems encountered were those that have been of concern from the outset of the privatization of healthcare. These examples do not indicate that privatization is the wrong direction; instead, they can be viewed as a warning that the problems of the healthcare industry over the past 40 years are complex and only partially solved by criticizing the poor management and cost containment procedures of the old systems.

Clinicians solving patient care problems are likely to conduct research examining patient care outcome and financial results, but corporations behave differently. They respond to market forces and attempt to shape and control the nature of the marketplace. Quick, forceful activity is often rewarded, and even subsequent mistakes can leave a few executives at the top of a corporation with fortunes. These are different cultures, and merging these cultures will be a challenging process.

Having burst into healthcare so dramatically, where is managed care likely to take us in the United States? Of course, no one is able to answer this question, but there are voices suggesting that the run of managed care is now threatened. The growth of managed care will be very difficult to sustain as the cost savings are likely to wither after the initial containment; the public will decry the lack of support by managed care of medical education, research, and care of the indigent; and, finally, the public disaffection with the clinical care policies of managed care companies will lead to more advocacy and more government regulation of managed care policies and practices (Ginzberg & Ostow, 1997; Kassirer, 1997). Moreover, the 20% to 30% profits needed to sustain capital investment in managed care organizations, given the added costs of their administrative expenses, will be difficult to sustain in the future. In particular, corporations are likely to increasingly turn directly to providers (hospitals and clinician groups) to save these additional managed care expenses. As corporations attempt to go directly to healthcare providers for contracts, leaving out managed care organizations, the bedrock of managed care activities is threatened. Moreover, in order to survive, "managed care plans will have to show that they have become better citizens: that they care about more than profits, that they do not skimp on care, that they support their just share of teaching, research, and the care of the poor, that they no longer muzzle physicians, and that they offer something special (including control of costs) by managing care" (Kassirer, 1997).

THE IMPLICATIONS OF CHANGING HEALTHCARE
ECONOMICS AND POLICIES FOR CHILD AND
ADOLESCENT PSYCHIATRY

Beyond Managed Care: Old and Detrimental Competitive Influences

A failure to understand and adjust to the influences of managed care and other changes in healthcare delivery services is detrimental to clinicians planning care for their patients. On the other hand, it can be a strategic error for clinicians providing mental health services to children and adolescents in the United States to focus solely on managed care as the single basis for their competitive activities. This is particularly true because mental health services for children and adolescents are either outside or on the periphery of managed care systems in most regions of the United States. While the influence of managed care on our clinical care is pervasive, as all healthcare systems adopt at least some of the techniques pioneered by managed care systems, it is less dominant because of its neglect of our subspecialty, which has a history of not being viewed as economically productive.

For those engaged in mental health services for children and adolescents in any country, one simple meaning of these developments is that attention to the development of improved treatments for our patients, in the context of sound financial practices, is likely to be a pathway to success. This perspective is amply evident in this book, but is difficult to put into practice in spite of the knowledge base available to clinicians. Child and adolescent psychiatrists, having discussed the competitive forces and progress in the general healthcare marketplace, must return to fundamentals and examine their competitive position, both its vulnerabilities and its potential.

The field of child and adolescent mental health, as a "low income producer" and a "personnel-intensive specialty," is afflicted with a pervasive lack of equity for its patients. Combining two sectors of medical neglect, children and mental illness, mental healthcare for children is easily shunted aside with familiar excuses, such as the idea that psychiatric care is not medical care (the brain is not an organ of the body) or that children with these problems are not suffering. The high prevalence of children urgently needing treatment and the probable greater number of children burdened with childhood psychiatric disturbances create a challenge to our profession and an alarming prospect to healthcare administrators unable to conceptualize concurrent savings that could accompany increased funding.

It is a mistake to portray administrators and third party payers as the sole source of doubt and caution. Regrettably, patients and families readily accede to efforts by healthcare purchasers, such as businesses on behalf of their employees, to reduce or eliminate psychiatric coverage, especially for children. The unrealistic notions that "this does not pertain to me" or "children don't have psychiatric disorders" are seductive to every business and to every individual seeking reduced healthcare premiums. Insurance companies and managed care organizations then bear the brunt of later accusations when coverage is needed but missing.

Competitive Obstacles

Commentaries on economic and management influences on the development of mental health services for children and adolescents typically include no discussion of some elements that remain concealed: (a) the unchallenged biases of third party payors against children and adolescents needing mental health services; (b) the common and unchallenged poor management practices by administrators with no knowledge about child psychiatric services that further undermine the economic productivity of child psychiatry; (c) the failure of professionals to join together nationally to specify the standard minimal resources needed by varied types of child and adolescent psychiatry service units in order to function (e.g., inpatient unit, outpatient clinic, etc.); (d) the minimal use of incentives for professionals in child psychiatric clinical services; (e) the political conflicts inherent in the process of achieving better resources for children and adolescents: professionals with these goals can be overridden by other professionals who gain administrative hegemony but are dependent for their prestigious positions on the administrators restricting the resources needed.

There has been a failure to recognize that efficient management practices have been sought by many child psychiatrists over the years (for example, adequate clerical staff and computerized patient information systems), but avoided by administrators in authority for short-term and political reasons; some child psychiatrists today do not understand this and then join in damaging criticism of prior child psychiatrist administrators. This is detrimental because it creates the illusion that mental health services for children and adolescents are so burdened by incapable professionals, and that the treatments are inherently so complex and expensive, that capital investment is foolish. This encourages administrative and financial neglect for this otherwise burgeoning field.

A related problem is that maintaining budget control at remote administrative levels to assure political control can lead to management errors due to impractical policies or procedures; a common bureaucratic error is the use of rigid budgets that must be spent in a prespecified manner based upon the procedures and budgets in other medical specialties, or an abstract annual goal set by administrators unaware of actual clinical and budget needs. Another common error is the reduction of a subsequent year's budget if the current year's budget is not fully spent, thereby encouraging questionable spending.

It would be naive to ignore the competitive forces acting upon child and adolescent psychiatrists. In the United States, child and adolescent psychiatry is a division of a larger department, usually psychiatry but sometimes pediatrics. Some child psychiatrist administrators, prior to the ascendence of managed care, attempted to establish more sensible administrative and financial structures and policies.

Initially encouraged in this effort by administrators, child psychiatrists usually confronted a sudden aversion to the idea once their plan was completed. Departments of psychiatry or pediatrics, or general hospital administrators, were unwilling to give up administrative and financial control of this group of professionals and patients. Presented with a viable plan, the chairpersons and managers would pull back, especially when the plan included establishment of a "cost center" of accounting for all income and expenses for child psychiatry. This reluctance to cede any management control would occur even though child psychiatry administratively would remain fully within the larger department.

Such a cost center, ceding control of a budget for child psychiatry, would encourage child psychiatry to establish profitable clinical activities if they were to expand their services. It also would expose instances in which child psychiatry received fewer personnel lines and other forms of budgetary support, or had money siphoned off to support other activities in the hospital. Simultaneously surprised and alarmed that a child psychiatrist produced such a plan, the chairpersons would plead changing budgetary or administrative circumstances that prevented them from following through with the plan.

In this way, child psychiatry activities were kept at an artificially reduced size, their more complex therapeutic services received less funding instead of more, and clinical and research initiatives were undermined. Child psychiatry then continued to be criticized as scientifically unproductive. Ironically, child psychiatrists were recommending some of the same policies that were later adopted out of necessity by administrators, who then criticized physician administrators as being incompetent.

Imaginative and potentially productive clinical and financial strategies are highly constrained, and usually impossible, while child and adolescent psychiatry is not an independent department in medical centers. One example of the results of these competitive forces is the current gradual absorption of selected child and adolescent psychiatric research activities by general psychiatrists and pediatricians. It is short sighted to direct criticism solely at managed care practices in the United States or individual political or economic influences in other nations. Competitive forces against child and adolescent mental health services have been continuous and have assumed many forms. These competitive pressures will not disappear. The competitive forces acting on mental health services and systems for children and adolescents must be confronted by those administering and providing these services if our patients are to participate in the dramatic medical advances of the 20th and 21st centuries.

REFERENCES

Annas, G. J. (1997). Patients' rights in managed care—Exit, voice, and choice. *New England Journal of Medicine, 337,* 210–215.

Ginzberg, E., & Ostow, M. (1997). Managed care—A look back and a look ahead. *New England Journal of Medicine, 336,* 1018–1020.

Kassirer, J. P. (1997). Editorial: Is managed care here to stay? *New England Journal of Medicine, 336,* 1013–1014.

Morgan, R. O., Virnig, B. A., DeVito, C. A., & Persily, N. A. (1997). The Medicare-HMO revolving door—The healthy go in and the sick go out. *New England Journal of Medicine, 337,* 169–175.

Ubel, P. A., DeKay, M.L., Baron, J., & Asch, D. A. (1996). Cost-effectiveness analysis in a setting of budget constraints—Is it equitable? *New England Journal of Medicine, 334,* 1178–1184.

Wolff, N., Helminiak, T. W., & Tebes, J. K., (1997). Getting the cost right in cost-effectiveness analyses. *American Journal of Psychiatry, 154,* 736–743.

Woolhandler, S., & Himmelstein, D.L. (1997). Costs of care and administration at for-profit and other hospitals in the United States. *New England Journal of Medicine, 336,* 769–774.

27

Challenges in Providing Mental Health Services for Children and Adolescents in India

SAVITA MALHOTRA

India has for a long time prided itself on its glorious past and a rich heritage of philosophy, art and culture, tradition, and values. Despite being a predominantly religious society, in the contemporary sociopolitical system India exhibits an admixture of old traditional culture and beliefs and modern, westernized values and lifestyles. There is also a considerable diversity of languages, religions, cultures, social practices, and levels of development across regions within the country. It has a predominantly rural population (70%), mostly dependent upon an agricultural economy. Modernization, technological and industrial development, and urbanization are relatively recent phenomena, seen only after independence from colonial rule which was achieved about half a century ago.

After independence, India decided to be a secular republic and a welfare state, where health services and education were to be provided free to all its citizens up to 14 years of age. As a sign of its commitment to the care of children, the Government of India adopted a National Policy for Children (1974) which in addition to the constitutional provisions provided, among other things, for

- protection of children against neglect, cruelty & exploitation;
- prohibition of employment of children under 14 years old in hazardous occupations;

- facilities for special treatment, education, rehabilitation, and care of children who are physically handicapped, emotionally disturbed, or mentally retarded;
- amendment of existing laws so that in all legal disputes, whether between parents or institutions, the interests of children are given paramount consideration.

Primary education for children has now (in 1997) been made a fundamental right in the Constitution of India. The status of children in India today needs to be evaluated against the backdrop of the ideology and guiding principals enunciated for their care.

THE STATUS OF CHILDREN

Study of some of the gross indicators of health of children in India (UNICEF, 1991) has revealed the following facts.

The infant mortality rate has been significantly reduced, from 160 per 1,000 live births at the time of independence (1947), to about 94 in 1988, being much higher in the rural areas (102 per 1,000) as compared to the urban areas (61 per 1,000). There is a very high interstate differential from 28 in Kerala to 123 in Uttar Pradesh. The infant mortality rate has been directly linked to social development (assessed on the parameters of the social and economic support available at home) and availability of pre- peri and postnatal infant care. At the all–India level, about 12% of preschool children (0–4 years-old) in rural areas, and about 29% in urban areas, have any access to healthcare.

Child mortality at 2 years of age is about five times higher among those who have illiterate mothers compared to educated mothers, twice as common among urban manual workers, and thrice as common among rural agricultural laborers than among the urban non-manual workers. Malnutrition and infectious diseases constitute the two major causes of mortality in children. About 40% of children between 1 and 5 years suffer from protein-calorie malnutrition. Over the years, the percentage of children suffering from severe malnutrition has decreased, but that of those with mild malnutrition has increased.

Only about 40% of rural and 70% of urban children between 6 and 14 years of age attend schools. Although, through successive policies, programs, and active efforts, enrollment for children in schools has recently increased substantially to nearly 90%, about half of these drop out by the end of 10 years of age. Despite free education in government schools, most parents are not able to afford the cost of books or stationery. Moreover, the education system is considered to be inappropriate or irrelevant since there is no immediate reward or gain, it is too long and slow, and it is uninteresting and not in keeping with their home environment or lifestyle. Parents of children in urban areas and in middle and upper socioeconomic classes, on the contrary, place a very high value on education and push children into a highly competitive and ambitious pursuit, sometimes to the extent of overburdening them.

These families make the best use of the educational opportunities in the country and contribute a significant amount of money, time, and energy into producing some of the best-qualified professionals in various fields. Thus, the index of social development, as judged by the availability and utilization of services in the health and education sectors, along with the economic situation of the society, is the key factor that accounts for regional and social disparities. Realities of life for people living in rural areas, as against those living in urban areas, or for those who are economically weaker vs. those who are affluent, are in total contrast. Nevertheless, there are certain characteristics of culture, value systems, and child-rearing practices that have greater uniformity across regions and may constitute a unifying link.

Philosophy of Child Rearing

Most Indians, particularly Hindus, who constitute about 70% of India's population, believe in the theory of "rebirth and karma," which states that the deeds of past lives influence the lifecourse in the present life. This belief in a preordained lifecourse exhorts people to accept what is available in the present life and to work for a better situation in the next life through "good deeds" in the present one. This ideology is held irrespective of social or educational status and exhibits itself in the individual's acceptance of life's difficulties, frustrations and failures in considerable measures. People have strong faith in religion, which provides a framework for cognitive appraisal, and an emotional and behavioral direction, to conduct themselves according to a set of prescribed rules and systems. Most people take recourse to religious solutions in the face of personal adversity. Traditionally, there is a strong family system in India where the family's honor and interest override the individual's interest or pursuits. All the members of the family have well-defined roles and responsibilities, with considerable emphasis on integratedness and cohesiveness. Most of the problems of individual family members are solved within the family system to the extent possible. With modernization and urbanization, the family system is changing from extended joint to nuclear, accompanied by changes in the prescribed roles of various members and an increasing focus on the individual rather than on the family as a whole. This is more of a western influence occurring as a result of globalization.

According to ancient Indian philosophy (RigVeda), man has an average life-span of 100 years, which is divided into four periods of 25 years each. The first 25 years of life is the period of "brahamcharya," which is a period of learning and celibacy. During this time the child is put through a formal and rigorous education which is a form of general experiential education for life and also (depending upon the ultimate aim) for different professions. Education is obtained under conditions of austerity and absence of pleasure. The second period, from 25 to 50 years is called "grahsth-ashram," which means "family life." During this period the person is expected to raise a family, pursue an occupation, and enjoy worldly material life. Pursuits like status, fame, pleasure, and sex are permitted during this period. The next phase from 50 to 75 years, is called "Vanprastha," which signifies a period of gradual withdrawal from the world, and preparation for the ultimate, i.e., renunciation. The fourth period, from 75 to 100 years, is supposed to be a phase of total renunciation of the family and of the world, called "Sanyas." The individual is expected to seek "Nirvana," which means freedom from the bondage of the birth-death cycle. The person undertakes contemplation, an awakening of the inner subtle self, and the merging of self with the cosmic soul.

These are general guidelines for life rather than being a rigid or closed system. Most people do not consciously think of these periods of life, but are culturally conditioned to follow them in a very broad sense.

This ideology is reflected in the way children are brought up and treated. Children are handled in an authoritative manner, inculcating great respect for social hierarchy. They are not praised lest they become vain, and they are encouraged to live a simple and sober life devoid of luxuries or material pleasures. Behavioral expectations from adults towards children, and vice-versa, are specified, but the needs of children are not particularly mentioned. The adults around them have a major responsibility for providing a loving, secure and protective environment for children. This is a deeply ingrained cultural value that determines the attitudes and behavior of adults towards the understanding of children's needs, ways of dealing with them, and providing solutions to their conflict situations. It is also worth mentioning that this value system is again changing as a result of the increasing influence of western societies and globalization. In the urban areas, which are exposed to western culture and lifestyles, the formal authority of the family and of the society over individuals is getting diluted. Children are beginning to be exposed prematurely to the adult world and share in it without imbibing or learning the basic values of life that would enable them to evaluate and discriminate between right or wrong.

Child Mental Health in India

Child health in India has been a matter of serious concern and accorded due priority and attention in the post-independence era. However, child mental health has remained neglected for many reasons. There were other overriding health problems like high rates of perinatal and infant mortality and a high prevalence of infectious diseases, malnutrition, etc. that needed intervention. For a young country like India, where about 40% of the total population is below 14 years of age, providing for basic needs and services for all the children required ever larger proportions of resources than could be allocated for this purpose, and this still continues to be a challenge. As such, the mental health needs of children were poorly recognized due to a lack of awareness in the community. General psychiatry itself has been struggling to find its own place in the medical curriculum and the profession. Due to inadequate training facilities for child psychiatry in India, general psychiatrists and pediatricians have virtually no exposure to child psychiatry, which, coupled with the lack of job prospects in the field, limits the options for general psychiatrists to pursue child psychiatry as a career. It is only recently that a few psychiatrists and psychologists have taken a keen interest in the discipline and are beginning to develop leadership and training resources in the country.

The need for improving the mental health status of children and adolescents cannot be overemphasized for various reasons. Any efforts at improving the prospects of survival for children without adequate opportunities for their optimal all-around growth in the physical, emotional, intellectual, and social domains will not bear the desired fruits. In fact, mere survival without attention to the quality and dignity of life is an antithesis to the definition of health. There is ample evidence to show that physical and mental morbidity coexist. It is also known that many adult psychiatric disorders have their roots in childhood. These can be extensions of disorders in childhood or consequences of adverse living conditions, traumas, or faulty upbringing in childhood.

Taking care of child mental health is likely to prevent psychiatric disorders and even contribute to the development of a healthy personality in adulthood. Above all, the state has a responsibility towards all citizens, including children, who have as much right to mental health as adults, if not more. The health of children must incorporate mental health within its envelope.

Most issues related to child mental health in India were deliberated upon by a group of experts in 1988 and have been summarized in the form of a book (Malhotra, Malhotra, & Varma, 1992). Indigenous systems of medicine prevalent in India for centuries, such as Ayurveda and homeopathy, were holistic in approach, as considerable attention was paid to the psychological characteristics of human beings (viz. temperament, constitution, lifestyle, and habits). However, the modern allopathic system of medicine approached illnesses as maladies of different organs or systems. It is only recently that the integratedness and interdependence of structural and functional units of the body are being understood and accepted and that ideas about mind and body are converging to postulate monistic theories.

There have been a few studies on the prevalence of psychiatric disorders in children in India, but very few of these are sufficiently methodologically sound to provide reliable estimates. For example, one of two population prevalence studies on urban children reported an overall prevalence of 8.2%, with enuresis and mental retardation being the most common problems (Verghese & Beig, 1974), in 4–12 year-olds, while the other reported a prevalence of 35.6% (Lal and Sethi, 1977) in 0–12-year-olds, with the most common disorders being mental subnormality and neurotic and allied disorders. Studies on schoolchildren have reported varying rates of disorders, such as 20.7% (Jiloha & Murthy, 1981); 12.5% (Gadda, 1987); 33.7% (Deivasigamani, 1990); and 9.3% (Malhotra, 1995). Deivasigamani (1990) used a two-stage assessment procedure, utilizing the Rutter B Scale for teachers for screening and clinical assessment for diagnosis. There was a very high false positive (48.4%) as well as false negative (30.4%) rate on the Rutter B Scale. The reported prevalence figure of 33.7% includes the false negative cases, who predominantly had enuresis as an isolated symptom, which is accepted by parents as a developmental phenomenon and not considered as a problem requiring treatment. In our epidemiological study of schoolchildren 4–12 years old (Malhotra, 1995), assessment was done at three stages: by a teacher, by parents, and by the clinic. There was very low concordance between the teacher's assessment on the Rutter B scale and the clinical assessment (33.3%). The concordance was much higher (66.7%) between the parents' assessment, studied on the Childhood Psychopathology Measurement Schedule (CPMS), an Indian adaptation of the Child Behavior Checklist (CBCL) (Malhotra, Varma, Varma, & Maholtra, 1988), and the clinical assessment. Children who were positive on both the teacher's assessment and the parents' assessment had a clinical diagnosis rate of 92.3% on the clinical assessment. Again, the screening instruments for this study missed 14% of the children who had a disorder on the basis of clinical assessment, predominantly enuresis (7.7%). Although there are methodological differences and limitations among the various studies, broadly speaking, the evidence points towards a prevalence rate of psychiatric disorder ranging between 7% and 20% among children in India, which is largely similar to those reported from several other countries. The findings also point towards low specificity as well as sensitivity of certain scales like Rutter's B Scale for teachers when applied to a sociocultural setting other than that in which it was developed.

The availability of some data on the prevalence of psychiatric disorders in children in India is sufficient confirmation of the idea that the status of children's mental health in India may be no different from that in the rest of the world. However, there are differences in the types of problems that are seen. Population studies, as well as clinic-based studies (Lal & Sethi, 1977; Malhotra and Chaturvedi, 1984), have revealed that neuropsychiatric disorders, such as mental retardation and epilepsy, are the most common disorders (40% to 50%) encountered, followed by neurotic and somatization disorders (15% to 20%), special symptoms (e.g., enuresis) (7% to 8%), and attention-deficit hyperkinetic disorder (5%). Disorders of conduct have been found in 5% to 7% of children with psychiatric disorders. This is similar to the absence of conduct disorder and the increased proportion of emotional and somatization disorders seen in Asian patients attending mental health clinics in both Asia and the United Kingdom (Nikapota, 1991; Stern, Cottrell, and Homes, 1990). Recognition of these differences in the presentation and prevalence of illness is important for understanding their etiologies, as well as for planning services for them.

In India, there are about 350 million children under 14 years of age. By the most conservative estimate of 10%, there will be about 35 million children with severe psychiatric disorder requiring immediate treatment. Psychiatric services for children are virtually nonexistent. There are approximately 3,000 psychiatrists in the whole country for a population of 980 million, of which only a few, i.e., a dozen or two, practice child psychiatry to any significant extent. There are only about 120 child guidance centers or child psychiatric clinics in the whole country, which are located in the large metropolitan cities, with a professional staff of about 400, including less than 100 psychiatrists (mostly general psychiatrists). The services offered at these centers vary considerably in scope and comprehensiveness. Many of these are services on a part-time basis (National Institute of Public Cooperation and Child Development, 1986).

There are only about half a dozen academic centers in the country in which any amount of significant research and teaching in child psychiatry is going on.

There are 286 institutions for mentally handicapped persons in India, out of which 90% are in the private sector. There are approximately 2,000 qualified professional staff members (special educators, psychologists, speech pathologists, audiologists, social workers, physical and occupational therapists) who serve in these institutions. A total of 12,200 mentally handicapped persons are enrolled in these institutions (Reddy, 1988). Considering that the prevalence of mental retardation is 3%, the services available to them, as well as to those with psychiatric disorders, is not more than a drop in the ocean. The wide gap between the need for service and the existing infrastructure and the resources, at hand or in the future, seems insurmountable. This is the challenge for the whole profession, the nation, and also the world.

Cultural Issues

There are multiple domains of interfaces between culture and psychiatric disorders, more so in child psychiatry. It is well known that the rates of behavior and conduct disorders are lower among children of Chinese origin than those of American (Chang, Morrisey, & Koplewicz, 1995), and that people of Asian descent utilize the child psychiatric services in the United Kingdom or United States much less frequently than the natives (Sue & McKinney, 1975; Stern et al., 1990). These findings require serious examination of possible differences in the perceptions, the tolerances, or attitudes of Asian parents that determines whether a child will be perceived as psychiatrically disturbed or brought to a psychiatric service for help. For example, in many epidemiological surveys in India, enuresis in children is not perceived as a problem and is often missed unless specifically asked about.

Childrearing patterns in India are characterized by loving, active care involving protective, nurturing mothering and a prolonged dependency relationship. This is coupled with a high degree of control, low autonomy, and strict discipline, which is enforced within the broad framework of the family system. De-emphasis on the expression of thoughts and emotions in children could explain the greater preponderence of neurotic, psychosomatic, and somatization disorders (Malhotra, Malhotra, & Varma, 1992). The ethnodynamics determine the psychodynamics (Neki, 1976), where the cultural ideal of an interdependent adult, not an autonomous, fully independent adult, is inculcated right from childhood through a prolonged dependency relationship between the mother and the child. Dependency has a negative, pejorative connotation in Western thought, which is not so in the Indian context. Thus, the culture influences the definition of normalcy or disorder; prescribes the values and ideals for the behavior of individuals; determines the threshold of acceptance of pathology; and provides guidelines for the handling of pathology and its correction.

Therefore, the western concepts of health and disease, assessment methods, and technology and models of intervention may not be directly applicable to the Indian setting. It has been found that Rutter's B scale for teachers has very low specificity and sensitivity when used with Indian children (Malhotra, 1995). Children have a greater number of behavior problems at home than outside home (Malhotra, Malhotra, & Varma, 1992), a finding that has now been acknowledged and accorded recognition in the International Classification of Disorders (ICD-10) system of classification under the category "conduct disorder confined to family context" (F91.0). Although there are indications that cultural factors must be taken into account while formulating hypotheses about and planning treatment of psychiatric disorders of childhood, a considerable amount of work still needs to be done to understand fully the interrelationship between culture and psychiatric disorders in children.

DEVELOPMENT OF CHILD MENTAL HEALTH SERVICES IN INDIA

Services

While attempting to plan mental health services for children in India, certain facts and realities need to be borne in mind:

1. The services are needed to cover approximately 350 million children under 14 years of age (this figure does not include about two thirds of adolescents).
2. 35–70 million children, a number that is likely to increase over the years, require treatment immediately.
3. The available strength of qualified professionals (psychiatrists, psychologists, special educators, social workers, etc.) working in the field of child mental health and mental retardation put together is around 2,500. The rate of increase in the number of professionals is likely to be much lower than the increase in the rate of population growth, leading to an ever-widening gulf between the needs and the manpower resources.
4. There are no training centers for child psychiatrists in India, and training overseas is unaffordable.

One thing that is immediately clear is that the western models of care by specialists are neither feasible nor desirable. India will have to develop indigenous methods and models of care which are not dependent upon specialists. All those who are involved in the care of children, i.e., parents, teachers, and pediatricians, should become the primary providers of mental healthcare. They can be given specific and short training by specialists (child psychiatrists and psychologists), and specialized child psychiatric centers can act as back-up facilities for more severe types of disorders. Parents and the community should be involved as full partners in the mental healthcare of children.

Mental health should also be integrated with general health services for children. The available infrastructure and network of health services for children can be used to take care of their mental health needs as well. This will require redefining the role and objectives of the staff, and providing them with adequate training to deal with mental health problems.

We will also need to prioritize the problems and disorders, so that the scarce resources that are allocated will yield maximum benefit. Some of the common but benign disorders, such as enuresis, may be given low priority.

Improvement in the mental health status of children is very closely linked to social development. Therefore, all steps need to be taken with true earnestness, to improve the general socioeconomic status, living standards, standard of education, and living environment of children and society.

Research and Development

There is a need to establish centers of excellence in the country that will serve to develop indigenous models and systems of care, as well as leadership. There is a need to develop a cadre of trained professionals who will take on the task of teaching and research. Investment in research is extremely important and necessary because India needs to develop its own methods of treatment and care that should be rooted in its sociocultural and philosophical traditions. The strong family system in India is a source of tremendous strength to its members, and this should be (a) strengthened further to act as a fertile ground for healthy personality development; (b) protected and supported as a sanctuary for containment and resolution of emotional problems and interpersonal conflict; and (c) guarded against influences favoring its disintegration and erosion, which are a serious threat as a result of globalization and westernization. For child psychiatry to be a scientific discipline, the need for systematic research cannot be ignored. Research should focus on (a) the study of antecedents and correlates of morbidity; (b) the development of assessment technology and tools that are appropriate for the population and the setting; and (c) the study of the community's resources and methods of handling problems. Taking the example of conduct and behavior disorders, which are seen at a relatively lower frequency in India as compared to the West, research can look into the methods of child-rearing that may have a preventive influence, and the methods of handling this problem in the community which may have a remedial effect. It is possible that the resources within the family or community may be able to meet the need for help, and professional help may not be necessary (Newth & Corbett, 1993).

Policy

Several national policies for children exist in India, in the health, education, labor, law, and welfare sectors and have been reviewed by Murthy (1992). However, there is an absence of coordination among and unsatisfactory implementation of these policies. The focus of these policies is general socioeconomic and educational development, which is highly significant and necessary for primary prevention of childhood mental disorders. Child mental health activities must address secondary and tertiary levels of prevention as well, particularly keeping in view the high rates of prevalence and the social burden of these disorders. There is a need to establish a comprehensive national policy on the mental health of children, which should focus on and monitor all other programs impinging on the mental health of children. Given the low number of professionals, the poor sensitivity of planners and policy makers, and the low social priority accorded to this field, the task is gigantic and quite difficult. However, it is the public need that should, and is expected to, act as a pressure lobby on politicians and planners. Therefore, enhancing the community's awareness and general sensitization to these needs of children should be the major task for mental health professionals.

It has also been observed that India's policies and programs have been influenced by international trends and goals that are far removed from its everyday realities. There is a need to identify priorities at the regional and national levels and then attempt to formulate a policy that should be commensurate with the local sociocultural conditions and expectations.

Child mental health professionals should work in close collaboration with the workers in other fields, such as education, social welfare, labor, and the law, so as to effectively guide the implementation of various programs as well as to affect the future direction of these policies and programs.

For any beginning worth its while, the foremost need will be to accord professional status and accreditation to the discipline, that is, child psychiatry, and the professionals, that is, the child psychiatrists. Unfortunately, in India, general psychiatrists are too few, as well as too busy in their work, so that they have neither time nor the orientation to work with children. On the other hand, there seem to be some reservations about the development of child psychiatry as a discipline in its own right, due to the apprehension that child psychiatrists will be superspecialists who may professionally be held in higher esteem. International trends and systems could provide a broad framework and professional support, within which systems of psychiatric care for children in India could be formulated. It is nearly a blank slate currently, offering tremendous scope, opportunity, and a challenge to mental health professionals.

REFERENCES

Chang, L., Morrisey, R. F., & Koplewicz, H. S. (1995). Prevalence of psychiatric symptoms and their relation to adjustment among Chinese-American youth. *Journal of the American Academy of Child and Adolescent Psychiatry, 34*(1), 91–99.

Deivasigamani, T. R. (1990). Psychiatric morbidity in primary school children—an epidemiological study. *Indian Journal of Psychiatry, 32,* 235–240.

Gada, M. (1987). A study of the prevalence and pattern of attention-deficit disorder with hyperactivity in primary school children. *Indian Journal of Psychiatry, 29,* 113–118.

Jiloha, R. C., & Murthy, R. S. (1981). An epidemiological study of psychiatric problems in primary school children. *Child Psychiatry Quarterly, 3,* 109–120.

Lal, N., & Sethi, B. B. (1977). Estimate of mental ill-health in children in an urban community. *Indian Journal of Paediatrics, 44,* 55–64.

Malhotra, S. (1995). *Study of psychosocial correlates of developmental psychopathology in school children.* Report submitted to Indian Council for Medical Research, New Delhi.

Malhotra, S., & Chaturvedi, S. K. (1984). Patterns of childhood psychiatric disorders in India. *Indian Journal of Paediatrics, 51,* 235–240.

Malhotra, S., Malhotra, A., & Varma, V. K. (Eds.). (1992). *Child mental health in India.* New Delhi, India: MacMillan.

Malhotra, S., Varma, V. K., Verma, S. K., & Malhotra, A. (1988). Childhood Psychopathology Measurement Schedule: Development and standardisation. *Indian Journal of Psychiatry, 30,* 325–332.

Murthy, R. S. (1992). Policies relating to children in India: Focus on mental health. In: S. Malhotra, A. Malhotra, & V. K. Varma (Eds.). *Child mental health in India.* New Delhi, India: MacMillan.

Neki, J. S. (1976). An examination of the cultural relationship of dependence as a dynamic of social and therapeutic relationships I: Socio-developmental. *British Journal of Medical Psychology, 99,* 1–10.

Newth, S. J., & Corbett, J. (1993). Behaviour & emotional problems in three year old children of Asian parentage. *Journal of Child Psychology and Psychiatry, 34,* 333–352.

Nikapota, A. D. (1991). Child psychiatry in developing countries: A review. *British Journal of Psychiatry, 158,* 743–5114.

National Institute of Public Cooperation and Child Development. (1986). *A report of Child Guidance Clinics in India.* New Delhi: NIPCCD.

Reddy, S. H. K. (1988). *Directory of Institutions for the Mentally Handicapped Persons in India.* Secunderabad: NIMH (National Institute for the Mentally Handicapped).

Stern, G., Cottrell, B., & Holmes, J. (1990). Patterns of attendance of child psychiatry out-patients with special reference to Asian families. *British Journal of Psychiatry, 156,* 384–387.

Sue, S., & Mckinney, H. (1975). Asian Americans in the community mental health care system. *American Journal of Orthopsychiatry, 45,* 111–118.

UNICEF. (1991). *Children & women in India: A situation analysis 1990.* New Delhi: United Nation's Children's Fund.

Verghese, A., & Beig, A. (1974). Psychiatric disturbances in children—An epidemiological study. *Indian Journal of Medical Research, 62,* 1538–1542.

28

The Economics of Mental Healthcare in the Context of Rapid Political Change in Hungary

AGNES VETRÓ

This paper gives demographic figures for Hungary and outlines the organization of its healthcare before and after the political changes of the past 10 years. The main point of the health system reforms has been that the former central financing has been changed to performance-based financing. The emphasis has shifted from centralized inpatient healthcare to basic services. This has entailed drastic decreases in the numbers of hospital beds and medical staff. Since even the long-established medical specialties were forced onto the defensive, the situation of child and adolescent psychiatry has been especially difficult lately. Its integration within psychiatry and pediatrics leads to the problem that these basic specialties often solve the problem of reduction of staff and hospital beds, and try to reduce losses within their specialties, by dispensing with child and adolescent psychiatry. Thus, the defense of the mental health of Hungarian children has been thrust into the background during these new political changes.

DEMOGRAPHIC AND HEALTH SERVICE FIGURES FOR HUNGARY

Hungary, located in central Europe in a region of 100,000 km^2, has 10,354,000 inhabitants, 52% females and 48% males. Some

Table 28.1 *Distribution of Inhabitants by Geographical Location in Hungary in 1992*

Geographical location	Inhabitants
Budapest	2,018,000
Other towns	4,417,900
Villages or isolated areas	3,918,900
Total	10,354,800

70% of the inhabitants live in towns (2 million in the capital, Budapest), and 30% live in villages or isolated settlements (Table 28.1).

In 1992 medical services for the population were provided by 37,255 physicians, 1,480 of whom were specialized psychiatrists and neurologists. For inpatient healthcare, 105,097 hospital beds were available. Patients with mental problems were treated in institutes with 17,225 patient beds (17% of all hospital beds) and 132 outpatient mental care units (Magyar Statisztikai Évkönyv, 1992–1993).

21% of the population was younger than 14 years old, with a slight preponderance of boys (Table 28.2). Their healthcare was provided by 2,704 infant and child specialists. 9,014 patient beds were available for child patients (the number of child and adolescent psychiatry beds was 204, i.e., only 2.1% of all beds available for children), and a well-functioning pediatric network operating under the concept of preventive care existed, independently of the family health service (Magyar Statisztikai Évkönyv, 1992–1993).

Table 28.2 *Distribution of the 0 to 19–Year-old Population According to Gender and Age in Hungary in 1992*

Age	Boys	Girls	Total
0–4	315,808	301,424	617,232
5–9	335,356	320,794	656,150
10–14	439,263	417,904	857,176
15–19	393,404	373,452	766,856
Total	1,493,831	1,413,574	2,898,405

PRINCIPLES AND AIMS OF THE RECENT HEALTHCARE REFORMS

Both the healthcare and insurance systems have undergone a basic transformation since the late 1980s. This process was speeded up by the political changes. In 1990, the Social Insurance Office took over the task of the financial regulation of the medical care system. Previously, this was under governmental direction. At present, 2.5% to 6% of the national income covers the finances of the Hungarian health system. This is equal to a $200 yearly expenditure per person, which is a very low amount compared to other countries. The greatest amount covers wages, which account for 49% to 61% of all expenditures. In spite of this, Hungarian healthcare workers are among the worst-paid employees in the country ("Előkészületek a valódi reformra?," 1996).

The rapid increase in expenditure required a basic change in the financial mechanism. The old income distribution system bore no relation to medical achievements and included many subjective elements; it was replaced by a new system that works according to the rules of the market economy. The Insurance Office provides facilities on the basis of legal contracts. The new law prescribes that the Insurance Office has to make contracts with every institution involved in medical service.

Earlier, the development of healthcare was facilitated by a concentration of modern medical techniques and a hospital system able to ensure a high quality of treatment. Nowadays, this has changed. The appearance and spread of modern diagnostic and therapeutic devices has led to a decrease in treatment time and the omission of some unnecessary hospital treatment (Köbl, 1995).

According to the Ministry of Welfare, however, the professional development of the health system was not followed by a reorganization of the healthcare delivery system. Hospitals still formed the basis of services. Thus, the number of hospital beds increased tremendously up to the end of the 1980s, leading to an unnecessarily high number of 110,000 hospital beds. Even in the summer of 1996, the health system worked with 93,000 hospital beds. Due to the reforms, a further 10,000 beds were taken away from acute care that year, causing 10,000 healthcare workers (including 3,000–4,000 doctors) to lose their jobs. In 1997, there was a further gradual reduction. The aim is to reach the Western European standard of 70,000–75,000 beds per 10 million inhabitants (Hegedüs, 1996).

Financing of the family doctor system costs much less than that of in- or outpatient services. Therefore, in order to compensate for these changes, there are plans to improve the family doctor system to a level of 1,000–1,200 patients per family doctor. These doctors would not only deal with already-developed diseases, but would also be responsible for prevention and the long-term care of patients.

The reforms are meant to achieve a system of referrals similar to those of the health maintenance organizations (HMOs) in the United States and the Fund-Holding system of England.

THE REFORMS AND THE NEW PRINCIPLES OF FINANCING

In 1993, hospitals received funds from the health insurance system according to central financing fees. Every institution received money according to their own budget calculations. This was an unfair system.

In 1995, a new decree was passed that stipulated standard financing fees throughout the whole country (the diagnosis-related groups (DRG) system). Nothing was straightforward. Institutions were still not equally financed because "correctional multipliers" were introduced on the basis of professional and institutional considerations (the correctional multiplier for pediatrics was 1.25, that for psychiatry was 0.85, that for county hospitals was 1.2, and that for university hospitals was 0.9). Restrictive limits were placed on hospital financing: the fund could not be greater than 120% or less than 90% of the original amount. Through this step, funds again became independent of performance.

In 1997 the restrictive limits were removed. A new DRG system was introduced, which is a variation of the U.S. DRG 12. The expectation was that the professional multipliers would lose their significance in the long run if the DRG system was adequate.

Financial funds were to be determined by two factors. The first is the hospital financing fund of the Health Insurance System (HIS), which is the amount of money that can be distributed among the inpatient services. The second is a strong connection between performance and income. If this type of financing works effectively, then its economic stimulating effect should form the structure of all healthcare institutions (Faggyas, 1996; NTE, 1996).

Table 28.3   *Specialty Outpatient Services in Weekly Consulting Hours per 10,000 Inhabitants*

Specialty outpatient services	Hours/week
Pediatrics and infant care	3.5–7.0
Psychiatry+substance abuse+rehabilitation	2.6–6.0
Internal medicine and related areas (general internal medicine, intensive care, contagious diseases, admission unit, hematology, immunology, metabolic diseases, gastroenterology, nephrology, AIDS, rehabilitation)	16.0–22.0
Total	120–180
Inpatient services	
Neurology and psychiatry	6.0–10.0
Total	12.0–22.0

HEALTH BILL T.2423

This bill of May 6, 1996, which is based on the above principles, stipulated the obligations of the health service and set standards for regional healthcare delivery. Under it, health institutions are obliged to ensure services in contracts with the HIS. Health institutions must ensure the conditions required to fulfill the services. In other words, the bill laid down the quality of service, the number of hospital beds, and the amount of outpatient time that must be financed by the HIS in each county in the various specialties. Table 28.3 shows the norms for pediatrics and psychiatry.

Throughout the bill, the multiple subspecialties, such as those within internal medicine, are detailed. Child and adolescent psychiatry is included in neither pediatrics nor psychiatry.

INPATIENT SERVICES

The bill stated that in the years 1996–1997, 52 beds must be financed per 10,000 inhabitants. This number is to be gradually reduced to 49 by the year 2,000. The suggested share of beds for pediatrics and infant care (Perinatal Intensive Center) was 6.5% to 8.5%, and the share for psychiatry (including mental rehabilitation) was 10% to 13%.

A motion to include provisions for child and adolescent psychiatry was unsuccessful, and the bill became law on July 3, 1996. Accordingly, Hungarian public health is not obliged by law to insure child and adolescent psychiatric services, which differs from the treatment of other specialties.

PRACTICAL CONSEQUENCES

Following the passage of the law, the counties convened County Conciliation Committees to define the total number of hospital beds and their distribution by specialty in the region. Furthermore, the counties could decide which institutions in which cities would have to reduce the number of its beds. In almost all counties, the number of pediatric beds had to be greatly reduced (there were too many beds and the utilization was low), which endangered the child psychiatry units integrated within pediatrics. Other counties reduced the number of psychiatric beds in order not to exceed the calculated number of beds per 10,000 inhabitants, even if the utilization was maximal. This endangered the child psychiatry units integrated into general psychiatry. It is obvious that all specialties were loyal to their own beds and cared less for the integrated, but less related specialties.

Thus in parallel with the political changes in Hungary, professionals in the field of child and adolescent psychiatry faced new problems.

BRIEF HISTORICAL BACKGROUND OF HUNGARIAN CHILD AND ADOLESCENT PSYCHIATRY

Child and adolescent psychiatry first developed on the borders of the areas of education, adult psychiatry, and pediatrics. It still bears the marks of this origin. The pioneer in the field was Pal Ranschburgh (1870–1945) at the Institute for Handicapped Children. Endre Schnell established the first Institute for Paediatric Mental Care in 1935, which became the prototype of future institutes for child and adolescent psychiatry. Blanka Loránd established the first child psychiatry unit in Hungary at the Institute of Psychiatry and Neurology in 1950. In 1960, Miklós Vargha became head of the children's ward at the Department of Neurology and Psychiatry of the Medical University in Szeged, which remains the only child psychiatry ward in a Hungarian medical university. Child psychiatry officially became a subspecialization in 1961.

THE PLACE OF CHILD AND ADOLESCENT PSYCHIATRY IN THE HUNGARIAN HEALTH SERVICE BEFORE AND AFTER THE REFORMS

In Hungary, several institutions are involved in pediatric mental healthcare. On one hand, this is advantageous because a multidisciplinary approach to these disorders is warranted, but on the other hand, overlapping and/or shortcomings appear in certain fields. The Ministry of Welfare (MW), which heads the structural reform of the health service, finances in- and outpatient psychiatry, with a contribution from HIS.

The reform administrators are counseled by the Board of Hungarian Specialists. A common Board of Specialists for child and adolescent psychiatry, child neurology, and child neurosurgery functioned between 1989 and 1995. In May 1995, however, child psychiatry was integrated into the Boards of Specialists of Paediatrics and Psychiatry. To avoid a split in the field, the two boards each appointed one of their members to act as a subcommittee for child and adolescent psychiatry, and their decisions on important issues are submitted by the two boards to the MW.

In 1996, a few of the terminated Boards of Specialists appealed to the MW, protesting against the boards' terminations. The MW dictated that those Boards of Specialists be refounded which have a basic specialization examination in Hungary and in the EUMS. Child and adolescent psychiatry did not get its Board of Specialists back, since this specialization did not belong among the basic ones in Hungary. However, numerous specializations which are not basic specializations in EUMS (e.g., human genetics, oral surgery, vascular surgery, angiology, etc.) did receive independence, probably for subjective reasons. Representatives of the field of child and adolescent psychiatry remained divided between the Board of Paediatrics and the Board of Psychiatrists, where their interests are not represented ("Újraszabályozzak a szakmai kollégiumokat," 1996).

There is a similar split between in- and outpatient services. Some child and adolescent psychiatry hospital wards and outpatient services are independent, while others are integrated into pediatrics or the adult psychiatry service. Therefore, they have no uniform organizational and functional order. Since the health law did not regulate the situation of child and adolescent psychiatry, its status is still uncertain.

Medical universities have a unique situation. They are supervised by the MW in regards to patient care activities, but their training activities are supervised by the Ministry of Culture and Education. The supervision of child and adolescent psychiatry services are divided in the same way.

CHILD AND ADOLESCENT PSYCHIATRY MORBIDITY STATISTICS IN HUNGARY

If we compare the results of Hungarian epidemiological studies with those in other countries, we find that psychiatric morbidity is rather high comparatively: depending on age and geographical area, it is 15% to 25% (Vetró, McGuinness, Fedor, Dombovári, & Baji, 1997). This means that 300,000–750,000 individuals are in need of psychiatric care from among the approximately 3 million children and adolescents in the population. Only a small proportion, 11,000, are actually registered by the child and adolescent psychiatry network, including neurological cases.

OBJECTIVE CONDITIONS OF CHILD AND ADOLESCENT PSYCHIATRY IN HUNGARY BEFORE AND AFTER THE REFORM

Outpatient Services

Child and Adolescent Psychiatry Outpatient Clinics

In each of the 19 counties, there is one child and adolescent psychiatry outpatient service, and in Budapest, there are seven such institutions, where approximately 40 child psychiatrists work. The equipment and staffing levels in these institutions greatly differ.

There are some where only one child psychiatrist works, and others with multidisciplinary teams. Patients are referred by pediatricians, family physicians, teachers, and parents (Gádoros, 1992).

Since child psychiatry has not received required hours for specialized clinics or outpatient clinics by law, its status remains uncertain.

The insurance office pays individually after medical interventions, so in many cases the most important factor determining the treatment of the patient is the price of the intervention. There is a fixed budget to cover the expenditure of the outpatient care units each month according to the points list calculated after the medical interventions. Thus, the sum paid to the individual units can change according to the points reached from month to month. In general, it becomes lower and lower, making it financially difficult for the units to function.

Since they are in competition with one another, all outpatient units show a strong tendency to enhance the number of interventions in order to acquire more points. In this situation, child psychiatrists cannot make a living independently or in private practice. They work additionally either as pediatricians or as psychiatrists.

Outpatient follow-up care activities have received basic financing (independent of achievement) up to the present, but since there is no law mandating the care of these patients, the existence of this optimal financing possibility depends on a sympathetic attitude.

Child Guidance Clinics

These outpatient services are generally headed by either an educator or a psychologist. In order to provide a proper psychiatric diagnosis and to attain acceptance of their therapeutic activities, they employ a child psychiatrist. Children with learning disturbances are generally referred by their schools. They are in close contact with boards that test learning capabilities, and these boards may direct the children to special schools or classes.

Family Counseling Centers

In every county, one or more family counseling services is run by the social services department of the local council. It is headed by either a psychologist or a social worker. This person's major role is to provide social services, but occasionally they act as child psychiatrists.

Table 28.4   *Status of the Child and Adolescent Psychiatry Hospital Beds Before the Health Reform*

	Number of hospital beds		
	Permitted	Functioning	Not functioning
Szeged[a]	44	36	8
Debrecen[b]	50	50	
Kerepestarcsa[b,c]	26	0	26
Szolnok[a]	35	35	
OPNI[c,d]	19	19	
Vadaskert[b,c]	24	24	
Gyula[d]	20	20	
Budai Regional Paediatric Hospital Neurotic Unit[a,c]	20	20	
Total	238	204	34

Based on the national study carried out by the Board of Specialists of Child and Adolescent Psychiatry, Child Neurology and Child Neurosurgery in 1994.
[a] All units integrated with pediatrics: 91
[b] All independent: 74
[c] All functioning hospital beds in Budapest: 63
[d] All units integrated with psychiatry: 39

Special Centers in Hospitals

These do not generally perform nursing, preventive, or rehabilitative work, but offer significant services for outpatient assessment of children and follow-up care of inpatients.

Other Special Centers

These function within the framework of various organizations (e.g., the College for Teachers of the Handicapped, hospital wards, private clinics of foundations, etc.) and specialize either in one disease (autism, hyperkinetic patients, post-traumatic stress disorder, etc.) or in the whole field of child and adolescent psychiatry.

The health reforms did not affect those institutions that were not already integrated into the healthcare system.

Inpatient Care

In Hungary, eight inpatient wards have been established since the opening of the first one 45 years ago (Table 28.4). Some are independent, while others are run within the framework of pediatric or adult psychiatric wards.

EFFECTS OF THE HEALTH REFORMS ON CHILD AND ADOLESCENT PSYCHIATRY INPATIENT SERVICES

Child psychiatry representatives were not invited to the County Conciliation Committee meetings, and thus child psychiatry beds were not protected. Before the reforms, the number of psychiatric beds per 10,000 inhabitants was 10, while that of pediatric beds was 9. After the reform, these numbers were 5–6 and 4, respectively. (The number of psychiatric beds is 10% of all adult hospital beds, and the number of child and adolescent psychiatry beds is 2.1% of all child beds.)

As a result, two child and adolescent psychiatry units had to be closed and one is endangered because of the planned closure of the mother institution (Paediatric Clinic of Buda). Another child and adolescent psychiatry unit integrated within pediatrics in Szolnok will be reduced to an 8–bed unit. Including these beds, there are at present 204 child and adolescent psychiatry hospital beds in Hungary. This means that there are 0.2 child and adolescent psychiatry beds per 10,000 inhabitants in Hungary, which is a very low number.

The introduction of the DRG system means that child psychiatric disorders receive low point scores. The mean time for treatment was established according to the practice in general pediatric wards. This is why autism, for instance, receives a categorization of 3–10 days of treatment and 0.7 points in Hungary, compared with 3.5 points in the United States. The calculated time is only sufficient to evaluate the various organic etiologies of the disorder and not enough for psychodiagnostic and treatment interventions.

The introduction of work-related financing has created new relationships and sometimes acts against the original purposes. According to the original logic of the financing mechanism, institutions are interested in working to maximize bed capacity and minimize time limits. Going over the minimum time limit means full payment according to the DRG system.

Due to the devaluation of outpatient point values, it is worth a lot more to hospitalize patients for the minimum time. That works against the reforms' goal of directing patients to cheaper levels of services.

THE RESOURCES FOR REMEDIATION AND REHABILITATION BEFORE AND AFTER THE REFORMS

The framework for remediation and rehabilitation in child and adolescent psychiatry is provided mostly by training institutions in an extern or intern form. Two types of special schools exist, depending on the intellectual capacity of the children, for more and less severe mental retardation. Special kindergartens and school groups have been established recently for patients with pervasive developmental disorders (mostly autistic patients). The plans for hyperkinetic children and those suffering from conduct disorders have not been determined. The status of school-age children with anxiety symptoms or depression is similarly unresolved.

Children with very low functional capacities live in group homes. These homes are integrated into the pediatric health service, and an organic focus is characteristic, instead of an intention to remediate or rehabilitate.

The political changes brought about the creation of numerous alternative services for chronically ill patients. Many associations and foundations have been formed to help the mentally ill. The preventive and rehabilitative activities of nonprofessional aides have resulted in new possibilities for the mental health of children.

TRAINING FRAMEWORK FOR CHILD AND ADOLESCENT PSYCHIATRY

Structural Modification of Medical Training

According to the new higher education law, universities and colleges must be reorganized to a standard financing method instead of the former fund financing (similar to health financing). As a result, for example, Budapest Medical University lost 302 million Forints from its original income, which entailed the laying off of 300 teachers. The University receives 510,000 Forints for each student, but the training costs a minimum of 860,000 Forints per student. Therefore, medical training is in a difficult position. Generally, new diagnostic, therapeutic, and surgical techniques are first introduced at the universities. In order to teach and apply them, a significant amount of money is needed ("Jövõképet az egészégügynek," 1997).

Child and Adolescent Psychiatry in the Curricula of Medical Universities

Since there is no independent department for child psychiatry at the medical universities in Hungary, the subject of child psychiatry is not included in the curriculum of medical students. Albert Szent-Györgyi Medical University in Szeged is the only institution with a Child and Adolescent Psychiatry Department, which is integrated organizationally into the Department of Paediatrics. The child and adolescent psychiatry ward developed a training system for medical and postgraduate students in collaboration with the Child and Adolescent Psychiatry Departments of the University of Würzburg (Germany) and the University of Glasgow (UK) within the framework of a 3–year TEMPUS JEP, but it has not been accredited at either a university or a national level (Parry Jones, Vetró, & Warnke, 1994). In Szeged, students may study child and adolescent psychiatry as an elective subject, but at other universities, even this option is not available. Most pediatric family practitioners do not know even the fundamentals of the subject. The universities have received 1.3 billion Forints in 1997 to improve medical training. Hopefully, child and adolescent psychiatry will receive some of that money.

Postgraduate Training Structure Modifications

Since MOTESZ (Association of the Scientific Committees of Hungarian Medical Doctors) became a member of EUMS, it has received accreditation rights. This has made it possible for some specialties to be present in the professional groups with the help of MOTESZ, and to have a chance to directly influence the specific professional work at a European level.

The problem is that postgraduate training is not well organized in spite of the above-mentioned advantages. The Haynal Imre University of Health Sciences was previously responsible for postgraduate training in the specialties. This task is now under each university's control. At a national level, the National Specialist Qualifications Examinations Committee supervises these activities. A new specialist qualifications order is currently being revised, which attempts to adjust the Hungarian specialist training to the standards of EUMS ("Új elnökség, új alapszabály a MOTESZ-ben," 1997).

Training Within Child Psychiatry

Since 1992 (a few years before the MOTESZ membership), our specialty has had the opportunity of being present in the CAPP Monosection Meetings of EUMS with observer status, and has arranged its specialist training program with the help of the Board of Specialists. This training program has not yet been accepted by the Specialist Qualifications Examinations Committee.

Specialization is supervised by the National Board of Specialization, which is in charge of examinations. To sit for the examination, 1½ years of practice is necessary at a child and adolescent psychiatry ward, one-half-year in pediatrics or general psychiatry, and one-half-year in a child and adolescent psychiatry outpatient unit. As a place for practice, any of the seven inpatient wards is accepted, as is a psychiatry service where a physician specializing in child and adolescent psychiatry works. The examination consists of a one-week practical examination (patient examination and diagnosis) and an oral examination.

There are more than 120 physicians specializing in child and adolescent psychiatry, but only 50–60 work in the child and adolescent psychiatry service. The others are retired or work either as pediatricians or in adult psychiatry.

Since the field is not represented at a departmental level at any of the universities, its prestige is rather poor. There are few candidates for specialization, because in Hungary, child psychiatry is a subspecialty; the training starts with specialization in pediatrics or in general psychiatry. Some child psychiatrists choose to return to their basic fields, where the prestige is higher.

One or two training courses are held annually for the preparation of candidates for specialization and training. There are places where discussions about scientific papers in specialty journals and supervision of treatment cases take place, each with a regional character. The child and adolescent psychiatry working groups of HIETE (Budapest), SOTE (Budapest), and SZOTE (Szeged) have a decisive role in these discussions.

Training in psychotherapy (3 years) has been conducted separately from psychiatry training for the past 5 years in Hungary. Every candidate to be specialized in child and adolescent psychiatry has to take part in a 1 year basic theoretical training course.

ACTIVITIES OF SOCIETIES

The CAP (child and adolescent psychiatry) Society was established in 1990, combining the children's sections of three societies (the Child Psychiatry Section of the Paediatric Society, the Child Neurology and Psychiatry Section of the Society of Neurologists and Psychiatrists, and the Child Section of the Society of Neurosurgery). The CAP Society has been admitted to MOTESZ under the name of the Hungarian Society for Child and Adolescent Psychiatry, Neurology and Neurosurgery. The society works in two independent sections (Section of Child and Adolescent Psychiatry, and Section of Child Neurology and Neurosurgery), which are separated professionally and financially. Common scientific sessions are held each year in different towns. The 1991 session was visited by the Steering Committee of IACAPAP. Members also deliver scientific lectures at the meetings of the Hungarian Psychiatric Society and the Hungarian Paediatric Society.

There are few departments where regular scientific work is performed in child and adolescent psychiatry. Three Ph.D. degrees have been conferred in child and adolescent psychiatry, all at the Albert Szent-Györgyi Medical University.

QUALITY ASSURANCE, ACCREDITATION, MINIMAL STANDARDS

Prior to the reforms, the levels of equipment at the hospital units and outpatient clinics differed greatly. The quality of service depended on the knowledge of the local head physician and also on the availability of monetary resources. The chase after DRG points induced hospitals to admit cases for which they lacked both knowledge and equipment.

In order to improve this process, the MW devised general minimal standards related to the functioning of hospitals and asked each

Board of Specialists to draft minimum personal and objective requirements. These are necessary standards for a unit's accreditation,
i.e., for permission to function. The MW at the same time offered
financial aid to those units where the minimum requirements were
not met, so that they could modernize their equipment.

The general minimum standards set for some specialties are very
high. Therefore, a great number of hospitals could receive only
temporary permission to function. In such cases, the basic requirements have to be met in 1–5 years. (One such requirement, for
example, is that each patient must have an area of 8 m² in the ward.
The fact that each patient's space is smaller than this in 70% to
80% of hospitals could bring about yet another wave of bed reductions.) The minimum standards for the different specialties are also
not uniform. Some built up dreams of future hospitals, whereas
others have respected the true necessary minimum standards.

Since child psychiatry is not included in the law, its minimum
standards (prepared by the subcommittee of the Board of Specializations) were not considered in outpatient or inpatient services. Thus,
this specialization cannot put forward any arguments in the debate
for development. At present, we work according to the standards of
adult psychiatry, which are less advantageous than those of child
psychiatry and do not consider the particular requirements of the
specialty.

DIAGNOSTIC AND THERAPEUTIC PROTOCOLS

The DRG system has brought about other changes as well.
Hospitals have started to prefer treatment models with greater point
values instead of the most modern ones with lower values. At the
same time, the accounting departments of these institutions are trying to economize as much as possible. To deal with this chaos, a
declaration of the basic principles of treatment became an important
and urgent task.

The increasing numbers of medical malpractice lawsuits also
made it necessary to defend doctors, to ensure that they had performed all the specified diagnostic activities and employed the latest
treatment techniques.

The MW requested the Boards of Specialists to prepare diagnostic
and therapeutic professional protocols which should be used as

guidelines in everyday work. Naturally, such a protocol (or "practice guideline") is only a suggestion; its application is not obligatory, but in special cases the doctor needs to explain any deviation. The development of the specialties is an ongoing process, and protocols follow this development only with a time-lag. This is another reason why their application cannot be obligatory. The future will involve the continuous reevaluation of these protocols, forming up-to-date profiles for the specialties and ensuring an improved quality of work. Those institutions that cannot meet these expectations in treatment will eventually languish. The training of specialized doctors will not be possible either, so the problem of supplying adequate staff will not be solved. In 1996, our subcommittee worked out the ICD-10 child and adolescent psychiatry categories, which were attached to the psychiatric protocol.

CONCLUSIONS

In summary, the new health reforms have changed the basis of the Hungarian health system and patient-care services. The Hungarian Medical Chamber (HMC), the representative of medical sciences and the medical profession, and also of the Hungarian population's health interests, is in strong opposition to the MW. After the new law went into effect, the HMC called together an ad hoc committee, the "catastrophe committee," to define the most urgent tasks. The HMC declared that nobody should believe that the Hungarian health services would be more effective after the reduction of the number of hospital beds. Just the opposite, the level of efficiency would become worse. The aims of the structural changes are correct, but the ideology behind them is not. Nobody knew in advance the demands and expectations of the population. A mathematical equation showing a surplus of hospital beds is a mockery of statistical methods. If there are surplus beds at all, then the development of the social services infrastructure should precede the reduction. Without an adequate social services infrastructure, certain patients could die unnecessarily. The responsibility lies with the legislators. The law now coming into being is unjustified from a professional point of view. It does not bring any economic benefits or savings. It even means extra expenses. It does not leave enough time for the changes, and it foreshadows the possibility of chaos. It destroys the structure of education, leading to a future decay of the professional level of care. It violates personal rights and reduces the population's chance of staying alive. Doctors are forced to break their pledges. The HMC disagrees with the intent of the law and has decided to submit an independent motion about the reform of the healthcare structure, in addition to their right to a statement as provided by law.

On these grounds and with the status of healthcare in such a chaotic state, it is understandable that sustaining the status and management of child and adolescent psychiatry is not an easy task. Since there is constant debate among the main specialties, it is difficult to get access to the financial opportunities of the HIS independently of adult psychiatry or pediatrics. Tendencies towards professional independence prove abortive, mainly due to the lack of interest with regards to both examination in the specialty and the independence of outpatient or inpatient units. During the 3 years since the reforms began, three MWs have promised support and given useful advice toward maintaining the independence of the specialty, but in practice, the situation has worsened. We do not have a Board of Specialists, since child psychiatry is not an independent profession, but we cannot be independent until we have a Board of Specialists. The circle closes at this point. The universities refuse to teach child psychiatry, because it would be an extra expense. The medical diploma received in Hungary is accepted in foreign countries, even if child and adolescent psychiatry is not among the subjects taught. EUMS only suggests the types of basic specialties that a country might need. Other specialties do not care about the matter, since the absence of Hungarian child and adolescent psychiatry does not endanger their European accreditation.

In any case, we can only hope that these are transitional difficulties which will cease in a short time. The situation will clear like the sky after a storm, and child and adolescent psychiatry will find its own place among the other medical professions (Vétro, 1995).

REFERENCES

Elōkészületek a valódi reformra? (1996, June). *Magyar Orvos, 4,* 4–10.
Faggyas, K. (1996, October). Elkerülhetetlen a finanszirozás reformja. *Magyar Orvos, 4,* 19–20.

Gádoros, J. (1992). A hazai gyermek és ifjúságpszichiátria Helyzetkép és javaslat. Psychiatrica Hungarica., 7, 193–203.

Hegedüs, E. (1996, October). Szükités kérdőjelekkel, Magyar Orvos, 4, 8. Jövőképet az egészségügynek. (1997). MOTESZ Magazin, 97(1), 16–20.

Köbl, A. (1995, November). Finanszirozási reform? Magyar Orvos, 3, 10–11.

Magyar Statisztikai Évkönyv. (1992–1993). Központi Statisztikai Hivatal Budapest.

NTE. (1996). Egészségügyi közgazdaságtan, MOTESZ Magazin, 96, 58–59.

Parry Jones, W. L., Vetró, Á., & Warnke, A. (1994). Teaching and training in child and adolescent psychiatry in Hungary. In T. Sensky, C. Katona, & S. Montgomery (Eds.), Psychiatry in Europe (pp. 179–191). London: Gaskell

Új elnökség, új alapszabály a MOTESZ-ben. (1997). MOTESZ Magazin, 97(1), 4–8.

Újraszabályozzák a szakmai kollégiumokat. (1996). MOTESZ Magazin, 96(3), 6–8.

Vetró, Á. (1995). Quo vadis child and adolescent psychiatry. Gyermekgyógyászat, 46, 102–108.

Vetró, Á., McGuinness, D., Fedor, I., Dombovári, E., & Baji, I. (1997). Epidemiological survey of behaviour problems among children of school age in Szeged. Psychiatrica Hungarica. 12, 193–201.

29

The Current Status of Mental Healthcare for Children in Russia

ANATOLY A. SEVERNY

ALEXANDER YU. SMIRNOV

ADVANTAGES AND DISADVANTAGES OF TRADITIONAL MENTAL HEALTHCARE FOR CHILDREN IN RUSSIA

Mental healthcare for children in the former Soviet Union was established in the 1930s. It was structured as a chain of regional child outpatient and inpatient clinics. All children from a particular district could have free service from the regional outpatient center for mentally ill children. If the disorder was severe and demanded hospitalization, the child could be sent to the regional hospital or, in complicated cases, to a specialty clinic. The main person in this system was the district child psychiatrist, who would have known the ill child, since his or her first visit to the clinic, and sometimes even several generations of the family.

This system had certain advantages:

1. The regional child psychiatrist actively supervised the children in the area. The psychiatrist did not wait until the patient came for help, but had the ability to summon or visit the patient, even in a period of remission, to prevent a relapse or to resolve problems at school. The psychiatrist could advise the patient to go to a daycare hospital or residential center.
2. A specific result of this active supervision was that it led to the prevention of homelessness. The regional psychiatrist arranged

for children to go to foster homes, group homes, hospitals, or special kindergartens, depending on the needs of the individual child.

3. This strictly managed system made it possible to obtain statistics about child mental disorders easily. Therefore, the planning of mental health services was facilitated.

4. All these services were free, a significant advantage to mentally ill children whose parents could not pay for hospitalization and more or less expensive treatment.

Apart from these advantages, mental healthcare for children in Russia (formerly, the Soviet Union) had many disadvantages:

1. Mental healthcare had been separated from systems of education and social services. Patients could not receive multidisciplinary treatments or remediation because they were limited by the provisions of the Ministry of Healthcare.

2. This system was very rigid, which led to lack of prevention and rehabilitation. The regional child psychiatrist was responsible for a population of up to 20,000 children and often did not have adequate time or facilities to create systems of prevention and rehabilitation for mental health in childhood. This entire system was oriented only towards the care of seriously mentally ill children or those with severe disabilities, and it had no organizing framework for these children when they were coming back to normal life after their treatment.

3. There was a lack of social and legal services for children with mental disorders and for their families. There was no law defending the rights of children with mental health problems. Therefore, many orphans and delinquent children could not obtain appropriate service.

4. There were no special services for children under the age of 4. Children could see a child psychiatrist only after this age. Many mental disorders appear in the first years of life, and this lack of early services led to the absence of preventive interventions.

5. The ridigity of the system prevented collaboration between governmental and nongovernmental organizations. The Ministry of Healthcare could officially collaborate only with government organizations that were under its auspices. The Ministry was not permitted to undertake joint projects with professional or public

associations. Responsibility for advancing new projects and developing new areas of expertise was held by institutes that were in competition, which resulted in controversial results emerging from these competitions.

All these disadvantages led to decreased quality and availability of mental healthcare for children. Many social problems arose due to the deterioration of the systems aiding the child's development.

Currently, 7% of all school-age children do not attend school.[1] About 1 million children are homeless.[2] The total number of orphans exceeds 500,000. The period of time for children awaiting placement in an orphanage is now several months. During this time, they are deprived of normal food and clothing and are exposed to physical and sexual violence.

One study, conducted jointly by the Independent Association of Child Psychiatrists and Psychologists and the Research Institute for Preventive Psychiatry of the Research Centre for Mental Health of the Russian Academy of Medical Sciences, suggests that as many as 40% of children are abused in families (Brutman, 1995).[3] In school-based studies, 16% of pupils are said to have been exposed to physical violence, and 24% to psychological violence. Also, many children have begun to use drugs. For example, 20% of all adolescents try drugs one or more times (Brun, 1995). As a result, child and adolescent criminality has grown twice as fast as in adults. In 1995, 80 adolescents in Moscow were punished for murder.

All of these factors are linked closely with the mental health of the child population. Recently, only 16% of adolescents were judged to be completely mentally healthy (About the Status of Children in the Russian Federation, 1994). Mental pathology among socially disadvantaged adolescents reaches 95% (Iovchuk, 1995). Unfortunately only 10% of all the children who need psychiatric help actually get it (About the Status of Children in the Russian Federation, 1994).

Our government has inadequate financial resources to maintain the proper mental health system for children. Last year we had no official statistical data about the prevalence and incidence of different childhood mental disorders. Moreover, in November 1995, the Ministry of Healthcare issued instructions which deleted the specialty of child and adolescent psychiatry from the official list of medical professions.

ACTIONS NECESSARY TO IMPROVE MENTAL
HEALTHCARE FOR CHILDREN IN RUSSIA

We make the following recommendations for improving mental healthcare for Russian children.

1. The following should be considered the main principles for the development of mental health services for children and adolescents:

• Prevention and rehabilitation should be the cornerstones of child mental healthcare.
• The multifactorial background of mental disorders and the needs of children demand a multidisciplinary system of service, with collaboration of specialists from many professions: psychiatrists, psychologists, educational personnel, social workers, etc.
• Mental healthcare cannot intrude into public life, but it should be organized to offer full access to children, adolescents, their parents, and all specialists who work with children.

2. A law must be developed to assure availability of psychiatric and psychological care for children. This law should give rights to children and their parents to demand equal opportunities to receive care.

3. The "Charity Tax Law" must be changed. According to this law, commercial companies can give only 2% of their profits to charity. Many companies would like to support child mental healthcare, but currently they donate only small sums, because they must pay taxes on the amount given to charity. At a time when the government cannot finance child mental healthcare sufficiently, attracting public or commercial money becomes very significant.

4. Federal child mental healthcare services must coordinate with the volunteer centers that have arisen in the last few years. This effort will be aided by the establishment of a Specialized Information Center. Now all these organizations are separate, which is detrimental to delivering complex mental healthcare.

5. Competition should be introduced for the support available for new programs for "Improving Mental Healthcare for Children." Currently, this program is administered and implemented by the

Ministry of Healthcare and its institutions. Meanwhile, many professional and public associations have been organized that have become very important for delivering services to children. These are more flexible and have the necessary experience, but cannot participate in governmental programs.

6. Interdepartmental assessment centers for children and adolescents should be established. Their main aim would be to assess and to prevent social disability, and to develop an individual social services program for each child who attends.

Some positive changes are already occurring on the local level. For example, Ludmila P. Rubina (Chief Child Psychiatrist of St. Petersburg) and her collaborators managed to organize a new system of child mental healthcare which includes prevention, treatment, and rehabilitation. This system contains:

- psychotherapy consultation studies in child polyclinics;
- child outpatient clinics (Regional Child Mental Health Centers);
- a crisis center for children and adolescents under severe stress;
- a hotline for children and adolescents;
- a psychiatric inpatient hospital, a hospital for children suffering from borderline psychopathology, and a psychiatric daycare hospital;
- an interdepartmental rehabilitation center, organized jointly by the Department of Healthcare and the Department of Education (the first in Russia).

Similar attempts, but on the local level, are being made in other cities as well, such as Yaroslavl and Tomsk.

The Independent Association of Child Psychiatrists and Psychologists (IACPP) is trying to support the new trends. Organized 4 years ago, IACPP has representatives in eight Russian regions. IACPP first began in Russia to carry out a program for prevention of homelessness and child abandonment. (Recently, they have been joined in their efforts by the Research Institute for Preventive Psychiatry of the Mental Health Research Center of the Russian Academy of Medical Sciences.) Also, programs for the prevention of school adjustment problems and a gifted children support program were realized; the number of projects is increasing.

In order to promote a multidisciplinary approach to the problems of child mental health, IACPP has organized four all-Russian conferences where the main focus has been on the collaboration of different specialists in determining tasks to be carried out in defense of child mental health. Now IACPP is finishing the preparation for the publication of the first *Russian Handbook of Psychology and Psychiatry of the Child and Adolescent*. Collaboration between diverse specialists has also generated a journal, the *Archive of Child Psychology, Psychiatry & Psychosomatics*, which is projected for publication by IACPP soon.

CONCLUSION

Russian child mental healthcare had certain advantages and disadvantages under the previous political system. The changing world has recently led to decreasing quality of services. Efforts to improve mental healthcare for children are being initiated by governmental and nongovernmental organizations. A new system of child mental healthcare should be based on the following principles: availability, a multidisciplinary approach, and primary attention being given to prevention and rehabilitation.

NOTES

1. Data of the Russian Ministry of Education (1995).
2. This data was reported during a session called "Listening on Education" (1995) in the Parliament of the Russian Federation.
3. Data of the Federal Committee for Problems of Youth (1994).

REFERENCES

About the Status of Children in the Russian Federation. (1994). Moscow: Governmental Report.
Brun, E. A. (1995), submitted.
Brutman, V. I. (1995), submitted.
Iovchuk, N. M. (1995). *School Disability: Emotional and Stressful Problems in Children and Adolescents.* Moscow.

30

Planning Mental Health Services for Children and Adolescents in Brazil

SALVADOR CELIA

The official theme of the IACAPAP Congress in Stockholm in 1998 is "Trauma and Recovery." We will consider how mental health planning for children and adolescents can diminish the deleterious effects of the present-day world, which include a great number of very serious risk factors, including stress and violence, that predominate from early in life. In developing countries and troubled areas of the developed world, this violence is part of what we call social violence and begins with scarce food and resulting hunger (Celia, 1994). In such a difficult, traumatic world, planning is an optimistic process, as we begin to review, understand, and apply studies on vulnerability, risk factors, and resilience developed by investigators such as Rutter, Garmezy, Cohen, Werner, and Anthony.

For example, the study by Emy Werner (the Kawai Longitudinal Study, 1991) followed 698 infants to the age of 30 years, monitoring the impact on development of a variety of biological and psychosocial risk factors, as well as stressful life events and protective factors in early and middle childhood, late adolescence, and young adulthood. The results showed that one third of this sample was considered at risk, because they had experienced moderate to severe degrees of perinatal stress, were born into poverty, were reared by mothers with little formal education, or lived in a family environment troubled by discord, desertion, or divorce or marred by parental alcoholism or mental illness. All of them encountered four or more such cumulative risk factors before the age of 10 or had records of delinquency, mental health problems, or teenage pregnancy by age 18.

Surprisingly, however, one out of every three of them (30 males, 42 females), or approximately 10% of the total cohort, instead developed into competent, confident, and caring young adults. Looking back at the lives of these 72 resilient individuals, Werner and colleagues found a number of characteristics in the individuals, their families, and those outside their family circles that contributed to their resilience. These characteristics were the presence of protective factors needed to counter the risk factors that existed in the lives of these individuals and that reinforced a positive outcome of development. To be more or less resilient, however, is not a matter of magic. Our responsibilities as healthcare professionals enlarge considerably as we participate at various professional levels; inform the public at large, as well as government authorities; act as advocates for children; and help to educate and train healthcare professionals at several stages of learning.

TRAINING

If we look at medical training, it is obvious that, at most medical schools, students are not prepared for the humanistic aspects of medicine, to view human beings as whole persons, and to practice preventive medicine: they are trained in the physical and pharmacological aspects of medicine. Lately, considering the rapid advances of technology, I often ask myself whether we are not actually training "medical engineers." I refer to the fact that no matter how welcome technological progress is, it is often ill used. True iatrogenic illnesses are perpetrated, for instance, in the modern, revolutionary neonatal intensive care units, where children are usually kept apart from their parents for longer periods than desirable. Studies have shown that this is a very damaging situation for the infants and their future development.

The vision of the physician's centralizing power is often harmful. The work of the healthcare team becomes dissociated, full of "fiefdoms." For instance, in the mental healthcare team, the psychiatrist, the psychologist, the social worker, and others may not integrate their activities, and the consequent fiefdoms prevent it from functioning smoothly. In community health also, despite good training, the physician often is not the best person to coordinate group work that must involve the community. I see training as an essential factor for carrying out action plans. This mental health training is the result of an integrated idea of "health," and only includes the term "mental health" for didactic purposes since, like the individual, health is unique and indivisible.

BONDING, DEVELOPMENT, AND PERSONALITY

As mental health professionals, we view individuals as biopsychosocial, environmental, and political beings, because of their assets, their contributions, their interactions and experiences, and their rights and duties. We try to protect the child and "humankind" with regulations and laws. We consider the child a fully-fledged citizen with rights. This means that when there is lack of means to adequately facilitate development, it is the "state" which must fulfill these rights, which include, for example, the right of the infant to experience adequate "bonding." When a child is born, that child has a father, a mother, a family, a community, a nation, and a flag. All this is inherent to the child even under the worst psychosocial circumstances, and the state which organize social policies founded on these basic social bonds.

These ideas are reinforced by an understanding of development according to the data described by investigators such as Stern, Emde, Zeanah, and Rutter, referring to the importance of context in the development of "continuity and discontinuity," contrasting with reductionistic theories and the fixation-regression model of psychopathology and development. In the continuous construction model there is no need for regression, and ontogenetic origins of psychopathology are no longer necessarily tied to specific critical or sensitive periods in development (Zeanah et al., 1991).

For theories acknowledging "continuity," the most significant focus is on internal representations, derived from the model of relations with one's caregivers. Stern (memory structure) and Bowlby (working models) contributed decisively to understanding these operational models which, when successful, can render the child ego-resilient (flexible, self-reliant, curious, motivated) and, consequently, a healthier adolescent and adult. These models become intergenerational, as we see from studies of mothers and infants

(Ainsworth), adults and their own childhoods (Main), and adults and their children (Main & Eichberg).

PREVENTION

We therefore view bonding and the formation of attachments as the core of environmental provisions favoring resilience when seeking to understand mental health.

I suggest that mental health begins with women, even in their childhoods. In childhood, girls need to acquire a practical knowledge of life which will make them better and literate citizens who know their communities, their rights, and their duties. This will make it easier for them to face risk factors such as teenage pregnancy, drug abuse, etc.

During pregnancy, integrated prenatal care is essential for satisfactory development of the infant and its interaction with the environment. The World Health Organization recommends 5 to 8 prenatal visits to the doctor. However, even when this recommendation is complied with, the mother may not receive sufficient attention and care. Surveys we performed on malnourished infants and their depressive mothers show that, surprisingly, all the poor mothers had had prenatal care, and nothing was detected which could have prevented the problem from occurring. Physicians and healthcare teams commonly lack the full vision necessary to understand all the phenomena of somatic and psychosocial change in the pregnant woman.

Equally, due value is not given to what we believe is a matter of public health: the prevalence of depression during the postpartum period. We know, from very recent studies, that 1 out of every 10 to 15 women has severe symptoms of depression, while another 50% have the so-called "postpartum blues" on the fifth day; they improve when the woman finds support in her environment or in the hospital (Cox, 1996; Murray, 1996). As Esquirol said long ago, many are "cured" at home, but we ask: how?

These depressions affect the family, the parenting couple, and the infant's development. They tend to occur in primiparae who have delivered by cesarean section and have had some mental health problem in their lives or among family members. Such depressions are too common in cultural settings such as Brazil, where being young, poor, black, a primipara, undergoing cesarean section, and having a premature baby is almost an identity profile—one we must prevent! Additionally, it is alarming that the number of cesarean sections in Porto Alegre, Brazil, is almost 68% in the better-off social classes.

We recommend that care be provided for pregnant women, and, if possible, to the couple, in an informative, operational group. This group, if necessary, should sometimes meet on weekends, because of the parents' jobs. In a survey performed in 1983 (Celia, Santos, Krowcrzuk et al., 1983) investigators saw that sociability developed more intensely in children up to 3 years of age whose mothers attended these groups than in children in the control group, whose mothers consulted healthcare centers but did not participate in groups while pregnant.

INFANT-PARENT RELATIONSHIP

Another survey (Celia, Alves, Behs, Nudelman, & Saraiva, 1992), on malnourished children and their depressed mothers, showed that one of the most important psychosocial factors which led the mothers of these children to become depressed was lack of support from the husband or partner. Among other psychosocial factors relevant to psychopathology, we also observed loss of familial roots (internal migrations), abandonment, neglect in childhood, unwished-for pregnancy, attempted abortion, short breastfeeding time as compared with the control group, and also short time of exclusive breastfeeding. The "father effect" must also be the subject of further studies and follow-up. The father's presence during delivery is an important factor for the mother's security and for triggering initial interactions (Brazelton).

Various positive steps can be taken to provide optimal conditions for the infant during delivery and in the first year of life. The use of a "doula" to assist the mother during labor and delivery should be increased (Kennel, 1993). Rooming-in is essential and must be sought, because it has clear beneficial effects on the development of infants (Kennel, 1993). To be born without violence is to prepare for humanity; it is the genesis of ecological man (Odent, 1982). Breastfeeding, which is so necessary to save lives, should be encouraged and fostered, but not to the point of iatrogenic problems. Campaigns must take into account ideas on femininity, motherhood, and respectfulness with regard to women, but not introduce more guilt into women's lives. Campaigns should actually begin in preschools, by not encouraging the use of bottle-feeding when little girls play with dolls.

We also use mother-infant participation groups as an "early intervention" technique up to the age of 3. Here we seek to follow the dyad, to provide reinforcement for beneficial behaviors, to encourage mothering, and, when possible, to promote better fathering. This activity helps diagnose problems in mother-infant interaction.

Since it is expected that by the year 2000 almost 50% of the female population will be working outside the home, caregivers must be found, possibly among the grandparents, as in China, or in the community. It is necessary to have daycare centers provide physically and emotionally appropriate responses to infants' needs. Studies by Rutter and others indicate the positive effects of good daycare centers on the development of infants (Haggerty, Rutter, Garmezy, & Sherwood, 1994).

The working mother, who generates income, can transform working into a new element of primary healthcare. Data suggest that a mother's income is usually used to pay for goods and services that maintain and improve the health and nutrition of family members, and thus their own self-esteem (Schuftan, 1995). Therefore, it can be seen that school, ranging from daycare centers, to kindergarten, to primary and secondary schools, is an excellent therapeutic factor for increasing resilience.

An environment where children feel welcome, protected, and cared for and where they can play and use their potential for games that foster creativity will help them to introject models of references, relationships, and group experiences. These can trigger the "social energy" that is the sum of positive energies available in individuals and that can be channeled and developed by group interaction. If the community has appropriate places for sports and leisure and social activities, children will become aware of significant caregivers who show them that they are important, valued, and necessary to the life of the community, now and in the future. Social mobilization in community culture creates healthy potentials and reinforces the esteem which is essential to citizens and to community life (Odent, 1982; Pavlovsky & Kessblman, 1990).

One example of this is Project Vida, founded 7 years ago in Porto Alegre. It is a cooperative program between the state government and the community that seeks to reinforce the citizenship and self-esteem of low-income people (malnourished infants, women with high-risk pregnancies, street children, the aged, the handicapped, women in general). The project takes a comprehensive approach to the areas of health, education, leisure, sports, technology, culture, and human rights in almost 60 in-house or external activities. These activities, which cover a large number of physical and emotional issues, are intended to foster the potential for resilience present in individuals and the community. The contact (togetherness) between different social groups and different age groups (grandparents, parents, children, adolescents) creates opportunities for bonding and development of attachment while maintaining individual and social autonomy.

One hundred twenty employees, trained to provide this care, work with a population of 4,000 persons. We believe that this care could also be given in less complex structures, such as schools, neighborhood associations, parish halls, etc., as long as it complies with the project philosophy.

PROGRAMS FOR ADOLESCENTS

Attention to the adolescent, always respecting his or her needs at this point in life, is achieved by giving priority to activities which will foster their potential for group play, where socialization becomes the significant operational matrix. Another experience in which we participated in Porto Alegre was organizing the Center for Adolescents. This is a physical space where healthcare is provided to teenagers, as well as education, leisure, sports, and culture. Some adolescents come to the center to obtain medical aid for drug problems; others seek social contact and the opportunity to develop their potential. When more specialized support is required, they and their families are referred to social services, such as a boarding school type of facility.

The concepts of acceptance and integration that are now advocated in the treatment of handicapped children should also be applied to these troubled adolescents. Schools now advocate integration of handicapped children (mildly retarded, high-functioning autistic children, borderline patients, etc.) into group activities, together with individual attention to each case, during school time if necessary, as well as establishing spaces for special activities and providing follow-up to individuals or small groups. If this model is followed, special schools will become less and less necessary, and primary and secondary prevention of adolescent problems will be emphasized.

In outpatient clinics belonging to health centers, group techniques should increasingly be used to care for adolescents and the family and, often, to reinforce parenting skills. It is equally necessary, especially in cases of depression, attempted suicide, and the anorexia-bulimia syndrome, which are more and more prevalent, to provide for the optimal but moderate use of psychopharmacological agents. Another modality which can be successfully developed is training adolescents to function as health agents in their communities, providing basic first aid and helping to prevent drug abuse.

One example of prevention was an experiment which took place at Canela, a small town in Rio Grande do Sul, where adolescents were mobilized in their schools and their community to participate in theater activities. They underwent changes in behavior and self-esteem and managed to mobilize the whole community for a theater festival that is prepared for throughout the year. A goal to be achieved through Winnicott's so-called transitional space is to favor creativity, which will become an important protective factor in life. The use of play space, beginning with the first parent-infant interactions, stimulates creativity.

A FINAL RECOMMENDATION

A final suggestion emphasizes the value of community participation in organizing healthcare plans. Leaders of community associations, teachers, parents, children, and adolescents can all contribute and share their needs, ideas, and experiences within the culture. Rio Grande do Sul organized such a "State Conference for Mental Health Planning" in 1992. Similarly, it is essential to focus on health team training, multidisciplinary work, and, in the medical area, the special role of the pediatrician.

In 10 years of training pediatricians in mental health, we have become increasingly convinced that it is useful for their participation as the main health agent to begin even in the prenatal period. The pediatrician is the physician most trusted by the family, a social organization which requires more and more support in our present-day world. As health promoter, the pediatrician can diagnose illnesses, prevent impairments, and advise parents, children, and teenagers throughout their development. In their psychotherapeutic functions, they can provide the best support to families and parents, reinforcing parenting skills and using "interactive guidance." The pediatrician creates a space for parents to talk and to get to know themselves, and can suggest steps to be taken. The pediatrician thus becomes a catalyst and an advisor on behaviors which the parents strive to achieve by developing their insight. It is primary prevention of emotional and behavioral disorders, using psychoprophylaxis, an integrated, ecological, ecosystemic view, that will best help us to develop our mental health goal. Obviously, the same education and the same base will be extremely valid in achieving secondary and tertiary prevention.

As we arrive in the 21st century we still face a great challenge: increasingly, we must find the strength to promote health and life projects, the only way to stand up to the great number of death projects still present in our society. I call on the reader to investigate and find factors that will promote life and that will reduce risk factors or render them less significant, so that individuals and their communities will be able to develop and use their own potentials.

REFERENCES

Celia, S., Alves, M., Behs, B., Nudelmann, C., & Saraiva, J. (1992, September). *Malnutrition and infant development.* Paper presented at Fifth International Congress of the World Association for Infant Psychiatry and Development, Chicago, IL.

Celia, S., Santos, A., Krowczuk, E., et al. (1983). Assistência materno infantil. Anàlises de uma experiência. Perspectivas. In *A criança e o adolescente brasileiro da década de 80* (pp. 13–28). Porto Alegre, Brazil: Editora Artes Médicas.

Celia, S. (1994). Sociocultural roots of violence: Street children in Brazil. In C. Chiland & J. G. Young (Eds.), *Children and violence* (pp. 163–170). Northvale, NJ: Aronson.

Cox, J. (1996, January). *Trouble psychiatrique du post-partum; Aspect socio-culturel de la "Maladie Mental Seven."* Personal Communication. Colloquium, Monaco.

Haggerty, R., Rutter, M., Garmezy, N., & Sherwood, J. (1994). *Stress risk and resilience in children and adolescents.* Cambridge: Cambridge University Press.

Kennel, J. K. (1993). *Pais-Bebê, a formação do apego.* Porto Alegre, Brazil: Editora Artes Médicas.

Odent, M. (1982). *Gênesis do Homem Ecológico.* Sao Paula, Brazil: TAO Editora.

Pavlovsky, E., & Kessblman, H. (1990). *Espacios y creatividad.* Ediciones Ayllu, Edición Buenos Aires, Argentina.

Schuftan, C. (1995). Atividades geradoras de renda para mulher: o novo elemento dos cuidados primários de saúde. *O Canguru, 3,* 38–46.

Werner, E. (1991). High risk children in young adulthood: A longitudinal study from birth to 32 years. In S. Chess (Ed.), *Annual progress in child psychiatry and child development.* New York: Brunner/Mazel.

Zeanah, C., Stern, D., et al. (1991). Implications of research on infant development for psychodynamic theory and practice. In S. Chess (Ed.), *Annual progress in child psychiatry and child development.* New York: Brunner/Mazel.

31

The Impact of Changes in Healthcare Systems on Psychiatric Care for Children and Adolescents in Hong Kong

T.-P. HO

BACKGROUND

Hong Kong is a rapidly developing city on the south coast of China. In the past three decades, a number of social changes have taken place. First, the population in Hong Kong doubled from 3.1 million in 1961 to 6.3 million in 1996 (Census and Statistics Department, 1961–1996). The proportion of youth in the population (aged under 20) dropped from 46% to 25%. The apparent aging of the population was counteracted by a constant influx of children immigrating from mainland China. This has created tensions in the education, social, and health systems, as they attempt to integrate these children into the society of Hong Kong. Second, the number of households has more than doubled, and the average size of a household has decreased from 4.6 persons in 1961 to 3.4 in 1996. The proportion of extended families among all households has decreased from 22% to 13% in the last decade. Third, the number of divorce petitions received in the past 20 years has been increasing at a rate of 5% per year. Fourth, the proportion of female participation in the labor force has increased from 23% to 49% in the past 35 years. The increase is more obvious in the child-bearing ages. Fifth, the manufacturing industry in Hong Kong has undergone a massive shift to south China. A significant proportion of the working population, especially males, has to frequently travel across the border. This often means a virtual absence of a paternal figure at home. The cumulative effects of these changes have gradually eroded the socio-cultural provisions for children and adolescents in traditional Chinese families. Many of these unmet needs have inevitably increased the demands on the social, educational, and medical fields.

Medical healthcare in Hong Kong is heavily subsidized by the government. Medical insurance is not popular. The total number of beds supported by public funding represents about 90% of all hospital beds in Hong Kong (Hospital Authority, 1995). On the other hand, most of the primary care services are provided by the private sector. There is no comprehensive primary healthcare service for the population. Following the establishment of the Hospital Authority, a wide range of initiatives were planned and put into action in the past few years. Among those changes that probably have the greatest impact on clinical care are the emphasis on evidence-based justifications of new developments, the clinical output-outcome-focused orientation, the development of a Patient Related Group (PRG) case-mix information system, and the linkage of resource allocation/management to these parameters. Similar to the experiences in other countries that have gone through these changes, psychiatry, not to mention child and adolescent psychiatry, lags behind in the implementation of these healthcare system changes. At the time of writing, the first PRG in psychiatry was chosen to be schizophrenia, which has yet to be finalized. No PRG has been chosen in the field of child and adolescent psychiatry.

EFFECTS ON CLINICAL CARE

To describe the impact of changes in the healthcare system on clinical care seems to imply that there are systematic, goal-oriented efforts aiming to achieve planned targets with certain strategies. While it might be the preferred scenario, both clinical and research experience at the front line speak to the contrary. Two studies carried out in local settings ought to be mentioned.

In a prospective study, of 100 consecutive referrals to a hospital-based child psychiatric clinic in Hong Kong, the help-seeking processes of the referred children were characterized by (a) a sequential pattern of lay consultations starting with the families, relatives, and then friends of the parents; (b) a detour via multiple professionals which included school personnel, social workers, general practitioners, counselors, and psychologists; and (c) a delay in reaching specialist services (Ho & Chung, 1996). Low awareness of services was the predominant difficulty parents encountered when they sought psychiatric care for their children.

Nearly all child psychiatric services in Hong Kong work in general hospital or specialty clinic settings. A community-based child mental health clinic came into being in the late 1980s. In a comparison study of child psychiatric patients attending hospital-based clinics (which require professional referrals) and community-based clinics (which accept parents' self-referrals), patients were found to be similar in demography, degree of social disadvantage, duration of chief complaints, maternal psychopathology, help-seeking behaviors and number of life events preceding clinic attendance, parental explanatory models of the child's problems, and expectations in treatment (Ho & Luk, in press). A major proportion of the parents of community clinic subjects reported that they attended the clinic because of recent knowledge of the existence of the service. Community clinic subjects have also gone through a large number of professional consultations. Given the gross similarity of the subjects seen at both settings, the tortuous help-seeking pathways, and the delay in reaching clinical services, one naturally wonders about the low availability and poor accessibility of child and adolescent psychiatry services in Hong Kong. Without appropriate treatment possibilities, some parents reported that they sought help for their children from herbalists and geomancers. Various helping strategies have been noted, including prescription of herbal medicine, advice on *Fung Shui* (geomancy), changing the child's name, and some religious rituals. Apart from reflecting congruity with the parents' expectations, the phenomenon partially speaks to the unmet needs of the parents and their children.

The above studies seem to suggest that a pool of disturbed children in the community are unable to reach child psychiatric services because the parents do not know about the services, and the professionals do not refer them for one reason or the other. Parents of these disturbed children tend to seek help from the people and professionals around them. Quite often, they have to go through a number of professionals before they eventually reach a child psychiatric service. There seems to be a lack of an organized healthcare delivery system for these disturbed youngsters. The problem is more acute given the lack of comprehensive primary care services in the territory.

The above-mentioned problems have to be appreciated from the context of current medical care in Hong Kong. It is unlikely that the much-needed improvement in resources will materialize in the near future. Indeed, the emphasis on evidence-based practice, development of PRGs, and linkage of resource allocation with output and outcome probably put child psychiatry in a disadvantageless position because of its labor-intensive treatment and relative lack of an empirical basis. Moreover, the current trend of establishing psychiatry units within general hospitals, rather than large mental hospitals, has increased the difficulty of securing resources. Given the short history and lack of professional identity of child psychiatry in the territory, the competition for resources with other well-established and technologically advanced subspecialties is not an easy task. Data collected from different hospitals and clinics reveals interesting variations in clinical practice, output, quality, and costs. Thus, as auditing becomes routine, standard treatment protocols have to be established. In this climate, professionals cannot help but be more conscious of cost-effectiveness in their clinical practices.

Given the restraints described above, plenty of work needs to be done, much of which cannot be within the scope of child psychiatry. Among professionals, one needs to establish child psychiatry as a respectable subspecialty. Public health education to demystify child psychiatric services is required. Networking with front-line workers to improve accessibility of the services is warranted. Establishment of community-based services can be an alternative service model. With the shortage of trained personnel in mind, it appears that child psychiatry services in the territory may have to play different roles for different childhood disorders. While direct clinical service is most often called for in severe disturbances and some neuropsychiatric conditions, child psychiatrists may utilize their knowledge of child development and psychopathology, and their skills in team work, to support front-line workers to handle disturbed children in their community settings.

REFERENCES

Census and Statistics Department. (1961–1996). *Hong Kong Census.* Hong Kong Government.

Hospital Authority. (1995). *Hospital Authority Annual Report, 1995.* Hong Kong.

Ho, T. P., & Chung, S. Y. (1996). Help-seeking behaviours among child psychiatric clinic attenders in Hong Kong. *Social Psychiatry and Psychiatric Epidemiology, 31,* 292–298.

Ho, T. P., & Luk, C. (1997). Comparison of child psychiatric patients in hospital and community clinics in Hong Kong. *General Hospital Psychiatry, 19,* 362–369.

32

Transitions for Mental Health Services for Children and Adolescents: The Polish Experience

JACEK BOMBA

The Mental Health Act indicates childhood and adolescence as a period of life requiring special preventive, therapeutic, and remedial care. The organization of services can be based on patterns of services developed in countries with a longer tradition and on the recommendations of international organizations. This desirable goal, however, will remain at a project stage if realistic factors are not taken into account. Assessment of specific community needs through epidemiological studies requires highly trained professionals and reasonable funds. This is more practical for the modifications of well-developed care systems.

Early exposure to fundamental information concerning the mental health problems of children, adolescents, and their families in undergraduate medical training is important, recognizing that the development of specialized services requires the support and cooperation of other physicians and forms a background for postgraduate training in child and adolescent psychiatry. Professional multidisciplinary associations of child and adolescent mental health clinicians play a very important role in creating standards and making recommendations for the improvement of care systems, and in lobbying for changes essential for the realization of any design.

INTRODUCTION

It is commonly agreed that mental health services should be available close to the community they are serving, and provide preventive, therapeutic, and rehabilitative measures. Guidelines developed by international organizations (e.g., World Health Organization, professional associations, etc.) can be followed, especially when there is no local experience or the existing system is dysfunctional. There is no doubt that epidemiological studies can provide solid data for assessing community needs for mental health services: the number of affected children, profile of disorders, and specific characteristics of the community (Orwid, 1981; Stomma, 1989). Another unquestionable factor to be considered is the impact of the economic and political situation of the community on the implementation of any conceptual design. Macrosocial difficulties (poverty, social crises, wars) result in the neglect of the needs of the weaker members of the community: infants, children, problem families, as well as the elderly (Bomba, 1994b).

So, when designing a system:

• one is able to follow the patterns of structures already developed;
• one should take into account the system already existing and its assessment by professionals and consumers; and
• one has to assess the economic and political situation, because designing realistically means designing ways and measures to overcome problems created by macrosocial conditions rather than only relying on a drastic limitation of goals.

THE POLISH PROJECT FOR THE ORGANIZATION OF MENTAL HEALTH SERVICES FOR CHILDREN AND ADOLESCENTS

The Project (National Board of Child and Adolescent Psychiatry, 1995) was developed by the National Board of Child and Adolescent Psychiatry in 1995. The legal regulations regarding healthcare and the National Programme of Mental Health Care formed a background for its shape. The main idea was to bring care close to its consumers. It aimed to achieve this by creating mental health clinics and daycare units for children and adolescents in all areas of the cities and in the country. The second issue emphasized was close cooperation between mental health services and the other services providing care for children and adults.

The project also provides a design for the framework of services. More specialized services were designed for the regional level. Family clinics, inpatient psychiatric units for children and adolescents, and halfway houses for adolescents were organized there. University departments supervise the mental healthcare system within a region and provide highly specialized services.

Implementation of the project requires radical changes in the system already developed in Poland. The modern history of child and adolescent psychiatry goes back to the last decades of the 19th century and has had enough time to establish its own identity. A part of this is the recognition of long-term inpatient treatment for children as essential. Due to the theoretical orientation of child psychiatrists and a complicated plethora of sociopolitical and economical factors, mental health services for children and adolescents form a part of the National Health System administered by the state and financed from the national budget. The most important (and the most expensive) part of the mental health services is formed by inpatient institutions providing long-term hospitalization, very often far from the child's home. At the beginning of 1995, the ratio of hospital beds for children and adolescents (0–18 years) in Poland was 0.7 per 10,000 population,, while the ratio of places in day units was only 0.2 per 10,000 population. It should be emphasized that the vast majority of hospital units were designed for children under 14 years of age. In addition, outpatient services are still too limited in number, and each of the clinics serves a child and adolescent population exceeding 200,000.

The strategy supported by the project is to almost double the number of outpatient services. It is believed that a clinic is capable of providing satisfactory care for a population of 100,000 children and adolescents if effective cooperation with other services exists. The other services supported by the project are day units. The goal is to establish a total number of day centers 10 times bigger than the number we already have (an increase from 13 to 104), to achieve an index of 0.7 places per 10,000.

The experiences of deinstitutionalization in psychiatry in many countries were broadly published (Crome, 1994; Talbott, 1985). The process is not easy and it is emphasized that closing down inpatient units has to be accompanied by the parallel development of alternative therapeutic programs in the community.

There is only one problem with the project: the number of Polish professionals. At the moment the National Health Service provides up to one psychiatrist and two clinical psychologists for a population of 250,000. The goals of the project cannot be achieved unless the number can be changed to closer to that suggested by the WHO (1 psychiatrist per 100,000 inhabitants).

IDENTIFYING BARRIERS TO ACHIEVING THE GOALS OF THE DESIGN

The low number of Polish clinicians for children is, as one can easily imagine, the direct result of resources allocated in the national budget to mental healthcare for children and adolescents. This is a political problem and, as such, should be solved with political measures. The National Board (supervising child and adolescent psychiatry), the Section for Child and Adolescent Psychiatry of the Polish Psychiatric Association (PPA, the organization of professionals in mental healthcare for children and adolescents), and professionals themselves (provided they share the concept of change presented in the project) are able to promote political solutions which will bring better financing for this domain.

One might well wonder whether government economic influences are the only, or at least the most important, barrier. Should we not look for factors blocking realization of the objectives of the project within child and adolescent psychiatry itself? The present, unsatisfactory status of mental healthcare is, in some ways, a consequence of the theoretical concepts of psychiatrists, both directly, as child psychiatrists had an opportunity to actualize what they understood as helpful and correct, and indirectly, as they influenced the way physicians were trained in their discipline.

TRAINING IN CHILD AND ADOLESCENT PSYCHIATRY

When attempting to increase the number of physicians choosing developmental psychiatry for their postgraduate specialization, one should look at the way the subject is presented to medical students.

Undergraduate Training

Twelve medical schools in Poland are obliged to follow the fundamental curriculum of medicine suggested by the Ministry of Health, which also provides resources for their training. The medical schools, however, are to develop their own curricula. Child and adolescent mental health issues are not explicitly named as a subject to be taught at medical schools. They form parts of other preclinical and clinical disciplines. Medical psychology (behavioral sciences) covers (among other such topics): growth and development, the life cycle, family styles, child upbringing, family violence, and child abuse. Within clinical psychiatry, specific issues of child and adolescent psychiatry should be taught. Pediatrics is supposed to teach the fundamentals of psychosomatics in childhood.

The number of Polish medical schools actually teaching developmental aspects of the behavioral sciences and developmental psychiatry is unfortunately rather small. The way the faculties of medicine use the liberty they have in designing undergraduate training programs reflects the very low position of child and adolescent mental health in the hierarchy of important issues for professors of medicine. The PPA Section of Child and Adolescent Psychiatry is confronted with the very hard task of changing this. There is a chance for positive change, especially as the number of professors of developmental psychiatry is growing.

Postgraduate Training in Child and Adolescent Psychiatry

A program for postgraduate training in child psychiatry was formally instituted for the first time in 1958 (Stomma, 1989). The program was available to psychiatrists and pediatricians. Joint efforts of the PPA Section of Child and Adolescent Psychiatry and the National Board of Child and Adolescent Psychiatry resulted in acceptance of the new program in child and adolescent psychiatry, also available to medical school graduates.

Until now, postgraduate training has been based on a tutorial system. A nationally recognized specialist was fully responsible for implementation of the training program for each individual. There has been evident improvement in the quality of training, but the number of fully trained child and adolescent psychiatrists is still below the actual need.

OTHER PROFESSIONALS

The role of other professionals in mental healthcare for children and adolescents has been recognized for decades. In Poland, this important group consists of clinical psychologists and educators (teachers). Nonmedical professionals form a majority of the PPA Section for Child and Adolescent Psychiatry members. Their undergraduate training is highly differentiated depending on the university they graduated from. However, since 1980, there has been established postgraduate training in clinical psychology for those who work within the healthcare system. While the first part of this training is in general clinical psychology, the second part is designed for those who specialize in child and adolescent clinical psychology.

The PPA Section for Psychotherapy established a certificate in psychotherapy in 1990. Training programs leading to board examination have to be recognized by this section. Among the programs already accepted are some that include psychotherapy for children and adolescents and family therapy. Family therapy has become especially popular among postgraduate students.

RECENT CHANGES AND THEIR IMPACT ON CHILD AND ADOLESCENT MENTAL HEALTHCARE

Reforms in the healthcare system declared in the political program of democratization in 1989 are occurring very slowly (Bomba, 1994a). However, as part of these changes, outpatient and other extramural services recently have been placed under municipal instead of central governmental administration. The change resulted in an increasing role for local professionals as well as consumer groups, nongovernmental organizations (NGOs) and others. Without their effective lobbying, the proposed project could not be turned into reality. Another change in healthcare was the introduction of a family doctor (general practitioner) system. It is anticipated that family doctors will take care of many early problems of child mental health. The program of postgraduate residency training in family medicine includes child and adolescent psychiatry, family psychiatry, and a systemic approach to medical problems. It is difficult to predict the influence of this change on the actualization of the goals of the project.

CONCLUSIONS

Planning the future organization of mental healthcare for children and adolescents can be based on patterns of services developed in countries with a longer tradition, as well as on the recommendations of international organizations involved in designing improved healthcare systems. This laudable goal, however, will remain in the planning stage if realistic factors are not taken into account.

Assessment of specific community needs is extremely difficult, as epidemiological studies require highly trained professionals and are costly. Therefore, epidemiological data can be obtained more easily for the modification of already well-developed care systems.

The early initiation of training in the mental health problems of children, adolescents, and their families during undergraduate training of physicians is very important, since the development of specialized services requires the support and cooperation of other doctors, (e.g., general practitioners). This early training forms a background for postgraduate training in child and adolescent psychiatry.

Professional, multidisciplinary associations of child and adolescent mental health clinicians play a very important role in creating standards, making recommendations for the improvement of care systems, and lobbying for changes essential for the realization of any plan.

REFERENCES

Bomba, J. (1994a). Opieka psychiatryczna w Polsce po przelomie politycznym. *Dialog, 1,* 81–85; Die polnische psychiatrie nach den politischen Wende. *Dialog, 1,* 96–91.

Bomba, J. (1994b). Children during political changes. In J. Y. Hattab (Ed.), *Ethics and child mental health* (pp. 34–42) Jerusalem: Gefen.

Crome, A. (1994). Die Psychiatriereform nach der Vereinigung Deutschalnds. *Dialog, 1,* 75–79; Reforma psychiatrii po zjednoczeniu Niemiec. *Dialog, 1,* 69–73.

Orwid, M. (1981). *Zaburzenia psychiczne u mlodziezy.* Warszawa: PZWL.

National Board of Child and Adolescent Psychiatry. (1995). *Projekt wytycznych w sprawie organizacji i zasad prowadzenia psychiatrycznej opieki zdrowotnej nad dziećmi i mlodzieza.* Warszawa: IPN.

Stomma, D. (1989). Zarys rozwoju psychiatrii dzieciecej. In A. Popielarska (Ed.), *Psychiatria wieku rozwojowego* (pp. 13–17). Warszawa: PZWL.

Talbott, J. A. (1985). The fate of the public psychiatric system. *Hospital and Community Psychiatry, 36,* 46–50.

33

Strategies for Responding to the Needs of Adolescents in Romania

TIBERIU MIRCEA

ATTACHMENT PHENOMENA DURING ADOLESCENCE

Adolescence is a fluid moment, a moment resulting from a concatenation of individual existential stages. It develops as a result of an evolution. In adolescence, we find the evolution and dynamism of individual biogenetic characteristics and specific psychological structures that act in relation to interactions with other persons, life events, sociocultural influences, and zonal specificities. The individual's fantasy life and imagination together complete this picture and complicate one's ability to investigate the complex and mysterious period of adolescence.

I would like to start with a metaphor. We can compare adolescence with a portrait that needs to be hung in a gallery of the different stages of human existence. The portrait is both unique and individualized; it is only of the youth who is going to be "exhibited." But until we come to the portrait, several preliminary phases are undergone—phases that are similar to those in photography.

Similarly, we can compare the phases of development from childhood to adolescence with the stages of photography. Thus, the child's genetic material can be compared to film quality, and the biopsychological characteristics of the parents, with the the brand name and quality of the camera. The film and the camera contribute equally to the quality of the resulting pictures. The distances, the shutter time, and the exposure time in photography can be compared with the time necessary to develop object relations regarding attachment processes and attachment figures in childhood development. Up to the age of 3, attachment style is still being established, as pointed out by Bowlby and other authors (e.g., Ainsworth, Main, and Sroufe). We can compare this period of time with the opening of the shutter and the imprinting of the image.

The qualities of the image are important because the final portrait depends on them. Any movement of the image or the camera will give a blurry picture, with no firm outline. In child psychology, these phenomena are equivalent to disturbed mental processes related to attachment models, as proposed by Ainsworth's "Strange Situation" paradigm: avoidant, ambivalent, and insecure attachments. Certainly, there are many other details that make up the picture and that are worth discussing, but we make this reference to attachment theory in an attempt to point out some highly significant influences.

In photography, developing the negative requires a special, high-quality developing solution. Likewise, preschool children find themselves in a continual developmental process based on their previous attachment experiences. Depending on these attachment experiences, they may have difficulties with problem solving or with interactions with friends and/or adults. In a nonlinear manner these attachment qualities will influence the vulnerability or, on the contrary, the psychological-structural invulnerability of the future adolescent. Even in the unconscious, different past experiences mix with new acquisitions and changes; similarly, the adolescent's portrait reflects and represents that person's first developmental stages, though certainly not precisely. If we come back to our metaphor, we can say that the negative is not identical to the portrait, but maintains its individuality. I would like to comment on this similarity between the negative and the picture.

During ontological development, we identify two stages of development—one lasting until 3 years of age, and the other the period of adolescence—as being similar in relation to attachment, noting the time discrepancy between the two stages (3 years of early childhood compared to 7 or more years of adolescence). The two stages have similar characteristics: the psychological process of a transition from a stage of undifferentiated self-centeredness to differentiated non-self-centeredness. Likewise, in early childhood, there exists a period of attachment clarification; in adolescence, an attachment clarification occurs as well.

I would like to propose a hypothesis regarding attachment in adolescence. Except in Sroufe's research, studies regarding the quality of attachment in relation to later development generally refer to attachment at an early age, and to a correlation with types of children and parents. This is an important issue because it allows us to suggest that even though we do not find the same attachment in maturity as in childhood, the child's parents transmit something to their children in early childhood that stimulates their attachment. Although this assertion is controversial (different authors, such as Kagan, argue this point), it leads us to hypothesize the existence of a more spiritualized form of attachment in adolescence as well.

Attachment structures itself through childhood interactions. Tizard's study indicated that a first attachment bond can develop at as late as 4 to 6 years of age. Rutter (1979) considers the best period for the development of attachment to be during the early years of life.

By putting these concepts together, we conclude that:

1. There is an obligatory and favorable period for the normal development of attachment in childhood (Rutter).
2. There is the potential for attachment development, even if this does not occur during the most favorable period (Tizard).
3. Attachment development in childhood is correlated with the type of later parental interactions with the child. (Main).

ATTACHMENT PHENOMENA AND PSYCHOPATHOLOGY IN ADOLESCENCE

Recent studies recognize that the reactive attachment disorder of infancy or early childhood (313.89, DSM-IV; American Psychiatric Association, 1994) alters psychological structure and makes this structure and its development vulnerable throughout childhood (Cicchetti & Toth, 1995). Thus, different forms of the disorder exist in adolescence as well as in maturity.

Adolescents' state of ambivalence in relation to their desire to become independent despite their continued dependency on their parents can be compared with Ainsworth's "Strange Situation" experiment. According to the analogy of Ainsworth's Strange Situation (The "Existential Strange Situation," as I call it), adolescents' reaction to the realities of their own existence can be classified as secure, avoidant, or ambivalent. The classification reflects how attachment was structured in early childhood, as well as the influence of life events and later relationships.

The adolescent tendency to "complete the reference figure," with an "idol" taken from art, public life, or literature, appears to be a means for satisfying the need for assured attachment. The fantasy life often compensates for the adolescent's uncertainty and offers additional security and identity.

Research on adolescence and young adults demonstrates (within the conditions in Romania) that the caregiver in the first years of life (especially the first 6 years) becomes a "figure of attachment." The research sample was made up of young Romanian students, interviewed using Main's Adult Attachment Interview. The research established that those students who were taken care of in early childhood by grandparents named grandparents as their attachment figures (100%), and not the parents who supported and took care of them during their schooling. The same study demonstrated that there was a significant correlation between the way the subjects were taken care of by their parents and their present relationship with their parents, as well as negative perceptions of their childhoods. Thus, most of the subjects felt rejected by their parents in childhood (more than 66%). An alarming number of subjects (more than 80%) described physical abuse, and more than 50% had a feeling of separation from or loss of their attachment figure.

Although it is likely that not all subjects were actually physically abused or mistreated, it is useful to take into consideration that they live with a retrospective image of parents who rejected them. This trauma is imprinted in their psychic processes. The image they have of their parents explains the adolescents' conflicts with their parents. Even those answers which did not reflect reality demonstrate an unpleasant image fastened upon in childhood. This could explain the adolescents' devotion to other figures, as well. The adolescent tendency to identify themselves with idols (artists, personalities, teachers, etc.) is what we call "teenage attachment."

ORGANIZATION AND FEATURES OF ATTACHMENT PHENOMENA DURING ADOLESCENCE AND THEIR INFLUENCE ON TREATMENT

We can conceptualize this kind of adolescent attachment as a result of the turning process from parental figures to existential figures to an "other." This other is a new focus of attachment, the person toward whom the adolescent will also orient sexual and psychoerotic impulses.

The four stages described by J. Bowlby can also be recognized in adolescence:

- the preattachment phase (11–13 years);
- the attachment-in-the-making phase (13–15 years);
- the phase of clear-cut attachment (15–18 years);
- the formation of a reciprocal relationship (15–18 years).

I propose the following attachment characteristics in adolescence:

- psychological clinging,
- imitation,
- opening toward another,
- horizontal communication.

Bowlby made the following comments on this issue:

> Attachment is presented as a system of behavior having its own form of internal organization and serving its own function. Moreover, in so far as sexual behavior has been discussed at all . . . it has been referred to as a system of behavior distinct from attachment behavior, and one having a different ontogeny and, of course, a different function. Does this mean, it may be asked, that in the new schema no links between attachment and sex are thought to exist? If so, does not this ignore one of Freud's greatest contributions? (Bowlby, 1969, p. 280).

We can conceptualize adolescence as a period of imprinting with the distinctive properties that Lorenz ascribes to imprinting:

1. that it takes place only during a brief critical period in the life-cycle;
2. that it is irreversible (later discussions denied this hypothesis);

3. that it is *supra individual learning*; and
4. that it *influences patterns of behavior that have not yet developed*, e.g., the selection of a sexual partner.

Attachment is specific to early childhood, but also occurs during a later, brief and critical period of time, as Lorenz mentioned; we define imprinting in adolescence differently than imprinting in childhood. Adolescent imprinting supports attachment. Through imprinting, the attachment object is established.

In adolescence there is the possibility of orienting oneself and choosing a specific "level of aspiration." Some adolescents can be oriented primarily on their physical characteristics. They invest in and remain attached to these physical features. Body building and sports are ways for adolescents to overtake and reconcile themselves with their body schemas and can lead to a consolidation of aspiration that remains at this level (the corporal level). Often we find adolescents with a kind of fury overflowing against their bodies, which they are trying to destroy through self-aggression or suicide attempts. At other times, they try to express themselves using different forms of expression, such as hair painting, hair dressings, corporal embellishments (tattoos, earrings, make-up, etc.). This kind of relationship, in which the body image is psychologically perceived, can traverse the path from the "object" to the "spirit," which can then constitute the adolescent attachment target.

A mental health service for adolescents should include a program that recognizes and helps with body image. Thus, there should be sports facilities where adolescents can train in body building and fitness and play sports. Special therapies, such as motion and body therapy, body expression, and psychodrama as "body presentation" can also be used. It is necessary during adolescence for the person to move from the body to the spirit.

Adolescents are in the process of making sense of their lives and of finding a partner, and they must enter the "portrait gallery" with figures that they like. For all these tasks, a *model is needed*. Parents do not fully satisfy an adolescent's needs in this regard. Adolescents need exemplary models that are superimposed on their ideals and that satisfy their imaginations, models that deserve the attachment, and with whom they can open up and communicate freely.

In the search for a practical solution that can respond to adolescent needs for attachment, the Psychiatric Clinic for Children and

Adolescents in Timisoara, Romania found a method. In this technique we used myths as *transactional objects* in forming the "transitional object, the adolescent spirit," in relation to the possibility of an equal and two-way interaction.

The myth was placed as an "available object" for the attachment of an adolescent who goes through a crisis. In referring to defense mechanisms of the adolescent (in a Freudian sense) we can say that we use a form of intellectualization.

USING MYTHS IN GROUP THERAPY WITH TEENAGERS WITH SOCIAL ADAPTATION PROBLEMS

The use of myth with teenagers in group therapy is the result of over 10 years of experience at our Clinic at Timisoara (Romania). In our methodology we use the myths of Icarus, Oedipus, Prometheus, Theseus, and Perseus, and from the strictly autochthonous myths, we use the myth of Manole.

For teenagers, the themes of the myths suggest reflections on the meaning of life: ideals, hopes, and spirituality versus the tendency toward perversion and triviality understood as murder of the soul and the slipping toward nihilism. Initially, all these would seem to be themes that are refused by teenagers, especially by those who are in opposition to the duplicitous world of adults in which people deny themselves in order to assert themselves.

Using these forms of group psychotherapy over the years, we have treated teenagers belonging diagnostically to the group displaying emotional and behavioral disorders and having suicide attempts in their past (of various etiologies). We have also treated some cases of depression that occurred after a remitted psychotic episode.

As in every group psychotherapy, the purpose was to bring the persons together, to make them interact and be in interrelationships, and to perform therapy, but at the same time, we aimed to confront them with an exemplary meeting centered on the symbolic function of myth.

In order to reach a more dynamic and receptive tone in the group but also to equalize the interactions and interrelationships within the group, the activities were monitored by the psychotherapist and cotherapist (who also directed the meeting protocol). The initial intervention was done by training one teenager (selected for high intellectual performance) and investing that person with "opening catalyzer" functions. The meetings were held once a week during the school year (about 28–30 meetings in total), with a closed group formed by 12 teenagers, 4 of them belonging to the catalyzer group and the other 8 displaying a problem related to the selection of the myth symbol.

The following stages of the group therapy gradually covered a series of methods:

- creation of an active situation by involving the teenagers in evaluation, symbolic decodification, and dialogue toward which they had to adopt an attitude regarding their own interpretation as well as that of another person, and having to express their agreement or disagreement through argument and motivations;
- psychological decoding through drawing and comments (following the same techniques);
- assumption of a part, through choice of a certain character, with psychodramatic interpretation of the myth (sequential or integral);
- creation of one's own script (screenplay) of the myth and analysis of this by the other members of the group.

COMMENTS AND CONCLUSIONS

Nowadays, teenagers do not suffer only from a poverty of instincts, but from a lack of traditions, as well. Their instincts no longer tell them what to do, and traditions offer them no sense of their own being or the dominance of their existential spaces while testing the path of "nonconformism." Thus, teenagers' alarmed cries for an understanding of life echoes the psychiatrist's cry for a new psychotherapeutic modality.

It is probable that our attempts at a new modality show our own subjectivism, but according to the evaluations that we have done, we can say at least that the myth can define and circumscribe a meeting space that "contains the metalevel but is consumed in interlevels." It can "steal" from the teenagers what they are trying most to hide, thus creating an entrance into an understanding of the other, an opening toward the other and the wish of being to-gether—outside of the realm of the bar or discotheque. But this path begins with reestablishing the teenager's attachment to values.

REFERENCES

American Psychiatric Association. (1994). *Diagnostic and statistical manual of mental disorders* (4th ed.). Washington, DC: American Psychiatric As-sociation.
Bowlby, J. (1969). *Attachment and loss* (Vol. 1). New York: Basic Books.

SUMMARY: RECONCILING EVOLVING ECONOMIC STRATEGIES AND THE NEEDS OF CHILDREN IN 21ST CENTURY SYSTEMS OF CARE

34

Designing Mental Health Services and Systems for Children and Adolescents: Observations and Recommendations

J. GERALD YOUNG

PIERRE FERRARI

> For parents love their children as part of themselves, whereas children love their parents as the source of their being. Also parents know their offspring with more certainty than children know their parentage; and progenitor is more attached to progeny than progeny to progenitor, since that which springs from a thing belongs to the thing from which it springs . . .
> Aristotle
> *Nicomachean Ethics*

All parents experience the enduring, complex challenge of being parent to a child. We feel the joy of our children's laughter and progress, the confusion of arduous decisions, the frustration of our mistakes, and the burdens of striving to repair problems that life can bring to a child from whatever sources. This book is devoted to examining how mental health professionals can design clinical services that help parents to nurture children, prevent the psychological mishaps that can cause pain and maladaptation (prevention), intervene when the child's development or behavior are moving off course (early intervention), and repair the psychological symptoms and suffering that too predictably oppress so many children (treatment). And all of these goals must be sought within the economically responsible frameworks of our various societies, all of which lack the resources to do all that we wish. The strains of these contradictory pressures vex us and lead to painful decisions. Yet, a book such as this refreshes us with the recognition that there is a growing consensus about pragmatic approaches to successfully solving these problems in novel and productive ways.

Reviewing the chapters in this book, we find evidence for the following observations and recommendations selected from among those presented within the chapters. They are not offered as final views on a topic, nor as the views of all the authors, nor even necessarily of the editors or of the International Association of Child and Adolescent Psychiatry and Allied Professions (IACAPAP), but as valuable points of view that are supported in significant ways by at least some experts and that enliven the exchange among professionals. As observations, we hope that they will guide debates about the best future strategies, and as recommendations, that they will guide the next phase of efforts to nurture and support children in need.

THE GENESIS AND PREVALENCE OF DEVELOPMENTAL PSYCHOPATHOLOGY: DEFINING THE NEED FOR MENTAL HEALTH SERVICES FOR CHILDREN AND ADOLESCENTS

Etiology

- The concept of developmental psychopathology encompasses the recognition that specific disorders in childhood and adolescence are not static, but dynamically changing with development and with the child's experiences with the molding influences of the environment, and that many disorders of adults are spawned during the developmental period.
- Genetic endowment has been decisively demonstrated as a durable foundation for a child's personality and intellect, subsequently to be shaped by the influence of his or her environment, particularly the family. It can also provide a vulnerability to maladaptation in many ways.
- The stages of a child's development build on the foundation of prior developmental stages.
- Problems of individuals can propagate themselves to descendants through multigenerational transmission of adaptive and maladaptive behaviors by means of both genetic and social transmission.
- Chronically traumatic or neglectful experiences during childhood mold mental images markedly different than those of children

benefitting from a "normal" childhood; these mental images reflect distinct neuronal pathways formed over many years.

- Social trends affecting the broad cultural shaping of how children are nurtured and educated seem so broad as influences that they are usually mistakenly discarded as unreachable targets for altering the fortunes of children: children caught in the cauldron of war, children neglected within the aridity of poverty and left to develop their own adaptive strategies, or children subjected to intense, repetitive images of violence through "entertainment" media, are common contemporary victims of this cultural pessimism and neglect.

- Everyday experiences are formative influences for children. Parental neglect and other damaging parental behaviors can be, in part, the painful results of daily demands and stresses acting on parents, who are then unable to carry out their parental responsibilities in an optimal manner.

- Invigorating advances in the neurosciences bring possibilities for reconceptualizing disorders, as well as for spawning improved treatments.

Principles of Intervention

- While we labor to better delineate pathways of compounded misfortune for children by obtaining more detailed research data, enough is known to provide much needed help to individual children to avoid great suffering and burdensome expenditures by social and educational agencies later. Early intervention is more effective, and it is cost effective.

- Factors affecting risk and resilience are well known, if not yet perfectly defined: genetic endowment; environmental provision, stimulation, deprivation, and trauma; the strength of each influence; the age at which each influence occurs; the mitigating effects of caring parents or other adults; and therapeutic interventions, whether preventive or in response to trauma or symptoms.

- Should healthcare planners wait for perfect understanding of the roles of each factor, and their interactions, before they take obvious steps of intervention? Waiting to establish adequate mental health treatment programs for children and adolescents at a later date is costly, just as postponing preventive interventions for young children is very expensive.

- Authentic knowledge is too often ignored, with complaints that it is incomplete. Simultaneously the children whose development is most hazardous lose the benefit of the application of this knowledge.
- Neuronal pathways underlying maladaptive mental images and behaviors are modifiable: through the interventions of caring adults, through fortunate changes in life circumstances, through determined efforts to better a child's life, or through treatment; but these experiences must be sufficiently substantive, enduring, and cumulative to alter previously stable mental images and neuronal pathways.
- The attraction of using preventive methods early in the lives of children is becoming not only more firmly supported by scientific data (both basic neuroscience and clinical research data), but more appealing from the economic and mental health systems points of view.
- There is an increased awareness of the continuity of childhood and adult illnesses. In effect, every treatment of a disorder in childhood or adolescence can be considered to be a preventive intervention for an adult disorder. In this sense all treatments in the developmental period are preventive.

Prevalence

- The prevalence of children meeting criteria for a psychiatric disorder steadily increased in multiple studies during the past 30 years, from 7% to 11.8% to 14%, and eventually to the current best estimates of approximately 20%.
- These rates are drawn from studies using differing assessment techniques and diverse populations, but the rates are comparable across studies. Improved assessment techniques (e.g., multiple informants and better assessment instruments and data collection methods) gradually led to the appreciation of this much higher rate of disorder among children.
- Approximately 2% of the children with definable disorders have serious disorders; 7% to 8% have moderately severe disorders. The remaining 10% to 11% have mild disorders.
- About half of the children with a disorder have another co-occurring (comorbid) disorder, a significant factor to be considered in service planning.
- All of these prevalence rates are problematic, however, because they are based upon specific definitions of disorders. Definitions raise or lower thresholds for disorders.

- If only symptom criteria are used, the rate is high, but when increasingly stringent criteria for degrees of impairment are included in the definition, then the rates fall accordingly; this creates a very broad range of rates, from 40% to 5%.
- This should not be mistaken as a technique for inflating prevalence rates; these are authentic numbers derived from the use of alternative techniques according to the purposes of the studies. For example, when attempting to plan for possible utilization of inpatient beds for children, the lower rates might be applicable, but when developing prevention programs, the higher rates must be considered.
- When planning mental healthcare systems for children, the real interest in prevalence rates might lie in their meaning for the future.
- Are childhood disorders evanescent reflections of particular stresses on children who are unable to protect themselves, but who bounce back as conditions improve? Regrettably, in *at least* one third to one half of the children, the disorders persist at an equivalent level in later years.
- Ultimately these prevalence data raise the fundamental question: Are these childhood disorders likely to evolve into adult disorders? If so, their significance for economic analyses of healthcare planning is magnified many times.
- At another level, investigators must ask what exactly they are studying. The use of prevalence rates when predicting needs and planning clinical services is increasingly accurate as the breadth of the diagnostic group is increased.
- What meaning do highly specific diagnostic categories have if planners have much better predictive powers using a very broad group, such as externalizing disorders? Should the emphasis for service planning rest on risk factors and causal pathways in preference to discrete diagnostic categories?

Assessment

- The evaluation of a patient is organized to generate diagnostic information and guide treatment planning. There is no single method for defining a psychopathological disorder, and three major techniques are utilized:

    - Categorical diagnoses: Traditional diagnostic categories defined by explicit operational criteria

- ◆ Dimensional diagnoses: Diagnostic categories generated by the frequency and severity of symptoms on assessment instruments, generating symptom groupings; this approach does not use preset categories
- ◆ Ideographic diagnoses: Highly individual descriptions of individual patients, such as a case description, while not favored in the past 20 years, continue to be used clinically because of the complexity of individual cases and are of increasing interest for treatment outcome studies and financial planning.

- Developing optimal diagnostic procedures has long been a clinical challenge that is now also becoming a significant challenge for financial planning.
- Assessment methods differ according to the purpose of the assessment. Clinical assessments, epidemiological and public health assessments, and clinical research assessments can differ in their format and content.
- Assessment procedures are a source of tensions, as investigators and clinicians attempt to simplify clinical evaluation methods but disagree about how to accomplish this. The need for economic efficiency makes it tempting to eliminate clinical techniques that are not highly structured, on the premise that they do not provide utilizable data and are clinically unproductive.
- Clinicians, even while striving to give more structure to clinical data generation and formulation, recognize that the elimination of clinical techniques like the psychodynamic clinical assessment interview deprives us of a major source of diagnostic information that guides treatment in unique ways.
- Efforts to achieve a simple and inexpensive assessment technique using one or two measures are repeatedly thwarted.
  - ◆ Direct interviews are necessary components of assessments not supplanted by easily administered checklists.
  - ◆ Multiple informants must be utilized, as neither child, parent, teacher, nor clinician is sufficient as a single source of data.
  - ◆ Multiple developmentally appropriate forms of assessment instruments for similar data are required in order to obtain information about the same symptoms from children at different ages.

- ◆ Particularly at younger ages, discrimination of developmentally normal behaviors from symptoms can be quite difficult and the source of controversy.
- ◆ Beyond diagnostic information, there is a need for accurate indications of both severity of impairment and level of adaptive functioning, which are important for practical treatment planning and financial planning.
- ◆ A method for combining parts or all of this information has become a subject of investigation in its own right.
- ◆ Discarding these assessment procedures eliminates opportunities for developing accurate clinical predictors that form the infrastructure of techniques for reliable financial estimates and service planning.

THE COSTS OF DEVELOPMENTAL PSYCHOPATHOLOGY: FINANCING, MANAGEMENT, AND QUALITY OF CARE OF MENTAL HEALTH SERVICES FOR CHILDREN AND ADOLESCENTS

Economic Influences on Mental Healthcare for Children and Adolescents

The Emergence and Meaning of Managed Care Organizations

- The existing system of healthcare services has been shaped over time by many incremental and empirical decisions, particularly by powerful providers (such as hospitals), payers (such as insurance companies and government), and professional groups.
- In many countries the choice of treatments is increasingly being made, or strongly influenced, by insurance companies on the basis of financial considerations, with little or no understanding of the child's overall needs.
- "Managed care, as this term has become used, is not care at all: it is a method of administration of healthcare as a business to increase the profits of corporations" (Cohen, Chapter 10).
- The objection of clinicians to managed care practices is not an objection to good business practices, but to the fact that it is easy to improve business practices and results in isolation from other considerations of patient care. It is both difficult and necessary to improve

business practices, clinical care, medical education for all physicians, and research to benefit patients and improve healthcare for the future.

- Linking clinical investigation to treatment is a concern if it appears to increase current costs, yet research is ultimately the most productive investment for cost containment.
- Expanding healthcare costs, novel methods of payment, and the emergence of managed care organizations have been pivotal influences on clinicians providing mental health services for children and adolescents in the past decade in many countries.
- The costs of mental illnesses are massive and the special characteristics of the economics of mental health systems and services make cost containment unusually complex.
- Knowledge of managed care concepts and practices is essential to clinicians in all countries. Even if managed care is not used, or is gradually replaced by other management paradigms, many of these strategies will be central to the new systems.

The Effects of Managed Care

- It is possible to "manage" mental healthcare, meaning manage the costs of this care, by one or more of several techniques:
    - the selection of the clinicians and facilities to be credentialed for inclusion as managed providers for an insured population;
    - a requirement for a clinician's treatment to be preauthorized, as well as continuing the need for authorization throughout a treatment, in order for the clinician to be paid;
    - the determination of facility and fee rates by the managed care organization;
    - the utilization of the clinician with the lowest salary or fee possible, as determined by the managed care organization;
    - the elimination of confidentiality between the clinician and the managed care organization;
    - the withholding of 10% to 20% of the clinician's fee for release back to the clinician at the end of the year if the managed care organization has been financially successful.
- More than 75% of U.S. companies currently use managed care organizations to supply healthcare for their employees.

- The network of *government* healthcare facilities in the United States (hospitals, residential treatment facilities, and clinics) has begun to establish contracts with managed care organizations. This will include the care of poor children with mental health problems, often quite severe. This public managed care movement is expanding rapidly and probably will have spread to all 50 states of the United States in some form by the year 2000.
- Many hospitals report that the length of stay on a child or adolescent psychiatry inpatient unit fell from 30–60 days to 5–15 days in only a few years. The single remaining admission criterion for many managed care organizations is that a patient is dangerous toward himself or others.
- Clinicians are distressed not only by the loss of personal income, but also by the demand for psychiatrists to focus their care predominantly on medication management, leaving no time to form a therapeutic relationship or to be able to engage the family and patient fully in the treatment process.
- It is very difficult to define quality of care and even more challenging to measure it through controlled outcome measures.
- Approximately 3 million children in the United States are eligible for Medicaid care but are not enrolled, and there are 7 million children with working parents who have no commercial health insurance because their family income is too high for Medicaid participation, yet they cannot afford to purchase insurance.
- It has been apparent for several years that a grave danger in the for-profit managed care takeover of the mental health service system for poor and severely ill children is that, ultimately, when the profits have all been taken, the for-profit organizations will likely leave the mental health business. This would leave the government agencies with no healthcare system.

Healthcare Economics

- Child psychiatrists are preoccupied with struggles to improve their clinical methods to help children, yet these activities are embedded within rapidly changing healthcare systems. It is essential for clinicians to consider the effects of these changes, yet it is difficult, due to the complexity of the two fields, which have different conceptual structures, vocabularies, and, most importantly, purposes.

- The economics of healthcare need to be examined in the context of the interrelated concepts of both quality of care and equity (equal opportunity of access to the requested health services) in times of limited resources.

- Although high quality of care is usually considered to be invariably tied to increasing expenditures, it is true that various programs of quality improvement and management have improved the quality of care without additional funding.

- These differing perspectives about the economics of healthcare partly reflect the difficulty of defining the product and quality of the healthcare system. Therefore, there must be a variety of ways in which one can enhance quality of care in addition to a financial infusion.

- Equity is a more complex concept than equal access to care. It includes equality of access, utilization, quality, and expenditures within the healthcare system, all within the context of a distribution based on needs.

- Healthcare enterprises utilize several approaches when adapting to current economic forces: competitive mechanisms, the principles of private enterprise, and ''value for money.''

- There are four ''protective mechanisms'' for maintaining conditions of equality in the face of limited resources: improving efficiency through incentives, reduction of waste, avoiding the inappropriate use of resources by optimizing healthcare services, and maintaining specified standards of equity.

- Efficiency is at the heart of these efforts, meaning *clinical* efficiency, or efficacy of treatment and quality of care. Administrative, managerial efficiency is, at best, a support mechanism, but this is usually not recognized in most administrative decisions in healthcare facilities.

- If clinicians fail to involve themselves in efforts to improve efficiency, market forces will operate in a manner that may be highly detrimental to patients and professionals. This gloomy possibility is already alarmingly near to reality in many countries.

- One way of framing the challenge of high-quality care to healthcare economists and managers is to point out that longitudinal studies conclude that about half the children with psychiatric disorders exhibit the same or similar disorders years later.

- The most persuasive indicator of the wisdom of investing in mental healthcare for children is a case example of how much is lost if society fails to intervene for a child with a specific disorder. Tracing the likely expenses generated by this untreated child in later years is very convincing.
- One example is a 13–year-old boy in London who refused to go to school for 1 year. Following an intensive treatment program, he returned to school for the subsequent 5 years—the only member of his family to remain in school after the age of 16. Using judgments and predictions of his likely life-course if he had remained untreated and of the costs to society of the associated problems the lack of treatment would entail, it was estimated that the cost to society of the behavior of this untreated individual would have been at least 500,000 British pounds over a lifetime. His treatment at age 13 cost 769 pounds, which suggests a 650–fold return on the treatment investment.
- It is for this reason that "Child and adolescent mental health services are the most underrated and neglected investment in healthcare today. They strengthen families, prevent decades of wasted life, teach self-help skills, increase productivity, reduce medical costs, minimize hospitalization, and reduce welfare costs, crime, and police, court, and prison costs" (Light & Bailey, Chapter 6).
- The question of needs inevitably becomes a central focus, as it becomes necessary to set priorities and define who should receive services.
- The unduplicated total of children with behavior, conduct, and emotional disorders is 10 times the number actually seen by mental healthcare professionals. This reflects the general observation that fewer than 10% of children who need mental health services actually receive them. This is a huge underinvestment.

Economics and Healthcare Management

- Concepts guiding improved management can be applied as explicit methods to achieve efficiency and prudent financial planning for clinical services.
- The most difficult endeavor when developing a mental health budget is the estimation of the cost of treatment. Many problems interfere with the estimation of treatment costs.
- Diagnostically Related Service Packages (DRSPs) are a structure for estimating the cost of treatments for specific disorders. The structure

ensures that managers can provide details indicating the specific derivation of the costs for each DRSP, enabling periodic revisions to improve the accuracy of the estimates.

- A more general benefit of the DRSPs is that they demonstrate that rational financial planning for the cost of treatments is possible. They are also more likely to reveal the comparative value of later improved treatments.
- One way of conceptualizing the goal of a sound financial budget for child and adolescent mental health services is that it is a profile of prevalences and a menu of DRSPs.
- A needs-based purchasing plan begins by assembling prevalence rates of specific disorders, the total populations for specific age and sex groups, and the number of actual cases. In order to estimate the cost of effective treatment plans by mental health teams, DRSPs should be developed.
- DRSPs for a child at a specific age with a specific disorder incorporate into the estimated cost of treatment information including age and sex of the child, diagnostic category, severity of the disorder, treatment level (outpatient, day patient, etc.), types of clinical services for assessment and treatment likely to be required, the number of hours for each professional involved, the rates per hour for the professionals, and the resulting "total package cost."
- Utilizing the incidence and prevalence of needs in the region, and multiplying them by the relevant DRSPs, generates a realistic budget. Additional costs must be added to this budget, such as those for supervision of the mental health team, in-service training, and consultation and training for other agencies.
- Using this management approach, early recognition and treatment will save money when compared to later recognition and treatment.
- Information is too often unavailable in health systems. For example, the business office and management team might have no budget for a unit, and repeated requests to obtain needed information are unproductive.
- A common source of serious inefficiencies in mental health units for children and adolescents is having too few secretarial staff, compelling professional therapists to do their own clerical work.
- Commonsense management principles are often violated because of bureaucratic needs with a complex history: for example, keeping inpatient bed days and costs low one year is sometimes rewarded

by providing less money to the unit the next year, a consequence which undermines motivation.

- This type of short-term cost reduction by "strict" managers who are rewarded at the end of a budget period can lead to long-term cost increases.
- The DRSPs often underestimate the actual costs of assessment and treatment, presumably due to the unrelenting pressure to reduce costs; however, underestimations can lead to accusations of cost overruns, the frustrated irritability of underpaid staff members, and inefficiencies as highly paid professionals use their time for jobs intended for less skilled staff.
- Cost management has reduced waste in the system, but it has generated new administrative expenses for these new activities and their associated personnel. Moreover, these new administrative systems often do not provide adequate reporting systems or clerical staff, so the new administrative requirements add to the workload of clinicians and reduce the time available for appropriate professional activities while the clinicians are doing the work of lower salaried clerical staff.
- Later savings will come from improved prevention and treatment.

Financial Management, Competitive Influences, and Child and Adolescent Mental Health Services

- No investment in children: This is a temptation at the time of every annual budget shortfall and is the political and economic background for the neglect of children and the need for advocacy.
- The field of child and adolescent mental health, as a "low income producer" and a "personnel-intensive specialty," is afflicted with a pervasive lack of equity for its patients.
- The high prevalence of children urgently needing treatment, and the even greater number of children burdened with mild to moderate childhood psychiatric disturbances, create a challenge to our profession but an alarming prospect to healthcare administrators unable to conceptualize concurrent savings that could accompany increased funding.
- It is a mistake to portray administrators and third party payers as the sole source of doubt and caution. Regrettably, patients and families readily accede to efforts by healthcare purchasers, such as businesses on behalf of their employees, to reduce or eliminate psychiatric coverage, especially for children.

- The unrealistic notions that "this does not pertain to me" or "children don't have psychiatric disorders" are seductive to every business and to every individual seeking reduced healthcare premiums. Insurance companies and managed care organizations then bear the brunt of later accusations when coverage is needed but missing.
- Commentaries on economic and managerial influences on the development of mental health services for children and adolescents typically include no discussion of some elements that remain concealed:
    - the unchallenged biases of third party payers against children and adolescents needing mental health services;
    - the underfunding of child mental health services;
    - the common and unchallenged poor management practices by administrators with no knowledge about child psychiatric services that further undermine the economic productivity of child psychiatry;
    - the failure of professionals to specify the standard minimal resources needed for varied types of child and adolescent psychiatry service units to function (e.g., inpatient unit, outpatient clinic, etc.);
    - the minimal use of incentives for professionals in child psychiatric clinical services;
- Budget control is maintained at remote administrative levels to assure political control; this leads to management errors due to impractical policies or procedures.
- In the United States, child and adolescent psychiatry is not an independent department and does not control its own budget, with rare exceptions. Therefore, child psychiatry activities were kept at an artificially reduced size, their more complex therapeutic services received less funding instead of more, and clinical and research initiatives were undermined. Child psychiatry then continued to be criticized as scientifically unproductive and administratively disorganized.
- Ironically, child psychiatrists were recommending some of the same management policies that were later adopted out of necessity by administrators who then criticized physician administrators as being incompetent.
- In the most general view, department chairpersons and administrators have very infrequently provided capital investment for a substantial new program within child and adolescent psychiatry. No

investment has resulted in a lack of change or improvement in an already underfunded subspecialty.

- Imaginative and generative clinical and financial practices will remain highly constrained and usually impossible as long as child and adolescent psychiatry is not an independent department in the United States and some other countries.
- It is short sighted to direct criticism solely at managed care practices in the United States or individual political or economic influences in other nations. Competitive forces against child and adolescent mental health services have been continuous and have assumed many forms.
- The competitive forces acting on mental health services and systems for children and adolescents must be confronted by those administering and providing these services if our patients are to participate in the dramatic medical advances of the 20th and the 21st centuries.

THE UTILIZATION AND OUTCOMES OF CURRENT TREATMENTS FOR DEVELOPMENTAL PSYCHOPATHOLOGY

Service Needs and Service Utilization

- Whatever directions are chosen for planning strategies, one is confronted by the single most dismal fact out of all these data: however you define disorder and impairment, very few of the children needing treatment actually receive it.
- If 20% of children and adolescents have a diagnosable disorder and 10% have unquestionably significant functional impairment, only 5% or fewer receive treatment, and even fewer receive it in clinical units designed specifically to provide mental health services. These are disturbing shortfalls certain to cause great suffering and substantial financial waste.
- In order to establish systems of psychiatric care for children and adolescents, data is needed to describe:
    - the number of children determined by a standardized method to have a psychiatric disorder with sufficient functional impairment to require treatment. A common estimate of children under 18 years old in a population needing treatment is 5%, according to multiple studies.
    - the number of children currently utilizing such services.

- Administrators fear that the creation of more services will lead to an expanding use of services, followed by subsequent protests that more services are required, and no halt to the cycle of demands: this is the old comment that "needs will expand to fit the available services."
- A less cynical view is that there is such a large number of underserved children requiring mental health services that the population has learned that the services are unavailable.
- Many families desperately need these services. Their provision will prevent later, expensive problems as these children grow into adulthood. Research data supports this concept.
  - The highest rate of service utilization (e.g., about 4%) is found where the most services are available, whereas the lowest utilization rate (e.g., about 2%) occurs where the density of services is lowest.
  - As the distance between one's home and the location of inpatient units increases, there is a decrease in the rate of inpatient treatment.
  - Regions with better outpatient facilities have higher utilization of inpatient services but shorter admissions to the hospital.
  - Patients from regions with less satisfactorily equipped inpatient and outpatient services are older, and have both a more severe psychiatric diagnosis and longer duration of treatment.
- These data suggest that better services can be more cost efficient in the long run, and there is a substantial pool of children who need such services.
- Research indicates that, even in countries with sophisticated psychiatric services for children, a large proportion of the group requiring treatment is untreated (estimated in the most conservative manner, typically at least one third remain untreated).
- Even more are left untreated when the entire group of significantly psychiatrically disturbed children is considered, not just those with the most urgent functional impairments.

Economic Planning and Treatment Outcomes

- Most managed care organizations, in spite of statements describing dedication to quality of care, actually are focused on cost reduction and improved administrative coordination.

- Managed care organizations give little attention to developing new clinical methods to improve clinical outcomes, such as reducing the duration of illness, preventing recurrence, and decreasing the ensuing levels of disabilities associated with these disorders.
- If clinicians fail to direct the effort to provide effective services, it is likely that efforts to develop services will continue to be determined more by economic factors than clinical outcomes.
- If most clinicians fail to document the outcomes they achieve, someone else will do so. These efforts are very unlikely to be consistent with the best interests of children and adolescents who have emotional and behavioral problems.
- It is no longer sufficient for clinicians or administrators to monitor only the *quantity* of clinician contacts. Serious efforts to improve the mental health status of a community require evaluation of the organization of systems of treatment services and prevention programs to determine the extent to which the actual risk of having disorders, and the level of disability associated with these disorders, is reduced.
- More children aged 9–17 are treated in school settings than are treated by child psychiatrists, according to multiple community studies. Planning must include this reality, or risk portraying a world of treatment missing one of its biggest components.
- There is a need to achieve some consensus about methods to assess the need for and outcomes of mental health services; failing this, we cannot instruct policy makers and purchasers of services about the contributions of these services towards improving the mental health and social functioning of their communities.
- Agencies and providers can consider developing "report cards" for use by consumers or undertaking population surveys.
- Studies of adults with serious mental disorders teach us that changing the organization of mental health services does not necessarily lead to changes in patient outcomes.
- Future endeavors to establish the effectiveness of mental health services will include a wider range of assessment procedures for management purposes. This requirement, stemming from the need for management efficiency, mirrors the clinical requirement for a broad array of assessment methods.
- "Recent focus on healthcare markets, interorganizational networks, and the management of care has paid too little attention to the actual nature of the services being provided and the barriers to providing

effective services. Efforts to monitor mental health services and outcomes are going to increase, not decrease. Without greater participation by clinicians and consumers in the evaluation process, it is clear that the interests of these two groups will not be well served by the solutions devised. If mental health specialists are going to maintain input into the services that are available, it is critical that they help set the criteria for evaluating services and participate in the design, implementation, and interpretation of evaluation efforts'' (Leaf, Chapter 8).

Treatment Outcome Research and the Design of Mental Health Systems for Children and Adolescents

- Policy debates are fueled by the tension between clinical needs and economic forces, which is mirrored in the internal tension of how best to use funding already available for child and adolescent mental health services.
- There is an ethical responsibility for child mental health professionals, organizations, and systems to consider the full range of child mental health needs and the full spectrum of potential ways in which available funds can be used.
- This is a task within the field: What do clinicians and planners know about treatment, how can they provide the most effective care to the children most in need, how do they balance the expensive costs for very disturbed children (e.g., autism) with the lesser costs for children with less severe difficulties, who are, perhaps, more likely to benefit, etc.?
- Therefore, when child mental health professionals move from the clinical setting, where they advocate for everything that child mental health patients need, to the policy setting, they too are confronted by the need to achieve a balance.
- The tension between clinical needs (for populations of children) and economic forces (how much is available and how it should be spent) becomes an internal tension for the child mental health professional working in a policy-setting situation.
- The designs for new systems of care are usually prepared by individuals who do not provide direct care. This brings to mind the problem of engineers who have never built a car designing the next model.
- Most new designs flow from administrative agendas from government, foundations, or other third party payers whose overriding concern is reducing costs. This is a laudable goal, but in isolation it is deceptive in its relative simplicity.

- There is an emphasis on community settings for services in all-new designs.
- Current knowledge of treatment is poorly applied; the development of treatment knowledge has outpaced its application, so children do not benefit sufficiently from what is known.
- Documentation of the need for better programs has not been matched with effective programs; there is a remarkable gap between the number of children who need treatment and those who actually receive appropriate care that meets standards.
- The magnitude of the problem is remarkable: 12% to 20% or more of all children have a diagnosable mental disorder and half (6% or more) are conservatively estimated to have a serious mental disorder.
- Most of these children receive no services and many receive inappropriate services. Care is concentrated in a small group of children in residential settings (hospitals, residential treatment centers). Most children's families do not have the resources to provide access to care.
- In brief, there is a need to design new systems of clinical care if we are to responsive to the needs of families.
- The recommended guidelines for the design of clinical services and systems are:
  - Programs should be decentered from national and state levels to the community and to families.
  - Fiscal constraint is essential.
  - The initial focus should be on children with the most severe mental disorders and on maintaining children in their communities.
  - This requires case management and development of a continuum of care, which implies the need for a flexible disposition of funds; financing schemes should allow shifts of funds among the types of services required by the child.
  - For most communities this requires an expansion of service resources in order to create missing components in the spectrum of required clinical services.
- There is ample evidence that children at risk can be given a continuum of care and children's services coordinated among the conventional agencies.
- The systems evolve uniquely in each community, according to each community's needs and characteristics, and according to which agency takes the lead in the development of the new program.

- Moreover, the systems continue to evolve, reflecting the need to change in response to altered demographics, economic conditions, etc.
- Children at risk can receive multiple, intensive services in their communities and this can result in lower rates of hospitalization and residential treatment.
- Communities need to be imaginative in developing the needed funds for services; for example, some communities generate funding pools and obtain waivers to provide ''wraparound funds'' that can be used to supplement therapy and provide support for children and families. This allows the programs to address the totality of the child's needs and to adapt to the child's changing needs.
- No individual model of care appears to be better than others. Objective evaluations of treatment effectiveness are very arduous and some researchers suggest that there is little data indicating that these treatments for children are effective.
- Other quasi-experimental research testing the effectiveness of systems of care services to children with emotional disorders has puzzling but encouraging results. Using much-expanded care, establishing a continuum of care, and giving individual children access to a broad range of high-quality services makes these children less likely to use hospital and residential treatment, but more likely to use intermediate services, to have more psychotherapy sessions, and to be in treatment longer.
- The clinical outcomes among treatment sites are similar: all outcomes improve, although the children with enhanced services have better scores on mental health measures and have costs 1½ times more per child than comparison sites.
- Therefore, not all studies demonstrate that a continuum of coordinated services improves access to care and treatment outcome.
  - ♦ Some experts suggest that there has been too much emphasis on how care is managed, when what is needed are more effective treatments.
  - ♦ Others also feel that the scientific literature does not adequately support the effectiveness of services in community settings, and that we need to learn more about what makes treatments effective.
  - ♦ Another view is that a critical factor is the inadequate research methodology at this time, and the lack of a result clearly indicating the advantage of a continuum of care does

not yet indicate that it is not optimal. Access to services is improved for children at risk, and children at all sites gain significantly in their functional capacities with a magnitude of gains greater than most studies.

- The evolving new paradigm is
  - ♦ one of patient-focused services for restructuring mental health services;
  - ♦ one in which clinical needs are foremost and professionals act in partnership with patients and families to make key decisions for care.
- This does not sound novel, but in the United States, new technology and institutionalization of services has transferred decision-making powers to health services institutions and to those providing financing.
- Guiding principles are that care be community and family based and comprehensive.
  - ♦ How could the view of children as embedded in families and communities have been ignored for so long? It was not ignored, as this has long been the view of clinicians, which is evident in the bitter battles occurring with managed care companies.
- It is essential to consistently provide mechanisms for testing assumptions.
- The complexity of defining specific outcome variables, when multiple categories of interrelated improvement can occur, is extraordinary.
- Child and adolescent psychiatric disorders generate costs for several systems over the course of a lifetime: the general healthcare system, schools, child welfare, the legal system, and the penal system. On the other hand, child mental health services may reduce the costs in other systems.
- Initially, improving access to child mental health services (making services available, reducing stigma, improving case finding in child welfare and pediatric systems, etc.) will increase the costs of the child mental health system. Nevertheless, savings in other systems will follow.
- Therefore, linkage with other systems of services for children is essential for mental health systems for children.
- Child pediatric disorders are sometimes short term (e.g., adjustment problems) and other times very long term. Economic models are

needed that encompass long-term illness and disability, including its economic and psychological impact on the family.

- Systems of care range from:
    - ◆ Least restrictive (e.g., school-based interventions, such as teaching teachers about behavioral approaches, prevention, and trauma programs)
    through
    - ◆ Moderately restrictive (e.g., outpatient therapy, family guidance, medication, group therapy, intensive home services, short-term hospitalization, day hospital programs, partial hospitalization)
    to
    - ◆ Most restrictive (long-term hospitalization or long-term residential treatment)
- Children and families should be able to move through the spectrum of systems of care, obtaining the kind of care needed when they need it. This should not require changing administrative systems and should maintain relationships with therapists as much as possible.
- Computer-based records are essential to these systems of care for patient management and transfer of information. Confidentiality is essential.
- While the models are clear, the application of the models is very slow due to various economic and political influences.

MODELS OF TREATMENT AND PREVENTIVE INTERVENTIONS FOR DEVELOPMENTAL PSYCHOPATHOLOGY

Models of Treatment and Their Effects

The Principles of Psychiatric Treatment for Children and Adolescents

- As risk factors accumulate, the probability of disorders increases.
- While the diagnostic classification systems are necessary and have a practical utility, most children seeing a clinician do not have circumscribed diseases with clear-cut treatments. Children need treatment because of an array of external and internal influences that have been active for a long time and are eventually expressed through

their particular behaviors and emotions. Children tend to have more than one "disorder" at a time, as defined by diagnostic classification systems.

- The multitude of often conflicting environmental demands and conflicting mental images within the mind of a child beset by many problems and stresses makes the development of a treatment plan a complex, imperfect process.
- There is no perfect measure in the clinical assessment that will define a child's illness or substitute for a carefully elaborated clinical and developmental assessment.
- Multiple types of treatments are available, can be explicitly defined, and are utilized for varying types of problems and symptoms at various times according to the professional judgment of the clinician.
- Children with behavioral problems in the United States receive psychosocial intervention more often in schools or some related component of the educational system than in any other location.
- Most psychotropic medications prescribed for children in the United States are prescribed by primary care physicians and pediatricians, not child and adolescent psychiatrists.
- Therapeutic trials investigating individual treatments, such as a drug, are typically short term and managed in situations that are artificial in relation to the complex problems of children and families in everyday life.
- The recent rapid development of new medications that have much more specific actions is providing clinicians with much-improved therapeutic pharmacological agents to help children. At the same time, however, these drugs have adverse effects, as well as unknown effects on the developing nervous system, and should be used judiciously.
- The enhanced understanding of genetic contributions to the psychiatric disorders of children and adolescents will enable a gradual capacity to target treatments more specifically, with a corresponding improvement in treatment outcome.
- Psychosocial therapies are not only as effective as pharmacological therapies, but are fundamentally required by each child and necessary to permit the fully beneficial effects of medications.
- Effective treatment of children or adolescents requires that treatment planning consider interventions affecting the children's inner mental lives and images, their behaviors and skills, their families, and their schools and communities.

- Two concepts of the therapeutic actions of psychosocial therapies are essential for understanding them: the manner in which therapy changes the psychological structures within a child through interaction with an adult clinician, and the processes through which self-understanding becomes an expanding healing process within the child.
- A child needs the assistance of adults in order to gradually gain the capacity for self-regulation, and this can be an essential component of the therapeutic encounters.
- The investigation of therapeutic action requires a careful breakdown of therapeutic settings into operationally defined, experiential, and replicable modules. For example, to make judgments about the advantages of inpatient vs. outpatient treatments for conduct disorders or other conditions requires the specification of the ways in which settings create, contain, and deliver particular treatments.
- The procedures for investigating treatment for child and adolescent psychiatric disorders, and mental health systems and services more generally, are well defined and available for clinical application.

Research Designs for Treatment Studies

- General guidelines for the design of treatment studies are already available that provide essential ingredients for enhancing preventive intervention techniques, as well as the quality of research data that emerges from these interventions.
- Among the highest priorities for research in this area are four issues that affect many aspects of treatment outcome research: the concept of risk status, the measurement of children's behavior, treatment contexts, and follow-up intervention systems.
- It is essential to develop a model of risk status that adequately captures the interplay of environmental stressors and protectors, personal coping skills, and children's behavior through appropriate measures of each sector.
- This is essential not only for accurate understanding of true outcomes and the causes of a child's disorder, but also for the choice of treatment among different children in relation to the relative contributions of these sectors.
- Measurement techniques can have an unintended, remarkably distorting effect on the results of an intervention study.
- Similarly, good treatment methods can appear unsuccessful when the treatment context is not considered.

- A valuable intervention might be described as useful in the short term, but erroneously said to have no long-term effects, because no follow-up services ("booster" interventions) are incorporated into the treatment plan.

Psychodynamic Therapies

- Psychosocial therapies, especially psychodynamic psychotherapy, attain their beneficial effects in patients in complex ways. Nevertheless, improved research techniques indicate the significant benefits that children and adolescents experience.
- Many child inpatients receiving primarily psychoanalytic psychotherapy as treatment show improvement years later at follow-up and function in a stable manner. The great majority function at normal levels globally and in their family functioning and social networks. They infrequently require hospitalization for psychiatric reasons following discharge.
- Methodology can be criticized in this type of study on the outcome of psychoanalytic psychotherapy, but it is nevertheless informative and has the advantage of reporting "real world" approaches to the treatment of children as inpatients and to their outpatient follow-up.
- One must take into account the changing profiles of a disorder during development when judging whether a behavior is symptomatic and deserving of treatment, and which therapy might be best suited for its treatment.
- The form and style of the treatment must be altered according to the developmental stage of the child in order to make the therapy understandable, attractive, and meaningful to the child or adolescent.

Prevention Research

- Recent studies indicate prevalence rates from 15% to 28% for psychiatric disorders in children and adolescents, varying according to the level of impairment used to establish the threshold for diagnosis. There is additional evidence suggesting increasing rates of psychopathology in children.
- Clinicians and planners must know how and when to intervene if the promised benefits of early intervention are to be fulfilled. Decades of early intervention research become their compass, guiding them as they design mental health systems and services.
- The expansion of prevention research is fundamental to the design of mental health services for children.

- The concept of prevention will increasingly extend to prevention of the psychiatric disorders of adulthood.
- Data now substantiates the beneficial effects of (a) early childhood nutrition on development; (b) intensive early interventions, such as Head Start, on short-term outcomes and school readiness; and (c) recently developed school-based approaches to the immediate safety and success of schools.
- There is an urgent need to document with rigorous research our understanding of which early interventions are beneficial and how they achieve their efficacy.
- Models for preventive intervention have been developed that can be used to select preventive intervention programs at varying levels of intensity and cost: universal preventive interventions, selective preventive interventions, and indicated preventive interventions for childhood mental disorders.
- The emphasis is shifting from the question of whether preventive interventions can be effective to that of which interventions and through what mediating mechanisms.
- The developmental neurosciences now describe the basis in brain biology for potential preventive interventions recommended for decades by psychoanalysts and child psychiatrists.
- Awaiting perfect knowledge about a childhood psychiatric disorder and related effective preventive interventions is a risky strategy.
- Many lives can be favorably affected by actively intervening as soon as reasonable data has accrued suggesting the efficacy of the interventions.
- Preventive interventions target identified influences on a child, termed "risk factors."
- Risk factors are defined as "those characteristics, variables, or hazards that, if present for a given individual, make it more likely in terms of statistical prediction that this individual rather than someone selected randomly from the general population will develop the disorder"; the risk factor must be active prior to the development of the disorder (Jensen, Chapter 13).
- Results of research on risk factors must reach the attention of other professionals and policy makers through knowledge exchange, and must reach parents and others for whom it is important through education. This will lead to a nurturing of the "preventive intervention research cycle," generating new data.

- Policy advocates and government and foundation managers must then engage in a process of risk assessment (that includes risk estimation, risk evaluation, and risk perception), which leads to all of the activities involved in risk management.
- These activities lie at the border between research, the provision of clinical services, and the design of clinical systems for service delivery. They are the essential steps that amplify the chances that the preventive interventions actually undertaken in the clinic or the community will be those most likely to be beneficial.
- Implementation of specific preventive intervention programs recommended by a governmental agency or a professional organization is a complex process derived from the interaction of all of these stages in occasionally unanticipated ways, as these programs extend into the sometimes volatile regions of personal freedom and human behaviors.

Models of Treatment and Preventive Interventions

Recognizing the Need for Treatment

- There are many unreferred children with psychiatric disturbances whose symptoms are unrecognized by their families.
- Epidemiological data vary according to the threshold set to define each disorder. Investigators and administrators question if the data are a true representation of the actual number of children afflicted with the disorders.
- In a similar manner, both the burden of care for clinics and our understanding of "true" prevalence rates are affected by the views of parents when observing the behaviors of their children. Do parents neglect behaviors that clinicians define as significant symptoms, viewing them as insignificant or as normal childhood phenomena? This question has infrequently been examined.
- Disturbances in many children are misinterpreted as minor and not requiring referral for evaluation and treatment because they are viewed within the context of relationships and stressful events within the family.
- This forestalls referral and both protects the family from a perceived criticism of significant family problems or psychiatric disturbances and perpetuates the child's disturbance. On the one hand, if these children are identified and clinical evaluations and treatment are

made available to them, the costs associated with this large group of children might be perceived as unnecessary and overwhelming.

- On the other hand, an unknown percentage of such children will go on to manifest more serious symptoms that will require substantially more expensive care; preventive interventions at this early stage in the development of symptoms might be decidedly more cost effective.
- Early intervention programs can be established in a cost-effective manner if developed gradually, following clear conceptualization of goals.
- For example, a mental health team consulting to daycare centers can be a cost-efficient method of preventive intervention. In an initial period of a few years, a team can establish the structure of these programs and serve many children.
- Such a project can be expanded and, over several years, serve a much greater number of children in more daycare centers.
- This model is of particular practical utility because it does not require establishing early intervention centers, but utilizes existing centers to initiate preventive interventions, provide training, and conduct research on the project as a whole.
- Improving efficiency—and, therefore, quality—means improving clinical efficiency.
- One example is a novel method that encapsulates how new clinical and economic efficiency can be achieved: a home treatment program to reduce the need for inpatient treatment for children and adolescents.
- There are compelling therapeutic advantages to home treatment in contrast to inpatient treatment, yet the treatment costs are less than half that of inpatient or day hospital units.
- Home treatment cannot be used for all children; most children do not fulfill the requirements for entry into a home treatment program, so it is applicable to only about 10% to 15% of inpatients as currently structured.
- Child and adolescent psychiatric nurses can be the therapists in the program, supervised by child and adolescent psychiatrists. The underlying methods employed within the home treatment program are behavior therapy and counseling for caregiving individuals to improve parenting competence.

- The eligible children can be afflicted with a range of psychiatric disorders and the typical duration of treatment is 3½ months and requires a total of about 40 hours of direct contact with the patient or caregivers, as well as 10 telephone consultations.
- There is a marked improvement in symptomatology, impairment, severity of the disorder, and various measures of functional adaptation following home treatment. The estimate of improvement by parents, patients, and therapists is 90% or more.
- There is no difference between the effects of home treatment and the effects of inpatient treatment, nor between the effects of home treatment by a specialized nurse who is supervised and home treatment by a child and adolescent psychiatrist.
- The improvements of home treatment patients followed up after 1 year remain stable.

Developmental Influences on the Design of Mental Health Services

Infants and Preschool Children

- Children of different ages require different assessment methods and treatments, as is evident from the radically different approaches to infants and adolescents. This demands that different types of resources be available.
- Different professional disciplines may have different approaches to a child's problems, and members of the same professional discipline may have different theoretical views of development and childhood disorders; while these differing views are sometimes confusing, they are more often complementary than competing.
- As preventive and therapeutic interventions are developed, it is important that they be codified, or "manualized," so that they can be better used and understood by clinicians.
- Even among preschool children, studies of the practices of pediatricians suggest that between 5% and 15% of these children have developmental or psychological problems sufficiently serious to warrant an evaluation. One quarter of these children may require some type of intervention. For populations selected for an increased risk status, the proportion who would benefit from an intervention goes up markedly.
- Categorical diagnoses are always subject to continuing research and controversy, but especially so in the youngest children for whom the markers of disorder are more ambiguous.

- The complexity of interventions in childhood is markedly increased because the child is not the only focus of the intervention; the younger the child is, the more this is the case. For example, for infants and preschool children, the intervention can be for parents, for parents and children together, for a child in school or for the school staff, for the individual child, or for the child in a daycare or school setting.

Adolescents

- Epidemiological studies suggest prevalence rates of psychiatric disorders in adolescence of about 20%. The prevalences of many of these disorders vary widely across cultures and the decades, as they are very susceptible to social influences.
- There are other psychological problems of adolescence, beyond the diagnosable conditions, that have significant morbidity, mortality, and economic costs associated with them: accidents and life-endangering and health-endangering behaviors (e.g., substance abuse, recklessness, risky sexual behavior, violence, etc.).
- Changing healthcare financing is having a profound influence on treatment methods for adolescents. Some of this influence is beneficial, but some might dilute or undermine the essence of certain therapeutic interventions.
- Many mental health problems in adolescents must be addressed within the context of their social situation, involving the school, pediatrician, police, etc.

Professional Training for Mental Health Services and Systems for Children and Adolescents

- If clinicians are to achieve sufficient treatment efficacy and efficiency, mental health systems for children and adolescents must utilize methods that are increasingly "evidence-based," indicating their validity for helping children. This makes research a first priority, and professional training must reflect this.
- Mental health treatment systems for children and adolescents must be integrated with other child service systems, and professional training must assure that trainees experience training within these interdisciplinary activities.
- Training in child and adolescent psychiatry should reflect major shifts in all aspects of mental health services, and should include

training in new elements facing clinicians, such as treatment efficacy, the influence of health economics on clinical care, cross-cultural issues, etc.

INTERNATIONAL MODELS OF MENTAL HEALTH SYSTEMS FOR CHILDREN AND ADOLESCENTS: WHAT IS THE REALITY WHEN WE PUT PRINCIPLES INTO PRACTICE?

The Organization of Clinical Care, Training, and Research

France

- In France the government took definitive steps to manage the mental health needs of children and adolescents as long ago as 1972. It created sectors of care for child and adolescent psychiatry, each of which has responsibility for prevention and treatment in its geographical area.
- The full range of services is provided in various facilities according to the intensity of treatment, and is free for everyone. Moreover, these services are provided in the context of integration with the services of schools, juvenile courts, and other relevant agencies.
- These mental health services are available to children who have already benefitted from a daycare system that is a model for the rest of the world and a significant preventive force on its own.
- All of these mental health activities are carried out by multidisciplinary teams composed of the full range of professionals needed for comprehensive services. Thus, a full mental healthcare network for children and adolescents is possible, although economic forces in all countries exert pressure for reduction of services.

The Nordic Countries

- One day of hospitalization for child psychiatric care can cost approximately four times the amount for adult psychiatric services.
- Immigration can cause numerous problems, even at the most elemental level. For example, in Sweden, over 70 languages are spoken in some of the public schools.

- Service utilization rates can be very low, even in highly developed countries.
- Child and adolescent psychiatry is a young discipline whose structure is still developing, as is true of the allied mental health professions. This means that it has inadequate resources and is vulnerable to the actions of other professional and nonprofessional groups.

Management Strategies for Mental Health Systems for Children and Adolescents

- Child and adolescent psychiatrists in developing countries describe their efforts to use the models of mental health systems in developed countries to develop their own. It is instructive to examine the reality of the mental health systems for children and adolescents in developed countries and to determine whether they have fully structured and effective systems.
- Observing difficult adjustments to altered economic conditions in developed countries can be instructive: colleagues in other countries can benefit from analysis of the problems encountered in those countries with the most advanced systems by not repeating mistakes such as the development of unnecessary or inefficient components in the mental health system. It might be hoped that these problems in administrative and financial management can be avoided in developing countries.

Germany

- Equity is not ignored in Germany, where it is explicitly stated that children with psychiatric disorders should be provided services comparable to those received by children with other disorders. The full range of mental health services is available to all citizens in Germany and is funded by a compulsory insurance system and by the government.
- Nevertheless, even in this developed country, there are notable gaps, such as in day hospital services and substance abuse programs.
- The universal problem of setting targets for reasonable levels of service is a complex process. In 1988, a special government report recommended that one child psychiatrist for 200,000 inhabitants was needed, which is far from the World Health Organization (WHO) recommendation of one child guidance clinic per 50,000 inhabitants. The fact that one of the economic powerhouses of the world lags

behind WHO recommendations illuminates the problems burdening all children with psychiatric disturbances.

- A significant advance in administrative planning for mental health services is visible in Germany, where the number of personnel needed for specific clinical activities is not determined according to the number of patients but according to the needs of the patients, meaning "the amount of care, support, supervision, and treatment that they need."

- This is a more rational approach that can also benefit the field as a whole as it documents the labor-intensive nature of much of child psychiatric practice, a reality that quickly becomes evident whenever an administrator is asked to provide equitable care for child psychiatric units, comparable to units for adults, and is immediately reluctant.

United Kingdom

- A detailed view of the process of organizing services within emerging structures for healthcare delivery in the United Kingdom has particular value because the National Health Service there has a long history and is a model for service delivery structures in other countries. Well-defined structures and procedures make the United Kingdom model useful.

- An initial step taken was to divide local medical services into purchasing authorities (for organization, planning, and funding) and providing organizations (for healthcare delivery), which avoids a centralized bureaucracy that underuses incentives and stifles initiative.

- The service providers in hospitals or community settings were reorganized into Health Care Trusts that vary in their components, clinical activities, and sizes.

- It is the responsibility of purchasing authorities to assure that the Trusts provide needs-based and cost-effective services in relation to government priorities, and to contract with them to do so. One means of accomplishing this is to set performance goals for the Trusts. There is a continuing dialogue between the two concerning all facets of the health delivery system.

- Preparation of a report on the management of child and adolescent mental health services precedes the establishment of the actual system for the region and guides its structure. The report includes several steps: a review of the literature concerning service delivery, position statements, and principles of practical services are developed; a hypothetical guide for purchasing services is prepared as a set of theoretical gold standards; interviews with service organizers and providers are carried out at selected service sites; and this fieldwork information is contrasted with and integrated into the theoretical standard.

- The definition of the diagnostic disorder and functional impairment through assessment is an essential activity because it determines the flow of patients through a four-tiered structural organization.
- The tiers range from general community services to highly specialized services in appropriate facilities that are not available in all units. Entry into each of the tiers is determined by a set of filters. The filters are also the locus of financial proposals and negotiations and service level agreements.
- Typical problems of centralized authority in health management creep in, as, for example, when there is little room for either over- or underperformance in an activity within any of the tiers, no matter what the reason, and performance is not invariably accompanied by clear incentives.
- Tier 4 includes low-volume, high-cost services that are the subject of continuing scrutiny and disagreement.
- Expensive services (e.g., an inpatient unit) can be funded by pooled resources in which several purchasing authorities purchase or establish shares (e.g., beds) in the most cost-efficient size for the specific service (e.g., 10–15 beds), and a portion of these pooled resources (e.g., 2–3 beds) can also be made available on a flexible basis to patients from other areas.
- While this organizational blueprint is nearly perfect, the resources do not match. Blueprint and resources do not map onto each other and service delivery falters at many points. Tiers 2 and 3, in particular, lack necessary resources.

Sweden

- Economic forces are too commonly judged as detrimental by clinicians who forget that economic systems also *build* mental health systems.
- However, the structure of the financial support can be weak and vulnerable, as in Sweden, where the social systems established in the 1970s and 1980s were heavily dependent on loans from abroad.

- Overuse of government services became a problem and some policies were wasteful, including providing a child allowance to everyone who had children regardless of income.
- This largesse has been substantially cut back, affecting child psychiatrists who endure reduced budgets along with very large increases in the number of referrals. Reductions in services have resulted that are familiar to clinicians in other countries, including reduced inpatient length of stay, more emphasis on day hospital care, and a reliance on outpatient care as the foundation of services.
- Formal priorities have been established to triage children entering this setting of reduced services. Nevertheless, mental health services for children and adolescents continue to be free in Sweden.

Israel

- A range of strategies are employed to manage disparate components of a mental health system in an era of changing healthcare policies.
- Healthcare management policies undergo rapid change because of spiraling costs, and the response in Israel provides an instructive example. In 1971, healthcare costs were 5.4% of the gross domestic product, thereafter rising to 7.8% in 1979 and to 7.9% in 1990.
- After 1978, although everyone could purchase health insurance from one of the health maintenance organizations (HMOs), the responsibility for mental health moved from HMOs to community clinics and hospitals managed by the state. Later, a commission took a realistic look at systemic problems that were also encountered in many other countries.
- For example, the Ministry of Health was both service provider and overseer of healthcare, a conflict of interest certain to encourage significant bias and eliminate competition. Similarly, hospitals encouraged hospitalization for treatment, as their budgets were based on bed occupancy. Psychiatric services were based in hospitals, with only perfunctory attention given to outpatient services.
- Recent reforms in Israel serve as a good model of typical elements of strategies emerging in many countries of the world. They include an emphasis on cost management and operational strategies responsive to market forces; utilizing autonomous, less centralized systems; and mechanisms for evaluation and control.
- Israel is specifically integrating mental health into general medical services provided by HMOs and converting state psychiatric hospitals to autonomous public trusts. Psychiatric care is being drawn

away from hospitals and moved to the community. The regional maldistribution of services is being corrected. A healthcare tax has been levied to pay for the services.

- Integrating mental health patients into general medical care improves equity, but also has beneficial effects on efficiency, because one fourth of general practitioner visits pertain to psychological problems.
- Changes in systems of reimbursement are integral to cost reduction policies. Alternative billing systems for hospitals are being considered in order to eliminate per-diem payments. For outpatient care, a mixed differential reimbursement based on a combination of regional capitation and fee-for-service is being considered.
- This combination of capitation and the use of diagnostic-related groups (DRGs) linked to a payment method via physician gatekeepers is similar to mixed systems developing in the United States and elsewhere. Fee structures will favor community facilities over hospital services two to one.

United States

- Soaring healthcare costs led to the emergence of cost containment practices largely pioneered by managed care organizations.
- While these practices have been beneficial in many respects, successful cost containment may have been transient and is not assured for the future, and some imprudent administrative and growth strategies have imperiled the future of managed care in the United States.
- Moreover, the 20% to 30% profits needed to sustain capital investment in managed care organizations, together with the added costs of their administrative expenses, will be difficult to sustain in the future. In particular, corporations are likely to increasingly turn directly to providers (hospitals and clinician groups) to save these additional managed care expenses.
- The special management competencies of managed care organizations were demonstrated in some sectors, but exaggerated in others. Similarly, controversies about quality of care and dissatisfaction among patients and physicians have led to a pursuit of patient rights and a reassessment of the likelihood of continuing acceptance of managed care.
- Nevertheless, many of the successful strategies and practices of managed care will continue in subsequent healthcare systems, whatever their form.

- For other nations assessing the utility of privatization for their own healthcare systems, their examination of the outcome in the United States must focus on both its successes and its failures. In an era of multinational corporations and an emerging international style of corporate administration, it will be attractive for other nations to join managed care systems seeking a global reach in what is already a global marketplace (wealthy patients may fly to other countries for care). All nations need to consider how these strategies ''fit'' their own needs and resources.

Developing New Mental Health Systems for Children and Adolescents

India

- The context of mental healthcare includes awareness of the locus of a country on the developmental curve of medical services for children. When struggling with fundamental health and social problems—the infant mortality rate, child mortality in the early years of life (especially due to malnutrition and infectious diseases), attendance at school, and other basic problems—attention to basic mental health services for children is postponed.
- Child rearing practices must be examined within the context of a child's culture.
- In some large, developing countries, a huge proportion of the population is young; for example, 40% of the total population of India is below 14 years of age (350 million children). A conservative estimate would suggest that 10% of these children, or 35 million children, have a severe psychiatric disorder urgently requiring immediate treatment. These figures do not include about 2/3 of the adolescents in India, who are 14 and above.
- Psychiatric services for children and adolescents are almost nonexistent, as only 10–25 psychiatrists in India practice child and adolescent psychiatry to a significant extent. There are no training centers for child psychiatry in India. Mental healthcare for children must be integrated within existing health, educational, and social services in India using models of care matched to Indian culture and resources.
- Methods of child rearing in countries where the prevalences of some disorders are low can be used as models for preventive intervention techniques in countries where the prevalences of these disorders are high.

- Data drawn from the existing epidemiological studies in India suggest a prevalence for psychiatric disorders among children in India of about 10% to 20%.
- "The wide gap between the need for service, the existing infrastructure, and the resources, at hand or in the future, seems insurmountable. This is the challenge for the whole profession, the nation, and also the world" (Malhotra, Chapter 27).
- Given the overwhelming disparity between the needs of such large numbers of children and adolescents worldwide for mental health services and the actual resources available, advocacy, public education, and public relations should be among the highest priorities of child and adolescent mental health professionals. Legislation on behalf of these children can be remarkably effective when attained.
- There are reservations among other medical specialists and professionals about encouraging the development of child and adolescent psychiatry as a fully accredited, respected, and funded discipline, and this must be a focus of attention, planning, and action on behalf of children.

Hungary

- The language of politicoeconomic pressures is similar in developed and developing countries. Recent Hungarian experience points out how economic influences that initially seem remote can threaten the existence of the mental healthcare system for children and adolescents.
- It is surprising, but the survival of these services can be tenuous when economic conditions deteriorate or change rapidly.
- The neglect of mental health services for children and adolescents is a symbol for neglecting the development of children and adolescents.
- In Hungary, decades of central financing were replaced by performance-based financing in the 1990s. Accomplishing this required many of the changes in service organization familiar in other countries, such as a shift from inpatient care to basic outpatient and other services, with a consequent reduction in the number of hospital beds and, therefore, of professional staff, leading to inevitable cutbacks among the medical specialties.
- A subspecialty like child and adolescent psychiatry, occupying a fragile position among much stronger medical specialties in most countries, is especially vulnerable to the effects of such changes. In

this instance the questions are not limited to how to make adjustments in clinical and financial organization and planning, but also extend to how to survive as a subspecialty when isolated politically and economically.

- Faced with reduced resources, the parent departments of psychiatry and pediatrics often begin to substantially cut back or eliminate the child and adolescent psychiatry activities, beds, and resources integrated within their departments.
- The bias against mental healthcare for children is vivid, and the uphill battle faced by advocates for children is painfully obvious. Demographically, 21% of the population in Hungary is under 14 years of age, yet less than 10% of the hospital beds are for children, and only 2.1% of these beds for children are devoted to the care of psychiatric disorders.
- Moreover, a very small percentage of the gross national product, 6% or less, is expended on healthcare, which is less than half of the proportion in the United States and other countries and minimizes the likelihood that child and adolescent psychiatry can find a place in the disposition of resources.
- The old funding system for healthcare in Hungary was not performance based, and the lack of incentives was destructive. The new system is structured to respond to the rules of the market economy: the 110,000 hospital beds available at the end of the 1980s was reduced to 93,000 by 1996, with a further decrease of 10,000 scheduled for 1996. The DRG system was implemented.
- Yet, in spite of such changes, equity was not achieved. For example, correctional multipliers were used in response to specific institutional and professional needs, restrictive limits for financing were put in place, and gradually the emphasis on achievement in the distribution of resources was eroded.
- By 1997, however, the restrictive limits were removed, a new DRG system was introduced, and again performance was emphasized in order to provide economic stimulation to the system.
- The changes that benefitted healthcare delivery were not beneficial for the subspecialty of child and adolescent psychiatry, which was included in neither psychiatry nor pediatrics in the health bill of 1996.
- Therefore, the public health system is not obliged to insure child and adolescent psychiatric services in Hungary. As beds were taken from both pediatrics and psychiatry and the specialties sought to

defend their own beds, the child psychiatry units were left unprotected and vulnerable.

- Attempts to regain subspecialty status for child and adolescent psychiatry through appeal, which some specialties were able to achieve, were unsuccessful. Needless to say, the prestige of child and adolescent psychiatry is not high in Hungary.
- More important have been the effects of these problems on the actual treatment of child and adolescent psychiatric disorders. Estimates of the prevalence of these disorders in Hungary are similar to those elsewhere (15% to 25%), yet the number of children actually in the network of services is probably less than 2% of those affected.

Russia

- Political and social upheaval in a country can rapidly contrast two mental health systems for children: those of the old and the new governments. While the new system might be an improvement, it often comes at a price.
- For example, the system in the former Soviet Union permitted the child psychiatrist to make direct interventions with any child rapidly, to easily obtain statistics to guide planning, to minimize problems such as homelessness, and to provide free treatment.
- Nevertheless, disadvantages were also apparent: health services were separated from social service agencies, severely limiting multidisciplinary treatments.
- There was also a lack of specific program areas central to child mental healthcare: prevention programs, social and legal services for children with mental illnesses, services for early childhood (under age 4), and the integration of efforts between governmental and nongovernmental organizations (including professionals).
- The Russia of today has inherited significant problems from previous decades, reflecting both limited economic resources and the low priority for children's services that is evident in other countries. Estimates of the depth of these problems include the fact that 7% of school-age children are not in school, 1 million children are homeless, and more than a half million children are orphans.
- The abuse of children appears to occur at a high rate, suggested to be 40% of the children in one study, with an estimated 16% experiencing physical violence and 24% psychological violence in school-based studies. But, as in other countries, accurate numbers are difficult to determine.

- Drug abuse is increasing, with more than 20% of adolescents trying drugs. Child and adolescent criminality is increasing at a rate double that among adults.
- A government report indicated that only 16% of adolescents were judged as completely mentally healthy, while 95% of socially disadvantaged adolescents were estimated to have psychopathology.
- These grim statistics are made more disturbing by the regrettable fact that only an estimated 10% of all children who need psychiatric intervention will receive it, due to the lack of financial resources. In 1995 there was no available data describing the incidence and prevalence of mental disorders among children and adolescents.
- The lack of recognition of the seriousness of these disorders, and of the financial wisdom of attending to them early in a child's life, was dramatically demonstrated when the Ministry of Health Care, in November 1995, eliminated child and adolescent psychiatry from the official list of medical professions.

Brazil

- An analysis of mental health systems painfully illuminates the pervasiveness and severity of the mental health problems of children because the data indicate that a very large percentage of the childhood population is affected in all countries, developed or developing. In developing countries these burdens are simply worse, sometimes staggeringly so.
- The magnitude of the problem is particularly evident when we recall that basic public health problems, such as malnutrition or infectious diseases affecting the brain, are mental health problems as well and must be resolved first.
- Imaginative solutions are needed. An example is the model used in Porto Alegre, Brazil, in which large projects, such as Project Vida, are in reality programs to wrap vulnerable families in services that lift them at many points: nutrition, immunizations, prenatal care, parenting skills, programs for adolescents, etc.

Hong Kong

- Limited awareness of mental health services can make the journey to the appropriate specialist's office a long one for a child. This delay often leads to the use of nonprofessional treatments for children.
- The transition to new healthcare delivery systems can amplify the problem of access to care transiently.

- Part of the problem is that other physicians do not refer patients as frequently as necessary, partially reflecting the lack of prestige of child and adolescent psychiatry.

Poland

- The history of child and adolescent psychiatry in developing countries is mirrored in many ways in the development and challenges of child and adolescent psychiatry in Poland.
- One advantage in Poland is that the status of the subspecialty itself is formally recognized and, accordingly, it is more secure.
- There are, however, familiar politicoeconomic threats to mental health services for children: poverty, social crises, and wars cause the neglect of the needs of weaker members of the community, such as infants, children, struggling families, and the elderly.
- In response to the need for more child and adolescent psychiatrists, there needs to be as strong an influence as possible early in the training of physicians to enable them to understand children, their needs, and their disorders in order to attract more students and more support within medicine generally.

Romania

- Treatment must respond to the changing features of a disorder during development when determining whether a behavior is symptomatic and deserving of treatment, and which therapy might be most appropriate.
- The forms and style of the treatment must be altered according to the developmental stage of the child in order to make the therapy understandable, attractive, and meaningful to the child. When this is not done, there is a risk that the patient will interrupt treatment or participate in only a partial, disinterested manner.
- Imaginative techniques are used in Romania to stimulate the participation of adolescents, such as group therapy using the themes from myths to generate discussions, psychodrama, and the preparation and analysis of screenplays.
- Treatment techniques can be devised to touch on important themes that reverberate throughout the developmental period, such as the central role of attachment. Planning need not be limited to chronological periods, such as adolescence, but can focus on developmental lines, such as dependent needs and impulses across the life cycle.

LINKING GOOD MANAGEMENT AND COMPASSION FOR CHILDREN

The observations and recommendations of the Venice International Working Group leave us confident and satisfied that a great deal is known about the treatment and prevention of psychiatric disorders in children and adolescents, and that this knowledge is the core of emerging solutions to the paradoxes presented by the economics of mental healthcare for children and adolescents. The application of this knowledge within systems of mental health services is the challenge that propels us forward.

We recall the words of memorable characters from Charles Dickens in a story so often told to children. As we travel through life, Scrooge can seem overdrawn and simplified, of little literary merit. At other moments he is disappointingly contemporary, and we recognize that the tensions illuminated in the story are always with us:

> "But you were always a good man of business, Jacob," faltered Scrooge, who now began to apply this to himself.
> "Business!" cried the Ghost, wringing its hands again. "Mankind was my business. The common welfare was my business; charity, mercy, forbearance, and benevolence were, all, my business. The dealings of my trade were but a drop of water in the comprehensive ocean of my business!"
>
> *A Christmas Carol*
> Charles Dickens

More than a century and a half later we debate the same controversy. Debate and regulations will stimulate us, but the answers will come from inventive new ideas linked to compassion for children.

ACKNOWLEDGEMENTS

We are grateful for the work and wisdom of the Venice International Working Group and the Executive Committee of IACA-PAP, whose efforts are reflected in this summary of their observations and recommendations. We give special thanks to Dr. Donald Cohen for his careful reading of the manuscript and helpful suggestions.

RECOMMENDATIONS OF THE INTERNATIONAL ASSOCIATION FOR CHILD AND ADOLESCENT PSYCHIATRY AND ALLIED PROFESSIONS (IACAPAP)

35

Mental Health Services and Systems for Children and Adolescents

---

THE VENICE INTERNATIONAL
WORKING GROUP AND THE
EXECUTIVE COMMITTEE OF THE
INTERNATIONAL ASSOCIATION
FOR CHILD AND ADOLESCENT
PSYCHIATRY AND ALLIED
PROFESSIONS

PREFACE

The International Association for Child and Adolescent Psychiatry and Allied Professions (IACAPAP) is the international organization of national organizations concerned with the mental health of children and families and the professionals who care for them. Organized in the middle 1930s, IACAPAP organizes international Congresses, publishes a book series, facilitates international communication among professionals and organizations, organizes study groups and other training activities, and consults with governments, foundations, and others concerned about children and families, especially in relation to psychiatric, developmental, and emotional difficulties. IACAPAP is a nongovernmental organization (NGO) within the framework of the United Nations.

In April, 1996, IACAPAP convened an international, multi-disciplinary group of leading mental health professionals in Venice, Italy, to consider issues relating to the mental and behavioral disorders of children and adolescents and approaches to treatment, including:

1. scope and impact of mental disorders of children and adolescents;
2. effectiveness of preventive and treatment approaches;
3. funding, organization; and evaluation of mental health systems;
4. differing national and regional models of mental health systems for children and adolescents;
5. mental health systems for specific groups of children, including infants and young children and adolescents.

The IACAPAP Working Group included experts in child and adolescent psychiatry, social work, psychology, developmental psychopathology, pediatrics, evaluation, mental health systems, and economics. The Working Group reviewed available knowledge and defined areas in need of future research. The report of the IACAPAP Working Group provides a framework for national plans for mental health systems. The Venice Declaration, with which this report ends, summarizes the Principles for Organizing Mental Health Systems for Children and Adolescents.

The Executive Committee
IACAPAP

MENTAL HEALTH SERVICES AND SYSTEMS FOR CHILDREN AND ADOLESCENTS

Child mental health services are a vital resource for developed and developing nations. These services are dedicated to promoting healthy emotional, cognitive, and behavioral development; detecting early signs of disturbance; and providing effective treatments for children, adolescents and families, based on the best available scientific knowledge.

National and regional mental health plans for children, adolescents, and their families should assure:

1. systems of care and treatment that are accessible to families of all social and economic backgrounds, that provide treatments that are least likely to disrupt children's normal relationships, and that are most likely to help children and adolescents towards normal developmental pathways;

2. the availability of mental health and associated services that are aimed at facilitating normal development and preventing disturbance, including family support programs, maternal and infant care, pediatric healthcare, early childcare, developmentally oriented schools, and community-based programs that support healthy development and reduce risk; and

3. a range of professionals (child psychiatrists, psychologists, social workers, educators, nurses, and others) who are well trained and able to engage in prevention, early intervention, and treatment services.

There is a natural sharing of responsibility among mental health systems, governments, and societies in alleviating environmental burdens, promoting competence, and guiding choices.

As with all situations involving public policy and the use of limited resources, it is essential to establish thoughtful priorities for the allocation of funds for mental health services for children and families. In determining priorities, a range of factors must be considered, including: the short- and long-term suffering, and disability associated with psychiatric and developmental disorders; the burden of illness on families; the cost to society of delayed treatment and of having individuals who do not function to their fullest potential; and the possibility of promoting development and competence through effective intervention. Also, in establishing priorities, there must be consideration of methods for providing the most well-established preventive and early interventive services to the largest number of children and families.

RISK, PATHOGENESIS, AND DISORDER

Children and adolescents are burdened by a range of serious and impairing emotional, developmental, and behavioral problems and disorders. A great deal remains to be learned about the basis for vulnerability to psychiatric disorders. Vulnerability to psychiatric disorders appears to reflect the interaction between a range of environmental and biological factors. Children are also exposed to many different types of traumatic experiences that jeopardize the emergence of social, emotional, and cognitive competence and the development of their central nervous systems.

High-risk situations include:

- psychosocial factors such as poverty, abuse, and neglect;
- war, migration, urban violence;
- chronic physical and mental illnesses in families, pre- and post-natal exposure to drugs, alcohol, HIV/AIDS, malnutrition, chronic infections, and other persistent and life-threatening illnesses.

The most vulnerable children are exposed to multiple forms of adversity. For example, children born into families that are drug abusing, suffering from psychiatric disorders, or living in great poverty are often born with constitutional vulnerabilities. These children experience the hardships of disorganized and violent early childhoods and enter school at great disadvantage. Failures build upon themselves, and the children are then exposed to other types of trauma in their communities. These often lead to experiences in the criminal justice system. Their entire lives are shaped by acute and chronic trauma that is not adequately buffered by resources in their families and community.

While there always have been children growing up in poverty, today they are exposed to new sources of trauma, including HIV/AIDS, drugs, and increasing rates of child abuse. Throughout the world, there is an increase in mobility caused by political changes and war; millions of children are living their entire childhoods as war orphans and refugees, and as displaced, homeless, and country-less individuals.

In addition to psychosocial factors, children experience serious emotional, behavioral, and developmental disorders because of in-born or emergent neurobiological dysfunctions. These neurobiological dysfunctions reflect genetic, toxic, infectious, dietary, constitutional, and other types of vulnerabilities and exposures. The disorders that emerge include the most severe problems of childhood, including mental retardation, autism, severe attentional disturbances, language disorders, tic syndromes, and other forms of impairments in the unfolding of basic social, linguistic, regulatory, and cognitive abilities.

Advances in behavioral and biomedical clinical services have added to the understanding of children's development and the structure and function of the central nervous system. This knowledge provides insights into the risk-factors associated with many forms of psychiatric and behavioral disturbances. New methods of cognitive, behavioral, and psychosocial treatments also provide the potential for prevention, early intervention, remediation, and treatment of a range of serious difficulties and disorders. Increasingly, molecular biology, neuroimaging, neuropharmacology, and other biological approaches are suggesting new ideas about pathogenesis of disorders and treatment. Currently available behavioral, psychological, and pharmacological therapies can profoundly improve the functioning of severely disturbed children and allow them to function adequately in the mainstream of society.

EMERGING MENTAL HEALTH SYSTEMS

Mental health professionals throughout the world have been creating innovative models of mental health services that are responsive to the new needs of children and families and that reflect new knowledge about pathogenesis and treatment.

These new services include approaches to acute care of traumatized children and families; delivery of services in the community; and treatment models for helping groups and individuals adapt to their traumatic experiences and move forward in their development. Most new models of care involve the collaboration among families, different types of mental health professionals (child psychiatrists, psychologists, pediatricians, nurses, social workers, educators) and community-based workers from the populations at risk.

At the same time as innovative models of treatment are being devised, governments throughout the world are engaged in reviewing the organization, goals, and financing of mental health and general health systems. This process of review and reform of mental and general health systems is being motivated by various factors, including:

- the recognition of the importance of population-based planning and public health;
- new approaches to prevention and early detection (for example, early intervention programs for preschool children, and school-based programs for facilitating social and emotional development and detecting children at risk);

- active participation of "patient populations" in their own health-care decisions;
- concerns about the financial implications (costs and benefits) of care.

The study and reorganization of mental health systems is being led by professionals with experience in health administration and finances (public health administrators, operations researchers, sociologists, economists, etc.) working with mental health professionals. In this process, the requirements of large-scale organization and financing are being balanced against the specific clinical needs of individuals and groups at high risk or in need of care. In the inevitable conflicts, administrators and professionals are turning to empirical research on the actual uses, needs, and outcomes of mental health interventions. This analysis of data is very useful. However, in these discussions, professionals concerned about children's mental health also have a responsibility to be advocates on behalf of children and families. They are the voice of children. For example, administrators currently are involved with developing systems that "manage care." This often means trying to reduce costs, with less concern for quality. In debates about "managed care," child mental health professionals should emphasize the importance of high-quality care that is clinically managed.

Child mental health professionals and other advocates for children can provide information to justify the belief that adequate funding of mental health services for children and adolescents is a shrewd investment. The allocation of funds for mental health services alleviates current suffering, supports families, and leads to better adaptation. Mental health services and enhanced development also reduce the costs of other publicly financed services (including special educational, long-term residential and treatment services, welfare and criminal justice services). They increase the likelihood that the individual will be a more fully contributing member of society.

Along with the analysis of *systems of care,* professionals are actively involved in studying and defining the efficacy (benefits in rigorous, experimental trials), and effectiveness (benefits in the usual, ordinary clinical situation) of treatments for specific groups of children and adolescents. Changes in healthcare delivery require changes in the education and training that are needed by professionals to provide care. The managers, purchasers, and users of mental health services are asking about the effectiveness of particular types of treatment, just as in other branches of medicine.

The design and implementation of studies to assess the short- and long-term impact of psychological treatments requires careful consideration of suitable methodologies. For example, studies often need to involve more than one modality of treatment and consider a range of outcomes (immediate improvement in symptoms, improved adaptation, longer term developmental consequences, etc.). Also, there are sensitive ethical concerns, including how to assign children to specific treatments, inform families, and maintain some control over "placebo" and nonspecific effects. Thus, empirical work in this domain may differ in some respects from the assessment of the efficacy and effectiveness of treatments for the medical illnesses (for example, the benefits of a particular medication for a specific indication, such as hypertension). The importance of rigorous research on child psychiatric treatment modalities requires that the field provide for the training and support of experts who are knowledgeable about therapeutic approaches as well as rigorous methodologies for assessment.

Both developed and emerging nations share the same set of concerns:

- What are the most effective treatments for children at high risk or who already suffer from developmental, psychiatric, and emotional disorders?
- How can these treatments be most effectively delivered by mental health systems?
- What infrastructure of professional training, research, and evaluation is needed to sustain a system of care and to evaluate its functioning?

FRAMEWORK FOR NATIONAL AND REGIONAL MENTAL HEALTH SYSTEMS

A systematic framework for planning mental health systems for a nation or region includes a series of related domains and considerations.

Ecological Sensitivity

Mental health plans must be carefully attuned to the culture and to the social ecology of the families and community being served, including specific historical and cultural factors, and must be respectful of the strengths, values, and goals of the children and families being served. In all ways, mental health systems must help facilitate optimal functioning, attempt to prevent and limit disability, and provide services that are nonstigmatizing. To the degree possible, mental health services should be provided within the normal context of a child's and family's life and in a manner that will offer the greatest likelihood of inclusion of the child with a mental or developmental disorder in society.

Developmental Suitability

Evaluation of children and adolescents and the provision of care rest upon a developmental model that includes the interaction between many different factors both in normal development and in the cause of disorders. The developmental model has several emphases, including:

- the hierarchical nature of development, in which competencies emerge over the course of time and in which adaptations at one point reflect early functioning as well as new capacities and challenges;
- changes in children's biological, psychological, and social functioning, including the ways they experience their world; changing demands and roles; and the rapid changes in their central nervous system; and
- the subtle interactions between inborn, constitutional, and environmental influences over the course of maturation.

In considering the emergence of disturbances, many factors may play a role, including both biological (constitutional, genetic, toxic, infectious, etc.) and psychosocial (family and community adversity) influences, and their interaction. Understanding a child or adolescent from a comprehensive, developmental point of view involves consideration of functioning in multiple personal domains (social, emotional, cognitive, linguistic, adaptive, motor, neurobiological) as well as various contexts (family, school, community).

Developmental diagnosis provides a longitudinal view of abilities and difficulties; helps define specific stresses and causative and contributory factors; and highlights potential resources and sources of resilience at present and that may be available in the future.

Spectrum of Integrated Care

A mental health system should offer a continuum of care that includes a spectrum of integrated services, closely related to a broad, developmental understanding of children's development.

Available services should include: early detection and intervention; acute treatment; longer term treatment; special education; family support and guidance; inpatient and residential services; rehabilitation; and other associated care.

The goal of the spectrum of care is to assure:

1. an emphasis on prevention;
2. early detection and thorough evaluation (diagnosis);
3. specific treatments that are closely related to the child's and family's individual needs;
4. the integration of psychosocial, psychiatric, educational, and associated treatment modalities, as needed, including family, individual therapy, pharmacotherapy, educational, occupational, and vocational therapies, etc.;
5. the provision of care for as long as needed, with changes in the nature and intensity of treatment as required;
6. availability of follow–up and rehabilitation programs to sustain and enhance the gains of treatment;
7. integration of services over the course of development, and across developmental transitions (e.g., from preschool to the school-age years, from school age to adolescence, and then from adolescence to young adulthood).

In indicating this broad range, it is also important to note that every region and nation will need to establish priorities, since no system today can afford to provide everything to everyone. Establishing priorities is ethically sound as well as necessary. In this context, we believe that emphasis in delivering mental health services should be placed on providing programs and care that will be most likely to affect the largest number of children, to reduce risk, and to minimize disability.

A consensus appears to be evolving among mental health professionals that relatively high priority in delivering mental health services should be given to caring for the following groups:

- younger children;
- children with major risk factors, including familial risk (such as
  being the offspring of parents who are psychiatrically ill) and individual risk (such as cognitive or intellectual disability or physical
  illness)
- children with the early signs of disorders for which effective treatments are available (for example, children with emotional, attentional, and behavioral disorders during the early school–age years
  or with anxiety, mood, and behavioral symptoms during the transition to adolescence).

In emphasizing priorities for care, it is also important to indicate
the importance of providing suitable treatment opportunities for all
children and families as well as the value of research that will expand the range of effective prevention and intervention for serious
disorders.

Accessibility

Mental health systems should be designed to assure that
all children and families have access to appropriate diagnosis and
care. The availability of care should be made known to children and
families. Younger children should have access to a system that will
allow them to safely and confidentially obtain assistance in situations of abuse and neglect. In certain circumstances, it is also appropriate for older adolescents to have access to care without requiring
parental permission (such as situations involving drugs or sexual
concerns, when adolescents are relatively independent or emancipated from their families, or when requiring parental involvement
as a precondition for care would block the adolescent from approaching or making use of a treatment service).

Care should be provided in a manner that is socially and culturally
acceptable, within geographic reach; and at costs that can realistically be afforded.

Consent

Children, adolescents, and their families should be provided with information about the nature of any condition that is diagnosed and the basis for the diagnosis. They should be provided with information about the recommended approach to treatment, any other treatment options that might be clinically indicated, the potential side effects of recommended treatment, and the potential dangers of not having treatment.

Parents and children maintain the right to consent to treatment or to terminate treatment at any time. Discussions involving consent and the provision of clinical information must be done in the context of clinical concern for the patient and family. When there is reason to believe that any type of information would be harmful for the child or family, there should be procedures of review that will assure that families and children are provided with suitable information in the most thoughtful manner.

Effectiveness

Children and families should be provided with treatments which reflect the current state of knowledge about pathogenesis and care. Clinicians should provide treatments that, to the best of their belief and knowledge, are most suitable and have the clearest evidence of demonstrated effectiveness. The cost of treatment should be balanced against short- and long-term benefits.

Professional Qualifications

The diagnostic assessment and treatment of children and adolescents should be conducted by professionals with competence in relation to child and adolescent development, the causes of developmental psychopathology, and varied treatment modalities.

Mental health systems require the expertise of several different types of professionals, including child and adolescent psychiatrists, social workers, psychologists, educators, pediatricians, nurses, and others. Most often, mental health systems will function best when professionals from different disciplines can work together in teams that make optimal use of their skills and knowledge.

The training of mental health professionals should include adequate academic and supervised clinical work. Mental health professionals should have continued education after graduation to assure that they remain knowledgeable about advances in the field.

Settings for Care

Mental health services for children and adolescents can be delivered in various settings. Preventive and early assessment services can be based in schools, community centers, childcare programs, and general health settings. Treatment may be provided in schools, special agencies, hospitals and clinics, residential and inpatient settings, and in children's homes. Child mental health services must be coordinated with all other services and programs that involve children at risk, including pediatric services and hospitals, criminal justice systems, social service programs for abused and neglected children, and special programs and schools for individuals with intellectual and learning disabilities.

Treatment should be carefully monitored for quality, continued effectiveness, and continued need. Medication should be used only for well-defined, proven indications and only for as long as required. Medication must be carefully monitored for benefits and side-effects.

When children are provided with services from more than one professional or agency, there should be specifically defined methods for assuring communication among professionals and integration of the various modalities of treatment.

Financing

Mental disorders are serious and often persistent conditions and may lead to long-term handicap and suffering. The financing of evaluation and treatment for mental, behavioral, and developmental disorders should be consistent with the financing of other persistent and potentially impairing medical disorders.

Also, children and adolescents with developmental and psychiatric disorders often require a range of ancillary services, including special education, occupational therapy, vocational rehabilitation, and the like. Their parents may incur special expenses relating to the need for additional help in the home and other associated costs. These ancillary expenses should be considered within the health system as medically indicated costs.

The primary goal of any health system must be to assure that individual patients receive suitable treatment. At the same time, the mental health system must strive to find the most cost-effective approaches to treatment and delivery of services. In this context, therapies for psychiatric disorders should be subjected to the same careful scrutiny for effectiveness, as with other medical treatments. Evaluation of the short- and long-term benefits of treatments (outcome research) is needed to assure that children are provided with care that is most likely to reduce their difficulties and enhance their development.

It is reasonable for a mental health system to consider cost–benefit analyses in deciding upon the value of a particular treatment program. Economic analysis of mental health services should include various parameters, such as definition of mental health needs within the population of children and adolescents; costs of treatment; and the ultimate savings to a society of providing care. There should be an attempt to allocate resources in such a way that the largest number of children in need of treatment receive the treatment that is economically the soundest investment, that is, the treatment that is most likely to improve the general welfare of children at a cost that society as a whole can tolerate. This principle of equitable access may deprive some children of the most expensive, comprehensive care in order to assure that more children will receive some degree of help.

High-quality mental health services are a shrewd investment: they reduce disability, improve functioning, and decrease the cost of other services (including medical, criminal justice, and welfare services). Early investment in treatment results in long-term savings.

Ethics

Diagnosis, treatment, and professional training must be conducted with a clear understanding of the ethical implications and potential ethical abuses. There are many ethical issues in child and adolescent psychiatry that are shared with other medical specialties, such as pediatrics. In addition, because of the special nature of mental disorders, their origins and treatment, and the information that is likely to become available, there are specific issues that are more salient in child mental health.

Ethical concerns in child psychiatry and allied professions include freedom of parents to select the caregivers and course of treatment, consistent with good medical practice; to terminate care; to have their child cared for in the least restrictive environment and with greatest inclusion in the general community; to know the basis for the diagnosis and the alternatives in treatment, including anticipated benefits and potential side-effects; to have opportunities for communication with all caregivers; to be provided with access to medical records; and to be given opportunities for observing treatment and the treatment setting, consistent with good clinical practice.

Parents and children have the right to anticipate that their care will be held in high confidentiality. Information should be provided to other professionals, insurance companies, agencies, government, or others only with their expressly given, free, and informed consent; parents should then be provided with copies of such information, if they so wish.

Children and adolescents are ethically entitled to receive care that is in their specific, personal best interest; that is, care should primarily be aimed at being helpful to the child or adolescent and his or her development. This care should be administered by competent individuals in environments that are most conducive to the child's overall social and emotional development and, as far as possible, within the mainstream of social life.

Mental health services should be nonstigmatizing. Thoughtful, valid diagnosis is part of providing rational care. However, children should not be "labelled" in ways that may deprive them of opportunities for education, socialization, future jobs, or the like based on a history of illness or treatment.

When there are trade-offs between the needs of children and the wishes and rights of adults, the rights of the child must be given paramount value. This is particularly important when children are at emotional or physical risk, as in child abuse, and when they are threatened with the disruption of the continuity of their relationships with their psychological parents (as in custody disputes). Similarly, children and adolescents have the right to expect that information they provide will be maintained as confidential, except as specifically indicated by clinical and other urgent considerations. No information should be provided to any agency or individual outside of the parents, without explicit consent: from the parents of young children, and from both parents and adolescents themselves, in relation to older children.

No information should be provided to the parents that is not in the clinically best interests of the child. In general, the right to confidentiality is closely related to the child's developmental needs and the roles of parents. For young children, there is generally no confidentiality in relation to parents, as parents are fully involved in the child's life. For adolescents, the presumption should be the preservation of the child's confidentiality, except with the assent of the adolescent and in emergencies.

The professionals who provide the treatment should disclose their own financial and other benefits. For example, families should be informed if a specific treatment is likely to lead to greater financial gain to the professional of if a treatment is being recommended because it is cheaper for the system but perhaps less effective. Clinicians have an ethical responsibility to inform parents about what they believe is the most suitable care, even if this may be more expensive for the system.

Within any mental health system, parents and children should be informed about whom they might contact if they have specific concerns about ethical issues or other aspects of their care, including the behavior or competence of the therapist. A patient advocate or ombudsman should be available to parents and children to listen to concerns confidentially; to assure the investigation of issues as they arise; and to oversee improvements in the system, as indicated.

The United Nations Convention on the rights of children provides a very important, internationally acceptable framework for ethical considerations. The actual implementation of the Convention, along with a system of accountability, would be a major achievement for children and families.

Research and Evaluation

While a great deal is known about children's development, disorders, and treatments, there are major questions in need of investigation. There are critical areas of ignorance in relation to pathogenesis and treatment. The long-term prognosis for the most serious disorders will be improved only through rigorous clinical investigation using advanced methods from various biological and psychological fields. Similarly, the development of new methods of intervention will depend on systematic investigation of risks and benefits. Service delivery research is essential to defining the benefits and long-term outcome of therapy and the most effective methods for organizing mental health systems. Research requires the collaboration of many different disciplines.

There is an ethical obligation for professionals to carefully evaluate and monitor what they are providing to patients.

Advances in knowledge about the causes, course, and treatment of mental, behavioral, and developmental disorders will require sustained, well-funded research programs. National mental health systems should include research and evaluation as essential components for assuring quality improvement.

When children and adolescents and their families are involved in systematic research, there should be safeguards to assure the highest level of scientific and ethical review. This includes careful assessment of the potential benefits, risks, and ethical implications of proposed research by formally designated Human Investigation (Helsinki) Committees. Before entering any research study, parents should provide fully informed, written consent and children should provide assent or consent, to the degree of their ability. In certain situations and for particular types of research, such as research in situations of trauma or involving large-scale interventions, the Human Investigation Committee can waive the requirement for individual consent if there are careful provisions to assure the highest ethical consideration. In general, participants in research should be able to withdraw at any time without the loss of standard clinical services.

Clinical investigation and research within mental health systems should be in the service of advancing knowledge about children's development and disorders and improving care and treatment. In no case should children or adolescents with mental disorders be subjects in research that is exploitative or of no benefit to their own situation. On the other hand, normal children should be allowed to volunteer to participate in research, with suitable consent procedures, as an expression of their voluntary, altruistic sharing in a socially important task that will advance knowledge and improve care.

Participants in research projects should be representative of the population in general and of the group of children and adolescents with the specific disorders or problems. That is, the children who are engaged in research should not be drawn from only one social, ethic, racial or gender group, but should reflect the diversity of their communities and of those who suffer from the condition.

When investigators perform systematic research, they assume the obligation to honestly and openly share findings with other professionals. Findings should be reported in a speedy and effective fashion to assure that the knowledge can be most broadly available.

Both positive and negative findings should be reported. In scientific reports, the rights of patients to confidentiality should be maintained.

Innovations

Mental health systems and specific methods of treatment are likely to continue to change dramatically in the coming years. It is thus essential for mental health systems to remain flexible. Knowledge will be advanced by the exchange of information among professionals from different disciplines and among regions and nations. Systematic, clinical trials that assess benefits of various therapeutic approaches will help shape the types of care that are provided. Thoughtful innovations will help assure the progressive advancement of the care of children and adolescents.

Declaration of Venice: Principles for Organizing Mental Health Systems for Children and Adolescents (1996)

The International Association for Child and Adolescent Psychiatry and Allied Professions (IACAPAP) is the international organization of national societies committed to child and adolescent psychiatry, psychology, and allied professions. For more than 60 years, IACAPAP has been an international advocate for children and families. A major goal of IACAPAP is to facilitate the provision of preventive and treatment services and to enhance the work of mental health professionals.

Mental health systems within nations and regions have overarching goals:

- to support families, teachers, social agencies, criminal justice systems, pediatricians, maternal and infant health services, and others in the community in the vital social task of raising children who function optimally;
- to provide access to services and programs, as soon as they are needed, for children who are first exhibiting signs of disorders and troubles;
- to deliver services that are as effective and safe as possible to all children regardless of their abilities to pay, race, ethnicity, legal status, nationality, or other personal characteristics, in order to reduce suffering, limit disability, and help promote the individual's fullest possible participation within the community.

To meet these goals, the mental health systems of nations and regions should include:

- a cadre of well-trained, committed professionals;

- a range of settings for prevention, evaluation, and treatment that are acceptable for use by families and that are nonstigmatizing;
- access to services for all families and children in need;
- suitable methods for financing;
- quality assurance and monitoring;
- evaluation and research; and
- ethical oversight, advocacy, and protection of the rights of children, including the implementation of the United Nations Convention on the rights of children.

IACAPAP asserts the importance to nations and individuals of well-funded, high-quality, ethically delivered, accessible mental health services for children and adolescents and their families. To assure the creation and maintenance of optimal mental health systems, government, private organizations, professionals, families, and advocates need to work together with shared commitment and values.

INDEX

abuse, 8, 10, 357
  child, 436, 446
  DSRPs for child, 75–76
accessibility, care, 452
accreditation, 349–350
Achenbach, T. M., 90, 92, 261
activity competence, 158–159
addictive disorders. *See also* drugs;
    substance abuse
  Nordic countries, 254–255
adolescents
  attachment phenomena, 385–387
  interventions' approaches, 232, 426
  level of aspiration, 390
  onset of endangering behaviors, 231
  poverty and, 11, 118, 446
  programs in Brazil, 367–368
  psychopathology and attachment
      phenomena, 387–389
  residential groups for, 272, 274
  in Romania, 385–392
  vulnerability, 234
age group
  clinical psychiatric syndromes and,
      85, 87
  Hungarian youth according to, 336
  psychiatric disorder and, 20
  psychopathological disturbances and,
      196–198
aggression, child's selfhood and, 8–9
Ahnsjö, Sven, 266
AIDS, 8, 446
Ainsworth, M., 386
alcohol, 190
ambulatory treatment, 249
  in Israel, 297, 299
  in the United Kingdom, 285

Angold, A., 21
anorexia nervosa, 174–175, 177, 368
  DSRPs for, 76–77
antisocial behavior, 161–162, 265
Anthony E. J., 361
anxiety disorders, 6, 19, 198, 201, 346
  phobic, 216
  therapies, 131
Asperger's syndrome, 133, 216–217
Association of the Scientific Committees
    of Hungarian Medical Doctors
    (MOTESZ), 347–349
at-risk children. *See also* high-risk
    children; low-risk children;
    moderate-risk children
  in Brazil, 361–362
  coping skills of, 148–149
  environment influence on, 149–150
  prevention interventions for, 184
  psychiatric disorders, 20, 125
attention-deficit hyperactivity disorder
    (ADHD), 20, 198–199, 253
  drug efficacy for, 132
autism, xix-xx, 128, 174–175, 177, 345,
    446
autonomy, post-therapy, 175–176
Ayurveda, 326

behavior
  change and psychosocial treatment,
      136–137
  early detection of maladaptive
      patterns of, 59–60, 447
  guidance to parents, 224–225
  measurement of children's, 160–163